SALT AND STATE
AN ANNOTATED TRANSLATION OF THE
SONGSHI SALT MONOPOLY TREATISE

Cecilia Lee-fang Chien

Center for Chinese Studies
The University of Michigan
Ann Arbor

*Open access edition funded by the National Endowment for the Humanities/
Andrew W. Mellon Foundation Humanities Open Book Program.*

MICHIGAN MONOGRAPHS IN CHINESE STUDIES
ISSN 1081-9053
SERIES ESTABLISHED 1968
VOLUME 99

Published by
Center for Chinese Studies
The University of Michigan
Ann Arbor, Michigan 48104-1608

Library of Congress Cataloging-in-Publication Data

Chien, Cecilia Lee-fang
  Salt and state : an annotated translation of the Songshi salt monopoly
treatise / Cecilia Lee-fang Chien.
      p. cm. – (Michigan monographs in Chinese studies, ISSN 1081-
9053 ; v. 99)
   Includes bibliographic references and index.
   ISBN 978-0-89264-163-5 (alk. paper)
      1. Salt industry and trade–China–History. 2. Song shi. Shi huo zhi.
Yan. 3. Government monopolies–China. 4. China–History–Song
dynasty, 960-1279. I. Song shi. Shi huo zhi. Yan. English. II. Title. III.
Michigan monographs in Chinese studies no. 99.

HD9213.C42C517 2004
338.4'76644'095109021—dc22

                                                                2003055689

ISBN 978-0-89264-163-5 (hardcover)
ISBN 978-0-472-03806-0 (paper)
ISBN 978-0-472-12750-4 (ebook)
ISBN 978-0-472-90145-6 (open access)

Printed and bound by CPI Group (UK) Ltd, Croydon, CR0 4YY

To my mother, Florence Chien,
and to the memory of my father,
Gabriel Y. T. Chien, 1922–2002

CONTENTS

Illustrations   vii
Preface   ix
Note to Readers   xiii
Maps   xv

PART ONE: INTRODUCTION

Pre-Song Salt Monopolies   4
The Historical Context of the Song Monopoly System   10
Early Salt Monopoly Operations   39
Government versus Merchant Distribution   49
Voucher Programs   62
Southern Song Realities   70
Salt in a Pre-Industrial Command Economy   81
Sources   85

PART TWO: ANNOTATED TRANSLATION

Brief Introduction to the *Songshi* Salt Treatise   93
Section 1: Pond Salt   95
      1. Xiezhou   95
Section 2: Sea Salt   141
      2. Jingdong   142
      3. Hebei   146
      4. Liangzhe   156
      5. Huainan   183
      6. Fujian   241
      7. Guangnan   257

Section 3: Earth Salt   275
              8. Hedong   275
Section 4: Well Salt   283
              9. Sichuan   283

APPARATUS

Song Reign Periods   301
Weights and Measures   303
Glossaries
        Place Names   305
        People   313
        Salt Monopoly and General Terms   318
Works Cited   330
Index   346

ILLUSTRATIONS

MAPS

Map 1. The Northern Song Empire   xvi

Map 2. The Southern Song Empire   xvii

Map 3. Yongxingjun (Shaanxi) Circuit   xviii

Map 4. Jingdongdong and Jingdongxi Circuits   xx

Map 5. Jingxibei and Jingxinan Circuits   xxii

Map 6. Jingji and Jingxibei Circuits   xxiv

Map 7. Hebeidong, Hebeixi, and Hedong Circuits   xxvi

Map 8. Huainandong and Huainanxi Circuits   xxviii

Map 9. Qinfeng (Shaanxi) Circuit   xxx

Map 10. Liangzhe and Jiangnandong Circuits   xxxii

Map 11. Fujian Circuit   xxxiv

Map 12. Guangnandong and Guangnanxi Circuits   xxxvi

Map 13. Jiangnanxi Circuit   xxxviii

Map 14. Jinghubei and Jinghunan Circuits   xl

Map 15. Lizhou, Chengdufu, Zizhou, and Kuizhou Circuits   xlii

TABLES

Table 1. Major Military Developments in the Song   25

Table 2. Pond Salt Production in the Northern Song   99

Table 3. Aggregate Liangzhe Salt Production   157

Table 4. Aggregate Huai Salt Production   183

Table 5. Annual Production of Fujian Salt   241

Table 6. Aggregate Guangnan Salt Production   258

PREFACE

The rich and unprecedented developments in virtually every aspect of Chinese culture during the Song dynasty (960–1279) have inspired scholars to delve into its many and diverse areas. In recent years in China, Japan, and the West the study of the state salt monopoly in the larger context of China's bureaucracy and political economy has generated rising interest.[1] My annotated translation and Introduction to the complete text of the salt monopoly treatise in the *Songshi*, the Song dynastic history, may be seen as part of this effort.

Through much of the imperial period, the monopoly stood second only to the land tax in generating revenues, particularly during the Song, when it provided over 50 percent of the state's cash income. Although the Song was arguably China's greatest age, its imperial administration felt fiscal pressures from the start. The government's central dilemma was how to maximize state revenues while improving its people's welfare. In response to ongoing military pressures, Song emperors assumed near complete control over the fisc in general and the lucrative salt monopoly in particular, their efforts arguably achieving the apex of court activism in the imperial era. They prohibited private individuals from trespassing on the state's monopoly revenues and established penalties for those who broke the law; they increased their personal control over financial decision-making by creating offices directly answerable to the throne; they presided over meetings on fiscal affairs and frequently inquired into the state's financial condition; and they had accounting records compiled to keep them informed of the overall fiscal process.

---

[1] Among the number of bibliographies which attest to the growth of the field, see Hans Ulrich Vogel's *Bibliography of Works on Salt History Published in China* (special issue of the Commission Internationale d'Histoire du Sel, Austria: Berenkamp Verlag Schwaz, 1992), which counts more than 700 titles between 1980 and 1989 and is to be continued for the periods before and after.

The state controlled the military, political, and economic resources necessary to maximize income, but even so it faced constraints. Each actor in the multi-layered and many-faceted salt trade, from the emperor, local officials, monopoly administrators, producers, and merchants, on down to consumers, had his own interests, interests often at odds with those of other actors. The state itself did not necessarily speak with one voice. The salt monopoly, which was key to the stability and prosperity of the dynasty, provides an excellent window onto the relationship between the government and the economy in the Song. The problems of the Song's bureaucratically managed economy are not unique, but rather resonate with problems generated by command economies elsewhere, both historical and in our own day.

The *Songshi* treatise, unlike any other source contemporary to the period, organizes the subject of the salt monopoly into an intelligible narrative that is unsurpassed in detail. As far as I know, no special study has been devoted to this work, nor does a complete English translation exist. Written in the language of memorials and policy pronouncements of a millennium ago, a language characterized by filler and convention, the salt treatise is replete with technical terms that relate to finance, politics, and the industry itself. The complexities of bureaucracy, political process, and factional debates are especially confounding for the latter-day reader. Song rulers perpetuated many institutions of the Tang and Five Dynasties, and they also introduced new institutions, creating the most complex administrative nomenclature in imperial Chinese history. I have tried to sort out these issues, inserting clarifying interpolations into the text and adding commentary where it seemed necessary.

I have used the punctuated Zhonghua Press edition of the *Songshi* for my translation, which averages about four parts annotation for every one part translation. I have corroborated, corrected, and supplemented lacunae of topic and time by referring to other major historical records. The running commentary offers my brief explication of how the *Songshi* editors presented policies and activities related to the salt monopoly. To paraphrase Denis Twitchett (1992), the writing of history was for historians not only a political act, but also an evaluative and interpretive one. I believe the *Songshi* editors, like Song officials, believed in maintaining a stable market and ensuring revenues, but these historians viewed the extreme controls of some officials (the Wang Anshi camp, especially) quite critically, and this is reflected in their treatment. But while the historians and bureaucrats may have differed on the means of generating state revenue, they did not greatly disagree on ends.

It is my hope that the introduction will enable readers to better understand the annotated translation by giving an overview of the dynamics of the monopoly against a backdrop of governmental centralization and foreign relations. This book will be useful to those interested in Chinese institutional history, economic history, fiscal administration, law, and historiography, as well as comparative bureaucracy and monopoly. Although some problems have necessarily been left unresolved, I trust that this endeavor will ease the task of future students in the field.

★   ★   ★   ★

The passage to completion of this book has been an odyssey for me in time, space, motion, and emotion. I thank Peter K. Bol of Harvard University for the inception of this work as a doctoral dissertation. I deeply appreciate his unfailingly open door, his candid reading of my drafts, and his confidence throughout the long haul, which helped me bring this work to fruition. His devotion to the field and to the facts continues to be an inspiration. I am further grateful to my graduate advisors Tu Wei-ming, who tried to keep me from losing sight of the forest, and Philip Kuhn, whose methodological questions and affection for documents are compelling.

Paul Smith of Haverford College went over the early draft with a fine-toothed comb; his queries could launch another tome. Peter Golas of the University of Denver gave essential advice at a late stage. I am indebted to a number of scholars for their generosity in sharing their manuscripts and visions: Bao Weimin and Liang Taiji of Zhejiang University; Lin Yimin of the Hong Kong University of Science and Technology; Liu Jiahe of Beijing Normal University; Seo Tatsuhiko of Chuo University; Hans Ulrich Vogel of the University of Teubingen; and Yang Weisheng of then Hangzhou University. I also express my thanks for the travel and research grants from the International Rotary Foundation, the History Department of Harvard University, and the School of Humanities and Social Sciences at the Hong Kong University of Science and Technology.

It has been a delight to work with Terre Fisher, who is an able and understanding editor indeed, and with Margaret Mirabelli, counselor and copyeditor extraordinaire. My thanks also to Amy Rock and Keith Pitts at Forward Thought Cartographic and GIS Solutions for their help in rendering the complexities of the Song salt system in the maps included here. I regret that it is impossible for me to acknowledge completely all the help that I have received on this odyssey from other colleagues, friends, and family members.

My pride and joy, YY, buoyed me daily with his sweet presence amid the reams of my drafts applied to his budding artistry. Finally, it is to D and M, who sacrificed the untold for their one and only, that I dedicate this book. Would that D had seen the fruits of my labor, but perhaps he does still, from on high. While I owe many, none bear responsibility for the deficiencies that remain.

NOTE TO READERS

Administrative units such as "fu," "zhou," and "jun," which were usually omitted from place names in the original text have been restored in this translation for the sake of clarity. The terms circuit (*lu*), county (*xian*) and directorate (*jian*), however, have been rendered in English to avoid an excess of transliterations. I also translate place names where this may be enlightening, such as "Northern Capital" for "Beijing," since in Song times this referred to the city of Damingfu, not present-day Beijing.

Emperors are referred to by temple name (*miaohao*), and because the *Songshi* normally gives only a reign period, I append a chart of Song emperors and their reign periods at the back of the book, where I also provide a table of Song weights and measures for the reader's ready reference.

Bolded, italicized numbers in brackets in the main text indicate the page on which text occurs in the *Songshi*. For ease of reading, I have inserted headings, block quotes, and some paragraph indentations.

I have rendered dates in month, day, and year order, or just month and year when no day was specified. I maintain the traditional stems and branches designations rather than convert them, so the date may be easily matched to the original sources.

Finally, the circuit maps indicate salt production sites, distribution routes and consumption within their regions. Prefectural boundaries are all laid out and prefecture names as well as the type of salt produced or consumed there are indicated at the site of the prefectural seat where salt activities would have been administered. The maps are not all drawn to the same scale; for their relative sizes, see Map 1: The Northern Song Empire, with its distance scale.

MAPS

Map 1 The Northern Song Empire

Map 2 The Southern Song Empire

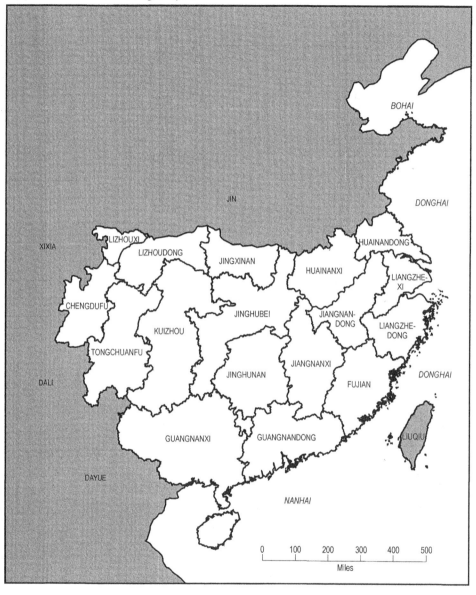

Map 3 Yongxingjun (Shaanxi) Circuit

XIXIA

HEDONG

Hengshanzhai Baoanjun

Huanzhou Yanzhou/
Yananfu

LUOSHUI

Qingzhou/
Anhua Danzhou

Fuzhou

HUANGHE Ronghe

Ningzhou Fangzhou Wenxi
YONGFENGQU

Xieliang Anyi

Binzhou Yaozhou Tongzhou Xiezhou/Sanmen
Hezhongfu

QINFENG Liyang Xiexian/
Jingyang Shanzhou

Qianzhou Gaoling HUANGHE
WEISHUI Huazhou Guozhou JINGXIBEI
Jingzhaofu/
Yongxingjun

Shangzhou

LIZHOU

JINGXINAN

◆ Xie pond salt consumer   ◆ Pond salt producer   ✦ ● ■ Major overland route
○ Other consumer   Major waterway

MAP 3

YONGXINGJUN (SHAANXI) 永興軍路

Anhua (xian) 安化縣

Anyi 安邑

Baoanjun 保安軍

Binzhou 邠州

Danzhou 丹州

Fangzhou 房州

Fuzhou 鄜州

Gaoling 高陵

Guozhou 虢州

Hezhong (fu) 河中府

Hengshanzhai 橫山寨

Huazhou 華州

Huanzhou 環州

Jiawa 賈瓦

Jingyang 涇陽

Jingzhaofu 京兆府

Liyang 櫟陽

Ningzhou 寧州

Qianzhou 乾州

Qingchengjun 慶成軍 (see Ronghe)

Ronghe 榮河

Sanmen 三門

Shanfu 陝府 (see Shanzhou, Xiexian)

Shanzhou 陝州

Shangzhou 商州

Tongzhou 同州

Wenxi (xian) 聞喜縣

Xieliang 解梁

Xiexian 解縣

Xiezhou 解州

Yanzhou 延州

Yaozhou 耀州

Yongfeng (qu) 永豐渠

Map 4 Jingdongdong and Jingdongxi Circuits

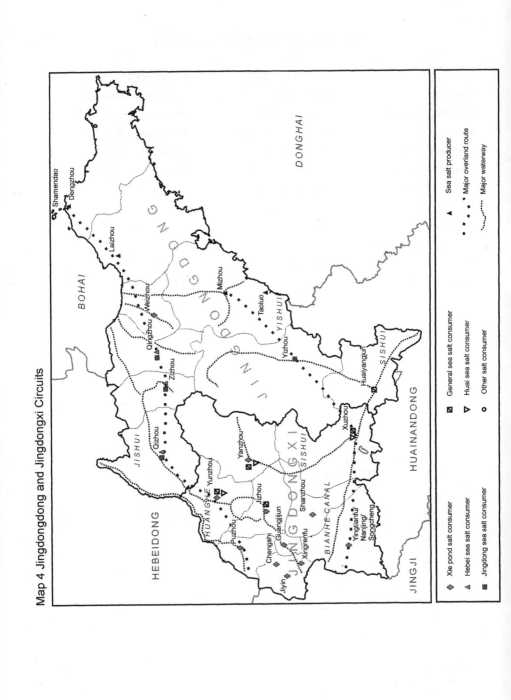

Legend:
- ◆ Xie pond salt consumer
- ▲ Hebei sea salt consumer
- ■ Jingdong sea salt consumer
- ▣ General sea salt consumer
- ▽ Huai sea salt consumer
- ○ Other salt consumer
- ▲ Sea salt producer
- ▪▪▪ Major overland route
- ⋯⋯ Major waterway

MAP 4

JINGDONGDONG　京東東路

Dengzhou　登州
Huaiyang (jun)　淮陽軍
Laizhou　萊州

Mizhou　密州
Qingzhou　青州
Taoluo　濤洛

Weizhou　濰州
Yizhou　沂州

JINGDONGXI　京東西路

Chengshi　乘氏
Guangjijun　廣濟軍
Jiyin　濟陰
Jizhou　濟州
Nanjing (fu)　南京府

Puzhou　濮州
Qizhou　齊州
Shanzhou　單州
Songcheng　宋城
Xingrenfu　興仁府

Xuzhou　徐州
Yanzhou　兖州
Yingtianfu　應天府
Yunzhou　鄆州

Map 5 Jingxibei and Jingxinan Circuits

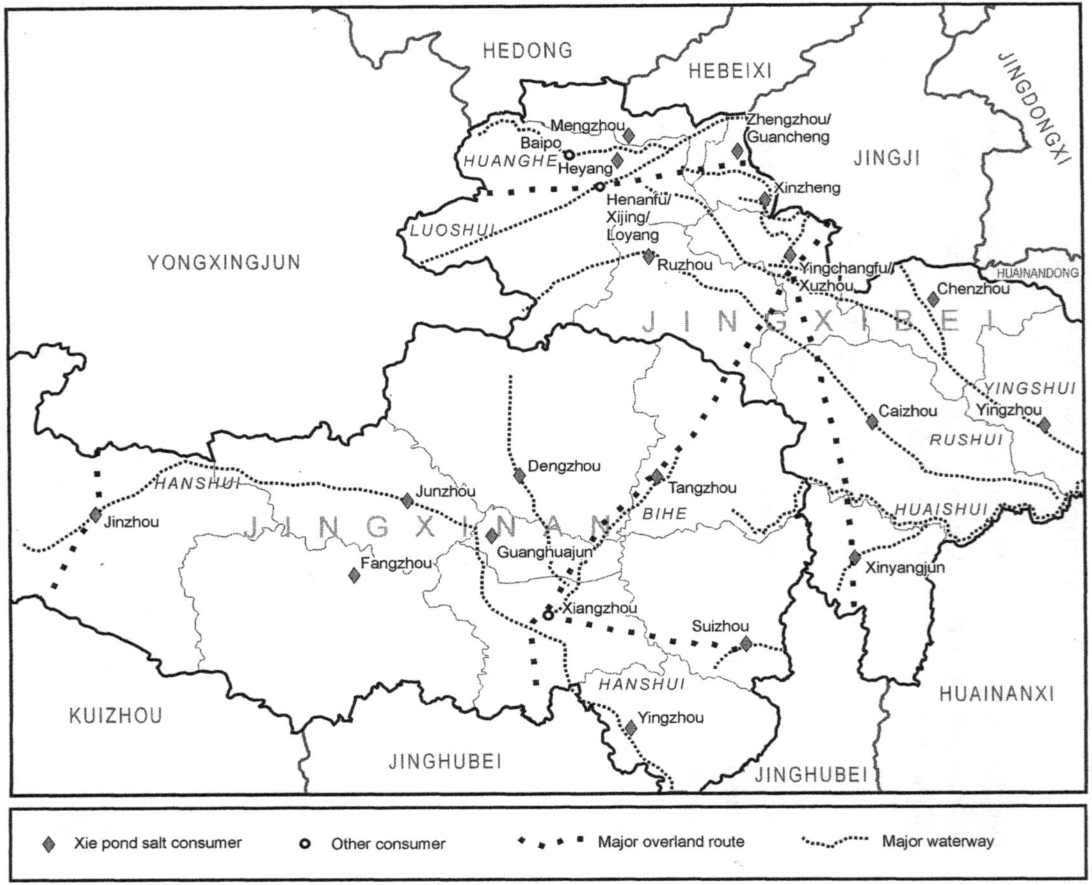

Legend:
- ◆ Xie pond salt consumer
- ○ Other consumer
- ····· Major waterway
- ▪▪▪ Major overland route

Regions and places shown on map:
JINGDONGXI, HEDONG, HEBEIXI, JINGJI, JINGXIBEI, HUAINANDONG, YINGSHUI, RUSHUI, HUAISHUI, HUAINANXI, JINGHUBEI, JINGHUBEI, KUIZHOU, YONGXINGJUN, JINGXINAN, HANSHUI, HANSHUI, BIHE, LUOSHUI, HUANGHE

Places: Zhengzhou/Guancheng, Xinzheng, Yingchangfu/Xuzhou, Chenzhou, Caizhou, Yingzhou, Xinyangjun, Mengzhou, Baipo, Henanfu/Xijing/Loyang, Heyang, Ruzhou, Dengzhou, Tangzhou, Suizhou, Yingzhou, Junzhou, Fangzhou, Guanghuajun, Xiangzhou, Jinzhou

MAP 5

JINGXIBEI 京西北路

Baipo 白波
Caizhou 蔡州
Chenzhou 陳州
Guancheng 管城
Henan (fu) 河南府
Heyang 河陽
Huazhou 滑州

Luoyang 洛陽
Mengzhou 孟州
Ruzhou 汝州
Weicheng 韋城
Xijing 西京
Xinyangjun 信陽軍
Xinzheng 新鄭

Xuzhou 許州
Yingchangfu 穎昌府
Yingzhou 穎州
Zhengzhou 鄭州
Zuocheng 昨城

JINGXINAN 京西南路

Dengzhou 鄧州
Fangzhou 房州
Guanghuajun 光化軍

Jinzhou 金州
Junzhou 均州
Suizhou 隨州

Tangzhou 唐州
Xiangzhou 襄州
Yingzhou 郢州

Map 6 Jingji and Jingxibei Circuits

HEBEIXI

JINGXIBEI

JINGDONGXI

HUAINANDONG

JINGXIBEI

JINGJI

Huazhou
Weicheng
Zuocheng
Changyuan
Suanzao
Fengqiu
Yangwu
Zhongmou
Kaifengfu/
Dongjing/
Bianliang
Xiangfu
Cheniiu
Weishi
Xianping
Yanling
Fugou
Dongming
Kaocheng
Yongqiu
Xiangyi
Gongzhou
Taikang

BIANHE CANAL

CAIHE

◆ Xie pond salt consumer

◆ Major overland route

⋯ Major waterway

MAP 6

JINGJI 京畿路

Bianliang 汴梁	Gongzhou 拱州	Xiangfu 祥符
Changyuan 長垣	Kaifeng (fu) 開封府	Xiangyi 襄邑
Chenliu 陳留	Kaocheng 考城	Yanling 鄢陵
Dongjing 東京	Suanzao 酸棗	Yangwu (xian) 陽武縣
Dongming 東明	Taikang 太康	Yongqiu 雍丘
Fengqiu 封丘	Weishi 尉氏	Zhongmou 中牟
Fugou 扶溝	Xianping 咸平	

Map 7 Hebeidong, Hebeixi, and Hedong Circuits

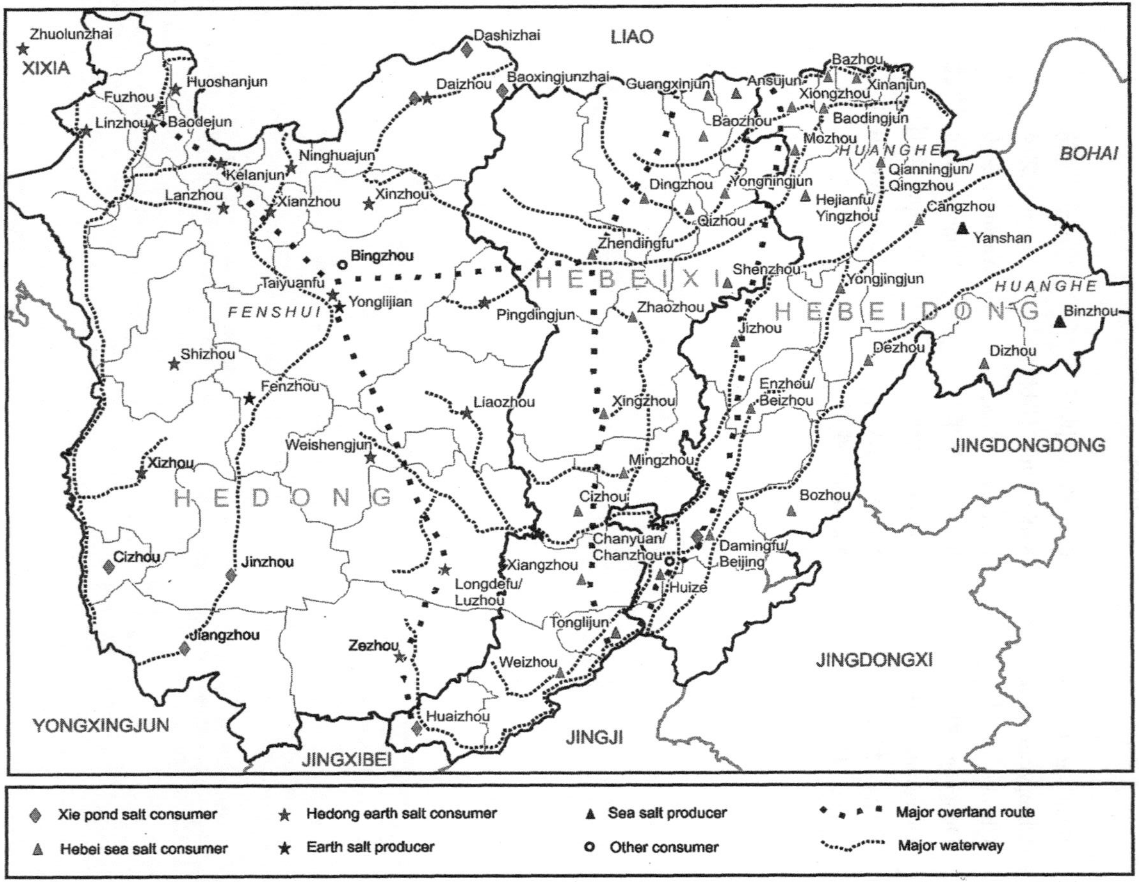

Legend:
◆ Xie pond salt consumer
★ Hedong earth salt consumer
▲ Hebei sea salt consumer
★ Earth salt producer
▲ Sea salt producer
○ Other consumer

◆ ▲ ▲ Major overland route
.... Major waterway

XIXIA
BOHAI
LIAO
HUANGHE
HEBEIDONG
HEBEIXI
HEDONG
FENSHUI
YONGXINGJUN
JINGXIBEI
JINGJI
JINGDONGXI
JINGDONGDONG

Zhuolunzhai
Dashizhai
Beoxingjunzhai
Daizhou
Fuzhou
Huoshanjun
Linzhou
Baodejun
Lanzhou
Kelanjun
Xinzhou
Ninghuajun
Guangxinjun
Anshijun
Bazhou
Xinanjun
Xiongzhou
Baodingjun
Mozhou
Qianninglun/Qingzhou
Hejianfu/Yingzhou
Yongninglun
Baozhou
Dingzhou
Qizhou
Zhendingfu
Shenzhou
Zhaozhou
Yongjinglun
Cangzhou
Yanshan
Dizhou
Binzhou
Dizhou
Enzhou/Beizhou
Bozhou
Mingzhou
Daminfu
Beijing
Huize
Chanyuan/Chanzhou
Cizhou
Xingzhou
Liaozhou
Pingdingjun
Bingzhou
Taiyuanfu
Yongjijian
Weishengjun
Fenzhou
Shizhou
Xizhou
Cizhou
Jinzhou
Jiangzhou
Xiangzhou
Longdefu/Luzhou
Zezhou
Tongliujun
Weizhou
Huaizhou

MAP 7

HEBEIDONG 河北東路

Bazhou 霸州	Daming (fu) 大名府	Qingzhou 清州
Baodingjun 保定軍	Dezhou 德州	Tonglijun 通利軍
Beijing 北京	Dizhou 棣州	Xin'anjun 信安軍
Beizhou 貝州	Enzhou 恩州	Xiongzhou 雄州
Binzhou 濱州	Hejianfu 河間府	Yanshan 鹽山
Bozhou 博州	Huize 惠澤	Yingzhou 瀛州
Cangzhou 滄州	Jizhou 冀州	Yongjingjun 永靜軍
Chanyuan 澶淵	Mozhou 莫州	
Chanzhou 澶州	Qianning (jun) 乾寧軍	

HEBEIXI 河北西路

Ansujun 安肅軍	Huaizhou 懷州	Weizhou 衛州
Baozhou 保州	Mingzhou 洺州	Xiangzhou 相州
Cizhou 磁州	Qizhou 祁州	Xingzhou 邢州
Dingzhou 定州	Shenzhou 深州	Zhaozhou 趙州
Guangxinjun 廣信軍	Tonglijun 通利軍	Zhendingfu 真定府

HEDONG 河東路

Baodejun 保德軍	Jiangzhou 絳州	Shizhou 石州
Baoxingjun (zhai) 寶興軍寨	Jinzhou 晉州	Taiyuan (fu) 太原府
	Kelanjun 岢嵐軍	Weishengjun 威勝軍
Bingzhou 并州	Lanzhou 嵐州	Xizhou 隰州
Cizhou 慈州	Liaozhou 遼州	Xianzhou 憲州
Dashizhai 大石寨	Linzhou 麟州	Xinzhou 忻州
Daizhou 代州	Longdefu 隆德府	Yongli (jian) 永利監
Fenzhou 汾州	Luzhou 潞州	Zezhou 澤州
Fuzhou 府州	Ninghua (jun) 寧化軍	Zhuolunzhai 濁輪砦
Huoshanjun 火山軍	Pingdingjun 平定軍	

Map 8 Huainandong and Huainanxi Circuits

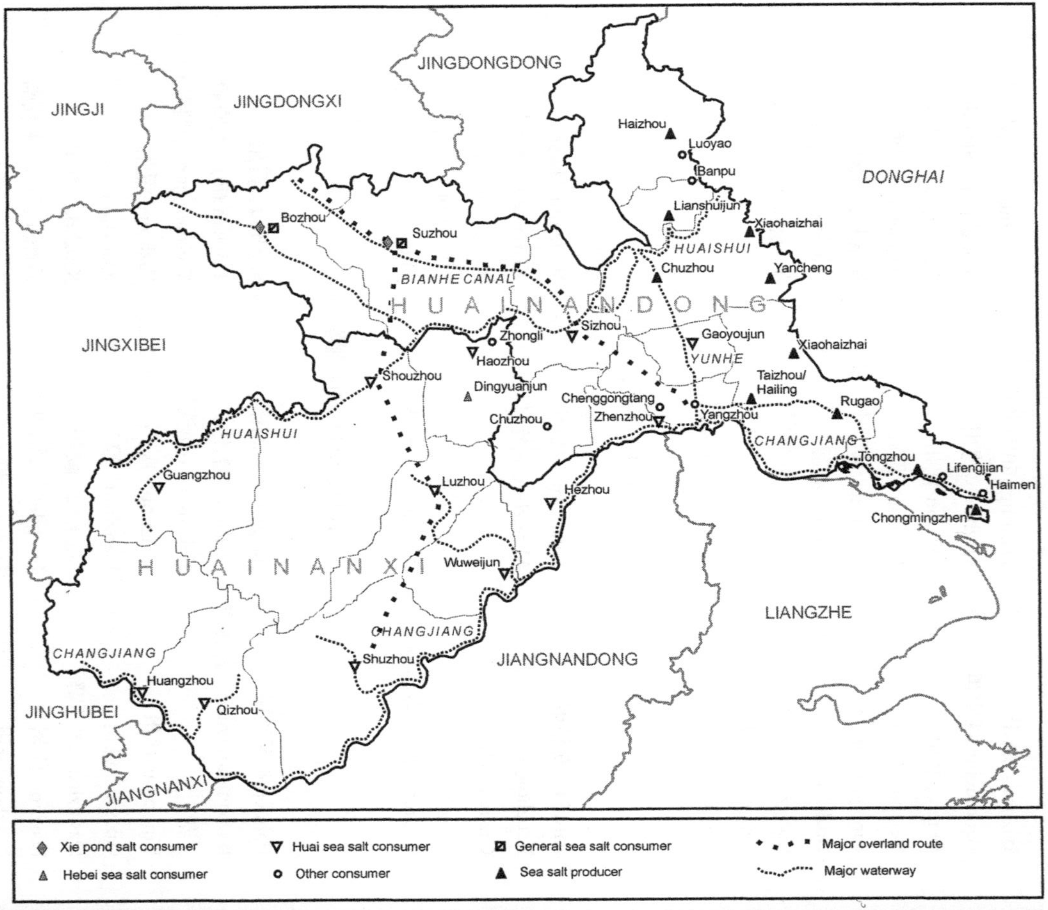

Legend:
- ◆ Xie pond salt consumer
- ▲ Hebei sea salt consumer
- ▽ Huai sea salt consumer
- ○ Other consumer
- ☒ General sea salt consumer
- ▲ Sea salt producer
- ▪▪▪ Major overland route
- ⋯⋯ Major waterway

Labels on map:
JINGJI, JINGDONGXI, JINGDONGDONG, DONGHAI, Haizhou, Luoyao, Banpu, Xiaohaizhai, Lianshuijun, Chuzhou, Yancheng, HUAISHUI, Sizhou, Gaoyoujun, YUNHE, Xiaohaizhai, Taizhou, Hailing, Rugao, CHANGJIANG, Tongzhou, Lifengjian, Haimen, Chongmingzhen, Yangzhou, Zhenzhou, Chenggongjiang, Zhongli, Haozhou, Dingyuanjun, Chuzhou, Luzhou, Haizhou, Wuweijun, LIANGZHE, JIANGNANDONG, CHANGJIANG, Shuzhou, JIANGNANXI, Qizhou, Huangzhou, CHANGJIANG, JINGHUBEI, Guangzhou, HUAISHUI, HUAINANXI, Shouzhou, Bozhou, Suzhou, BIANHE CANAL, HUAINANDONG, JINGXIBEI

MAP 8

HUAINANDONG　淮南東路

Banpu　板浦
Bozhou　亳州
Chengongtang　陳公塘
Chongmingzhen　崇明鎮
Chuzhou　楚州
Chuzhou　滁州
Gaoyoujun　高郵軍
Hailing　海陵

Haimen (dao)　海門島
Haizhou　海州
Lifeng (jian)　利豐監
Lianshui (jun)　漣水軍
Luoyao　洛要
Rugao　如皋
Sizhou　泗州
Suzhou　宿州

Taizhou　泰州
Tongzhou　通州
Xiaohai zhai　小海 ???
Yancheng　鹽城
Yangzhou　揚州
Zhenzhou　真州

HUAINANXI　淮南西路

Dingyuan (jun)　定遠軍
Guangzhou　光州
Haozhou　濠州
Hezhou　和州

Huangzhou　黃州
Luzhou　廬州
Qizhou　蘄州
Shouzhou　壽州

Shuzhou　舒州
Wuweijun　無爲軍
Zhongli (xian)　鍾離縣

Map 9 Qinfeng (Shaanxi) Circuit

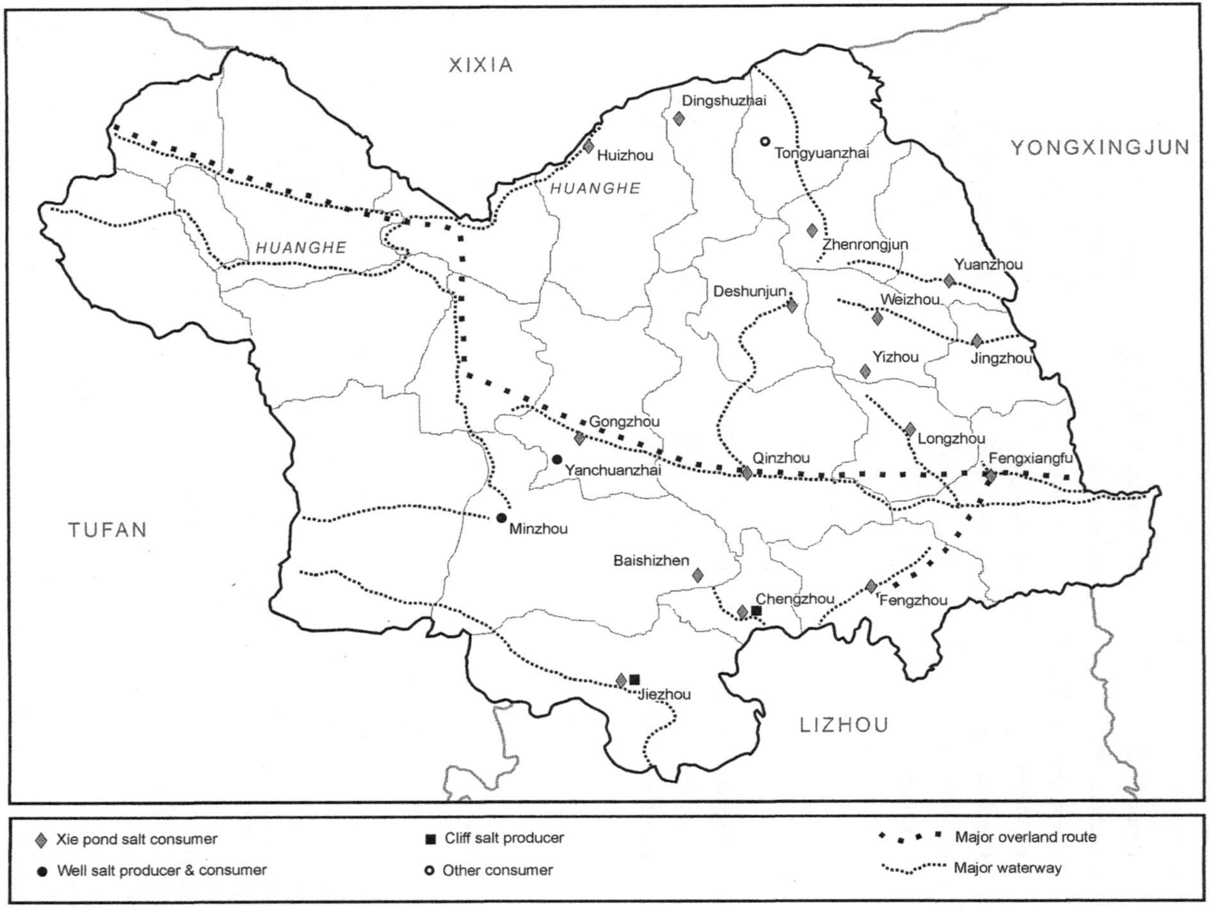

YONGXINGJUN

Yuanzhou

Jingzhou

Fengxiangfu

Zhenrongjun

Weizhou

Yizhou

Longzhou

Fengzhou

Tongyuanzhai

Deshunjun

Qinzhou

Chengzhou

LIZHOU

Dingshuzhai

Gongzhou

Baishizhen

Jiezhou

Huizhou

HUANGHE

Yanchuanzhai

XIXIA

Minzhou

HUANGHE

TUFAN

◆ Xie pond salt consumer   ■ Cliff salt producer   ■ Major overland route

● Well salt producer & consumer   ○ Other consumer   ⋯ Major waterway

MAP 9

QINFENG (SHAANXI) 秦鳳路

Baishi (zhen) 白石鎮

Chengzhou 成州

Deshunjun 德順軍

Dingshuzhai 定戍寨

Fengxiangfu 鳳翔府

Fengzhou 鳳州

Gongzhou 鞏州

Huizhou 會州

Jiezhou 階州

Jingzhou 涇州

Longzhou 隴州

Minzhou 岷州

Qinzhou 秦州

Tongyuanjun 通遠軍

Weizhou 渭州

Yanchuanzhai 鹽川寨

Yizhou 儀州

Yuanzhou 原州

Zhenrongjun 鎮戎軍

Map 10 Liangzhe and Jiangnandong Circuits

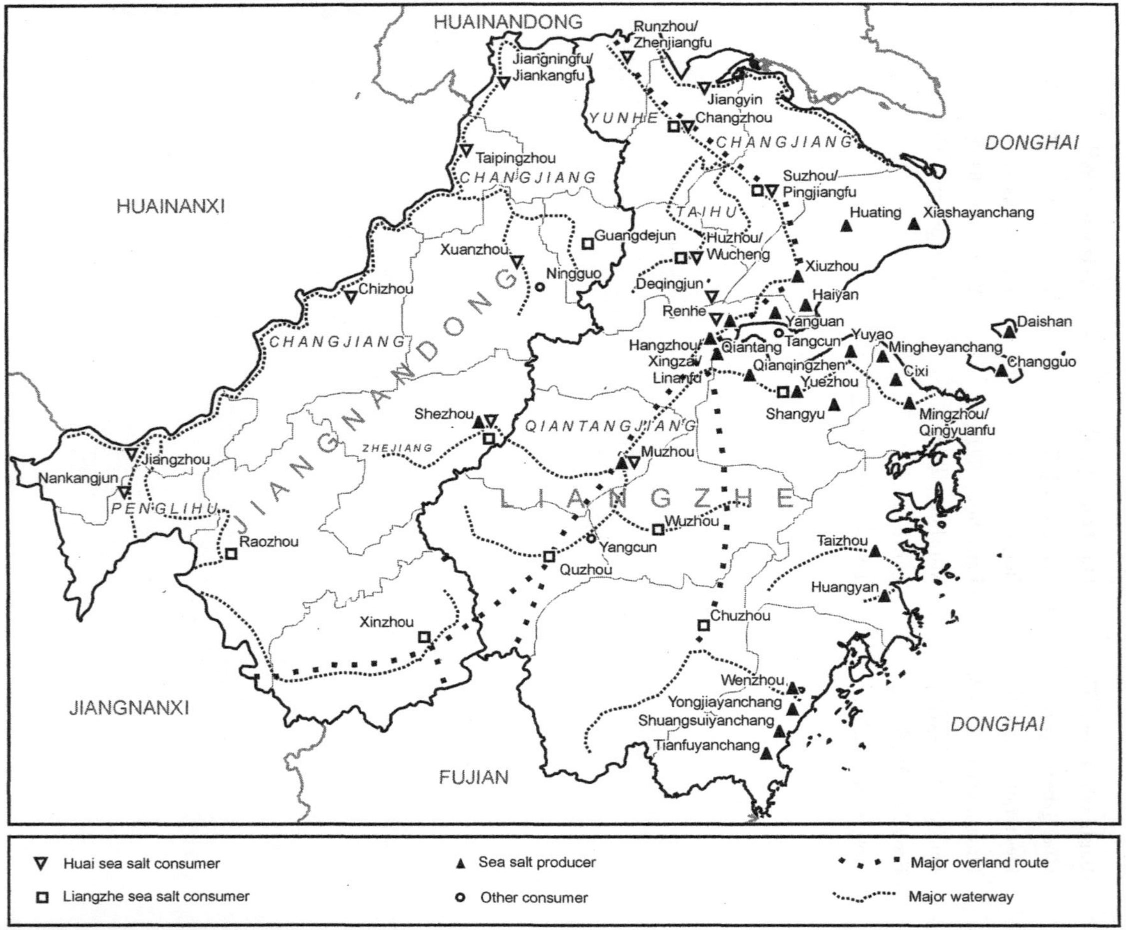

DONGHAI

HUAINANDONG

Runzhou/
Zhenjiangfu

Jiangningfu
Jiankangfu

Jiangyin
Changzhou

Suzhou/
Pingjiangfu

Huating
Xiashayanchang

CHANGJIANG

YUNHIE

TAIHU

Xiuzhou

Huzhou/
Wucheng

Haiyan
Yanguan

Tangcun
Yuyao
Qiantang
Qianqingzhen
Mingheyanchang

Daishan

Cixi
Changguo

Mingzhou/
Qingyuanfu

Deqingjun

Renhe
Hangzhou
Xingzha
Linan

Yuezhou
Shangyu

Guangdejun

Ningguo

QIANTANG JIANG

L I A N G Z H E

ZHEJIANG

Muzhou

Yangcun

Taizhou

Huangyan

Xuanzhou

CHANGJIANG

Taipingzhou

Shezhou

Quzhou

Chuzhou

Wenzhou
Yongjiayanchang
Shuangsuiyanchang
Tianfuyanchang

HUAINANXI

Chizhou

J I A N G N A N D O N G

Xinzhou

FUJIAN

Jiangzhou
Nankangjun

PENGLIHU

Raozhou

JIANGNANXI

DONGHAI

▽ Huai sea salt consumer
□ Liangzhe sea salt consumer
▲ Sea salt producer
○ Other consumer

▪▪▪ Major overland route
····· Major waterway

MAP 10

LIANGZHE 兩浙路

Changguo (xian) 昌國縣
Changzhou[b] 常州
Chuzhou 處州
Cixi (xian) 慈溪縣
Daishan 岱山
Deqingjun 德清軍
Haiyan 海鹽
Hangzhou 杭州
Huzhou 湖州
Huating 華亭
Huangyan 黃巖
Jiaxing (fu) 嘉興府 (see Xiuzhou)
Jiangyin (jun) 江陰軍
Kuaiji 會稽 (see Yuezhou)
Lin'an (fu) 臨安府
Linpingjian 臨平監 (see Renhe)

Minghe (yanchang) 鳴鶴鹽場
Mingzhou 明州
Muzhou 睦州
Pingjiangfu 平江府
Qianqingzhen 錢清鎮
Qiantang (xian) 錢塘縣
Quzhou 衢州
Renhe (xian) 仁和縣
Runzhou 潤州
Shangyu 上虞
Shaoxingfu 紹興府 (see Yuezhou)
Shiyan 石堰 (see Yuyao)
Shuangsui yancheng 雙遂鹽場
Suzhou 蘇州
Taizhou 台州
Tangcun 湯村

Tianfu (yanchang) 天富鹽場
Wenzhou 溫州
Wuxing (jun) 吳興郡 (see Huzhou)
Wuzhou 婺州
Xiasha (yanchang) 下砂鹽場
Xingzai 行在
Xiuzhou 秀州
Yanguan chang 鹽官場
Yangcun 楊村
Yinxian 鄞縣 (see Mingzhou)
Yongjia (yanchang) 永嘉鹽場
Yuyao (xian) 餘姚縣
Yuezhou 越州
Zhenjiang (fu) 鎮江府

JIANGNANDONG 江南東路

Chizhou 池州
Guangdejun 廣德軍
Jiankang (fu) 建康府
Jiangningfu 江寧府
Jiangzhou 江州

Nankangjun 南康軍
Ningguo 寧國
Raozhou 饒州
Shezhou 歙州

Shengzhou 昇州 (see Jiangningfu)
Taipingzhou 太平州
Xinzhou 信州
Xuanzhou 宣州

Map 11 Fujian Circuit

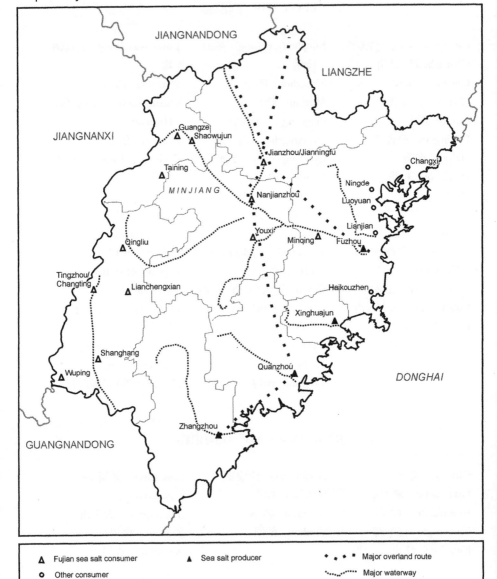

Legend:
- △ Fujian sea salt consumer
- ○ Other consumer
- ▲ Sea salt producer
- ◆ ● ■ Major overland route
- ⋯⋯ Major waterway

MAP 11

FUJIAN 福建路

Changting 長汀

Changxi (xian) 長溪縣

Fuzhou 福州

Guangze 光澤

Haikou (zhen) 海口鎮

Jianning (fu) 建寧府

Jianzhou 建州

Liancheng (xian) 蓮城縣

Lianjiang (xian) 連江縣

Luoyuan (xian) 羅源縣

Minqing 閩清

Nanjianzhou 南劍州

Ningde (xian) 寧德縣

Qingliu (xian) 清流縣

Quanzhou 泉州

Shanghang 上杭

Shaowujun 邵武軍

Taining (xian) 泰寧縣

Tingzhou 汀州

Wuping (xian) 武平縣

Xinghuajun 興化軍

Youxi (xian) 尤溪縣

Zhangzhou 漳州

Map 12 Guangnandong and Guangnanxi Circuits

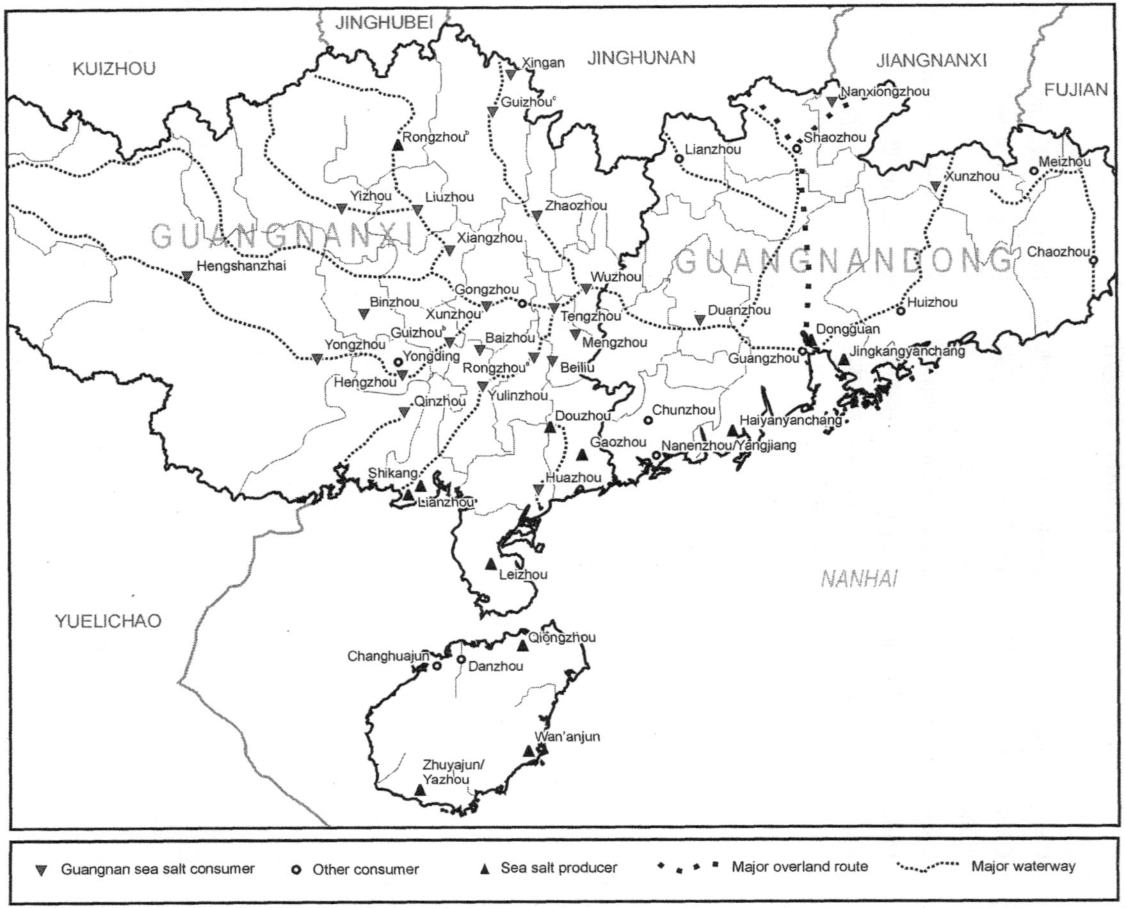

FUJIAN

JIANGNANXI

JINGHUNAN

JINGHUBEI

KUIZHOU

GUANGNANDONG

GUANGNANXI

NANHAI

YUELICHAO

Meizhou

Chaozhou

Xunzhou

Nanxiongzhou

Shaozhou

Huizhou

Jingkang/Yangchang

Dongguan

Lianzhou

Guangzhou

Duanzhou

Haiyanyanchang/Yangjiang

Xingan

Guizhou

Zhaozhou

Wuzhou

Tengzhou

Mengzhou

Beiliu

Chunzhou

Nanenzhou

Gaozhou

Douzhou

Huazhou

Rongzhou

Yizhou

Liuzhou

Xiangzhou

Gongzhou

Baizhou

Rongzhou

Yulinzhou

Leizhou

Binzhou

Xunzhou

Guizhou

Yongding

Qinzhou

Yongzhou

Hengzhou

Shikang

Lianzhou

Hengshanzhai

Qiongzhou

Danzhou

Wan'anjun

Changhuajun

Zhuyajun/
Yazhou

▼ Guangnan sea salt consumer   ○ Other consumer   ▲ Sea salt producer

◆◆◆ Major overland route   ••••• Major waterway

MAP 12

GUANGNANDONG　廣南東路

Chaozhou　潮州	Haiyan (yanchang)　海宴鹽場	Nanenzhou　南恩州
Chunzhou　春州	Huizhou　惠州	Nanxiong (zhou)　南雄州
Dongguan 東筦	Jingkang (yanchang)　靜康鹽場	Shaozhou　韶州
Duanzhou　端州	Lianzhou　連州	Xunzhou　循州
Guangzhou　廣州	Meizhou　梅州	Yangjiang (xian)　陽江縣

GUANGNANXI　廣南西路

Baizhou 白州	Jingjiangfu　靜江府 (see	Wan'anjun　萬安軍
Beiliu (xian)　北流縣	Guizhou[c])	Wuzhou　梧州
Binzhou　賓州	Leizhou　雷州	Xiangzhou　象州
Changhuajun　昌化軍	Lianzhou　廉州	Xingan (xian)　興安縣
Danzhou 儋州	Liuzhou　柳州	Xunzhou　潯州
Douzhou 竇州	Mengzhou　蒙州	Yazhou　崖州
Gaozhou　高州	Qinzhou　欽州	Yizhou　宜州
Gongzhou　龔州	Qiongzhou　瓊州	Yongdingjun　永定軍
Guizhou[b]　貴州	Rongzhou[a]　容州	Yongzhou　邕州
Guizhou[c]　桂州	Rongzhou[b]　融州	Yulinzhou　鬱林州
Hengzhou　橫州	Shikang (xian)　石康縣	Zhaozhou　昭州
Huazhou　化州	Tengzhou　藤州	Zhuyajun 朱崖軍

Map 13 Jiangnanxi Circuit

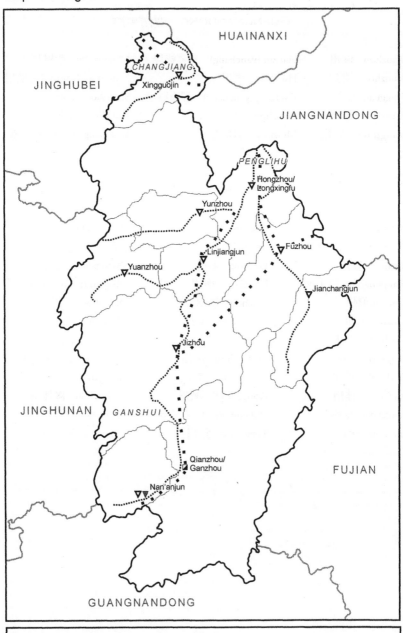

HUAINANXI

JINGHUBEI

CHANGJIANG

Xingguojin

JIANGNANDONG

PENGLIHU

Hongzhou/
Longxingfu

Yunzhou

Fuzhou

Linjiangjun

Yuanzhou

Jianchangjun

Jizhou

JINGHUNAN   *GANSHUI*

Qianzhou/
Ganzhou

FUJIAN

Nan'anjun

GUANGNANDONG

▣ Jiangxi sea salt consumer	▽ Huai sea salt consumer		Major overland route
▼ Guangnan sea salt consumer			·····•···· Major waterway

MAP 13

JIANGNANXI　江南西路

Fuzhou　撫州

Hongzhou　洪州

Jizhou　吉州

Jianchangjun　建昌軍

Junzhou　筠州

Linjiangjun　臨江軍

Longxingfu　隆興府

Nan'anjun　南安軍

Qianzhou　虔州

Xingguojun　興國軍

Yuanzhou　袁州

Map 14 Jinghubei and Jinghunan Circuits

▼ Guangnan sea salt consumer	● Well salt producer & consumer	✦ ● ■ Major overland route
▽ Huai sea salt consumer	○ Other consumer	Major waterway

MAP 14

JINGHUBEI 荊湖北路

Anzhou 安州

Dingzhou 鼎州

Ezhou 鄂州

Guizhou 歸州

Hanyangjun 漢陽軍

Jianglingfu 江陵府

Wushatouzhen 烏沙頭鎮

Xiazhou 峽州

Xuzhou 敍州

Yuezhou 嶽州

Yunzhou 雲州

JINGHUNAN 荊湖南路

Chenzhou 郴州

Daozhou 道州

Guiyangjian 桂陽監

Hengzhou 衡州

Quanzhou 全州

Shaozhou 邵州

Tanzhou 潭州

Yongzhou 永州

Map 15 Lizhou, Chengdufu, Zizhou, and Kuizhou Circuits

QINFENG

YONGXINGJUN

TUFAN

Xingzhou

Yangzhou

Wenzhou

Xingyuanfu

JINGXINAN

Xihezhou

L I Z H O U

Lizhou

Jianzhou

Bazhou

Daningjian

Mianzhou

Langzhou

Kuizhou

Yilong

Yongkangjun

Pengzhou

Zizhou

Pengzhou

Yunanjun

Hanzhou

Fuguozhen

Wanzhou

Chengdufu

Pengxi

Shizhou

Qiongzhou

Suizhou

Zhongzhou

Pujiangjian

Lingjingjian

Gongzhou

Chongqingfu

Lizhou

Rongzhou

Changzhou

Qianzhou

Jianwei

Gongjingzhen

Rongzhou

Fushunjian

Luzhou

Nanjingjian

Yujingjian

Z I Z H O U /
T O N G C H U A N F U

K U I Z H O U

JINGHUBEI

DALI

GUANGNANXI

◆ Xie pond salt consumer	▲ Sea salt producer	✦ ⋅ ■ Major overland route
○ Other salt consumer	● Well salt producer & consumer	⋅⋅⋅⋅⋅⋅ Major waterway

MAP 15

CHENGDUFU 成都府路 (S. Song YIZHOU 益州路)

Hanzhou 漢州
Jianwei 犍爲
Lizhou 黎州

Linqiong 臨邛 (see
  Qiongzhou)
Lingjing jian 陵井監
Mianzhou 綿州

Pujiang jian 蒲江監
Qiongzhou 邛州
Yongkangjun 永康軍

KUIZHOU 夔州路

Chongqingfu 重慶府
Daning jian 大寧監
Kuizhou 夔州

Qianzhou 黔州
Shizhou 施州
Wanzhou 萬州

Yunanjun 雲安軍
Zhongzhou 忠州

LIZHOU 利州路

Bazhou 巴州
Jianzhou 劍州
Pengzhou 蓬州

Wenzhou 文州
Xihezhou 西和州
Xingyuanfu 興元付

Xingzhou 興州
Yangzhou 洋州
Yilong 儀隴

ZIZHOU 梓州路 (S. Song TONGCHUANFU 潼川府路)

Changzhou 昌州
Fuguozhen 富國鎮
Fushun (jian) 富順監
Gongjingzhen
Luzhou 瀘州

Nanjing (jian) 南井監
Pengxi 蓬溪
Pengzhou 蓬州
Rongzhou^c 戎州
Rongzhou^d 榮州

Suizhou 遂州
Yujing (jian) 淯井監
Zizhou 梓州

PART ONE
INTRODUCTION

INTRODUCTION

The salt monopoly in premodern China is a near-perfect vehicle for understanding the Chinese political economy generally. The monopoly possessed the same type of organization, personnel, methods, and character as any other Chinese bureaucracy of the time, the only difference was one of function: it was charged with monitoring production, supervising transport, and selling its product. The universal demand for salt and both the large-scale and highly localized nature of its production made this industry an ideal target for revenue extraction under a centralized bureaucratic regime.

The monopolies evolved into a major source for the revenues sought by bureaucrats over China's long history. When the fiscal and geopolitical context became especially aggravated in the Song period, generating pressures like never before, this provided the backdrop to debates over the salt monopoly. Within the state hierarchy, diverse and contending voices emerged to battle over the conflicting imperatives of collecting revenues for the state and protecting the people.

In the course of organizing the salt industry, the government needed different groups of agents to implement and enforce its policies. The state called on salters to produce, under strict regulation; it frequently relied on professional merchants, who, while not salaried or ranked, operated subject to obligations and restrictions imposed by the state, and as such may be seen as quasi-official. Both producers and merchants managed to work around restrictions to their own benefit and at great cost to the government. But it was government officials themselves who caused the greatest problems in the system: they were the most flagrant violators of the monopoly law.

So what can be said about the monopoly as a system of government control? How successful was the salt monopoly, and for whom? How did the state manage competition for resources and to what extent did the center dictate the activities of local governments? How did the system

3

mediate and monitor itself? And finally, what was the impact of the monopoly on key participants? This study of the *Songshi* salt treatise will point to some of the broader political and economic contexts in which the monopoly operated, as well as filling in its account of the monopoly itself. We begin with a brief description of salt-related institutions that preceded those of the Song.

Pre-Song Salt Monopolies

Chinese legend traces the salt industry to Susha Juzi, a government minister of the Yellow Emperor, who lived with his clan near the sea and was skilled at decocting salt. The fabled emperor Shun was said to have been involved in the trade of lake salt.[1] From ancient times, in China as around the world, salt's unique role as a basic necessity with no ready substitutes has given it not just cultural significance but great importance as a strategic resource. When the Yellow Emperor won a battle against tribesmen over control of a salt lake in Shanxi, he was accepted as leader throughout the Yellow River plain, and henceforth salt became key in the process of assimilating tribal peoples.[2] During the Spring and Autumn period (770–476 B.C.), in the competition between states to become hegemon (*ba*), the ruler of Jin opted not to move his capital near a salt marsh on the advice that rich resources make a people lazy and their ruler poor.[3]

A Critical Work in Early Political Economy

The *Guanzi*, one of the first great works on political economy in China, provided an ideological basis for monopoly that persisted for

---

[1] Guo Zhengzhong 1997, 2–3, 19–22. We must acknowledge Guo Zhengzhong's painstaking work on the development of the Chinese salt industry in general and that of the Song in particular. See also Guo Zhengzhong 1990a, which presents 900 pages on salt production, trade, and policy.

[2] *Kongzi sanchao ji*, cited in Chen and Zeng 1991, 513; *Shiji* [*SJ*] 1.3; Qian Gongbo 1964, 160.

[3] Salt continued to weigh on Duke Cheng's (?–600 B.C.) mind when he dreamt the Chu ruler had "pickled" (*gu*) his brains (see Legge 1960, vol. 5, 209, 358–60). Legge renders this "sucked his brains"; I interpret based on the original meaning of *gu* as salt.

two thousand years, from the Han dynasty to the end of the Qing.[4] This treatise, probably collated by adherents of Guan Zhong (?–645 B.C.), a major figure in the establishment of Qi as the first hegemon among the Chinese states, asserted that because everyone needed salt, increasing its price even incrementally would reap huge returns:

> If you were to announce a head tax on all adults and children, everyone would certainly complain and oppose it. But if you implement a salt tax policy, one hundred times the profits will accrue to you, the ruler, while the people will be unable to escape it. This is what is meant by managing finances.[5]

According to the *Guanzi*'s logic, the cost of salt to consumers would effectively include a tax, yet spare them a separate payment. By controlling both the production and distribution of salt, the state could prevent disparities between rich and poor, as well as increase state revenues.

While statesmen before the Qin unification (221–206 B.C.) recognized the fiscal value of salt, the nature of China's monopoly came to be predicated upon a united empire. In contrast to other powers across Asia and Europe at other periods, where governments had to content themselves with charging transit tolls (France) or merely regulating sales or some other stage of the industry (Venice), China's centralized bureaucratic government could tightly monitor the sources of salt as well as the stages of production and distribution.

The Han Monopoly

In the early decades of the Han dynasty (206 B.C.–A.D. 9), emperors embraced enlightened taxation of the land and appeasement of the powerful Xiongnu empire beyond the Great Wall. When Han Wudi (r. 140–87 B.C.) broke with this policy, he embarked upon a general military offensive as well as more concerted development of the territory he already held. This led to a fiscal burden that China's small farmer economy could not bear alone, and the need arose for a

---

[4] The Republican period specialist Lin Zhenhan articulates this in the entry "*yanfa*" in his *Yanzheng cidian* (1988).

[5] Yan 1996, Haiwang 72, 537–41. See also *Tongdian* [*TD*] 10.15a–24b; *Guanzi* [*GZ*] 22.2a–4a.

new revenue source. In 119 B.C., for the first time in Chinese history, Wudi instituted an empire-wide state monopoly of salt, concentrating its production, transport, and sale in official hands.[6]

In the system of monopoly prohibitions (*quejin*), also referred to as monopoly sales (*quemai*), the Han state restricted entry into the market, took ownership of all salt, and assumed command over production, which had been in the hands of small local producers. The government provided equipment and funds to workers, often landless peasants it had drafted into salt production. It specified the size of evaporation pans to facilitate reckoning how much was manufactured each day. In what was also a monopsony, the product was not the producers' to dispose of freely; all salt had to be submitted to the state, which punished private production. After collecting the salt, the state undertook to transport it to points of distribution.[7] It implemented empire-wide sales to consumers in which the price greatly exceeded the costs of production and distribution.

The Han salt administration ran separate from and parallel to other central and local government administrations. Salt taxes accrued to the central fisc, under the aegis of the Office of Agricultural Supervision (*danong*, later *dasinong*), which established salt and iron offices around the country, controlled prices, and managed distribution.[8] From at least the early Han period iron had become a key industry in connection with salt, and even a major sector in its own right. The link between salt and defense meant that there were many more salt and iron administrators in the north than in the south at this time.[9]

Upon Wudi's death, the monopoly came under broad criticism. In 81 B.C., a Salt and Iron Debate, called at court to deliberate over continuation of the monopoly, turned into a classic confrontation between Confucians and Legalists. On one side, the "literate and virtuous" (*wenxue xianliang*) Confucians sympathized with the common people and argued against the monopoly that placed such a burden on them. They regarded commerce as incidental (*mo*). The

---

[6] *Hanshu* [*HS*] 59.2641.

[7] *SJ* 30.1429.

[8] *HS* 19.731, 732n; *HS* 24.1174–75; *SJ* 30.1441, 1428–29.

[9] *HS* 28.1591; Bao Zhao's "Wucheng fu" (Song of Wucheng), from *Wenxuan* [*WX*] 11.6–7.

state's true foundation (*ben*), they argued, was the agrarian economy based on small peasant households. But in the context of a centralized bureaucratic state, neither the Confucians nor the merchants could stand up to bargain with the ruler the way feudal lords did in the medieval West. The Legalists, on the other hand, most of them bureaucrats represented by the powerful Sang Hongyang (152–80 B.C.), Wudi's privy councilor (*dasinong zhongcheng*) and chief of fiscal affairs, stressed the financial deficit and the absolute necessity of maintaining the salt monopoly as a prime revenue source.[10] Sang Hongyang won the day because the land tax was insufficient to support the government, but the controversy over salt continued down to the Song era and beyond.

The Tang Monopoly

Since the Chinese monopoly was based on a unified empire, for several centuries after the collapse of the Han, salt production fell back to the localities. However pronounced the need for salt-generated income, no mechanism or authority existed for imposing a state monopoly until the Sui (589–618 A.D.) restored a centralized bureaucracy. The Sui rulers instituted a no-tax salt policy that allowed the people to produce salt freely. But their other policies provoked rebellion: extensive public works such as the Grand Canal and massive land and sea campaigns placed a heavy burden on the populace and eventually led to the dynasty's downfall. The succeeding Tang dynasty (618–907) also refrained from taxing salt at first, and it was local government administrators who managed salt except in a few areas directly controlled by the central government.[11]

Salt and other resources were still considered possessions of the state even when it did not attempt to control or tax them. With the acute concentration of land ownership in the 680s, peasants lost their

---

[10] *Yantielun* [*YTL*] 1.6b–9a.

[11] Before the An Lushan Rebellion, government policy was not clear-cut. Salt regions were administered differently from place to place: local or circuit authorities supervised lake salt production in Shaanxi; a central government office oversaw producers' tax payments of sea salt; and prefectures collected taxes on the well salt of Sichuan. *Jiu Tangshu* [*JTS*] 48.2106–2110; *Xin Tangshu* [*XTS*] 54.1377–81. For how the Tang monopoly operated, see Twitchett 1970, 49–58.

holdings and the Tang agrarian system (*zuyongdiao*), which had aimed at allowing every family sufficient land to live off in exchange for taxes in grain, corvee (labor service, *yong*), and cloth, became impossible to maintain. The state lost the revenue stream it needed and fiscal pressures were exacerbated when the self-supporting militia system (*fubing zhi*) collapsed and was replaced with professional soldiers who had to be paid. Moreover, the creation of regional governorships on the frontier increased the autonomy of military leaders and quickly led to crisis. The crisis broke wide open in 755, when one military governor, An Lushan, (703–757) attacked the Tang capital. To generate income for the effort against him, a Hebei prefect, Yan Zhenqing (709–785), turned to ad hoc salt taxation the next year. In 758 Diwu Qi (712–782), the salt and iron commissioner (*yantieshi*), pushed to extend this emergency measure.[12] He envisioned popular production, with the government procuring, transporting, and selling the salt. Such an arrangement was only one step removed from the total monopoly of the Han.[13]

In 759 the Tang instituted this salt monopoly empire-wide.[14] The court divided its administration regionally for the first time between the eastern sea salt and western pond and well salt regions. These two regions were gradually subdivided into smaller units, the better to monitor specific extraction methods. Liu Yan (715–780), the salt commissioner in 760, reorganized the monopoly into one using merchant distribution, thereby reducing the state's formerly active role in transport and sales.[15] He established monopoly agencies and branches in trade centers around the country to supervise production and the sale of salt to merchants. These branch offices were called salterns (*chang*), the lowest level at which salt production and distribution were conducted. Here officials sold salt wholesale to merchants after adding a set tax. While the procurement price paid to producers remained fixed, the excise tax was gradually boosted as needs became more urgent.

---

[12] *XTS* 153.4856. For the development of the salt administration from about 758 to 820, see Twitchett 1954, 60–89; Hino 1963, 1–56.

[13] Chen Yande (1991) argues that the salters' lot improved from the Han to Tang.

[14] *XTS* 54.1378; *JTS* 49.2116, 2119, 2130.

[15] *XTS* 53.1368; *XTS* 149.4798. For analysis of Liu Yan's government-merchant profit sharing, see Bao Xiaona 1982.

At this point direct government involvement ended. Merchants could freely transport and resell the salt. And yet merchants were not free agents, but were registered with the state: While salt merchants enjoyed a special status above other merchants, were exempt from corvee and the land tax, and benefited from protections of the government, they were obliged to fulfill a government sales quota and answered to the central government offices. The merchants passed on the cost of taxes, including illegal transit fees levied by local officials, to the consumer, who had no choice but to pay. The great essayist Han Yu (768–824) supported Liu Yan's reforms: "The state's monopoly on salt allows merchants to manage transport, pay a tax, then sell to consumers. In this way, the people rich and poor all contribute to the national revenues, making it unnecessary for the state to get involved."[16]

At the beginning of Liu Yan's administration, the annual salt revenue from the lower Yangzi and Huai River areas added up to only 400,000 strings; twenty years later, by 780, it had soared to 6 million strings, or more than 50 percent of the Tang's cash income.[17] By about 800, merchants who had already become the state's registered agents ran the trade between the Yangzi valley and North China, and between Sichuan and Zhejiang.[18] Regional and interregional transportation systems became tightly entangled with the salt monopoly: salt revenues were used to finance corvee labor and maintain key routes, particularly the canal system. This is why one individual was often called upon to hold both transport and salt posts. The success in reaping revenues from the south was due in large part to the tremendous growth of the Yangzi valley. Indeed, the fiscal system changed radically in the late eighth century so that income from commercial taxes began to surpass those from agrarian taxes, a trend that would become even more pronounced in the Song. When the emperor died and the new chief councilor had Liu Yan executed, the monopoly sank into disarray. Provincial military governors took

---

[16] *Han Yu ji* [*HYJ*] 41.313.

[17] *HYJ* 41.313. On salt revenues, see *XTS* 54.1378; *Zizhi tongjian* [*ZZTJ*] 226.7286. On total cash income, see Twitchett 1970, 35; 52n20; 55n36.

[18] Hino 1963, 35. Seo (1982a; 1982b) provides models of Tang local control over pond salt and sea salt, respectively.

control of their regions' salt administration, effectively stripping the court of its grip on revenue from the provinces.[19]

The Han established the principle of salt regulation, and in that era debate had centered on the pros and cons of maintaining a total monopoly. The Tang, which created a more bureaucratic financial machine, had inherited no uniform policy on the administration or taxation of salt. The financial requirements of fighting the An Lushan Rebellion, however, led first to the implementation of government-administered salt sales, later replaced by sales through merchants, who paid a monopoly tax to officials for the right to retail salt. By the Song era fiscal and geopolitical demands had become even more complicated, and so the complexities of the monopoly system grew. Debate now centered on how best to improve the monopoly's ability to generate revenue; its necessity was a given.

The Historical Context of the
Song Monopoly System

Overarching Political Concerns

In 960 the soldiers of Zhao Kuangyin, commander-in-chief of the Later Zhou (951–960) palace army, launched a coup that would enthrone Zhao as founder of a new dynasty, the Song (see Map 1). The successive military uprisings of the Five Dynasties, culminating in the coup that brought him to power taught the new emperor, Song Taizu (r. 960–976), a valuable historical lesson. The Song founder's guiding principle became "strengthen the trunk and weaken the branches" (*qianggan ruozhi*), that is, bolster the central government at the expense of local authorities. One key advisor noted, "The way to manage this now is simply to take power back from the generals, control their money and grain, and gather their crack troops [under court control]. Only thus can one ensure the stability of the empire."[20]

---

[19] For salt policy in the Five Dynasties, see Zheng Xuemeng 1982. For salt taxes during the Five Dynasties, see Kiyokoba 1984.

[20] The advisor was Zhao Pu (922–992), no relation to the emperor: *Xuzizhi tongjian changbian* [*XCB*] 2.49.

So Taizu replaced his military commanders with civil officials and transferred the best troops from the former regional commands into his "palace army" (*jinjun* or *jinbing*), which not only defended the capital but also the border, so in fact it served as the regular army. He also drafted the rootless into prefectural armies (*xiangjun, xiangbing*) to weaken the rebellious potential of the locales. From the early Song control of the military remained a key factor in executing the will of the court, yet ironically it ultimately debilitated the dynasty both defensively and financially.

Besides the goal of domestic control, the Song faced an unprecedented external challenge, the constant threat of invasion by nomadic states beyond the Great Wall. From the dynasty's very establishment, the Khitan Liao (907–1125), a comparably large empire with a superior military hemmed the Song in on the northeast. A second threat came from the Tangut Xixia (1038–1227) to the northwest. A third was the Jurchen Jin (1115–1235), who succeeded the Liao. The historical idiom "to go deer hunting on the Central Plain" (*zhulu zhongyuan*) has long been a metaphor denoting competition for political control over the Chinese empire, a goal the Song, Liao, Xixia, and Jin all pursued. While the Song remained an equal, though in fact a lesser equal, in the emergent interstate system, the imperial government was constantly engaged in building its military to ward off attack, contain border region predations, and occasionally to launch its own missions.

Of prime Song territorial concern was a large tract of land known as the Sixteen Prefectures of Yan Yun. This region, which included the Beijing area and present-day Datong, had been lost to the Liao empire during the Five Dynasties. The court never reconciled itself to the loss of this territory, and the unity of the empire would not be complete until it had been recovered.[21] This irredentist ideology only became more entrenched after the additional losses of the Southern Song, when Hangzhou was called the "temporary capital" for 150 years (see Map 2). It would remain the subtext to the continued inflation of the Song military.

The threat of attack by its powerful neighbors determined much of the Song's foreign as well as domestic policy, yet diplomatic exchanges and the peaceful trading of goods also continued in frontier

---

[21] *Liaoshi* [*LS*] 4.44–5.

areas along the line of the Great Wall. Envoys established markets for conducting government-authorized trade, including most notably Liao and Xixia exports of sheep, horses, carpets, and salt to the Song, while the Song exported agricultural and manufactured products to the steppe peoples. Control at the border regions had important implications both for security and overall relations, including trade.

Statism and Fiscalism

What was distinctive about the Song government's approach to the economy may be summed up in the terms "statism" and "fiscalism." Statism, a system in which control over economic, political, and social affairs is both extensive and concentrated in a central state organization, arguably reached a peak in the Song period. The fiscal policies of the Song were activist and interventionist. Having said this, we will see in this account of the salt monopoly that even the "predatory state" would not necessarily choose to engage in the total "economic bleeding" of its populace.[22] This was due not only to various and competing bureaucratic interests and players, but also to the sheer cost of enforcement, including ultimately and most extremely the potential collapse of social order. In principle the monopoly system was meant to maximize revenues for the state while not unduly burdening the people.

Furthermore, Song was notable for direct bureaucratic intervention in commerce and a command economy geared to generate resources, or what one might term fiscalism. Rather than simply regulate, the state continually sought new and ingenious methods by which to increase income. The motivation behind this economic activism included the overall political, military, and fiscal context of the times. While the "ancestral tradition" of the Song founding fathers was honored in its general aspects, the bureaucracy continually created new institutions to address changing conditions and perceived needs, and took a distinctively pragmatic approach to institutional reform. This activism was particularly well expressed through innovations in the state's monopoly of salt.

Debates raged at the Northern Song court about this general approach to the economy. On one side, the fiscalists, epitomized by

---

[22] See Levy 1988, 3–4; Schumpeter 1954, 6–7.

Wang Anshi, advocated developing income from new sources (*kaiyuan*) for the state coffers. The conservative side, represented by Sima Guang, advocated frugality and belt-tightening (*jielüe*). Wang's New Policies faced heated opposition from conservatives, as can be seen in the argument below, recorded at a meeting called by Emperor Shenzong:

> Wang declared, "The national deficit is not really the problem. The problem is, officials are ignorant of handling fiscal matters."
>
> Sima Guang countered, "Those who know how to handle fiscal problems only extract money from the people!"
>
> "That is not the case at all. Those who know how to handle fiscal problems do not raise taxes but still can maintain sufficient revenues."
>
> "Nonsense! The wealth of the empire lies in the hands of either the people or the government. Your schemes to extract wealth from the people are worse than raising taxes. Your kind of argument is just like that of Sang Hongyang who deceived (Han) Wudi!"[23]

Factional struggles and their attendant policy swings were to plague the Northern Song until its demise. At Shenzong's death Zhezong (r. 1085–1100), who was only a child, initially fell under the sway of the conservatives and his grandmother, who supported the conservative faction leader Sima Guang. Within months of taking office, Sima Guang, as chief councilor, had annulled the New Policies. Sima was by no means the first high official to denounce the "three excesses" in government expenditure—excessive troops, supernumerary officials, and excessive spending—which were bankrupting the treasury.[24] But neither did his fiscal approach win the day for long.

After 1094 Zhezong's approach shifted, for both Sima Guang and the sovereign's grandmother had died. He demoted the conservatives and appointed Wang Anshi's supporters Zhang Dun (1035–1105) and Zeng Bu (1036–1107) to be his chief councilors and restored various of the New Policies. Under Huizong (r. 1101–1125) the chief councilor Cai Jing moved to bar Sima Guang's associates from holding office in the capital and conducted a general purge of hundreds of

---

[23] The ideological terms invoked here remind us of the Han dynasty salt and iron debates. *Songshi* [*SS*] 327.10543, 336.10762–64.

[24] *SS* 188.4628–29. See *XCB* 42.880–83, 884, 897–898 for statements by Sun He, Wang Ji, and Wang Yucheng; *XCB* 52.1152 for Wang Sizong's words; *XCB* 112.2623–26 for Fan Zhongyan's criticism; *SS* 287.9648; and *Luancheng houji* [*LCHJ*] 21.4214–19.

conservatives.[25] Cai Jing made himself out to be Wang Anshi's successor but did not pursue the urgent task of reform. With the fall of the Northern Song, the conservatives managed to return to power for good and new contentions arose in place of this old debate.

Salt in Politics

Of course, the broader Song economic debates also touched on the salt monopoly policy. Throughout the dynasty, salt policies oscillated due to the conflicting interests of the groups involved in fiscal decision-making. From the emperor down to the county administrators, numerous vested interests competed within the state hierarchy. Conflict over revenue allocation at the operational level commonly shook center-local relations. Within the central government, clashes occurred between branches and organs that represented different philosophies, functions, and responsibilities. In the circuits, interagency competition developed among the intendancies.

It is difficult to generalize about what stand an official of a particular category or level would take, since a policy position might be determined more by an individual's political stance or character than by his job. Remonstrance officials, other policy critics, and various censors often memorialized on popular misery. They endeavored to protect salters, merchants, and consumers from excessive state intrusion. In contrast, the professional fiscal experts, including salt intendants, military intendants, and saltern officials, typically sought to maximize revenues and aggressively pursued state needs. They often looked upon the wretched producers as "stubborn and slippery" types.[26] Prefectural and county "father-and-mother" officials (*fumu guan*), charged with maintaining the well being of the public, also tended to sympathize with the real difficulties salters faced. They were generally tolerant of infractions committed out of desperation. Lastly, the emperor himself was caught between the contradictory aims of benefiting his people and augmenting revenue for the well being of the state.

---

[25] *SS* 19.367–69.

[26] *Song huiyao* [*SHY*] 26.13b.

Salt and Interstate Relations

The court also tried to regulate the salt trade as an element of foreign policy with the Liao, Xixia, and Jin; in fact salt had long played an important role in China's relations with minority peoples. Once the nomadic states had implemented bureaucratic governments and instituted their own salt monopolies, salt became the major concern of all.

The Liao empire produced pond salt for its own consumption while it exported sea salt produced on the Bohai coast into Song territory. Liao salt was so pure and white that its ambassadors presented it as a gift to neighboring states.[27] From the Liao's founding, the royal tribe claimed ownership of salt and instituted a liberal commercial tax system.

In the 920s, having taken possession of the Sixteen Prefectures of Yan Yun and its sea, pond, and earth salt resources, the Khitan Liao had inherited the monopoly system of that predominantly Han-populated territory. But a century later an uprising by people of the region prompted the institution of a tax system there, too, as in other Liao territories.[28] Most Chinese merchants near the Song border traded salt illegally with Liao merchants, and from the early Song Hebei salt regulations were relaxed to discourage competition from Liao salt. In the mid 1040s the Song emperor opted to abolish the government distribution of salt there altogether.[29]

Economic factors were probably more important in the Song relationship with the Xixia than with Liao and Jin. Xixia salt was celebrated for its fragrance, savoriness, and medicinal value. The Song battled the Xixia over its major ponds in present-day Ningxia and repeatedly attempted to control the trade of its famous blue and white salts. Chinese officials recognized the fiscal significance of the salt trade to the Xixia's "very life and survival" and so used it for political leverage. When relations were cordial, the Song imported Xixia salts; when they soured, the Song prohibited imports. This forced the Xixia to be less aggressive and more willing to compromise, and their "salt diplomacy" allowed the Song to "stabilize the barbarians' hearts" through the gains to be had from private trade.[30] Xixia salt's significance

---

[27] *Xu Zizhi tongjian changbian* (Taipei edition) [*XCBt*] 61.1375.
[28] *LS* 59.926.
[29] *SS* 181.4429, *XCB* 159.3852–53.
[30] *LS* 4.44–45; *XCBt* 284.6b; *SS* 257.8973.

for the Song monopoly was even clearer. By its efforts to halt illegal and unregulated sales, the court sought to prevent the undercutting of state revenues from pond salt sales. But the reason smugglers persisted was the slowness of the Song's pond salt delivery and the fact that Xixia salt was cheaper and better. Pond salt sold for over twice as much as the favored blue salt.

The Jin salt administration, also modeled on that of the Song, was more developed than that of the Liao. Jin's sea and pond salt production and revenues actually surpassed those of the Northern Song at times. The Song's eventual peace accord with the Jin meant it relinquished the salt resources of Hebei, Jingdong, and Hedong, allowing later Jin annual production to reach over 242 million catties. By 1151 the Jin had converted from government to merchant sales. Illegal trade between the Song and Jin thrived, and high volumes of salt flowed into Song areas, backed by the Jin government, which was keen to get Song goods.

*   *   *   *   *

The Song monopolies, together with the land tax, provided the bulk of state revenues. The salt monopoly in particular was organized to support the expenditures of the court and the military, so it is no surprise that the form of the salt administration and the shape of salt programs would be determined by the interests of the central government as it worked to secure revenue. An examination of the overall administration into which the monopoly bureaucracy fit will help explain the systemic stresses on and the workings of the monopoly itself.

Consolidating the Administration

Over the first few decades of the Song, Taizu and his successor Taizong (r. 976–997) proceeded to reshape the government, from the court down to the counties, into a centralized machine unprecedented in Chinese history. This process took place in three major areas: the military, the civil administration, and the fiscal organs, of which the salt monopoly was a key part.

Military Centralization

The highly centralized military control Taizu achieved meant that the Song was never plagued by regional warlordism as had been the case in the late Tang and throughout the Five Dynasties. In the celebrated (perhaps apocryphal) tale of "dissolving military power with a cup of wine" (*beijiu shi bingquan*), he feted former top commanders, then persuaded them to relinquish their posts in exchange for generous retirement packages. He "temporarily" filled these posts with civil officials, then gradually made those positions regular. He transferred the best troops from the former regional commands into the palace army and regularly rotated troops out to the frontier so that generals had little opportunity to build constituencies personally loyal to them: "Troops should not know their commanders; commanders should not know their troops."[31]

The Song founder drafted the rootless into prefectural armies, which did not fight but provided support services, such as water control, animal husbandry, and the transport of salt.[32] In the beginning the regional support troops were few in number and well disciplined.[33] Increasingly the court engaged disaster victims in their numbers as an explicit means to forestall banditry.[34] Taizu declared, "That which can most benefit one hundred generations is none other than cultivating the army (*yangbing*). In a year of disaster and famine there may be rebellious common folk, but [if the army is looked after] there will be no rebellious troops."[35] This strategy became a central legitimation for maintaining a large and expensive soldiery.

The collapse of the Tang's self-supporting garrison militia system (*fubingzhi*) led to its replacement by a mercenary standing army in the Song. At its height in the Northern Song, the standing army grew to over one million men, with non-combat support troops making up to half of the total number. In the Southern Song troop strength again

---

[31] *SS* 188.4627.

[32] See Ouyang Xiu's "Yuan bi" (The origin of national problems) in *Jushi ji* [*JSJ*] 60.1100; *XCB* 164.3957, 517.12300, 12305; *SS* 187.4571.

[33] *SS* 189.4639, 194.4825.

[34] *JSJ* 1100; *XCB* 164.3957, 517.12300, 12305.

[35] *Jingyusheng ji* [*JYSJ*] 1.28a. For Song recruitment of combat and support troops see *SS* 193.4799–4824.

reached this figure despite the halving of territory. All soldiers, whether combat troops or logistical support, were paid professionals who, along with their dependents, had to be supported for life. Attendant costs of arms manufacture and maintaining military installations, particularly on the border, meant that a huge outlay of resources was needed to support the military establishment.

As central as the military continued to be for the dynasty, the Song rulers actually downplayed its role and promoted the political and cultural superiority of their civil officials. Song emperors encouraged the commitment and identification of the bureaucracy with the dynasty to increase political support. They expanded the civil service examinations, fostered the prestige of scholar-officials, and provided them with unprecedented benefits, including high salaries, titles, and "shadow privilege" (*yin*)[36]: "Imperial favor for the civil servants in the Song was never considered enough, while the people's wealth never remained with them."[37] Overrecruitment led to additional budgetary difficulties. It was not so much the amounts of remuneration, but that so many needed to be supported. The problem of "superfluous officials," that is, officials with only nominal functions became second only to that of the bloated military, and together they formed the germ of the Song's intensifying fiscal crisis.

Administrative Centralization

Taizu also applied administrative controls, beginning with the chief councilor (*zaixiang*), the paramount civil post in government. Taizu split the authority of this post between left and right councilors, then divided it further into vice and junior councilors, so there might be as many as nine such officials at any one time.[38] He further constrained this dominant office by bolstering other key branches of the central administration, notably the Finance Commission (*sansi*) and

---

[36] By the *yin* privilege, high officials could confer civil service status on heirs without their having to pass the examinations; this became a most important channel for recruitment into the civil service during the Song.

[37] See *Nianer shi zhaji* [*NSZJ*] 25.6a–10b.

[38] Later, the holders of this office were allowed to play a powerful role, and a series of notorious chief councilors succeeded one another in the twelfth and thirteenth centuries.

the Bureau of Military Affairs (*shumiyuan*).[39] He regularly rotated the heads of these agencies and held separate audiences with them so that only he was privy to all information.

The circuits (*lu*) were formalized in the Song as an intermediate tier between central and local government; they were meant to strengthen control by the central authorities. The highest officials in the circuits were the specialized intendants whom the central government appointed to muster resources from the prefectures grouped beneath. These officials administered distinct areas of responsibility such as judicial, fiscal, military, monopoly, or transport matters. They shared common duties of surveillance over the prefectures and counties in order to maintain social stability. Each intendant was responsible for a different group of contiguous prefectures, but every circuit did not have each type of intendant. Since fiscal intendants came to hold more power, the number of circuits for a given period was reckoned according to how many were served by a fiscal intendancy.[40] Split as they were in duties and jurisdictions, circuit intendants were unable to dominate a region, and functioned largely as coordinators, not autonomous governors.

At the local level, the Song founders appointed prefects (*zhizhou*) and county magistrates (*zhixian*) provisionally for a term of thirty months. They stated that "the post is not regular, the term is not permanent" to discourage local officials from taking independent initiatives.[41] Although circuits were normally intermediaries, under certain circumstances they could be bypassed through direct lines of communication between the prefectures and counties and the central government.

Fiscal Centralization

The most crucial aspect of central control grew out of the Song's more robust economic management. The early emperors reversed the

---

[39] *SS* 161.3773.

[40] Tan Qixiang 1982, "Compiling Principles for the Liao Dynasty and the Northern Song Dynasty Period Map-Group," item 6. For the order of protocol, see *Qingyuan tiaofa shilei* [*QYSL*] 4.10b, and *SS* 182.4437. For an intendant's qualifications, see *XCB* 471.9b.

[41] *Ye Shi ji* [*YSJ*] 14.813–14.

fiscal structure inherited from the late Tang and Five Dynasties, which allowed local control of surpluses, allocation, audits, and accounting. The Song founder, for example, decreed that aside from what they needed to cover routine operations, prefectures must forward their land taxes and monopoly revenues to the capital each year.[42]

The two basic sources of income in the Song were the agricultural or land taxes (*tianfu*) and the monopoly taxes. The land tax system included the Double Tax (*liangshui*), paid twice yearly and reckoned on the land owned, and "miscellaneous fees" (*zaqian*). What had been provisional miscellaneous fees under the Tang became routine with the early Song, including taxes on salt and tea, even though these ought to have fallen under independent monopoly regulation. Lines between categories of taxes were often blurred to the benefit of the government, making them the bane of the people. Since military conscription had been divorced from agricultural production the Song state increased peasant taxes to cover army costs. Early on this became a primary factor in the growth of Song annual income and expenditure, though the trend was for monopoly revenues to rise at a faster rate, especially during the transition to the Southern Song.

The Song also regulated corvee labor service (*zhiyi*, *seyi*) more tightly. Corvee could be commuted to a cash payment, but with the proliferation of types of labor extracted under the Song, many households were ruined by the burdens it imposed. Thus Song land taxes were generally heavier than those imposed by the Tang, but exactions could not be increased indefinitely. The only way to cover growing expenses was to turn to the monopolies.

Central Agencies and the Salt Bureaucracy

As domestic consolidation and external threats generated a need for enhanced revenues, the government bureaucracy grew rapidly. In the first century, Song rulers overlaid the Tang-based governmental structure with irregular ad hoc agencies whose proliferation intensified over the course of the dynasty. Within the bolting general administration, government monopolies became enormous agencies.

---

[42] *XCB* 5.139. The scholar Ye Shi (1150–1223) noted that for Taizu to restrain the local military, the first step was to reassert authority over finances (*YSJ* 11.772).

In the first fiscal half of the Northern Song up to the 1070s, the most powerful fiscal unit in the central government was the Finance Commission. The Finance Commission, literally the "three fiscal agencies," was an aggregate of the Salt and Iron Bureau (*yantiesi*), the Tax Bureau (*duzhisi*), and the Ministry of Finance (*hubusi*). The Salt and Iron Bureau, in turn, was comprised of seven sections, including the Capital Salt Supply Section (*duyan'an*), the Tea Section (*cha'an*), the Iron Section (*tiean*), the Commercial Tax Section (*shangshuian*), and the Special Preparations Section (*shean*), the Military Section (*bing'an*), and the Armaments Section (*zhouan*).[43] It is clear from this bureau's organization that management of the empire's key monopolies was from the outset linked to the support of defense efforts.

Salt was a key segment of the monopoly system and the salt administration would develop an especially complex system of operational distinctions. Initially subordinate to the Salt and Iron Bureau, the Monopoly Goods Bureau (*quehuowu*) directed the collection of taxes on monopoly goods and the financial organs charged with issuing vouchers used in the salt trade. Merchants paid for these vouchers primarily in cash at the Monopoly Goods Bureau, with its main office in the capital, and later, at branch offices in major urban centers. The Bureau itself did not handle product.

All the ostensibly specialized circuit intendancies also took a hand in salt administration, particularly when the lines between them blurred at the onset of some difficulty, such as military threat or operational problems. Sometimes the overlap in jurisdiction occurred due to deliberate court efforts at playing them off against each other. The fiscal intendant (*zhuanyunshi*), who normally ranked above the others, oversaw tax collection and revenue distribution; at times he concurrently supervised the salt monopoly and coordinated general administration. The judicial intendant (*tidian xingyu, tixing anchashi*) supervised judicial and penal operations but sometimes was called on to manage the transport of salt, tea, and tax grain. The military intendant (*shuaifu, shuaichen, anfushi*) was charged with defense and functioned as the predominant authority in frontier regions where he coordinated civil and military affairs. The ever-normal granary intendant (*tiju changpingguan; tiju changping gongshi*) was responsible for grain storage, transport, and price stabilization, but also for suppressing

---

[43] *SS* 162.3808–9.

smuggling and other infractions of the law and monopoly duties like oversight of tea and salt quotas to ensure state revenues.

Controls intensified in the mid to late eleventh century with the establishment of special Salt Intendancies (*tiju yanshisi*) in the southeast. Salt intendants were direct representatives of the court delegated to manage salt affairs alongside the fiscal intendant. They sometimes also supervised a subordinate official (such as the *goudang gongshi* or *yangou*, *ganban gongshi* or *yangan*) who had charge of overseeing salt revenues and conducting audits. This man was dreaded by local officials and the populace alike.

In production regions, salt officials charged with the problem of smuggling (*tidian siyanshi, tiju xunzhuo siyan, duda xunzhuo siyan guan*) were to apprehend anyone engaged in illegal trade. In the Southern Song, the central government required different intendancies to file a copy of their annual report with one another as a means of creating competition between them. Intendants cognizant of wrongdoing on the part of colleagues but taking no action were to be punished.

By the accession of Shenzong (r. 1068–1085), the Song faced deficits every year. Shenzong, who admired the Legalists and their motto: "enrich the country and strengthen the army" (*fuguo qiangbing*), promoted the reform-minded Wang Anshi to be chief councilor and backed Wang's New Policies. These reforms were wide-ranging, but first and foremost they were aimed at augmenting the state's income.[44]

In 1069 Wang Anshi created the Finance Planning Commission (*zhizhi sansi tiaolisi*) to manage the New Policy reforms. This organ absorbed the functions of the now-defunct Finance Commission. But other officials pressed for a return to the traditional Ministry of Revenue (*hubu*, to be distinguished from the *hubusi* above) within the Department of Ministries (*shangshusheng*), and in response a year later Wang retired the Finance Planning Commission. By 1083 he had redirected fiscal command as well as authority over the salt industry to the Ministry of Revenue. This ministry (formerly the *hubusi*) no longer operated parallel to the old Salt and Iron Bureau but above it, where it was administered by Wang as chief councilor and directly controlled by the emperor. The Salt and Iron Bureau was discontinued and its Armaments Section merged into a Directorate for Armaments (*junqi jian*) under the Ministry of Works (*gongbu*).

---

[44] *SS* 327.10542; *XCB* 324.7799.

The Monopoly Goods Bureau now came under the authority of the Court of the Imperial Treasury (*taifusi*), which managed non-grain receipts, supervised tax collection on monopoly goods, and sold salt vouchers. This restructuring brought the revenue-generating arm of the monopoly under more direct court supervision and control.

The Fiscal Context and the Burden of the Military

Warfare or its threat played an enormous role in shaping Song court concerns and government policy; to no small degree it drove the development of the salt monopoly. Here we will examine key military and bureaucratic developments that created increasing financial pressures, resultant policy initiatives, and their impact on the state and the people (see Table 1).[45]

Moving from Surpluses to Fiscal Imbalance

At the beginning of the Song, surpluses of grain, cloth, and currency led Taizong, brother and successor to the dynasty's founder, to declare in 978, "Today's resources are piled mountain-high—we shall never exhaust them!"[46] Indeed, the Song state was flush enough in the early years to provide its troops with extras like firewood money, winter clothing, relocation funds, and festival rations.[47]

But from the very establishment of the dynasty, the Liao to the north posed a constant threat. Song founder Taizu had worried about Kaifeng's geographic vulnerability—the Liao cavalry could reach it in three to four days—but decided to maintain it as his capital due to economic considerations. The capital's security required heavy protection and several hundred thousand soldiers were posted in its vicinity. At the end of Taizu's reign army strength numbered 378,000, half of them palace regulars, and half prefectural support troops.

Aiming at total unification, including recovery of the Sixteen Prefectures of Yan Yun lost but a generation before, and riding the momentum from his incorporation of the Wuyue and Northern Han

---

[45] The importance attached to the military can be seen in the *Songshi*'s nearly 400-page Military Monograph, which treats the military at length.

[46] *XCB* 19.436.

[47] *SS* 187.4576, 194.4840–41.

kingdoms into Song territories, Taizong decided to direct an attack on the Liao. His effort was in vain, however, and after a second defeat at Liao hands, he abandoned further military action and turned instead to domestic consolidation. Taizong rapidly augmented the civil service and nearly doubled the army to 666,000 men.

The reign of his son Zhenzong (r. 998–1022) marked a peak of prosperity for the Song. Total income in the first years of the 1000s stood at 50 to 60 million strings, climbing to 140 to 150 million strings by the end of this reign.[48] In 1005 the court signed a peace treaty with the Liao at Chanyuan in present-day Henan, but preferring vigilance, Zhenzong actually stepped up preparedness: "The border is short of troops. The court must establish a policy, lest we be sorry. Only if we ensure the safety of the remote areas can we rest easy."[49] A minimum wage was set for low-ranking regulars that increased their pay and remained the standard thereafter.

The court spared no expense to maintain its troops, including several hundred thousand cavalry mounts, until the chief councilor voiced unease at the cumulative cost of this number of horses. By Zhenzong's later years the army had ballooned to 912,000 men, less than half of whom were combat-ready regulars.[50] In addition to military expenses, the cost of rapidly expanding bureaus, lavish pay increases of several hundred percent, and indiscriminate promotions across the administration gave some cause for worry.[51] The problem of supernumerary officials had already been raised in the first few years of Zhenzong's reign when it was recommended that their numbers be cut back drastically.[52] "Jade and coarse rock are all mixed in together. They become the burden of the people and will exhaust the treasury."[53]

---

[48] *XCBt* 66.4b–5a; *SHY* 12.2a; *Bao Xiaosu zouyi ji* [*BX*] 1.23a.

[49] *SS* 187.4573, 189.4642.

[50] *SS* 187.4576.

[51] *SS* 6.115, 161.3769, 168.4003–10, 171.4116, 172.4134.

[52] *SS* 6.115.

[53] *SS* 168.4009–10.

Table 1.   Major Military Developments in the Song

Emperor	Date	Event	Troop Strength
Taizu	961	Policy of civilian rule laid out	
	970s		378,000[1]
	979	All lands unified by the Song	
Taizong	986	Defeat by Liao	
	995-97		666,000[2]
Zhenzong	1005	Chanyuan Treaty with Liao★	
	1017-21		912,000[3]
	1038	Founding of Xixia	
Renzong	1041-48		1,259,000[4]
	1044	Treaty with Xixia★	
	1049-53		1,400,000[5]
Yingzong	1064-67		1,162,000[6]
Shenzong	1068-77	*Baojia* system instituted	568,600 regulars, 227,600 support[7]
	1072-73	Offensive against Xixia	
	1078-85		612,200 regulars[8]
	1080-82	Defeat by Xixia	ca. 1,000,000
Zhezong	1086-93		550,000 regulars, 300,000 support[9]
	ca. 1090s	Defeat by Xixia	
Huizong	1115	Founding of Jin	
	1125	End of Liao; Jin invades	
Qinzong	1126	Loss of north to Jin	
Gaozong	1127	Beginning of Southern Song	
	Late 1120s		10,000
	1142	Treaty with Jin★; imperial armies established	
	1160		318,000
Xiaozong	1163	New treaty with Jin★	
	1163-1189		800,000-1,000,000
Ningzong	Early 1200s	Defeat by Jin	
Lizong	1227	End of Xixia	
	1234	End of Jin	
	1260	Accession of Kublai Khan	
Duanzong	1276	Mongol armies enter Hangzhou	
Bing	1279	Suicide of last emperor; Mongols occupy all China	

★= annual tribute paid by the Song

[1] SS 187.4576; *WXTK* 152.
[2] SS 187.4576; *WXTK* 152.
[3] SS 187.4576; *WXTK* 152.
[4] SS 187.4576; *WXTK* 152.
[5] Wang Zhi, *Zhongshu bei jian*, quoted in Wang Shengduo 1995, 774.
[6] SS 187.4576.
[7] XCB 228, 350; SS 189.4645.
[8] XCB 350; SS 187.4579.
[9] XCB 472.

Moreover, with the conclusion of the Chanyuan Treaty, Zhenzong's advisors encouraged his predilection for massive and diverse ritual sacrifices to secure his longevity.[54] Traditionally part of an emperor's aggrandizement since the time of Qin Shihuangdi, such activities in fact posed a colossal drain on a dynasty's resources. Although Zhenzong's reign is considered the "Golden Age" of the Song, it was in fact a period in which the court began to engage in financial waste on a prodigious scale.

The Emerging Problem of Deficit

Beginning as early as 997 and continuing throughout the dynasty, high officials characterized the court's financial difficulties as having three major sources: superfluous troops and officials (*rongbing, rongyuan*), and excessive spending (*rongfei*). These burdens were likened to "the load pulled on a rickety cart by a scrawny horse up a mountain," sure to result in disaster.[55]

By far the most significant factor was the cost of the enormous army. Zhenzong's son, Renzong (r. 1022–1063) spent much of his four decades engaged in military build-up for a possible confrontation with the Tangut Xixia (1038–1227) to the northwest.[56] Although no major conflict with the Liao occurred under Renzong, there were frequent alerts, which caused the emperor to station hundreds of thousands of soldiers in the northeast as well.[57] By the 1040s the army had reached 1,259,000 men, the peak of the dynasty. This included over 800,000 palace army soldiers on the frontier, and 400,000 support troops. Of the total income during Renzong's reign, 80 to 90 percent was drained by the military.[58] The economy had to be squeezed for the funds, and by 1045 the court had collected nearly 20 million strings in commercial taxes, including the salt and wine taxes—compared to only 4.5 million strings collected under Zhenzong. Of the 60 million strings in total cash receipts, the military

---

[54] *SS* 6.103, 7.135–38, 8.172, 282.9539.

[55] *Luancheng ji* [*LC*] 21.5a.

[56] *SS* 10.206–8, 195.4854–55, 196.4882, 198.4931, 4933–35.

[57] *XCB* 112.2623–26. Also see Cai Xiang's memorial in *Guochao zhuchen zouyi* [*GCZY*], 121; *Duguan ji* [*DGJ*] 1.11a, 7.4a; *Sushui jiwen* [*SSJW*] 4.3a–b.

[58] *XCBt* 124.10a.

consumed 50 million. Bureaucratic promotions continued to drain treasury reserves: by the early 1050s, the Song employed more than 20,000 officials, twice the number at the time of the Chanyuan Treaty. These combined costs eventually created the Song's first recorded budget deficit in 1065.[59]

Between 1043 and 1044 Renzong's chief councilor Fan Zhongyan[60] had targeted these key financial problems by proposing a ten-point plan. He proposed replacing the paid military with the self-supporting Tang-era *fubing* system. He attacked excessive pay and lax recruitment standards and proposed cutting the numbers of officials who had gained office by virtue of shadow privilege. Five of his ten points dealt with relieving the peasants' corvee and tax burden. But conservatives and other strong interest groups blocked his relatively moderate proposals, since they believed the status quo to be the best path—certainly it preserved their interests. This policy battle prevented the reduction of government expenditure and plunged the bureaucracy into bitter factionalism.

Wang Anshi Attempts to Stem Deficits

By the ascension of Shenzong in 1068 the court faced deficits every year. Not long after assuming the throne, the emperor promoted the reform-minded Wang Anshi (1021–1086) to be his chief councilor and backed Wang's New Policies, instituted largely between 1069 and 1073.

At first Shenzong tried to boost the effectiveness of the bureaucracy, but like other Song sovereigns he ultimately fell back on showering generous remuneration and benefits on officials, their servants, and the imperial clan, simply exacerbating the financial problems of the court.[61] The reorganization of the bureaucracy from 1069 also resulted in complicated lines of responsibility for finance, so

---

[59] See discussions of when and whether deficits actually occurred in Smith 1991, 351n86.

[60] It was Fan who famously pronounced what became the credo for future Confucian activists: "True literati are the first to worry about the empire's troubles and the last to rejoice in its happiness."

[61] *SS* 161.3769; *LCHJ* 15.4505. *SS* 170.4080–81, 4090–91, 171.4101–24.

the expense of tracking costs may have increased. Military expenses also mounted.

When the Xixia repeatedly broke the 1044 peace accord in the early years of his reign, the twenty-year old Shenzong adopted an aggressive policy.[62] His first major action against the Xixia occurred from 1072 to 1073, when in just six months costs mounted to over 12 million strings. Between 1080 and 1082 Shenzong launched another expedition against the Xixia mobilizing nearly one million men, reorganizing commanders, and stiffening military law.[63] But Song losses were great and the Song had to pay reparations as a result, quite the opposite of what the emperor had hoped for. It was these military offensives that exerted a direct and relentless pressure on Wang Anshi's efforts to "enrich the country and strengthen the army."

Wang's comprehensive reforms—economic, fiscal, military, and administrative—have been described as revolutionary and socialistic, but his aims clearly were not to overturn the social and economic order but rather to bolster the state's revenues. Compared to Fan Zhongyan's earlier reforms, Wang Anshi's were, out of necessity, much greater in scope and depth. Among them were low-interest government loans, changes in the corvee system, new land registration programs, and curricular changes for civil examinations. His most important innovations, however, were in the military arena. In the early 1070s Wang established peasant militia units (*baojia*) to address the lingering fear that there were still too few troops. The *baojia*, designed to make defense everyone's business rather than a specialized activity, provided a more cost-effective supplementary force on the northwest frontier.[64] The *baojia* law combined a militia with the organization of local society by grouping households into units for maintenance of local order as well as to undergo military training. The government did not pay them but awarded land and tax exemptions.[65] Wang also advocated "using barbarians to fight barbarians" on the Xixia border, noting that if the Song enriched the minorities there, they could also direct and influence them.[66]

---

[62] *SS* 15.272, 277–78.

[63] *XCB* 327.7870; *SS* 191.4747, 195.4858–59.

[64] *SS* 190.4711, 192.4767–89, 196.4899.

[65] *SS* 190.4711, 192.4786.

[66] *SS* 191.4759.

During a second round of hostilities and reforms in the 1080s, the court combined the *baojia* system with local archer squads to cut costs further.[67] Local archers had been trained and organized earlier under several previous emperors. They placed no burden on the state granaries: when peace ruled, they worked the land; when hostilities broke out, the state equipped them and sent them to the border. Senior conservative ministers such as Sima Guang strongly opposed the use of the local archers and the *baojia* because they placed upon the peasants multiple burdens of crop raising, military training, and horse rearing.[68]

While the New Policies did appear to increase revenues, in the long run they did not achieve Wang's goals of agricultural development and consistent revenues gains for the court. They did not improve the peasants' lot but rather shattered their livelihoods, thereby in fact ruining the tax base. Conservatives criticized Wang for only seeking immediate results and duping the emperor.[69] Backed by both the weight of tradition and general bureaucratic inertia, the conservatives eventually won out. But coping with the fiscal stresses of the time was indeed difficult, and the conservatives proved equally unable to devise initiatives that would solve the problems of the fisc. In the end, Shenzong's military adventures against the Xixia resulted only in casualties and squandered resources.

The New Policies Restored

Shenzong's son, Zhezong (r. 1085–1100), was only a boy at the time of his ascension and initially was captive to senior conservative forces at court. Their fiscal policies relieved the burden on the masses to some extent, but were unable to stem the decline of state revenues. This opened them to political attack, which led the sovereign to restore the fiscal measures of his father's era.

After Zhezong's first decade, he managed to become his own man. He demoted conservatives and appointed Wang Anshi's supporters as his chief councilors. Attempting to defuse popular resistance to

---

[67] *SS* 190.4727, 191.4735, 4739, 192.4771.

[68] On the rural militias, see *SS* 190.4707–8; on the *baojia* see *SS* 190.4711, 192.4786, 198.4941, 4946–47.

[69] One should bear in mind that it was the conservatives that later wrote the history of this period and took no pains to hide their condemnation.

restoration of the New Policies, the reformers reduced taxes and corvee by half. The measures taken by this 1094 reform movement succeeded in reducing opposition, yet also sacrificed state income.

During Zhezong's reign the military declined seriously. In his second year a censor revealed problems of bogus recruitment and soldiers' stipends: as many as 80 percent of the forces in Fujian could not pass muster. They had simply been recruited as bodies to rack up numbers for payments that were no longer forthcoming, in any case. Around 1086 Sima Guang voiced worry about the numbers and quality of both central and local military men "in their camps eating and drinking and enjoying themselves, becoming arrogant and lazy . . . completely useless to the war effort."[70] By 1090 palace army men were so numerous that the government could not afford to promote even the most capable soldiers.[71]

When the Xixia invaded in the last years of the eleventh century, the court's defensive posture changed into an offensive one. The chief councilor opposed the return of any territory and wanted to pare down the amount of tribute paid. He also encouraged the emperor to act as commander-in-chief. Relatedly, the Bureau of Military Affairs in the mid-1090s successfully argued that prefectural officials hampered strategic decision-making and so commanders ought to decide matters unimpeded, as they had under Shenzong.[72] The court managed to mobilize its troops and launch an offensive against the Xixia, but they were roundly beaten. High officials reported that the central government treasuries were empty and the circuit intendancies deficient. Social crises grew more severe.

Cai Jing's Fiscal Reforms

Under the rule of Zhezong's younger brother Huizong (r. 1101–1125), one of the greatest fiscal problems was arguably sheer dissipation. Through a shared interest in the arts, the purported reformer Cai Jing (1047–1126) gained the favor of Huizong, and was appointed chief councilor. Cai was in and out of power several times but Huizong's fiscal administration can broadly be said to be his handiwork.

---

[70] *SS* 189.4629.

[71] *SS* 191.4749.

[72] *SS* 18.340–41, 351; 188.4630, 190.4886–87.

Cai's early purge of conservatives silenced criticism of his reforms, which continued in line with Wang's New Policies.

His diversion of treasury wealth into the privy purse allowed Huizong to conduct one monumental construction project after another.[73] Perhaps the most notorious extravagance was the "flower and rock flotillas" (*huashigang*), for which officials ransacked homes in the southeast for rare stones, plants, wood, and the like, packed them onto convoys of boats, and shipped them to the capital to adorn the houses and gardens of the elite. This ruined many families and caused some of the responsible officials to hesitate at the wisdom of such ostentation. These excesses helped spark the Fang La Uprising in 1120, though by that year Cai was already out of office.

In addition to court extravagance during Huizong's first decade, officials reported the Xixia border situation to be "a fiscal disaster."[74] The troops were in a state of near collapse, yet the court continued to recruit, rounding up "riffraff from the marketplace," unsuitable soldiers who could not be disbanded for fear that they would soon form roving bands to prey upon the populace.[75] When in 1116 the emperor had an inventory conducted, he concluded that nearly one trillion weapons had to be manufactured. Towering sums were needed to produce this weaponry and maintain craftsmen working under an accelerated schedule.

A chief characteristic of Cai Jing's policies was their redistribution of revenues such that the central government gained at the expense of local governments. This tendency emerged whenever the court encountered fiscal difficulty, but was particularly extreme under Cai's administration. A major target of reform was the salt monopoly, where exploitation reached new levels. Historians of the period have long blamed Cai Jing for setting policies that brought down the dynasty, and yet his extractive methods, perceived as effective at filling state coffers, would be copied assiduously by the Southern Song court.

Meanwhile, the Jurchen Jin (1115–1234) had risen rapidly in the northeast, subdued the Xixia, then toppled the Liao in 1125.[76] The Song ruling group, Huizong, Cai Jing, and the eunuch Tong Guan

---

[73] *SS* 182.4452, 472.13721–28.

[74] *SS* 190.4718–20, 4723.

[75] *SS* 193.4805–7, 4810.

[76] *Jinshi* [*JS*] 44.992, 997.

(1054–1126) developed a naive initiative intended to take advantage of this: by creating an alliance with the Jin, they believed they could regain the Sixteen Prefectures of Yan Yun to the greater glory of the Song. When the Jin turned around and attacked them, Huizong abdicated in favor of his eldest son, Qinzong (r. 1126), but Qinzong was unable to untangle the court's military and fiscal predicament in his one year on the throne. The Jin captured Kaifeng, then led the hapless Qinzong, Huizong, and over a thousand palace courtiers into captivity in the far north. The huge gap between troop strength on the books and their effective numbers in the field belied the political void that led to the end of the Northern Song.

The Southern Song Restoration

In 1127 the one remaining member of the royal house, Qinzong's brother Zhao Gou, was enthroned as Emperor Gaozong (r. 1127–1162) of the Southern Song.[77] The dynasty's precarious beginning was plagued by a dire need for income. As Gaozong's small court roved about in search of safe haven from the Jin, he issued vouchers for salt, tea, wine, and vinegar on the spot to get desperately needed cash. Alert merchants pursued the retinue to snap up these vouchers. The literati who had lost their sources of income with their flight south were granted by the court large, renewable stipends to tide them over comfortably.[78] This set an expensive precedent that proved difficult to break with.

At the inception of the Southern Song, Gaozong praised the general Yue Fei (1103–1142) and other commanders who advocated the recovery of the north, for their merit in resisting the Xixia and the Jin. Loyal defense by these men's family armies at a time when reassembled troops numbered less than 10,000 had proved crucial to the court's survival in the early years.[79] But Gaozong later may have come to view their progress toward recovery of the north (leading perhaps to a restoration of the former emperor) as a threat. In 1142 the emperor and his chief councilor Qin Gui (1090–1155) reached an

---

[77] For a thorough, detached monograph of Gaozong's period, see the Japanese scholar Teraji Jun (1995).

[78] *SS* 170.4082.

[79] *SS* 187.4570.

agreement with the Jin that ceded them territory north of the Huai River. It also stipulated annual tribute and the Song's reference to itself as the subordinate of the Jin.[80] With the conservative faction in power for good and the issue of reforms out of the picture, new debates developed between men who advocated recovery of the north and those who supported accommodation with the Jin.

At the same time Qin Gui recalled the top commanders to the capital, had Yue Fei killed, relieved others of their authority, and united their armies under imperial command.[81] This represented a return to unity of command versus empowering the generals as had occurred under Shenzong, in order to preserve Gaozong's security. Thus the troops encamped in prefectures across the remaining Song territory now became the imperial army (*yuqian dajun*), a new fighting force. Troop strength rebounded until in 1160, there were over 318,000 soldiers. Having proved too sorry in training and discipline, former palace troops who had been responsible for defending the border were retired to agricultural and other labor and no longer functioned as military men.[82] This early reorganization of the army meant added costs for the new Song regime.

To counter this pressure, a new organization was devised for the privy purse and imperial treasury in which the distinction between the two became increasingly unclear. Power over both lay in the emperor's hands and he often used portions of both as a war chest, which increased the ability of the court to react with force and effect, particularly during periods of unrest. Notwithstanding the court's efforts to raise revenues, most notably by its exploitation of the salt monopoly, by 1147 the Southern Song deficit amounted to about 2 million strings and would reach 3 million by 1154. The government had already fine-tuned land taxes to the highest possible level, so revenue from the monopolies was critical. Officials asserted that "the court's major expenses rely completely on salt and tea revenues," and "military expenses are covered primarily by the salt quota." Near the end of Gaozong's reign, salt revenue comprised over 50 percent of central government income.

---

[80] *SS* 28.529, 30.556, 563, 570–71, 31.582.

[81] *SS* 187.4583.

[82] *SS* 193.4821.

Short-lived Improvements Lead to Crisis

Xiaozong's reign (r. 1163–1189) saw widespread economic reconstruction and achieved perhaps the best fiscal footing of any period during the Southern Song. Around 1168 annual expenditures were reported at over 55 million strings, roughly equal to revenues.[83] The salt monopoly brought in over 21 million strings, wine about 14 million strings, tea about 2 million strings, and spices and alum combined over 1 million strings.[84]

Under Xiaozong the military rallied and the court toyed with the idea of retaking the north. Xiaozong also substantially built up the navy, with bases along the Yangzi River and the coast. Yet the emperor did not send out his troops heedlessly. It happened that the Jin ruler Shizong (r. 1161–1189) had also just ascended and Xiaozong decided to defer to him, but referred to himself as a nephew of the Jin ruler rather than his subject. When he requested a reduction in the Song's annual tribute, the two sides agreed to a new settlement in 1163, which brought on a forty-year cessation of hostilities. Even so, the Song did not dare let up readiness and increased its forces to an astounding total of between 800,000 to 1 million troops of all categories, approaching the Northern Song peak.

In the brief rule of Xiaozong's son Guangzong (r. 1189–1194) deterioration of the administration nullified these achievements. Intrigue at court was followed by at times violent factionalism under Guangzong's son, Ningzong (r. 1194–1224). Under Ningzong fiscal decline began to accelerate. During this period the imperial armies had grown to 400,000 soldiers, meaning annual expenditures of 80 million strings, not including the cost of the old palace regulars, the prefectural support troops, and equipment. A court relation, Han Tuozhou (1152–1207), hoping to solidify his position as chief councilor, launched a Northern Expedition against the Jin, but was defeated in a matter of months. In 1208 the Jin court took advantage of the Song's suing for peace to increase the annual tribute, and a few years later the two sides were again fighting. From then on, the Southern Song suffered from nearly continuous warfare.

---

[83] *Huang song zhongxing liangchao shengzheng* [*HSZLS*] 47.3a.

[84] *Jianyan yilai chaoye zaji* [*CYZJ*] 14.1a–b, 14.12a; *SHY* 55.27a–28b.

Collapse of the Military and Fiscal Administrations

Although toward the end of the Song much attention was paid to military technology and weaponry, which had developed to a highly advanced level, these efforts merely added to costs rather than overall effectiveness. Morale was low: "Out of one thousand men, one hundred are old or weak, and when they encounter the enemy they are the first to run so that the entire regiment is rendered useless."[85] At the death of Ningzong, the chief councilor Shi Miyuan had Lizong (r. 1225–1264) enthroned on the basis of a false mandate, further betraying the depth of the court's moral decrepitude. Under Lizong, the state's two great concerns remained management of the military and the "incurable disease" of the budget deficit. In the 1250s annual income was 120 million strings while expenditures had reached 250 million.

Prefectures remained responsible for paying for their own troops, yet their ability to generate revenues had become severely curtailed when the circuits diverted their resources to the support of the imperial military. Counties were staffed by the literati who resented being posted to that bottommost tier of the bureaucracy, where the pressures were "like falling into a pot of boiling water." Once land and monopoly taxes could be augmented no further, the government increasingly issued paper money until it held no value. It was only a matter of time before the Mongols moved in to demolish what remained of the dynasty.

Monopolies in the Song Fisc

Over the course of the dynasty the largely ongoing increase of annual monopoly revenues, especially salt revenues, occurred in spite of, or perhaps due to, the escalating fiscal stresses, which in turn encouraged an aggressively fiscalist approach to policy design. Here is a brief comparison of the roles of the major monopolies.

---

[85] *SS* 194.4839.

The Role of Salt

In Zhenzong's reign, in the first years of the eleventh century, salt revenues reached 3.3 million strings.[86] This was out of 26 million strings of annual cash income and total revenues of approximately 60 million strings. Fifty years later under Renzong in the 1050s, salt income had tripled to 9.1 million strings,[87] out of 37 million strings in cash income, while the overall budget had only doubled to 126 million strings. By Shenzong's reign only two decades later, salt income doubled to 20 million out of 60 million strings of cash receipts as total income shrank. Even near the end of the Northern Song in Huizong's reign salt revenues doubled again to 40 million strings while the whole budget then was likely less than 80 million.

After the Southern Song reconstruction in the 1160s salt revenues had recovered to at least 23 million strings with cash income at 60 million strings; in Xiaozong's time only ten years later salt revenues reached the high point of the entire dynasty at approximately 31 million strings with cash income holding steady and total income around 80 million strings; in Ningzong's reign in the early 1200s, salt income managed to claw its way to 22 million strings, of an actually increased budget of 106 million; finally under Lizong by 1256 some twenty years before the fall of the dynasty, salt revenues still reached 13 million strings but in the face of huge deficit: 120 million strings in, 250 million strings out. After this figures are unclear.[88]

The Role of Other Monopolies

If the salt monopoly was the major contributor to the state budget, the wine monopoly was the next best revenue generator, wine being important for social, religious, and medicinal purposes, with potentially unlimited consumption. In the mid-Northern Song, wine revenues on occasion surpassed those of salt. Since wine production was much more difficult to monitor, however, the

---

[86] *XCBt* 209.16a.

[87] *XCBt* 209.16a.

[88] For tables on Northern and Southern Song salt revenues over time and by region, see Guo Zhengzhong 1988, 674–79; for a simpler table but with sources, see Wang Shengduo 1995, 700–4.

government implemented various local controls: in urban areas only officials could produce and sell wine under monopoly control; in the countryside the government franchised wineries for a fixed-rate fee and levied annual taxes on production and sales. Local governments were allowed to manage a greater proportion of wine revenues than was the case for salt.

Tea, the third major monopoly, was by the Song an important element of daily life. The main production areas included the southeast and Sichuan. Like salt, tea was tightly regulated, with similar mechanisms and policy swings between government and merchant distribution until the latter prevailed in the mid-eleventh century. From the twelfth century on, tea and salt were combined into a single agency at the circuit level.

Iron and other mined monopoly products largely were minted into hard currency or used to manufacture weapons and agricultural implements. Iron also went into casting the heavy pans used in salt production, which could withstand high temperatures and transmit heat readily. Iron was important in salt-drilling technology as well. In the early Northern Song, salt and iron were consolidated in the Salt and Iron Bureau.

Currencies in Play

The variety of currencies used in the Song and their manipulation by the state resulted in a highly complex system of financial instruments and this had its repercussions in the development of the salt trade.

Precious and semi-precious metals circulated in the Song, with more widespread use among the lower levels of society than before. Gold and silver (along with silk in bolts of a standard length and breadth) were used for large transactions, including the annual tribute paid to the Song's neighboring states. Copper cash (*tongqian*) was the accepted medium for ordinary transactions across most of the empire although copper shortages encountered later in the dynasty contributed to a decline in the minting of copper coins. Iron cash (*tieqian*), second most common currency in the Song, played an especially prominent role in copper-poor Sichuan and in some border areas where the government tried to prevent the export of copper coinage.

Paper money was also employed for larger transactions and came into its own in this period. The origins of Song paper money are attributed to the Tang period. Long-distance transport of the heavy hard currencies—always a risky proposition—by tea merchants led to the adoption in 806 of "flying money" (*feiqian*). After depositing cash in the capital from profits realized from their trade, merchants were given a draft to receive hard currency when they returned to the tea-producing south. These two transfers of cash without direct physical transfer led to the term "flying money." The first true paper money in the world, called "exchange notes" (*jiaozi*), appeared in early eleventh century Sichuan, where the bulky iron cash circulated. By the Southern Song taxation in cash exceeded that in kind, largely due to the use of paper currency. The *jiaozi* were succeeded by "check notes" (*huizi*), which the government began issuing in 1160. At first *huizi* had a certain period of validity and were issued in limited quantities, but by the late Southern Song the validity period had been dispensed with, and the notes were continually printed.[89]

By the Southern Song the central government began to engage in discussions of how to adjust the ratios of exchange between paper currency, cash, silver, gold, and other monetary instruments. The Ministry of Finance discussed such measures in 1166; other discussions occurred in 1172 and 1173.[90] It was eventually decreed just what forms of money the Monopoly Goods Bureau and the voucher sales offices could use, and the exchange rates between them were set.[91]

The government frequently resorted to the overissue of paper money to cover budget deficits and meet military expenses. When bills were issued at an accelerated pace with no regard to reserves to back them, bounding several hundred percent in the half century from about 1200 to the 1250s, to about 1 billion strings worth, they depreciated severely. The Song court was forced to enact various countermeasures to deal with the devaluation, one of which was to buy up bills with Huai-Zhe salt profits generated from sales of above-quota salt, as decreed in 1174.[92] By the end of the Song paper currency had fallen into such discredit that its use was discouraged in later dynasties.[93]

---

[89] *SS* 181.4403–13.

[90] *SHY* 27.21b–22a, 42a.

[91] *SHY* 28.53b–55a.

[92] *SHY* 28.1a–b.

[93] *SS* 181.4403–13.

Among all the forms of revenue it collected—grain, cash, and monopoly goods—the government considered salt to be the decisive factor in guaranteeing the value of the others. Paper money depended upon sufficient reserves of precious metals and the main source for those reserves, in turn, was income from the salt monopoly. In its efforts to guarantee salt revenues that would stabilize the entire fiscal system, the government turned to manipulation of the salt laws. These included switching from merchant to government distribution in certain areas and wringing ever more out of its voucher programs. When, by the late Southern Song, merchants became financially unable to continue trading and the court had no wherewithal to mediate the situation, salt revenues crashed, taking the rest of the economy with them.

Historical developments naturally helped shape the behavior of the government at large, and concerns of the purse in particular. Military expenses remained the single biggest drain on the Song treasury, but the court's other policies and directives also contributed to the state's endless appetite for revenue. This configuration of forces forms the backdrop to the Song monopolies and highlights the motivations and constant urgency behind the manipulation of monopoly policies.

Early Salt Monopoly Operations

An Overview of the Salt Industry

The Song bureaucracy managed to impose itself on the salt industry's every aspect, from raw materials and equipment, producers' labor and knowledge, and the product itself, to the middlemen, trade routes and storage, and final delivery. At some points the state merely regulated existing relations and activities; at others it reshaped the nature of the trade completely.

The populace had initiated salt production and developed manufacturing techniques long before government functionaries ever intruded. The monopoly administration, therefore, did not concern itself with the preparatory stages—for example, readying the ground, constructing raised fields, and the use of animals and equipment in these activities—but strictly supervised actual production. Having dismissed the Han era policy of engaging officials directly in production, the Song court made immense efforts at grassroots regulation, directing workers and regulating their activities, materials and equipment, determining output, and setting production quotas. The salt administration also was charged with providing salters what I will call production funding (*benqian*, literally "capital"), to help them carry out their work.

Procurement followed processing. The monopoly asserted that the salt was not the producers' to dispose of but belonged to the government. Salters had to submit all output, be it quota salt or above-quota salt, at the production site. Here the government procured the quota salt cheaply, then resold it to merchants or directly to consumers. It paid a higher price for above-quota salt, lest it leak into more lucrative channels. The imperial court tied the major sales districts to the pond, sea, earth, and well salt production areas.

Transport and distribution were conducted either by the government (*quejin, guanmai*) or by state-controlled merchants (*tongshang*). As we will see below, the pros and cons of these distribution schemes would be an ongoing topic of debate and the impetus behind repeated monopoly policy swings. The state outlawed all other salt trade.

State-run storage depots facilitated the transfer of product from producer to consumer. The most common type was located in production areas along waterways; another type, situated at well-traveled intersections, served as transfer stations between the monopoly and its distributors; a third type, located near towns, functioned as direct sales centers where consumers could go to purchase salt.

Revenue from government salt distribution went to local governments to cover administrative expenses; revenue from merchant salt distribution went to the central government to allocate as it saw fit, but primarily paid defense expenses. Over time the portion going to the central government would increase.

The state reaped different types of income from its monopoly. It sold salt at a price many times the procurement cost, wholesale to merchants or retail to consumers. When merchants sold salt, the state taxed the proceeds; it also leased salt franchises to individual bidders. It relied on the inelastic demand for salt to raise household taxes, compelling people to buy quantities of salt based on how much land they owned, in addition to paying regular land taxes. Since salt revenues basically underwrote the military, the state went all out to maximize monopoly income by every feasible means.

Salt Production Regions

The four main types of monopoly salt (*queyan*) produced in the Song—pond, sea, earth, and well salt—had distinct natures and methods of extraction, which meant a regionally based salt bureaucracy.[94] Two basic production methods were used: evaporation, which resulted in a kernel salt (*keyan*) of relatively coarse texture, such as pond salt; and boiling, which resulted in a fine granular salt (*moyan*) such as sea, earth, and well salts.

The *Songshi* treatise first considers lake or "pond" salt (*chiyan*), which came from Xiezhou, near present-day Yuncheng ([Salt] Transport City). This was located in present-day Shanxi, at the Yellow River bend where the ancient Chinese state first emerged.[95] Pond salt was drawn from one sinuous lake six kilometers by fifty kilometers that sprawled across the counties of Anyi and Xie; hence it was sometimes considered two separate ponds. Its manufacture was the simplest and cheapest of all: producers evaporated salt lake water under the sun in a series of fields, then drained it to dry on mats. Pond salt may generally be considered to fall into the category of official production. This categorization refers not so much to the production personnel but rather, the government's direct ownership, use, and management of the ponds, raw materials, and tools.

Sea salt (*haiyan*), the biggest revenue generator for the Song as a whole, was produced along the coast from Hebei Circuit through Jingdong, Huainan, Liangzhe, Fujian, and Guangnan circuits. Huainan was the biggest sea salt producer; its revenues comprised two-thirds of the total earned from sea salt. Liangzhe was second, but it was perhaps

---

[94] Kawakami Kōichi (1992) concentrates on production rather than administration or policy. He addresses salt manufacture in this order: (1) Sichuan well salt, 1–58; (2) Hedong earth salt, 59–84; (3) Shanxi Xie salt, 85–184; (4) southeastern sea salt, 185–484.

[95] According to tradition, when the Yellow Emperor killed a defiant tribal chief, "his blood became transformed into the brine of the salt lake at Xiezhou and his limbs were rent asunder (*jie*); this is why we call it Xie Pond today." See *Kongzi sanchao ji*, cited in Chen and Zeng 1959, 513; *SJ* 1.3; Qian Gongbo 1964, 160. As a name, the character "jie" is pronounced "xie."

more important administratively since regulations developed for Liangzhe were often adopted as the standard in other circuits. Manufacture entailed evaporating seawater in beds, percolating it, then boiling it in cauldrons until the salt crystallized.[96] Since it was impossible to monitor the extended coastline and its seawater, production by the populace under official supervision (*cuijianzhi*) became the rule in many parts of the region. This category of "popular production" refers to private ownership by producers of production resources.

Earth salt (*jian*), extracted from alkaline soil, was produced primarily in Hedong (present-day Shanxi), as well as in a few areas in Shaanxi, Jingxi, and Hebei. Yonglijian in Hedong produced the greatest volume. Earth salt production was primarily managed by bureaucrats and employed corvee labor. Since output was low, its financial contribution to the state was minimal, and revenues went to the prefectures. Further, since it was produced close to Xixia and Liao territories, earth salt had to compete with salt smuggled from across the border. It was mainly consumed locally in Hedong and was important only during the Northern Song.

Well salt (*jingyan*) was produced in the circuits of Chengdufu, Zizhou, Kuizhou, and Lizhou (in present-day Sichuan and portions of Yunnan, Guizhou, and Hubei). While income from well salt did not constitute a large percentage of state revenues, this product was important for the region and tended to remain within it. Sichuan salt revenues went to the fiscal intendancies of those circuits rather than going directly to the court. Well salt, obtained after intensive prospecting from veins deep underground, was the most arduous and costly to manufacture. Initially, "well households" (*jinghu*) engaged in low-productivity digging to extract brine with traditional tools such as the manually operated capstan, leather bags, and wooden buckets. This meant creating a large-mouth well with boards lining the walls. Salters then boiled the brine using the intense heat generated by igniting nearby natural gas veins (*huojing*). The government assumed ownership and managed these wide-mouth wells. In the 1040s Sichuan salters revolutionized well salt production. Using technology that would contribute to modern oil drilling such as the round-bladed drill, bamboo cylinders for the well shaft, and uni-directional sluice

---

[96] See *Xixi congyu* [*XXCY*] *shang*, 25b.

gates, they created deep small-mouth or "standing tube" wells (*zhuotong-jing*), whose opening at the ground surface was as small as a bowl.

These four main regional varieties of manufacture generally produced a white crystalline salt, but there were many additional distinctions among salt types in the Song period. These included red, white, blue, and black salts, depending on their translucence and purity, rock salt (*shiyan*), also known as "cliff salt" (*yayan*), as well as such specialties as "horse-teeth salt" and "smelly salt."

Total annual production of nearly 220 million catties at the beginning of the dynasty breaks down as follows: sea salt (over 151 million catties) was followed by pond salt (over 45 million catties), then well salt (over 16 million catties), and finally earth salt (annually over 6 million catties). Income figures for around the year 997 show that total salt revenue was approximately 2.4 million strings.[97]

The Salt Producers

The total number of salter households in the Song is estimated to have reached 60,000 to 70,000, or over 100,000 workers.[98] Given the diversity of its production regions, the tendency to preserve historical names, and the salt industry's key place in state resources, it is little wonder the Song had more terms for these salt producers and the production process than any other dynasty. Many names reflected the differing modes of manufacture and the degree of state control exerted upon production. Salters were not permitted to change occupation, relocate, conceal the amount of salt they produced, or privately deal in their product. If they violated this law, their punishment was much harsher than that meted out to the average person.

For pond salt work, authorities forcibly registered local residents as "section households" (*qihu* or *xihu*). They were to produce the required quota salt (*keyan*) annually in exchange for cash wages, a rice stipend, and exemption from other requisitions. The Northern Song administration moved to systematize the direct hiring of labor, eventually offering terms ranging from temporary to three-year and

---

[97] *XCB* 97.20a.
[98] Guo Zhengzhong 1997, 247.

lifetime positions.[99] As with the other major types of salt production, the government often drafted soldiers and convicts to supplement the regular workforce, even though these rootless laborers were not the most stable workers, tending to quit easily or loiter in town markets.

The government established sea salt "pavilion salterns" (*tingchang*) and compelled independent salters along the coast to register as "pavilion households" (*tinghu*) or "stove households" (*zaohu*). Administrators then were to provide them with the production funds to cover the cost of fuel, brine, labor, supplies, and taxes.[100] Within a given period, sea salters had to produce a certain quota of salt (*zhengyan*). But they were expected to sell all the salt they produced to the government, including any above-quota, so-called "floating salt" (*fuyan*).

Earth salt producers, like those in other regions, were local producers whom the government had registered. There was one difference however: earth salters might be excused from service after serving for a number of years, or in a place where local salt resources had been exhausted due to some natural disaster. Another avenue for leaving salt production was one household finding another to replace its labor. Earth salters were commonly called "salt boiler households" (*jianyanhu*); those affiliated with a government salt directorate in Hedong Circuit were known as "pan households" (*chenghu*). They used pans or cauldrons of various shapes to boil down salt extracted from the briny soil of their locales. Unlike pond and well salts, earth salt production sites tended to be scattered. After gluts occurred in the late Northern Song, employment for earth salters was changed to a rotating system, rather than using permanent laborers.

Producer families of well salt were generally termed "well households" (*jinghu*). But there were further distinctions: some worked the government-managed wells, some franchised salt wells, some simply paid taxes on wells they ran independently, while others purchased brine to boil down. Regular laborers were normally called "salt artisans" (*yanjiang*), while those with technical knowledge who supervised the drilling were called "well artisans" (*jingjiang*). The government eventually gave up trying to monitor the new, easily-concealed

---

[99] Guo Zhengzhong 1990b, 425; *SHY* 23.34a; *SS* 181.4415–16; *XCB* 109.2545. See also Kawakami 1974, 59–61, 66–67.

[100] *SHY* 26.1a, 27.1b, 3b, 28.29a. For corroboration of southeast production figures, see Guo Zhengzhong 1983, 77–115.

small-mouth wells so those came to be privately run, a degree of latitude awarded to none of the other major salt producers.[101]

Units Within the Salt Monopoly

Government control of the production, storage, and distribution of salt was centered on a system of agencies and facilities. The basic unit of production was the saltern (*chang*). The term "chang" is not specific to salt; it refers to processing sites generally, including mines and forestry enterprises.[102] *Chang* also entails different levels of usage that are not always specified. Sometimes it refers to the place of production and as such is an abbreviation of *yanchang* or *tingchang*.[103] At other times *chang* refers to offices that oversaw various functions. The production-supervisory *chang* (*cuijianchang*) was the point at which boiling officials (*jiancha zhuyan*) oversaw production. These were subordinate to procurement-sales *chang* (*mainachang*), the point at which procurement officials (*mainaguan*) bought salt from producers and sold it to merchants. There were also branch salterns (*zichang*) affiliated with procurement-sales *chang* as opposed to production-supervisory *chang*.[104] Small saltern operations were called *wu*. For our purposes here, general production *chang* or unspecified *chang* will be glossed as "salterns" or "saltworks."

Among the largest administrative units were the salt directorates (*jian*), established in the early Song to regulate production and distribution. Their specific powers and functions evolved over time and differed by region, but those in the sea salt regions may be considered the model. In the early to mid-Northern Song the court established three directorates in Huai, and seven or eight in Liangzhe. Each had jurisdiction over several saltworks. Directorates reported to their prefectures and for a time were administratively equivalent to a county.

---

[101] Su Shi (1037–1101) was one of the first to describe the new type of well (*SHY* 23.22b; *Dongpo zhilin* [*DPZ*], 3721). Hans Ulrich Vogel, a German specialist on the premodern Chinese salt industry, considers the small-mouth well to be a crucial breakthrough in the pre-industrial age, one that occurred in China long before it did in the West (Vogel 1991; 1993).

[102] Yoshida 1993, 2n4.

[103] *Ting* appears with and without the "man" (*ren*) radical (*SHY* 23.24a–b; *JTS* 48.2109).

[104] *Siming zhi* [*SMZ*] 3.24b–25a; *SHY* 23.14a–15a.

The early southeastern directorates were charged with three functions: supervising production, procuring product, and sales. Empowered to carry out such comprehensive functions, the directorates were plagued by abuses that arose from the overlap of all their activities at one site. They were gradually dismantled over the course of the mid-to-late Northern Song, although their locations often retained the name of the original unit.

When abuses at the large directorate sites compelled the state to separate their functions into distinct agencies and locales, the directorates were broken down into production works (*cuijianchang*), procurement storehouses (*shouyancang*), distribution storehouses (*zhiyancang*), and other such agencies, each with its own specialized officials. When the government required that salters deliver their product to storehouses rather than handing it over at the saltworks, this proved exhausting for these producers, since some storehouses were as distant as 200 *li* from production sites. So the government relocated a number of the storage facilities, leading to the institution of specialized procurement salterns (*mainachang*), which were affiliated with several surrounding saltworks.

These production and procurement facilities were now generally subordinate to the circuit salt intendancy, rather than to the county or prefecture in which they were located. But it was the host government that usually paid official salaries connected with such facilities. This led to dissatisfaction on the part of local governments and a call for the procurement salterns to cover their own staffing expenditures, which were often as not "of no concern whatsoever to this prefecture!"[105] Tensions were complicated further in the Southern Song when *mainachang* "interference" prevented production units from directly relaying petitions to the circuit salt intendancy. Procurement and production works had originally been intended to operate independently as equal units, not as superior and inferior.[106]

The many close connections remaining between the former directorates and the *chang* into which they had been split—in terms of term of office, personnel, location, and name—continued to impede the intended separation of their functions. But the evolving top-down

---

[105] *SMZ* 6.30b–31a.

[106] At times in the southeast these two types of operations took over the other's function and on occasion they were even joined into one unit.

structure still marked a success for the central government at the expense of prefectural governments. The transformation of the directorates had been aimed at greater systematization and closer control under court auspices in an effort to increase revenues. This process was escalated during Shenzong's reform period, and the *mainachang* became another tool by which the court could collect, control, and sell greater amounts of the salters' product. The state's procurement concerns would come to drive production and its management.

Coping with Production Problems

When quotas rose and funding fell, salters resisted, engaging in smuggling, fleeing, even turning to banditry or open rebellion. Salter operations were also subject to fluctuations in the weather and natural disasters, but the more serious challenge to state revenues from salt came from its producers, who were chronically unable to meet their basic needs. Their easiest form of resistance and a way to make up their losses was to illegally boil and sell.

The Northern Song's attempts to cope with various kinds of smuggling led its key reformer, Wang Anshi, to believe that salt crimes could not be eliminated because the laws were not severe enough. He believed that if twenty or thirty families in a village of one hundred smuggling families were wiped out, none of the rest would dare continue their activities. Wang's protégé Lu Bing served as the influential Huaidong and Liangzhe judicial and salt intendant in the 1070s and his programs reflect Wang's severity, with its tendency toward social engineering solutions.

Several new control mechanisms emerged under Lu Bing's direction. He elaborated on policies probably instituted in the 1030s regarding supervision over production in the southeast. A production-supervisory official (*cuijianguan*) determined when boiling would commence and conclude, based on local regulations. A foreman (*jiatou*) recorded the firing schedule and the amount of salt produced. A supervisor examined the accounts and calculated each household's production quota.[107] Lu's "stove head" (*zaojia*) system applied the *baojia* policy to salter households in the southeast with the goal of increasing surveillance over the boiling process. When the state

---

[107] *SHY* 27.11b–12a; *Aobo tu* [*ABT*], plate 46; Yoshida 1993, 148–49.

uncovered illegal activity, it punished all households in the unit. Lu Bing convicted countless "smugglers," including the elderly, women, and children, and exiled over 12,000 people.[108] His "regiments and palisades" (*tuanzha*) system created guarded compounds surrounded by walls or moats for a dozen salter families, a stove house and storage facilities.[109] Enclosures were built mainly in Liangzhe and Fujian, and these villages continued to operate into the early Southern Song, some developing into large communities.

In the Southern Song the remaining salt-producing territories comprised six southeastern sea salt circuits and Sichuan. Gaozong's early policies to revitalize the industry after the calamitous years of Huizong and devastation of the war included a number of measures geared to helping sea salters resume production. First, the government allocated money, materials, and draft animals as well as extending loans to assist producers in resettling and getting to work again. Second, the court pardoned households that had fled, and reduced taxes and corvee to allow them to concentrate on meeting production quotas. The corvee exemptions proved so attractive that some great families posed as salters just to avoid the labor service.[110] Third, the state granted payment of production funds to salters in advance of production while also paying a good procurement price for the final product. Xiaozong continued the more enlightened of Gaozong's policies, aiming to provide production funds on time, reducing quotas, relaxing punishments, amending abuses at procurement, and increasing the procurement price. This resulted in the highest levels of production for Huai-Zhe salt yet seen.

These policies may be best understood in the light of state benefits from them. Illegal production both undercut revenues and sparked social unrest but persisted as part of a vicious cycle the state could not seem to escape: the greater its budgetary pressures, the higher the taxes and government salt prices, the more frequent the state's failure to pay out production funds, forcing producers to make contraband salt and so pave the way for illegal sales. The government distribution system in particular perpetuated these abuses.

---

[108] *SS* 182.4437, 331.10670.

[109] *ABT*, plates 1, 2, 4, 47; Yoshida 1993, 115, 116, 117, 149.

[110] *SHY* 27.10b–11a.

Government Versus Merchant Distribution

Overview of the Debate

Since the nature of salt production and its techniques was not so susceptible to the tides of policy changes, Song disputes over the salt monopoly revolved principally around the post-production stages of transport and distribution. These debates stand out for their number and ferocity, akin to the overarching debate over pursuing new revenues versus economizing, of enriching the state or providing for the people.

The two basic policy positions supported either (1) government transport and direct state distribution of salt (*quejin, guanmai*), or (2) government-regulated merchant transport and merchant distribution (*tongshang*). Which type (and there were permutations of each) was implemented in a given region depended on the local situation and structures inherited from the Tang and the Five Dynasties.

Boundaries between the two main distribution zones and the distribution areas of the major types of salt were strictly demarcated for most of the Song. While its policies within a region did fluctuate, the importance the court attached to regional boundaries was consistent. Signs, often lengthy stone inscriptions carved into cliff faces at points where travelers and merchants were likely to pass, explicitly stated, "Monopoly salt must not exit this boundary." These notices empowered local authorities to make arrests; they also offered rewards to informants, and warned of the legal consequences of violations.[111] The rigid boundaries, however, would also be a factor in the state's inability to alleviate distribution imbalances.

With government distribution, the state decided how much salt should be moved from a given locale then commanded both local militia and civilian inhabitants to transport it to points of sale. With merchant distribution, the state directed traders to move predetermined amounts of salt from a designated location and retail it in a specified locale.

Initially the Song relied upon government distribution, especially in the southeast, in line with past practice, but also allowed merchant distribution in certain locales. The type of distribution used within

---

[111] Ou Delu 1989.

each district could change fast and frequently. At the beginning of the Song the court rescinded and reinstated a merchant distribution policy for pond salt at least five times in the course of a decade. It is fair to characterize the general development of the monopoly thus: for its first fifty years, government and merchant distribution were both employed; merchant distribution came to hold sway over the next sixty years to 1068, with the success of a merchant voucher policy; a reversion to expanded government distribution occurred over the thirty-odd years to 1100; and for the last twenty-five years of the Northern Song merchants again became the vehicle of choice under a new voucher policy. Overall the pattern of policy swings favored the expansion of merchant sales, which fed revenue to the center to apportion.

Issues in Government Distribution

Government distribution of salt was initiated as a way to solve certain problems: it would generate revenues for the government, deliver a daily necessity to even the remotest areas of the empire, and manage a key resource across most Song territory. In practice it fell short, causing serious negative side effects that resulted in government losses and misery for the people.

The Labor Burden

Government transport of salt was generally conducted via the salt convoy (*yangang*) system. Under this system, monopoly functionaries called on the populace to move a designated amount of salt as part of their corvee labor obligation. These convoy laborers (*gangyunren*) were divided by functions specific to water and overland transport, such as captain, sailor, boat punter, cart puller, driver, and hauler. The boats or carts were grouped into convoys (*tuangang*). Each boat convoy (or flotilla) might comprise ten to thirty boats and carry on the order of 5,000 bags or 1.5 million catties of salt. During Shenzong's reign at least 170 convoys, or over 1700 boats, were in regular use. At first the government built or purchased these boats and carts, but later it expected transporters to use their own. Government transport demands became increasingly burdensome. Salt officials began to appropriate villagers' boats, carts, and beasts of burden, and forced the peasants to cut lumber and fulfill many other additional labor services. According to regulations the government was to provide convoy labor with food, a stipend, and regular rest periods, but these workers often had to turn to begging and became exhausted by the punishing labor.[112]

Pilfering and Contamination

Government distribution efforts were also hampered as desperate corvee workers took advantage of their access to the product. Locks, seals, inspections, and the supervision of a convoy overseer (*yagangren*) were meant to guarantee the volume and quality of the government salt, but these measures were commonly ineffective. A tare allowance of several percent was reckoned to account for a normal amount of wastage en route.[113] According to a 1033 memorial by Wang Sui, a vice-chief councilor, when salt left the Huainan seacoast for the interior, it was clean and uncontaminated, but in the course of convoy transport, the many levels of personnel who came into contact with the shipment stole some and adulterated the remainder with dirt, sand, and even feces to maintain the appropriate net weight. This meant not only significant losses of product, but the further the salt traveled, the more inedible it became. The problem was so pervasive that even the dowager empress complained at the contamination of the salt eaten at court.[114]

Gluts

Where salt was government distributed, periodic gluts were common over the course of the dynasty. This was one factor in the government's being unable to pay salters when they submitted their quota. Gluts occurred for every type of salt, in both salt-rich and salt-poor areas, from the coast to the interior.

Five major gluts of Xie pond salt occurred over the course of the Northern Song. At times these were separated by only a few years so that they were in effect continuous. The first, in the first quarter of the eleventh century, totaled nearly 400 million catties, valued at 22 million

---

[112] *XCBt* 167.10a; *SHY* 46.3a.

[113] *SHY* 46.2b.

[114] *SS* 181.4417.

strings.[115] The second, between 1028 and 1032, saw "mountains of salt, upon which have grown large trees around which one can wrap one's arms."[116] The third glut, in 1034, was said to equal ten times the output of a normal year.[117] The fourth, between 1039 and 1040, saw salt again piled "mountain-high,"[118] and the fifth occurred between 1060 and 1063, accumulating quantities sufficient to distribute for ten years.[119] Officials attempted to deal with these massive accumulations by pardoning the salters half their production quotas and devising ways to sell it off to merchants, none of which succeeded.[120] In the end Xie salt surpluses were alleviated only when flooding at the ponds caused so much damage that production did not reach its former capacity for years afterward.

There were at least eight major surfeits of Huai-Zhe sea salt. The first, in the 970s, occurred at the Lifeng salt directorate, which operated eight salterns. There officials could only helplessly "sit by and watch the surpluses [pile up] before them."[121] The second, in 1033, overflowed available storage and lay exposed to the elements; it amounted to 750 million catties, valued at one year's cash income for the entire state.[122] The third, occurring from 1041 to 1043, saw 150 million catties accumulate at Taizhou[b] salterns; the fourth, around 1158, saw over 180 million catties accumulate at Wenzhou salterns. The fifth, between 1162 and 1164, of more than 150 million catties, forced the state to construct up to 4,000 new storehouses.[123] During the sixth, around 1169, and the seventh, in 1174, only a third of the procured salt in Zhedong could be distributed annually.[124] The eighth, in 1184, was of nearly 140 million catties. Some time in the later Southern Song the Huai-Zhe region succeeded in dispensing only

---

[115] *SHY* 23.30, 36.16; *XCBt* 86.16a; *SS* 181.4416

[116] *XCB* 109.2545.

[117] *SHY* 23.36.

[118] *JSJ* 45.310; *XCBt* 129.17b.

[119] *SS* 328.10586.

[120] *SS* 181.4413–26.

[121] *Gongshi ji* [*GSJ*] 51.2a–b.

[122] *XCB* 113.2655.

[123] *SHY* 27.10.

[124] *SHY* 28.1b–2b.

100,000 of its 900,000-bag annual distribution quota.[125] Fujian and the two Guangs produced much less sea salt, but still experienced gluts in 987, 1028, 1143, 1160, and 1187–1189.[126]

Gluts occurred even in salt-poor areas of Sichuan in 1005, 1065-1066, 1086, 1088–1091, and 1195. And they occurred with earth salt at Hedong's Yongli directorate between 998 and 1003. Measures to slightly reduce the price of government-distributed salt, or to sell it off to merchants at a better price did not succeed in moving sufficient quantities to alleviate these gluts.[127] In the most drastic cases, production had to be completely closed down for several years.[128]

Shortages

While salt gluts occurred in one region, another might experience shortages. Shortages could occur over the long-term in a particular locale but could also spread across circuits and even the entire empire for certain periods. They occurred in both the Northern and the Southern Song. Even well-known salt production areas for all the major types of salt experienced shortages from time to time. "The people have not the wherewithal to provide salt for their own parents, wives and children, nor even livestock" was a common refrain.[129] The price of government salt was often too high for the poor to afford and so folk in the mountains might go for months or years without processed salt. During the 1130s a major salt shortfall extended across the circuits, and the price shot up to more than 2,000 cash per catty.[130] Many died of their long-term deficiency.

One factor where shortages were chronic was the inflexibility of distribution boundary lines. These could cut off supply between circuits or between rural and urban areas. Thus a shortage in one area could not be remedied by surplus in another district, for fear of encroaching on another's sales territory, even though it meant assisting a neighboring circuit.

---

[125] See *Qingzheng cungao* [QZCG], 864.

[126] *SHY* 23.22, 24, 26.29, 30, 27.6, 28.32, 35.

[127] *SHY* 28.34, 36.5; *XCBt* 369.12b–13a.

[128] *SHY* 23.38.

[129] *SHY* 24.12.

[130] *SHY* 26.3.

Maldistribution also occurred due to infrastructural and organizational factors. It was not so much oversupply—even producing regions experienced shortages and low-producing areas experienced gluts—as production capacity generally exceeding distribution capacity. Because salt is a heavy, bulky good that tends to absorb moisture and spoil easily, timely transport and passable routes were critically important. Many regions had only poor roads or waterways. But in the end the high price of government salt in relation to other sources of salt proved the greatest obstacle to its effective distribution. When the government was unable to sell its salt, then producers became impoverished and the court grew concerned at the disruption of its income. People had to turn to illegal methods to make up lost income or even secure this necessity for their own consumption.

Smuggling

Smuggling posed a significant problem for the salt monopoly, particularly for the sales of government-distributed salt. Again, the price differential between government salt and the often better quality product that was smuggled from region to region was a key factor. People naturally chose to eat the cleaner, cheaper smuggled salt, providing a ready market for smugglers who exploited any and all loopholes in the system to trade without getting caught. Clandestine production and sales clearly and consistently undercut official salt sales.[131]

The main smuggling regions were the same ones that produced the most salt: Huai and Zhe in the southeast. Around the 1060s the official Huai salt price stood at forty-seven cash for usually less than a full catty, while smuggled salt there cost only twenty cash for a catty and a half.[132] Smugglers also worked the border, transporting Liao, Xixia, and Jin salt into northern prefectures. In 998 the government marketed Xie pond salt at thirty-eight to thirty-nine cash per catty, while the nomads' blue salt was being openly sold for no more than fifteen cash. Small wonder the illegal trade in salt continued to flourish.

---

[131] For example, *XCB* 44.941; *JSJ* 7.837; *Su Shi ji* [*SSJ*] 73.3451. Zhang Xiaoye uses a legal and economic approach to understand the social phenomenon of smuggling in the Qing, which she argues was an economic activity to deal with need; see Zhang Xiaoye 2001.

[132] *SS* 182.4443.

Smugglers included not only producers, merchants, and soldiers, but also salt administrators, intendants, and inspectors. The most successful smugglers were sure to have close links with officialdom and lawful merchants. Even threat of severe penalties failed to deter them.[133]

Official Performance Imperatives

The salt monopoly, as a bureaucracy, naturally traded in its own evolving set of rules, regulations, and performance expectations. As noted for the imposition of extra duties on corvee workers, official abuses and even regular policies imposed a certain burden from one level to the levels below. An evaluation system (*mokan*) reviewed every grade of salt monopoly official and every local administrator with regard to the productivity of their work in procurement, storage, transport, and sales. These reviews could determine promotion or discharge.

How to heighten the effectiveness of government distribution among the southeastern sea salt circuits became an especially pressing question for the later Northern Song court. Under Shenzong, a Huai fiscal vice-indendant, Jiang Zhiqi (1031–1104), devised a new personnel evaluation system to spur officials to sell greater amounts of salt. Each prefecture in these eight circuits was required to declare annual tax figures to their respective fiscal intendancy and, based on these numbers, the intendancy would determine the locations with the highest and lowest salt revenues. After noting the names of the relevant prefects and prefectural officials, it would forward the information to the Ministry of Finance for reward and punishment. When all circuits' salt intendancies were compared against their old distribution quotas for annual increases or decreases, the best and worst performers again would be determined for appropriate reward or punishment.[134]

---

[133] In September 2002, the central government and local Sichuan authorities cracked the largest salt smuggling syndicate on the mainland in recent times. The syndicate used the train system and trucks to transport uniodized salt from a legitimate salt factory in Shandong to Sichuan. Then through local produce companies it sold the salt as regulation salt. Police surmise syndicate leaders connived with plant workers to carry out their operations. See "Chuan dao zuida siyan jituan" 川搗最大私鹽集團 (Sichuan smashes the largest salt smuggling syndicate), *Shijie ribao* 世界日報, June 20, 2003, page A9.

[134] *XCBt* 337.2b; *SHY* 24.24a.

Closely related to this, Shenzong initiated a policy that awarded special bonuses to salt officials who exceeded their sales targets: they were to receive up to 1 percent of the portion of revenues above their quota. In 1096 under Zhezong the court approved a new apportionment for the southeast: as much as 50 percent of the above-quota sales revenue would be awarded to any fiscal intendancy generating such sales. These policies succeeded in achieving record levels of distribution.[135] But while they resulted in increased sales by county, prefecture, and circuit salt officials, they meant corresponding hardship for local residents.

Head and Household Taxes

Salt administrators were known to sometimes make concessions to merchants, but understanding and satisfying consumer needs was the furthest thing from their minds. Bureaucrats, who could be held accountable for gluts and corresponding drops in revenue, responded with a variety of mechanical or irregular practices to meet, and beat, distribution quotas. Under government sales, consumption became a sort of involuntary service.

In principle, government quotas for salt sales were based on head count in the quota area. Many taxes were imposed by head count, on everything from infants to livestock.[136] Where salt gluts occurred, retail sales could turn into imposed distribution (kefu) that went far beyond normal needs. Circuit intendants forced salt upon the prefectures, where local officials in turn forced it upon the intimidated populace, who had no desire to buy the expensive, foul-tasting product.[137] If an administrator refused to do his part out of concern for the well-being of the populace, he was branded an obstructionist and likely to suffer demotion.

The amount of salt forced upon the consumer varied from one prefecture to the next. It also differed by household, with adult males of the highest ranked households (shanghu) required to buy approximately twice as much as those of lower ranked households (xiahu). In one Guangxi prefecture, an adult male of a master household

---

[135] Wenxian tongkao [WXTK] 15.36b; SHY 24.34a.

[136] SS 182.4453; XCB 112.2623, 115.2702.

[137] SHY 26.5a, 38b–39a, 27.5a–b, 28.8a–b.

(*zhuhu*) was required to purchase over 19 catties or nearly 12 kilograms annually, far beyond the current dietary requirement of 2000 milligrams of sodium daily, or 7.2 kilograms annually.[138] The regulations and records do not indicate transactions for all districts, therefore we cannot determine the full extent of the imposed distribution.

Even the normal demand for salt became a lever for raising household taxes. A prime example is the "silkworm salt" (*canyan*) system inherited from the Five Dynasties. This system was originally intended to alleviate the cash-flow problems of silkworm raisers by allotting them salt in advance of silk production. In time, this allotment became simply another mandatory form of salt distribution. After about 1041 officials no longer fronted salt for the silk, but still required payment as if they had.[139] From the early 1100s, even if consumers did not want the silkworm salt allocated to them, they still had to pay 60 percent of its value in cash, effectively changing the silkworm salt system into a tax. The practice then became the basis for the Southern Song "adult male salt silk" (*ding yanjuan*) and "adult male salt money" (*ding yanqian*) policies, which created new and formidable financial burdens for rural families.[140]

Finally, bureaucrats also targeted various types of consumers and even occasions on which salt purchases were required, for example, floating salt for fishermen, seasonal salt for monks, preserved-foods salt for shop owners, contract salt on the occasion of a property sale, winning-a-case salt, losing-a-case salt, scholarship salt, corvee salt, completing-the-corvee salt, long-life salt, afterlife salt, and the like.

---

[138] *SHY* 24.23a–b, 28.31–33; *XCB* 335.8068–69.

[139] *XCB* 18.398–99, 181.438990; *SHY* 24.27a–b; *SS* 181.4427.

[140] For Southern Song debate on silkworm salt distribution, see *SHY* 26.8b. For a general explanation, see *Taizong shilu* 977, cited in interstitial commentary of *XCB* 2.44, and *XCB* 18.398–99. A counterpart was the "harmonious purchase" (*hemai*) policy, which originated in the pre-Tang period of division but came into its own during the Song. In the spring, local governments "prepurchased" silk from inhabitants before they had produced it, offering to pay them in cash at a "harmonious" price. Ultimately, prefectures gave neither money nor salt for the silk in the summer or fall, even after the quantity so "purchased" had been produced. By the beginning of the Southern Song, this transaction had essentially become a routine tax (*SHY* 27.10b–11a, 28.57b–58a; *SS* 182.4446, 4448, 183.4465, 4473).

Reaching the System's Limits

Generally speaking, the inflow of revenue was more stable under government than merchant distribution, because the government could raise the salt price as needed. Still, the difficulties this system posed gradually weaned officials away from too-heavy dependence on it. A vivid exchange between Renzong and the executive censor (*yushi zhongcheng*) Zhang Fangping as early as the mid-1040s sums up the range of problems generated by government distribution. When a finance commissioner proposed resuming government distribution of Hebei sea salt so the state could better reap income, Renzong readily agreed. Zhang then raised a challenge based on the historical suffering of Hebei inhabitants under the high cost and other burdens of the monopoly. He further argued that higher government prices would encourage the smuggling of Khitan salt, which might lead to conflict with the nomads, a scenario even salt revenues would not be sufficient to cover. He asked the emperor, "How can we possibly impose the monopoly again?" Swayed by these arguments, the emperor decided to hold off on government distribution in Hebei.[141]

But the system's various burdens could engender even graver dangers for the state, leading to serious social turmoil and political disaster. Under pressure from official predation, popular uprisings occurred periodically. Salt bandits in Jiangxi and Fujian during the mid eleventh century swept through the countryside after the harvest year after year, attracting hundreds of the disaffected to take up arms against government soldiers.[142] With its many serious flaws, government distribution could not be successfully sustained across the empire over the long run.

Parameters of Merchant Distribution

As organizational and other problems with government distribution prompted the court to explore and expand its other options, merchant distribution would develop into a much broader program. From the start, the state regulated its merchant distributors as tightly as it did its salt producers. Merchant sales should not be

---

[141] *SS* 181.4429, 318.10353–59; *XCB* 159.3852–53.
[142] *SS* 182.4441–42; *XCB* 189.4569, 190.4595, 195.4719.

confused with private trade or a free market, therefore. No matter what their form of participation, merchants always operated as part of the monopoly. It was precisely this control over the merchant salt trade and retailing that disinclined the court to seriously tackle problems in the government distribution system.

The state set particular routes along which merchants were to transport the salt and designated locations at which they could sell it. But unlike the relatively immobile producers who could more easily be coerced into carrying out their duties, merchants could not be forced to engage in this trade. What drove them was the prospect of profit, so the limits of government exaction were simple: as soon as merchants could make no profits, they stopped participating. This meant the government had to maintain a balance, extracting income and savings from merchants who assumed the burden of transport, yet refraining from extreme measures that would dampen their motivation to move product. To meet its needs, especially in times of war, the Song state devised various devices to reap not just income but also services from merchant distributors.

Supplying the War Front

From 985 in the face of Liao forays south of the Great Wall the government instituted a border provisioning system through which merchants would transport fodder and grain to supply the military in the remote areas in exchange for vouchers for pond salt and other trade goods. The weakness of this distribution scheme was the opportunity it provided for merchants to inflate the prices of the supplies that they shipped north. For example, merchants might inflate the price of lumber they had transported to 1,000 cash, for which officials might award them as much as 220 catties of salt. This worked out to government income of only 4 cash per catty, which the state normally sold for ten times as much. Such arrangements caused the Song considerable revenue losses in the early years.

Vouchers for Cash

In the late 1040s a new voucher plan divorced provisioning from the salt trade so that merchants paid cash directly for salt vouchers. This bypassed the problem of inflated provisions pricing and would have a major impact later when merchant distribution became a permanent and nearly universal policy across the empire. The complicated bureaucratic controls over voucher use and their cross-filing with various offices made falsifying difficult, and merchants were increasingly forced to jump through new hoops as the fiscal situation required. In the following section we will take a focused look at the types of voucher programs the state devised since they were to remain central for so long, not just in the Song monopoly, but through subsequent dynasties.

Franchising

Franchising (*pumai, maipu*) was another tool of the monopoly. Resorted to in the latter half of the eleventh century in the face of deficits, the state contracted out salt tax collectorships, either to officials or to merchants. Appointed by the government, official franchisees could not be acting salt administration bureaucrats or their relatives. Merchant franchisees had to submit to a bidding process and all franchisees had to possess certain assets and make payments according to a set schedule, be it annually or monthly. After paying the flat sum estimated to be the amount of taxes due, a wealthy individual assumed both the right to buy and sell salt and the authority to collect any additional salt taxes, which would be forwarded to the government.[143]

During Shenzong's reign Lu Bing, the Zhe salt intendant, allowed wine franchisees to also take on salt franchises. These were limited to the same sales territory as that for their wine, and within this area the individual basically held a monopoly.[144] The income from such sales could be considerable.

In Sichuan, the franchisee was typically awarded complete command over salt production, transport, and distribution. The franchise program here was in large part sparked by the rise of new technology, which allowed creation of small-mouthed wells that easily escaped state surveillance, and so remained under private operation. Most of these wells, as well as many poorly managed large-mouth

---

[143] Guo Zhengzhong 1997, 277. These terms have been connected to a Song coin-toss game used to draw business: if the customer won, he gained goods, including possibly salt.

[144] *XCBt* 230.17b–18a.

government wells, eventually came to be franchised. Despite repeated petitions from Sichuan circuit fiscal intendants that the relatively light taxes paid by franchisee households be increased to aid the struggling local and circuit governments, Renzong's court denied the requests. This was presumably because the volume of activity and income from franchising itself, fees that fed into the central government, were plentiful.[145]

Under Shenzong, the reformer Wang Anshi grew concerned that even though this program generated significant tax revenue, it adversely affected the income from government salt distribution.[146] In practice, franchising often degenerated into another form of government distribution, with those who had bought the franchises taking advantage of this authority in the villages to behave even worse than the regular bureaucrats.[147]

Cash Surcharges

Since revenues from merchant distribution were dependent on merchant participation, when, for various reasons, merchants chose to withdraw, salt taxes were diminished. A merchant might encounter natural disasters or bandit gangs as he plied his trade, but worst of all was the array of commercial taxes and surcharges levied by circuit and local officials. These, cumulatively, could bankrupt even the wealthy merchant, never mind the illegal but common incidental fees, detentions, and confiscations, all of which damaged the credibility of the merchant distribution system among its participants.

Dumping Salt

Finally, merchants like consumers were not immune to the repercussions of pressure on officials to meet sales quotas and avoid accountability for gluts. Salt bureaucrats dumped extra salt on merchants through numerous schemes: They would dole out extra bags, increase

---

[145] Zhao Xiaogeng 1994, 173; Guo Zhengzhong 1997, 278. For a study of well ownership, see Zhang Xuejun 1984.

[146] *SS* 182.4436.

[147] *SS* 182.4443; *SHY* 24.20b.

the volume per bag, and extend the deadline by which merchant salt had to be sold.

But the merchants could go elsewhere or engage in illegal trade, thus officials facing their own performance reviews often found themselves competing for merchant business. As binding regulations on merchant movements went by the wayside over time, traders naturally chose dispensary locations where they could obtain the most salt at the best price. This then fed the official malpractice at the distribution sites. The extent to which officials succeeded in learning to manipulate merchants and their activities will become apparent in the next section, on changing voucher policies in the merchant distribution system.

Voucher Programs

Of the different merchant sales arrangements that generated revenue for the government, voucher programs were the most widespread. Through these programs the Song dispensed salt wholesale to merchants who were then entitled to transport and sell it. The consistent attention paid to voucher law over the course of the dynasty suggests that the sale of vouchers generated the bulk of the government's cash revenues. Needless to say, the state closely guarded its extensive voucher-printing operations.[148] The schemes by which the state deployed vouchers allowed it to accomplish various ends over time; they primarily generated income but also secured vital services.

Salt for Provisioning Services and Jiaoyin Vouchers

The Khitan attacks of the 980s necessitated supply lines to the Song troops and horses on the embattled northwest border. Few merchants were willing to journey there, however, so the government offered special voucher certificates (*jiaoyin*) as an incentive. From 985 the government used *jiaoyin* to entice merchants to not only convey the army's provisions to the northwestern front, but to also transport

---

[148] *SS* 182.4450–51; *SHY* 27.40a; Dai Yixuan 1957, 141. Dai Yixuan's was the first major work from China on the salt trade. It takes an institutional rather than regional approach and gives relatively short shrift to the Southern Song.

gold, silver, and silks to the capital where money was in short supply.[149] This process had two "legs." The first, called *ruzhong* or *zhongmai* ("sales to the center"), referred to merchants bringing in and selling goods specified by the government to the government. The second, *zhezhong* or *zhebo* ("equitable exchange"), referred to the government's payment of merchants in *jiaoyin*, whose value was based on the value of the supplies carried and the distance traveled. Issued by the Monopoly Goods Bureau, these vouchers could be redeemed in the capital for cash or for certain desirable products in the circuits where those commodities were produced.

In the mid 990s, under a Three Items Policy (*sanshuofa*), vouchers could be redeemed at government offices for cash, tea, and incense or ivory. Vouchers for other goods were gradually added, including alum *jiaoyin* and in particular salt *jiaoyin* or *yanyin*, which entitled a merchant to distribute the lucrative Xie pond salt.[150] In the late 1040s when the northeastern border situation turned grave, sea salt was added under the Four Items Policy (*sishuofa*) to attract additional merchant interest. Voucher programs changed frequently in line with changing defense needs, but they also played to the competitiveness of salt distribution by merchants. Via *jiaoyin* vouchers, the state was able to achieve an important service objective.

By the 1030s and into the 1040s, however, troubles arose within the voucher system. Merchants had learned to inflate the price of supplies they shipped north to increase profits. This caused the state to suffer losses.[151]

New Chaoyin Vouchers Generate Cash

In 1048, in the face of continued tensions with the Xixia, Fan Xiang (?–1060), the Shaanxi judicial intendant and Xie salt commissioner (*zhizhi Xie yan*), targeted the management of Xie pond salt for a number of reforms. He cancelled the government sales program for Xiezhou salt in favor of merchant distribution that used a new *chaoyin* voucher. As a consequence, by the mid-Northern Song

---

[149] *SHY* 36.5a–6b.

[150] For this policy's impact on merchants, see Kawahara 1979.

[151] *SS* 181.4417.

the exchange of goods for salt vouchers had been largely replaced by cash payments.

Fan Xiang introduced certain innovations that would enhance revenues the salt industry generated for the state. First, Fan's *chaoyin* program disengaged border provisioning from salt distribution. The state issued these vouchers to any merchants who could pay for them in cash, gold, silver, or paper money at the Monopoly Bureau offices in the capital and in certain prefectural cities.[152] This move effectively eliminated the problem of price gouging. Second, Fan correlated each voucher to a certain quantity of salt, regardless of the salt price at the time a voucher was turned in. Third, he required merchants to retrieve salt from the site designated on their vouchers to prevent imbalances and regulate the trade. Lastly, Fan Xiang had merchants manage salt transport, which spared prefectures the cost of corvee labor.[153]

Although voucher programs had been used before, even in pre-Song times, only after Fan Xiang's elaboration did the system become institutionalized and central to the government's financial policymaking. Fan's scheme both saved local governments outlay for supplies, corvee costs, and management and generated enough revenue to cover as much as 80 percent of border defense costs. For this reason, merchant distribution became, and remained, the preferred policy for salt distribution in the Song and subsequent dynasties.[154]

---

[152] The state also required merchants to find a reliable shopowner to act as guarantor, and on issuing the voucher would provide a receipt that had to match the tear of the other portion, which was filed with different offices. Yang Lien-sheng 1952, 57; *SS* 181.4403–13, 4416–18; *SHY* 23.35a, 27.21b–22a. The term *jiaoyin* sometimes was used interchangably with *yanchao*, complicating interpretation (*Shantang xiansheng qunshu kaosuo* [*STKS*] 57.822). See also the analysis of pond salt production and distribution in this period by Qian Gongbo (1964).

[153] *SS* 4417–18. Fan Xiang also augmented the state storage network to stabilize salt prices and prevent speculation. Storage sites became a matter of debate when merchants found storehouses more convenient because of their accessible locations, but storage at the salterns was cheaper for the government. For saltern distribution, see *SS* 182.4435; *SHY* 25.4b–5a, 27.2a–3b, 27.24b–25b. For storehouse distribution, see *Hainingzhou zhi gao* [*HNZG*] 19.11b–12a; Liang Gengyao 1988, part 2, 18. The history of the separation of production and distribution functions is described by Lu Yihao, minister of finance, on 9/7/1128 (*SHY* 25.32b–33a).

[154] *SS* 181.4418; Guo Dongxu 1997, 296. Saeki Tomi (1987) traces salt through a tripartite historical division. He devotes 118 pages to the Song, and

Fan's scheme was not perfect, however, because it led to record-breaking production and gluts, and also because the court periodically flooded the market with vouchers to cover costs of its large-scale defenses against Xixia, in effect reducing the value of salt.[155] Nevertheless, the state continued the salt voucher program because it produced more revenue for the center than alternative systems.

Reform Period Adjustments

Another important figure in the history of the monopoly was Xue Xiang (1016–1081), who succeeded Fan Xiang in the Xie salt commission from 1060 to 1068. Not only did Wang Anshi recommend Xue, he invited him to come up with new means to gather revenue. During this eight-year period Xue implemented a number of measures that both enhanced and expanded the government's use of the salt trade: To boost distribution and sales, he abolished commercial taxes on voucher salt in the northwest and cut the selling price of Xie salt in the face of cheaper Xixia salt.

Xue also established the institution of markets where nomadic traders were given Xie salt vouchers for their horses. One aim in doing so was to phase out the central government's use of silver and silk in horse procurement and instead have the regions contribute more toward the horse trade.[156] When at first this failed because nomads had their own salt, Xue adjusted the program so the salt vouchers could be redeemed for goods from Sichuan; Sichuan merchants then cashed in the vouchers for silver. This policy had the drawback of increasing the number of vouchers in circulation, which eventually led to their loss of value.

By 1071, with the backing of Wang Anshi, Xue had become central finance commissioner. He also remained involved in the Xie salt administration and developed several major policies at this time in Shaanxi. One was a new program offering *xiaochao* vouchers (of smaller denominations, presumably easier to use). The addition of this new type of voucher was expected to increase revenues, but in fact

---

650 pages to the Qing. He highlights Fan Xiang above all others in the Song (see 239–61).

[155] On the overissuing of vouchers in this period, see Yuki Tōru 1977.

[156] *SHY* 26.7a, 27.12b–22a; *XCBt* 192.8b–9b.

simply created gluts of vouchers. Because the populace in the Xie region was accustomed to eating the cheaper blue salt from the west—no matter that it was prohibited—even the handier pond salt vouchers did not lead to greater income.[157]

Xue also set up new centers for voucher purchases and salt sales, though these turned out to be a transitional vehicle to resumed government distribution of Xie salt. He apparently allocated large sums to Yongxingjun Circuit to buy up vouchers and concentrate them in government hands, then cancelled the merchant trade. This change of policy in the northwest accorded with the thrust of Wang Anshi's New Policies.[158]

In the face of a cash shortage during Wang Anshi's reform period, some pond salt vouchers were again used to pay merchants who transported provisions up north. This created problems reminiscent of those that had necessitated Fan Xiang's initiatives in the first place. Nonetheless, throughout the reform period government distribution in the pond salt region continue to expand at the expense of merchant distribution. Successors to Xue Xiang continued not only to stray from Fan Xiang's cash-for-vouchers policy, but in some areas they even banned merchant distribution.[159] New government distribution institutions were devised as part of the reformers' resolve to expand state powers and reduce merchant competition.

---

[157] *Fan Zhongxuan ji* [*FZXJ*] *juan shang*.30b–31b.

[158] Xue was a controversial figure, but he seems to have managed to meet the enormous expenses of the local prefectures even in the face of northern attacks. To what extent he actually increased revenues, however, is unclear because when he got wind of an impending investigation, the relevant evidence went missing. In the end, by departing from Fan's voucher policy, the cash-for-vouchers exchange was affected but Xue likely expected that the court would see more direct salt income than it had under Fan's program.

[159] Attempts were made under Shenzong to resuscitate the devalued salt vouchers. Old vouchers were bought back at 30 percent of their original value, and any remainders could be exchanged for new vouchers after a complex process involving imperial approval. In the end this scheme failed because the new vouchers could only be acquired in increasingly restricted areas of the empire, and vouchers generally continued to be overissued in border areas.

A Universal Voucher Policy

By Huizong's first decade, however, as officials were reporting the Xixia border situation to be a disaster, merchant trade of salt had again become the rule.[160] Under Cai Jing's administration the salt policies for both the northwest and the southeast were reworked, turning government distribution in these regions into merchant distribution and thereby diverting more revenues to central coffers.

Merchant Privileges and Retailing

Cai began by granting apparently generous privileges to merchants. One was an exemption from the old salt boat tax (*lishengqian*) on merchants in transit.[161] More critical was the "yellow flag" proof given to voucher-bearing merchants so they did not have to wait in line behind government convoys. These and other advantages attracted increased numbers to the salt trade, including prefectural officials who had to pose as sellers, since, as officials they were prohibited from engaging in trade.[162]

Within two years of the new policy, in the mid-1110s, the reorganization of the salt trade was so successful the Monopoly Goods Bureau was amassing 40 million strings annually.[163] But this hamstrung the fiscal intendancies, which used to control much of the salt income. The voucher program becoming widespread across the southeast as well as the north meant that virtually all income went to the capital, and the circuits felt the pinch.

In 1110 Cai Jing had been forced out of office, and the new chief councilor Zhang Shangying promoted a policy that revived government distribution, combining it with merchant distribution. Half of the salt was designated for government transport to the circuits where merchants were responsible for retailing it (*zhuanlang*). The other half was reserved for regular merchant distribution, giving priority to those who paid cash or held all new vouchers. The

---

[160] *SS* 190.4718–20, 4723.

[161] *SHY* 24.32b, 37a.

[162] *SS* 182.4444–45; Guo Zhengzhong 1997, 309; Guo Zhengzhong 1990a, 356, 818–19.

[163] *SS* 182.4452–53.

zhuanlang policy was begun in Liangzhe and adopted in other southeastern circuits.[164]

New Levels of Red Tape

By 1112 Cai Jing was back and had largely overturned government distribution in the southeast. In 1113 he implemented his voucher policy empire-wide. This shrank the few areas in which government sales continued to be carried out, reducing overall the losses through pilfering and embezzlement, and alleviating shortages of salt in remote regions.

As he moved the southeast to merchant trade, Cai Jing also devised an increasingly complex voucher program. The process of trading in salt now involved many layers of red tape. First, a merchant had to apply to the government to trade, pay for vouchers in cash at the Monopoly Goods Bureau or one of its branches, then register in the voucher record. Only after his paperwork was verified and he had found a reliable shopkeeper to act as guarantor was he able to obtain the official vouchers. He would then take the vouchers to a pre-determined dispensary site where he would claim a designated amount of salt after personnel there matched his records with the official records and determined the order in which the merchant would receive product.

Next, based on the voucher specifics, other specialized personnel confirmed his packages' content and weight, sealed and stamped the bags and reminded the merchant of his sales destination as they sent him on his way. On the road, he had to pass numerous checkpoints and undergo further inspections. When he arrived at the point of sales, he had to show his vouchers and register before the seals to his shipment could be opened, and further, he had to obtain an approval notice to sell. Finally after selling the salt, he had to return all vouchers and empty bags within one year; none of these items were to be reused.

Cai's later universal voucher program created further regulation and complications: Long vouchers (*changyin*), to be used at designated points outside the circuit where the salt had been produced, were valid for one year; short vouchers (*duanyin*), which circulated within

---

[164] Zhang also reversed another Cai policy: the expansion of sea salt sales into Xie salt territories. Zhang expanded the Xie salt sales area and even supported a ban on sea salt in some northern regions.

prefectures near the production site, were valid for three months. If a merchant had not sold his stock by the deadline, administrators destroyed his vouchers and confiscated his goods. Cai Jing's "bag policy" stipulated that all pertinent information be attached to each bag, including location of purchase, weight, destination where the salt could be sold, and the name of the salt master (*yanzhu*) at the production point. Special officials ensured that seals were not tampered with between production and storage, and between storage and distribution.[165]

Voucher Exchanges and Fees

Cai Jing also formulated a rotation law (*xunhuanfa*) by which the state frequently issued new vouchers that merchants were required to trade for old issues, then imposed a cash surcharge (*tiena*) on the exchange. Related to this was the tactic of exchanging new issues for old at a stipulated ratio according to the proportional voucher exchange law (*duidaifa*). For example merchants with old Jianyan period vouchers had to buy new Shaoxing second year, ninth month vouchers. Anyone already holding ninth month vouchers had to buy eleventh month vouchers, and so forth as time went on.[166] The ratio was 40:20:40 of the eleventh month to ninth month to Jianyan vouchers. This compelled merchants to hand in a mixture of old and new vouchers, again at a loss, typically making three such fee payments before receiving their portion of salt. If a merchant was unable to continue converting his vouchers, then the money he had already expended was lost to him; it enriched the state without his getting any goods in return.[167]

The vagaries of engaging in the salt trade had become discouraging: "The old vouchers turn into waste paper," one critic railed, and "useless vouchers accumulate like rotten pulp," runs another account.[168] For these schemes that bilked merchants, forcing them to pay multiple times for the same good, the attendant censor (*shiyushi*)

---

[165] See *SHY* 27.14a–b on the miscellaneous officials at warehouses.

[166] *Jianyan yilai xinian yaolu* [*XNYL*] 60.2015. For more on the complex *duidai* and *xunhuan* policies, see Dai Yixuan 1957, 307–35; Worthy 1975, 105n 7.

[167] *SS* 181.4425, 182.4452.

[168] *SS* 181.4425–26.

Mao Zhu criticized the Monopoly Goods Bureau, saying that it imposed surcharges at the expense of business. He maintained that merchants ought to be reimbursed for the old vouchers with salt.[169] Only when merchants trusted the government would they consider the vouchers worth trading.

Once vouchers had been dissociated from the provisioning system, monopoly checks, cross-checks, and the filing of receipts in different offices prevented misuse of the vouchers themselves. Compared with attempts to keep tabs on the amount of salt processed by producers, the system of vouchers was difficult to tamper with and highly successful within its revenue objectives. But the administration tended to overissue them, and their value often depreciated. And when the manipulation went too far and the price too high, merchants simply abandoned the trade. The government then had to resort to perks to restore interest.

The Song's voucher programs accomplished various ends over time: securing services and amassing cash, as well as allowing the state to dump salt and squeeze merchants. While Fan Xiang had tried to ensure the value of voucher salt to maintain levels of both government revenues and business profits, a half a century later Cai Jing merely enticed merchants into buying vouchers, then devalued them. Fan's policy had been aimed at meeting defense needs; Cai's supplied revenues for many nonproductive ends and imperial whim. Nevertheless, Cai's administrative and financial manipulation not only developed tighter regulations, with each stage requiring more inspections, receipts, and guarantees than previously, he also succeeded at generating vast sums for the privy purse. His program would remain the model for the Southern Song.

Southern Song Realities

Production Developments

In the early Southern Song four of the eight main salt producing regions had been lost to the Jin. Yet this still left the prolific Huai and Zhe regions, which together generated 70 percent of Southern Song

---

[169] See Mao Zhu's statement in *SS* 182.4445–48.

salt production. Salt income in this period helped to replace the losses in land taxes that followed the shrinkage of Song territory.

Overall, output for this period was shaped by three main factors: the stratification of salt producers and changes in their relations with the bureaucracy, a major technological advance, and increasing levels of hardship among lower-level salters, which led to rampant illicit production. As of old, the sticking point for the state was not so much quantities produced, but the effectiveness of management and distribution strategies.

Producer Stratification

At the beginning of the Southern Song, Gaozong launched a multi-pronged program to restore the salt industry's vitality in the wake of wartime transition. Especially in Huai-Zhe, he pardoned absconding households, allocated money and materials to help salters settle back into their production areas, and reduced taxes and corvee obligations. These exclusions proved so attractive that certain great families actually posed as salters just to avoid labor service.[170] At the same time Gaozong applied stricter punishments against smugglers.[171]

From the beginning of the Southern Song, the government classified sea salt producers in a three-tiered hierarchy based on the size of their operations, and then provided funds and levied taxes accordingly. Sichuan salters were also divided into upper, middle, and lower households, and their well capacity and household rank were periodically adjusted in a process known as "investigating and clearing out" (*tuipai*).[172] Liangzhe, one of the most densely populated and developed regions, subdivided its upper of the three tiers so that there were four, and sometimes five, classes of salt producers.[173] Salter stratification was aimed at better organizing production duties, with the higher or larger salters operating at an increasingly managerial level, while lower or smaller producers did the actual production labor.

---

[170] *SHY* 27.10b–11a.

[171] *SS* 182.4454. For a vivid analysis of monopoly controls in Liangzhe with tables of statistics, see Worthy 1975.

[172] *Huangshi richao* [*HSRC*] 71.6a; *SHY* 26.5a.

[173] *HSRC* 80.6b–7a; *SHY* 26.5a.

Because upper-level households already commanded certain assets, the state came to grant them crucial privileges such as authority over small government wells (in Sichuan). Upper household members might stand in for low-ranking salt officials. Prosperous salters could hire servants and were chosen to be "heads" responsible for taxes. Thus they often played dual roles: toward bureaucrats, they represented workers and accepted production funds on their behalf; toward lower salt workers they represented government saltern officials, pressed producers for product, and distributed funds.[174] Ultimately, high-level salters ceased to engage in production at all, but became an elite in their own right, standing with the administration and functioning as the workers' point of contact with the lowest level of the salt bureaucracy.

A Production Revolution

In the latter half of the twelfth century Xiaozong resumed Gaozong's policies of producer support, making timely payments of funding, reducing quotas, increasing procurement prices, and relaxing punishments. About 1174 one of the greatest advances in sea salt production was discovered. Called the "stone lotus test" (*shilianshi*), it allowed producers to double capacity and lower costs by determining the salinity of prepared sea brine to within at least 10 percent. This saved precious fuel in processing.[175] The stone lotus test led to a sudden 50 to 60 percent rise in productivity. Huai-Zhe salt produced under Xiaozong consequently reached its highest levels, and later bureaucrats referred to it as the glorious "ancestral salt quota."

Later, by the mid-Southern Song, Liangzhe production also rose at a rapid rate, exceeding its own Northern Song levels and even surpassing the Huai region in terms of numbers of active stoves.

Increased Burdens on Producers

Huang Zhen (1213–1280), having served in various salt-related posts toward the end of the dynasty, including procurement-sales official (*mainaguan*) and subordinate in the Zhexi Salt and Tea

---

[174] *HSRC* 80.2a–b, 3b–4; *ABT*, plate 46; Yoshida 1993, 148–49.
[175] *SHY* 28.20b.

Intendancy, had often memorialized passionately on the plight of salters, but even he made favorable comments about their circumstances during Xiaozong's reign.[176] This, however, did not translate into a better life for them in the long term, because the government soon renewed its efforts to tap the salt industry for more income.

All classes of salters were required to pay a surcharge in cash (*tienaqian*) for every 100 catties of salt that they produced, though for the lower households this was a regressive charge. A salt merchant of Huainan in the 1180s described nonstandard weights and procedures used to shortchange producers at procurement. Producers also suffered in the conversion of silver into copper and from fluctuations in the value of paper money.[177]

The most flagrant and devastating abuse at the hands of the state concerned reduced payments made to salters to support their work. The first half was to be given to them before production began; the remainder immediately upon submission of their quota of goods, when the actual amounts owing on both sides could be determined.[178] In the Northern Song this had already been reported as problematic; by the Southern Song the situation became grave enough to cause wholesale impoverishment of salter households. Bureaucrats failed to pay salters on time, if at all; instead salter funds went toward the bureaucrat's personal entertaining, gift-giving, and money-lending.[179] When officials did pay the funds owed, various parties took their cuts and soon the funds might be whittled down to nothing.[180] Huang Zhen counted at least twenty-two "routine operating fees" levied on a single share of production funds in Zhedong.[181]

---

[176] *HSRC* 77.3b.

[177] Saeki 1987, 200.

[178] The regulation on these two equal installments is described on 1/25/1160 in *SHY* 27.1b.

[179] *HSZLS*, 63; *SHY* 26.33b–24a, 27.5a.

[180] *Shupu* [*SP*] xia.27a.

[181] *HSRC* 71.5b–6a; *Huating xianzhi* [*HXZ*] 9.14a–15a; *Songjiang fuzhi* (Chongzhen) [*SJFZc*] 29.2a–b.

High Production Leads to Losses for the State

For the government, advances in production technology meant reduced costs per unit produced, but the salinity test also had serious implications for clandestine production, in which all levels of salters colluded. Recognizing this, Ye Heng of the Ministry of Finance advised in 1171 that the administration concentrate on monitoring production areas rather than pursuing sellers. The government added staff, heightened salter mutual responsibility for crimes, and organized patrols to confiscate contraband.[182] "But salt profits are too irresistible for anyone to care about the law. Everyone [producers] flocks together in large groups and the situation easily turns into social unrest."[183]

New Merchant Regulations

In the Northern Song, Huai and Zhe salt had fallen primarily under the government distribution program, with both the court and local governments benefiting. When this spawned abuses, merchant voucher distribution gradually took its place to become the norm by the Southern Song. The joining of the Huai-Zhe distribution systems made increasingly far-flung sales possible and would generate the bulk of the dynasty's salt revenues.

But the revenues were still not sufficient. New strategies were tried out to generate greater income. In the first decade of Gaozong's reign alone, salt policy swung as many as ten times between merchant and government sales, and the court repeatedly imposed, then rescinded, specific controls over traders.[184]

New Merchant Taxes

One of the earliest changes made under Gaozong loosened voucher restrictions. But two influential figures in the salt monopoly, Zhang Chun (fl. 12th cent.) and Lü Yihao (1071–1139), the Jiangdong military intendant (*anfu zhizhishi*), then right chief councilor, first instigated a sharp tightening of those same controls. Then in 1132 these

---

[182] Guo Dongxu 1997, 301; *SHY* 48.122.

[183] *SP xia*.26b–27a.

[184] Guo Dongxu 1997, 296; Guo Zhengzhong 1990a, 849.

two men proposed discarding the proportional voucher exchange program in favor of a straight surcharge policy (*tienafa*), according to which merchants had to pay a commercial tax (*tonghuoqian*) of 3,000 cash per bag within ten days of receiving product. The regulation not only increased costs for merchants, it also categorized as smugglers anyone who had paid for but not yet sold his salt before the onset of this program and failed to pay the tax retroactively.[185]

This measure prompted general dismay. The right grand master of remonstrance (*you jianyi dafu*) Xu Fu (?–1140) criticized the policy as merciless and unacceptable to popular opinion. He petitioned that the state take into account the risks of sea transport and the complications of storage, and reckon the surcharge only after a merchant and his goods had actually arrived at a sales destination. In the first month of 1134 Lü Yihao and Zhang Chun managed to restore the bag surcharge policy, but by the ninth month it had been abolished.

But by the 1160s the bureaucracy again imposed numerous surcharges on salt merchants—a transit tax, a stationary tax, transaction fees for the purchase or exchange of vouchers, and a fee for payment in paper money, which might get a merchant precedence in obtaining salt. It was through this multitude of taxes and fees that the state recouped its losses from selling salt to merchants at a lower price than it did to consumers in government distribution regions.

Other Strategies for Using Merchant Distributors

In 1135 a new policy emerged whereby merchants were subject either to the old *duidai* proportional exchange or to a new payment measure (*nna*) but not both. This new method was apparently meant to add some charge on above-quota salt without making merchants jump through the *duidai* hoops. This plan is credited to Zhao Ding (1085–1147), commissioner of the Bureau of Military Affairs (*shuxiang*) before he became left chief councilor. He rejected the ongoing issuing of vouchers as "a short-sighted view that does not take into account that it is merchants who hold power over profits."[186] Zhao felt his solution would not only ease impositions on merchants and gain their

---

[185] *XNYL* 58.1967.

[186] *XNYL* 80.2537–38.

trust but also boost state income; it seems to have originated from the perspective of merchant interests.

About 1240 during Lizong's reign a new Intendancy of Tea and Salt (*zhizhi chayansi*) had been established for Huai and Zhe. Its satellite offices were set up across the region and quickly grew in number. Besides being charged with supervision of salt transport and sales, this new intendancy collected "aiding the army" fees (*zhujunqian*) and other merchant surcharges. Its aim was clearly to augment salt and tea tax revenues.[187]

Sichuan Contract Markets

In Northern Song Sichuan, salt administration had first passed through a stage of government management, then turned into private operation of the salt wells by the mid-eleventh century. But the first decade of the Southern Song marked an important new trend toward the localization of fiscal authority in Sichuan, where control came to rest largely in the hands of the Quartermaster Bureaus (*zonglingsuo*).[188] In 1132 the quartermaster Zhao Kai (1066–1141), using the statutes of Cai Jing's period as a model, established contract markets (*hetongchang*) in all Sichuan prefectures and market towns. Here merchants dealt directly with producers yet exchanges were conducted under the watchful and covetous eye of the state, which collected a local products tax from salters and a voucher tax from merchants, both at a high rate. The contract markets also allowed state agencies to realize income from the price differential in exchanges that took place between producers and merchants.

But this system had a number of problems. The government issued a set number of vouchers to merchants to obtain product at various wells, but because volume was so variable, production at some wells fell behind and so salters owed salt. At the same time functionaries often taxed salters for more than they had actually produced, resulting in bankruptcies, and this led to the escalation of private drilling and covert trade. Another quartermaster, Yang Fu (fl.

---

[187] *Jiankang zhi* (Jingding edition) [*JKZ*] 26.58b–62b.
[188] Hartwell 1988, 64.

twelfth cent.), vowed to crack down on these unlawful activities and closed over 2,000 small-mouth wells.[189]

The heavy Southern Song reliance on merchant sales in the end meant an over-concentration of resources in the hands of the central government at the expense of the local governments, which consequently were compelled to extort income from the populace. Given these contradictory forces and concerns, it is no wonder that rulers were constantly adjusting their policies. Policy swings and attempts to devise new vehicles for state income seem to have originated on the one hand from the government's desire for immediate revenue and on the other from the desire to keep merchants interested. The result was frequent changes and resorting to methods reminiscent of Cai Jing's especially when fiscal circumstances worsened.

Official Abuses

One of the cardinal principles of Song government held that officials at any level were strictly prohibited from privately engaging in profit-making activity.[190] In the Northern Song officials were proscribed from selling salt, including voucher salt, and running retail shops. After 1123 some conditional flexibility was practiced. But no matter what policy was in effect, bureaucrats took every opportunity to pursue profit through the salt trade. They regularly took advantage of their positions to create obstacles to the proper order of salt distribution, engage in the voucher salt trade, even managing their own voucher businesses.

Official Noncompliance

The early Southern Song court, more than the Northern Song, targeted its official agents for their abuses. Illegal salt sales had reached an alarming level and in general posed a more serious problem in the Southern Song. And it was government personnel themselves who were the greatest violators of the salt laws. The sheer volume of regulations delineating normative standards, material incentives, and

---

[189] *SS* 183.4475–76, 374.11596–600.
[190] *SHY* 25.15a, 26.27a–b, 29b, 32a.

punishments for civil and military officials, clerks, even high officials, clearly reflects the scope of the problem.

Civil officials in the Southern Song were notorious for their negligence, tardiness, laxness, and outright larceny, especially at points where they extracted income or submitted it.[191] Other personnel, including transporters, patrolmen, and imperial and prefectural troops, turned to theft, harassment, blackmail, and demanding bribes and favors. They sometimes acted in league with smugglers.[192] Officials used aliases to pass themselves off as merchants. A notorious chief councilor at the end of the dynasty, Jia Sidao (1213–1275), once secretly dispatched someone to sell a hundred boatloads of salt for him in the capital itself. Jia is immortalized in the lines:

> On the rising blue tidal bore, on the river last night,
> Boat after boat passed by, loaded with the chief councilor's salt.
> They say it's all destined for the chief councilor's soup,
> But how does he manage to drink so much?"[193]

Interagency Obstructionism

Local officials and salt administrators often stonewalled each other at the salterns. Local officials were to oversee the salterns but not directly administer them; in fact, they were normally prohibited from entering the facilities. Whether because of this restriction or due to sympathy for the people in their jurisdiction, prefectural and county officials often turned a blind eye to producer violations committed inside the saltworks. In the first decades of the Southern Song local officials were grouped with salt officials with regard to rewards and punishments; this was meant as an incentive for them to comply and cooperate with their salt administration counterparts. For their part, saltern administrators did not always cooperate with local officials in their investigations into salt collection irregularities or the maldistribution of production funds.[194] This mutual checks arrangement,

---

[191] *SHY* 25.12a–b, 26.3a–b, 4a–5a.

[192] *SHY* 26.3b–4a, 17a–18b, 32.21b–22a.

[193] *Xihu youlan zhi yu* [*XYZY*] 5.88.

[194] *SHY* 26.13a–b, 27.41b–42a.

however, was not always clearcut: a county official might also serve as a salt bureaucrat, even though this created an accountability issue.

The court often fell back on combined office holding to minimize similar obstructionism between intendants. For example, the fiscal intendant might also concurrently hold the posts of judicial intendant, military regulator, or ever-normal granary intendant. At times tea and salt intendant posts were joined and later made concurrent with fiscal and judicial intendants so that one individual controlled several powerful areas of responsibility. In 1145 the post of tea and salt intendant was further combined with that of ever-normal granary intendant (*tiju chayan changping gongsi* or *tiju changping chayan gongsi*). But the court also intentionally created competition among intendants by requiring lateral communication between them: In the first half of the Southern Song intendants were required to file copies of their annual reports with one another and to inform on colleagues.

Local vs. Central Competition for Salt Income

Local government officials exercised a certain degree of latitude in exacting fees to support their offices, but the circuits increasingly moved to curtail this as the Southern Song wore on. The central administration had repeatedly attempted to switch the Guang and Fujian regions to merchant distribution with the aim of helping the center to a bigger piece of the revenue pie, but that form of distribution was a bad fit and could not be implemented. Surely, these regions were poor, but perhaps more crucial was the opposition of local officials.[195] As soon as a voucher policy was put in place, prefectural and county revenues would tumble, leading naturally to new exactions on the populace to make up the shortfall. Even with government distribution of salt, after 1165 as much as 80 percent of the annual sales income went to the Guangxi fiscal intendancy, and only 20 percent to the prefectures.[196] In the more productive Huai-Zhe region there were more revenues at stake and the center

---

[195] For the factors behind Fujian government distribution, see Xu Weiqin 1988.

[196] Although after discussion, Xiaozong moderated this (*SHY* 28.3b; *SS* 183.4468).

and circuits secured an even greater percentage of revenue, with the local governments receiving proportionately less.

Superfluous Salt Bureaus and Bureaucrats

By the late Southern Song the state had created an inordinate number of salt offices, all of which had to disburse the salaries of officials and clerks out of their own funds. Branch offices in the circuits introduced many burdensome requisitions on both merchants and producers. While these exactions cancelled out any returns the populace might realize, corrupt salt officials were also embezzling monies meant for the public coffers. Huang Zhen, knowing the faults of the system intimately, argued for a reduction of branch offices and excess staff. After listing 500 bureaucrats and hangers-on affiliated with one office, including wine and tea servers, fanners, and assorted family members, he asked sarcastically: "Do ten sheep need nine shepherds?"[197]

Final Failure

In its last fifty years the monopoly experienced unstable revenue streams and the accelerated breakdown of both the government and merchant distribution systems.[198] Under the slack Lizong (r. 1225–1264) and Duzong (r. 1265–1274), Huang Zhen and other officials had to pacify salters by actually paying the hundreds of thousands of strings that were owed to them.[199] In his first year Lizong reduced merchant surcharges, but he later established the new salt and tea bureaus to collect new fees from salt merchants.[200] The merchants' yellow flag privilege became a dead letter once salters had become too destitute to produce and merchants had insufficient salt to sell.[201] In the 1230s the court appointed an official to deal specifically with meeting quotas (*zhuguan wenzi*), an indication of the urgency driving

---

[197] *HXZ* 9.15a–16a; *SJFZc* 29.3b–4b. See proposals by Huang Zhen in *Songjiang fuzhi* (Jiaqing) [*SJFZj*], 374, 766–67. See also *HSRC* 71.7a, 19a.

[198] *Xuechuang ji* [*XCJ*] 1.8b–10b.

[199] *HSRC* 80.2b, 77.1a; *SS* 424.12664.

[200] *SS* 182.4456.

[201] Guo Zhengzong 1997, 311.

the search for revenue. Huang Zhen summarized the situation: "The people's daily life grows ever harsher, the troops weaker, the deficit worse, the literati more shameless. The deficit is so acute that prefectural and county coffers are empty, the central fiscal office is unable to disburse funds, and the country has rapidly fallen into a state from which it is unable to recover."[202]

The multitude of pressures on small producers meant either fight or flight. Like peasants, salters could deal with gross exploitation by walking away; in the final years of the dynasty half of the Liangzhe producers did just that.[203] At one Yuezhou³ saltern, only thirty-eight out of more than ninety households remained. The devastation of many middle and lower salter households provided the background to peasant rebellion. From the beginning of the thirteenth century to the end of the dynasty, at least one hundred uprisings were led by or involved salters and salt-starved peasants. Soldiers stood by or joined in, while officials, seeing that passions ran high, dared not act.[204] In Liangzhe, from the mid-1220s to the 1260s, violent insurrections broke out in Wenzhou, Mingzhou, and Xiuzhou.[205] The leaders included two salters, referred to only as Xu Erbaijiu (Xu "Number 209") and Ye Sanqiansi (Ye "Number 3004"); their lack of proper given names probably indicates low status.[206] By the time Huang Zhen proposed reforms, Mongol armies neared Hangzhou. In 1276 young Gongdi (r. 1274–1276) surrendered to the Mongol forces.

Salt in a Pre-Industrial Command Economy

In the end, Guan Zhong's dual aims of boosting revenue and improving the public welfare via the salt monopoly may have been mutually incompatible: a successful monopoly from the state's point of view meant high, predictable returns, which inevitably meant hardship for the populace. The salt monopoly succeeded in covering the state's expenditures. However, from production to procurement, storage,

---

[202] *HSRC* 69.1a–4b.

[203] *SS* 424.12664; *HSRC* 96.8a–b; *Yuanshi* [*YS*] 97.2496.

[204] *SHY* 28.52a.

[205] *SS* 407.12290, 424.12663–64.

[206] Guo Zhengzhong 1997, 308.

transport and sales, the monopoly ended up crippling the more vulnerable among its constituents.

The Song state rose and fell on both self-imposed and external constraints. When the Song imperial house faced (or provoked) stronger nomadic neighbors whom it was never able to fully contain, it built up a gigantic and expensive military establishment that proved impossible to reduce. The more ineffectual the army became, the greater the feeling that it was not large enough. Yet the court, having learned hard historical lessons, would no longer risk allowing military men to exercise power, instead favoring the civilian literati. As defense and bureaucratic growth created deficits, the search for ways to extract revenue grew ever more intense.

Statesmen who championed seeking new sources of income rather than curtailing expenditure in this pre-industrial economy did not recognize the implications of perpetual tax increases as they rushed to meet the ever-rising costs.[207] Fiscal conservatives sympathized with the common people but were unable to devise a viable policy to meet revenue needs. On the other hand, sheer fiscalism, lacking a component for popular protections, appears not to have been conducive to long-term economic development, not to mention political stability. When even monopoly taxes could no longer be increased, the dynasty was doomed.

In the end the salt monopoly's impact must be reckoned by the distinct effects it had on various socioeconomic classes among the disparate major players—producers, merchants, and consumers. The social stratification of salters and merchants led to new political alignments and severe conflicts of interest. Regardless of region, poor salters led a poverty-stricken existence while rich producers gained privileges and stood on the government's side, the differences in their wealth perpetuated and exacerbated by their relationship to the state's agents. Thus high-ranking producers and rich merchants shared benefits with officials, while the system was largely capricious in its treatment of

---

[207] *SS* 327.10543, 336.10762–64. Paul Smith has examined one of Wang Anshi's reforms, the Sichuan Tea and Horse Agency, and sheds light on conflict between the center and the locales and how changes in the local elite affected the later state's ability to exploit the economy. He argues that by the Southern Song, the government destroyed its successful monopoly on Sichuan tea through taxation (Smith 1991).

the lowest-level salters, the smallest merchants, and village consumers, who suffered greatly.

The system also encouraged widespread corruption among the primary agents of the state, the officials. The behavior of each level of bureaucrat involved in the salt monopoly was directly affected by the regular performance evaluations on which their careers rested. And these evaluations directly reflected the need to augment state income, intensifying the demands bureaucrats placed on producers, merchants, and consumers alike. The abuses committed to meet these exigencies contributed to the ruin of the salt industry and of Song rule itself.

The excesses of the monopoly often provoked smuggling or worse—popular unrest and open rebellion—which would lead to a new round of maneuvering and policy adjustment. For despite the fact that the Song had created a highly centralized bureaucratic machine capable of exerting awesome control over the salt industry, it still had to perform a balancing act. It ultimately had to take into account the interests of the producers, merchants, and consumers, if not actively accommodate them.

This leads us to the source of the oscillations and functioning (or malfunctioning) of salt policy: the often conflicting voices within the so-called monolithic state. Official interests and approaches differed by levels of government, branches of government, and organs of government, each of which represented differing responsibilities and philosophies. Emperors remained concerned about their good name and the appearance of a fair system. Fiscal appointees tended to be most aggressive in the pursuit of revenues, while local officials tended to be more sympathetic towards the population in their jurisdiction. Policy critics tried to protect the populace from undue state impositions.

For centuries, from the very start of the government monopoly system under the Han, critical issues had remained unresolved. What was the government's proper role in the empire's economic organization? What was an appropriate tax burden? Which worked better, a command economy or market-driven enterprise? How could conflicts between central and local interests be resolved? As the Song state addressed these problems, its responses set the tone for future discourse on the subject and framed most of the solutions subsequent dynasties would experiment with.

*   *   *   *   *

Scholars consider the Song salt monopoly to have been the model for those of the Yuan, Ming, and Qing, even as Song statism and fiscalism were nominally rejected. The Song's monopoly practices can be located in later imperial practice in the form of administrative regions, regulations, and the system of punishments, and rewards.[208] The trend begun in the Song of increasing reliance on merchant distribution would carry through to the Republican era.

The Yuan court did not try to regulate the amount of salt produced, so quantities forced on consumers surpassed those of the Song, and salt revenues comprised as much as 80 percent of the budget. When the Yuan continued to increase production quotas, mass uprisings brought that dynasty down. The Ming pursued a more cautious policy, and salt taxes amounted to only about 40 percent of its income. The Ming discontinued support payments to salters and required merchants to retrieve salt directly from them, bringing to an end the system of government procurement. But the key Ming innovation, in the last decades of the dynasty, was granting the right to procure and sell salt only to specially licensed merchants, a system that lasted through the Qing. Under the Qing, salt income had dwindled to only about 10 percent of government revenue. The state ceded transport and distribution to authorized merchants, who passed this right on to their descendants. Salt merchants came to possess the greatest aggregate income of any commercial group. At the end of the imperial period, under a new system of management, salt no longer played a role as a major source of state revenue.[209]

---

[208] Saeki 1987, 286. Kawakami Kōichi likewise considers the Song to be a turning point in the elaboration of the salt monopoly for later periods. See Kawakami 1992, preface.

[209] For later dynastic developments, see *YS* 94.2386–93; *Mingshi* [*MS*] 80.1931–47; *Qingshi gao* [*QSG*] 123.3603–40, as well as the extensive secondary literature in English and especially Chinese and Japanese. In the People's Republic today, the government has required the iodization of salt, and consumption of iodized salt exceeds U. S. levels. This process is prohibitive for the average small producer, and by creating a salt police force the government has succeeded in maintaining its monopoly over the salt supply and shut down private producers and merchants. However, in the northwest with its vast salt lakes and low average annual incomes, smuggling remains commonplace: see "Salt Police Enforce One of the Oldest Economic Policies," *South China Morning Post*, October 24, 2002, page 10.

Sources

The *Songshi* itself was assembled under a senior Yuan official, Tuo Tuo (1314–1355). Compiled within a mere two and a half years, it was hastily printed in 1345.[210] Scholars regard the work as disorganized, stylistically inferior, and full of minutiae, but I believe that its very value lies in this level of detail.[211] The *Songshi*'s editors excerpted memorials in full or in part, including imperial responses, making the work equivalent to a history of legislation.

Out of 496 chapters, 162 are monographs (*zhi*), or guidelines to administrative practice. Of those, the economic monograph (*shihuozhi*) is one of the best of its kind.[212] At 413 pages, it is longer than that in the Tang, Yuan, Ming, or even Qing dynastic histories. *Shihuo* is commonly rendered as "economy," but at the time it essentially referred to political economy, conceptualized from the top down, in line with the scheme of the cosmos: the ways of Heaven and the ways of Man were followed by the Eight Agricultural Functions, of which food (*shi*) and money (*huo*) were the most important.[213] The *shihuozhi* was consequently divided into two parts: the first dealing with activities directly related to the people's livelihood, including land taxes and corvee; and the second (because "the government ought not seek profit") covers commercial activities, including trade taxes and monopolies.[214] I have also referred to other *Songshi* monographs, including the emperors' biographies (*benji*), geography (*dili*), selection of officials (*xuanju*), officialdom (*zhiguan*), the military (*bingzhi*), penal law (*xingfa*), and biographies (*liezhuan*).

The sixty-four page salt treatise is the first and longest of the economic monographs. At times it seems the account given in the *Songshi* could have profited from inclusion of contemporary material from other sources, for example, the argument for government trade

---

[210] For compilation of dynastic histories and analyses of *SS* primary sources, see Cai Chongbang 1991, 188–91; Jin Yufu 1944, passim; Twitchett 1992, passim; Balazs 1964, passim; and Yang Lien-sheng 1961, 45–46.

[211] Gao Zhenduo 1982, 603; Franke 1961, 118.

[212] Gao Zhenduo 1982, 605.

[213] See the *SS* "Shihuo" preface, which mentions the *hongfan* ("great plan"), collected in Legge 1960, vol. 3, 320–344; *SS* 173.4155.

[214] *SS* 173.4157.

of salt could have greatly benefited from information provided elsewhere. What the *Songshi* omits, however, does not necessarily follow from political considerations. Much of the neglected material represents substantial chunks of time, especially in the Southern Song.

Since most of the *Songshi*'s original documents are no longer extant, the parallel histories rise in value as independent and complementary sources.[215] The *Song huiyao*, also known as the *Song huiyao gao* or the *Song huiyao jigao*, is one of the most valuable works concerning Song political and economic history. An encyclopedic compendium on the history of institutions (*dianli*), it was begun under Renzong and continued under the five remaining Northern Song emperors and the first four Southern Song emperors.[216] It includes the imperial daily calendars (*rili*), veritable records (*shilu*), and national histories (*guoshi*). Of the original 2,200 chapters, most were destroyed by the invading Yuan armies; only 500 chapters remained extant in Ming times, and only a tenth of the whole survives today.[217] A draft copy of the surviving chapters was shipped north; hence, it is referred to as a *gao*, a "draft" document. In the Qing, Xu Song (1781–1848) reassembled the 500 chapters preserved in the Ming *Yongle dadian* while he was working on Tang records. This explains why the heading of the Song salt material reads, "Complete Records of the Tang" (*Quan Tangwen*). Today the remaining 200 sections retain scribal errors and mistakes in pagination and chapter numbers that accrued along the way.[218]

Almost everything contained in the *Songshi* salt narrative is paralleled in the *Song huiyao* in much fuller form, which suggests that the *Songshi* compilers ran the data together. The economy, one of the largest topics treated in the *Song huiyao*, includes the salt treatise, which exceeds 300 pages, or five times the *Songshi* coverage. I drew upwards of 320 citations directly from the *Song huiyao*, more than from any other source. And this did not include material that would have been difficult

---

[215] For Song historical writing and Chinese historiography through the Qing, see Jin Yufu 1944, 97–222; Balazs 1964, 134–49.

[216] For analyses of all imperially commissioned *huiyao* that comprised the SHY, see Jin Yufu 1944, 121; Li Zongtong 1953, 126.

[217] Gao Zhenduo 1982, 626; Balazs counts 2,442 chapters (Balazs, 1964, 149).

[218] For its tortuous history, see Chen Zhichao 1995, 5–7; Jin Yufu, 1944, 121–22; Balazs and Hervouet 1978, 177–78; Gao Zhenduo 1982, 626.

to integrate into the *Songshi's* regional treatment because it either was not directed to a specific circuit or applied to all. The *Song huiyao* covers each salt region in far greater depth than the *Songshi*: Xie: 59 versus 14 pages; Hebei: 6 versus 4 pages; Jingdong: 2.5 versus 1 page; Huainan: 129 versus 27 pages; Liangzhe: 40 versus 3 pages; Fujian: 48 versus 5.5 pages; Guang: 121 to 3 pages; and Sichuan: 19 to 11 pages. Only Hedong is shorter: 3 versus 5 pages. (These figures exceed the total 300 pages due to rounding off and double counting where topics overlap.)

Song huiyao salt coverage devotes nearly 200 pages to the Northern Song, especially pond salt, and only 100 pages to the Southern Song. This is an artificial distortion, however, because the circuits that were lost to Southern Song received no coverage in any source. For those that remained, *Song huiyao* coverage is balanced, and in some cases two-thirds to three-quarters of the discussion is devoted to Southern Song events. While the *Changbian* (see below) is one of the richest sources on the Northern Song monopoly, the *Song huiyao* provides in-depth coverage of the monopoly for the later period, from about 1100 until 1214.

Li Tao's (1115–1184) encyclopedic *Xu zizhi tongjian changbian* (also called *Changbian*) is another most important source on Northern Song institutions. Li completed this annalistic history (*biannianti*) in about 1183 as a continuation of Sima Guang's *Zizhi tongjian*, but Li had the advantage of being a contemporary to the period. He located hundreds of now nonextant sources, including private histories, occasional notes, and biographies.[219] By the Qing, only 520 of the *Changbian's* approximately 1,000 chapters survived. I have drawn over 200 annotations from it, and the *Songshi* editors also copied from it en bloc.[220] The *Changbian* frequently collates with the *Song huiyao*, but quotes shared texts in briefer form. It emphasizes descriptions of social institutions and behavior, but covers the monopoly in detail from the 1020s until the 1090s, particularly pond salt and sea salt.

Li Xinchuan's (1166–1243) chronologically organized *Jianyan yilai xinian yaolu* is a sequel to the *Changbian*. One of the key sources on the reign of the Southern Song founder, it is alternatively known as

---

[219] Balazs and Hervouet 1978, 73; Li Zongtong 1953, 106.

[220] Jin Yufu 1944, 115; Li Zongtong 1953, 106. For works that may fill gaps in the *XCB*, see Balazs and Hervouet 1978, 74.

Gaozong xinianlu. It was readied for printing in the early 1250s but went unpublished until the Ming. Yuan compilers of the *Songshi* never discovered this work, and it can be used to fill in gaps in the account of the early Southern Song.[221] Its sources include the imperial calendars and national histories. Its 200 chapters emphasize military and political affairs, but also provide socioeconomic information. Salt coverage focuses on the southeast during the war and reconstruction, particularly the 1130s. Coverage of the peaceful period between 1140 and the end of Gaozong's rule is more limited. The same material can often be found in the *Song huiyao*.

Li Xinchuan's *Jianyan yilai chaoye zaji* is another chronological encyclopedia and the companion volume to his *Xinian yaolu*. Even though the last two of four collections have been lost, what remains still provides a useful record of administrative, military, and economic institutions in the Southern Song, particularly for the first four reigns. Its treatment of wealth and taxes (*caifu*) is considered one of the best. The *Chaoye zaji* is strong on the monopoly in the early to mid-Southern Song, especially for sea salt, devoting more attention than other works to production and technologies. This work can be usefully paired with the *Aobo tu*; it contains revenue figures, regional comparisons, and some of the best production figures for the southeast and Sichuan.[222]

Ma Duanlin's (1254–1325) 348-chapter *Wenxian tongkao*, which he compiled in 1322 or 1339, was written according to the model of Sima Guang's *Zizhi tongjian*. It is a comprehensive history (*tong*) of institutions and a critical examination (*kao*) of documents. Its category of monopolies (*zhengque*) is not found in the dynastic histories. It is especially strong on the Northern Song reform period, for which it provides salt production and population figures. It corroborates the *Song huiyao* and *Changbian* but adds unusual detail.[223]

Huang Zhen's (1213–1280) *Huangshi richao* is a collection of his writings in 97 chapters, including reports and communications on his salt management experience. It stands out for its authenticity in

---

[221] Balazs and Hervouet 1978, 81; Gao Zhenduo 1982, 615.

[222] For more historiographic discussion, see Balazs and Hervouet 1978, 179–80; Balazs 1964, 145.

[223] See *WXTK* 15.1a–42b, 16.1a–34b. For more on the significance of *WXTK*, see Balazs and Hervouet 1978, 174–75; Jin Yufu 1944, 203, 205.

depicting the local realities of the late Song monopoly. Huang served in various salt administration capacities in Liangzhe and wrote frankly on abuses, even at the cost of alienating power holders.[224] Huang Zhen was particularly concerned for the producers, and his petition on how to relieve their plight is found in the *Songjiang fuzhi*.[225] He also left a record of monopoly operations in the *Yinxianzhi*.

Chen Chun's (fl. 14th cent.) *Aobo tu* is probably the first extant work in the world to deal exclusively with salt production techniques, specifically at the Xiasha saltern in Huating County (Zhexi), the same region that Huang Zhen describes. This private source touches on administration, quotas, and stratification; it includes forty-seven illustrations, each of which is accompanied by a description and a poem. Though compiled around 1334, the illustrations were drawn earlier.[226]

Yao Kuan's (1105–1162) *Xixi congyu*, in two chapters, is a collection of miscellany drawn from his extensive knowledge. It details sea salt production and includes ratings of seawater salt content, boiling techniques, and testing procedures.

Shen Kuo's (1031–1095) *Mengxi bitan*, in one chapter recorded between 1086 and 1093, includes descriptions of varieties of salt as well as analysis of the hardships of overland salt transport.

Zhang Ruyu's (*jinshi* 1196) *Shantang xiansheng qunshu kaosuo*, in 212 chapters, is also entitled *Shantang kaosuo* or *Qunshu kaosuo*. Written by 1210, it is an encyclopedia in four collections on subjects including finance, wealth, and taxes. Along with Zhang's insights, it contains overlapping classifications but quotes otherwise lost books, provides Song army figures, and defines types of salt vouchers.

Fang Shao's (1066–post 1141) *Bozhai bian* is a miscellany that appeared in two versions, describing the court and commonalty from 1086 to 1117. The three-chapter version contains details regarding topics such as the Fang La Uprising provoked by Huizong's requisitions. Fang Shao writes knowledgeably about salt—such as

---

[224] For Huang's life and career, see SS 438.12991–94; "Ben zhuan" [BZ], 1a–5b; *Shaoxing fuzhi* [*SXFZ*], *Renwu zhi*, vol. 4. 42.2b–3a; *Song Yuan xuean* [*SYXA*] 86.1a–2a; *HXZ* 11.26b–27a; *SJFZj*, 40.16b; *Jiangnan tongzhi* [*JNTZ*], 113.30a–b.

[225] For salter hardships and Huang Zhen's indictment of the system, see *HSRC* 71.5b–21a, 77.1a–4a, 80.3b–12b; *SJFZc* 29.2a–b, 3b–4b.

[226] See *ABT*. Huating was the old name for Songjiang.

variable yields at salterns in the circuit—based on his residence in a Liangzhe village.

Tuo Tuo's *Liaoshi*, in 116 chapters, was compiled in 1334. It bequeaths a relatively inconsistent record, but provides a different perspective on Song-Liao relations than that found in the *Songshi*.[227] A private work that helps correct the *Liaoshi*'s inaccuracies is the *Qidan guozhi*, which is attributed to Ye Longli (fl. mid-1300s).

Tuo Tuo's *Jinshi*, in 135 chapters, provides a picture of the Song's relations with the Liao, Jin, and Xixia. Numerous quotes of Gaozong's submission impress upon the reader that the center of gravity from the late Northern Song onward lay in the Jin.[228] Such a feeling of a lord-vassal relationship is nowhere to be found in the *Songshi*. The *Jinshi*'s main sources were the veritable records and unofficial histories. The history of Jurchen development is the focus.

Finally, I have touched on, though not yet in a thorough manner, other genres of history and literature that seem promising.[229] Literary collections of the literati and other sources may provide further accounts of the salt monopoly: the voluminous *Quan Songwen* and *Quan Songshi*, for example, are punctuated editions that await more exhaustive probing.[230]

---

[227] *LS*, preface, 2; Li Zongtong 1953, 94.

[228] See, for example, *JS* 77.1751–56, Zong Bi (original name, Wo Chuai).

[229] Local histories can provide valuable checks against the one-sided treatments written by the metropolitan bureaucracy. Gazetteers (*difangzhi*), which detail the history, geography, and local culture of a region, take up where the *Song huiyao* salt record leaves off, from 1214 to the end of the dynasty, but only a fraction are still extant. Perhaps 200 gazetteers appeared in the Southern Song. See Balazs and Hervouet 1978, 135.

[230] Other types of writing can provide particulars related to the salt industry: daily jottings, anecdotes, facetiae, satire, and travel diaries. Most were written by city inhabitants who had obvious affection for their native places. An entire literature of nostalgic reminiscences arose after both the Northern and Southern Song downfalls. For example, Naideweng's *Ducheng jisheng* [*DCJS*] includes the food-related topics of markets, businesses, and eating establishments; Wu Zimu's *Mengliang lu* [*MLL*], describes night markets, noodle shops, and vegetarian restaurants, among others. Zhou Mi's *Wulin jiushi* [*WLJS*] includes wine establishments and eateries.

PART TWO
ANNOTATED TRANSLATION

Brief Introduction to
THE *SONGSHI* SALT TREATISE

The salt treatise appears in chapters 181, 182, and 183 of the Songshi, *corresponding to sections 3, 4, and 5 of the monograph on Political Economy (Part 2). After an opening passage unrelated to salt, the salt discussion begins without further ado, separated only by extra spacing from what has gone before. The salt treatise opens with a brief statement on the four main categories of salt: pond, sea, earth, and well. Each category corresponded to a distinct geographic region with its own extraction techniques and geopolitical concerns. Within each region, the* Songshi *discusses places where a given type of salt was consumed as well as where it was produced. The order in which the* Songshi *treats the different categories is telling: the first, pond salt, outweighed any other type in the Northern Song; the next, sea salt, eclipsed pond salt in the Southern Song; the third, earth salt, contributed minimally but still meant more to central revenues than did the last category, well salt, which was consumed in the region where it was produced and ultimately impossible to monitor. The treatise might have been organized in a number of ways: by salt quality, which was a function of grain size, profit rates, personnel functions, common problems, or other criteria. Instead, the editors chose to examine the monopoly by circuit. Though two or more circuits might be grouped as a single monopoly region, the circuit was the discrete unit for which policy was enunciated and in which success was measured. The treatise's organization stemmed from the overall Song bureaucratic structure. A circuit-level salt administrator managed local officials and set annual production quotas.*

[p. 4413] There were two types of salt: kernel salt (*keyan*[2]), or what the *Zhouguan* termed pond salt (*guyan*), drawn from ponds; and powder salt (*moyan*), or what the *Zhouguan* termed loose salt (*sanyan*), produced from sea brine, well brine, or saliferous earth.[1] When the Song unified the

---

[1] The *Zhouguan* or *Zhouli* [ZL] was one of the Thirteen Classics and believed to be the work of the Duke of Zhou, prime minister to the founders of the Zhou dynasty. The *yanren* entry in the ZL's "Tianguan" chapter states: "The office of salt is in charge of salt affairs. It supplies salt for various needs. At sacrifices, salt made

93

kingdoms, all salt revenues of the empire accrued to local governments. Government sales (*guanyu*) or merchant sales (*tongshang*) might be practiced depending on the conditions in each prefecture (*zhoujun*).[2] [Song salt] policy changed frequently, but the prohibition of private sales was consistently emphasized.

---

from brine is used. For feasts, rock salt (in the shape of a tiger) is used. For the king, queen, and heir apparent, a sweet-tasting rock salt is used. For seasonal culinary changes, pond salt is prepared." For both *guyan* and *sanyan* see *ZL*, 108. *Gu* was synonymous with *keyan* of the Xie pond; see *Shuowen jiezi* [*SWJZ*] 12 *shang*.3a; *Hedong yanfa zhi* [*HDYFZ*] 1.2a–b.

Salt was categorized according to grain size: the greatest difference was between kernel and powder salt, but many further distinctions were made, for example, black salt (*heiyan*), red salt (*chiyan*), soft salt (*rouyan*), smelly salt (*chouyan*), and horse-teeth salt (*machiyan*). See *WXTK* 15.4b. Shen Kuo noted more than ten types of salt produced by minority tribes and asserted that the Song industry produced "no less than several tens of varieties" (*Mengxi bitan* [*MBT*] 11.21a).

[2] Paul Smith, writing on the Sichuan tea monopoly, has rendered *tongshang*, as in *tongshang difen* (free-trade zone), as "free commerce" or "free trade"; I prefer "merchant sales" or "merchant trade" because the word "free" in an economic context conveys a set of relationships different from those within a monopoly. See Smith 1991, 143.

Section 1
POND SALT

This first section comprises fourteen pages or one-fifth of the treatise. Sun-dried pond salt came almost entirely from one highly productive "pond," a salt lake in Xiezhou, Yongxingjun ("-jun" indicating a military prefecture) Circuit, near present-day Yuncheng, Shanxi. It was the simplest and cheapest kind of salt to process, requiring little technology and energy except that of the sun. Because the salt lake was eventually lost to the Jin at the beginning of the Southern Song, coverage in the Songshi dates entirely from the Northern Song. The Songshi first offers generalities concerning pond salt production, workers, consumers, and pricing up to about the year 997. It says little about actual production techniques for this or any other type of salt, because at this stage, there was little official interest in salt as a source of revenue.

During the Northern Song, Xie salt was widely distributed in the northeast and the interior. It reached five to seven circuits beyond Yongxingjun (modern Shaanxi and the southwest corner of modern Shanxi where the Xiezhou pond lay). The state administration sold salt in thirty-one prefectures or capital cities across six circuits while allowing merchants to sell in a comparable number of prefectures in two circuits.

Chapter 1: Xiezhou

Northern Song

[p. 4413] The two ponds from which pond salt was produced were located in Xie and Anyi counties in Xiezhou [Yongxingjun Circuit, Map 3].[1] The land was divided into sections (*qi* or *xi*), then pond water was fed

---

[1] See Introduction for details. The northern end of the elongated salt lake was called Xie Pond and the southern end, Anyi Pond.

This is one of the oldest large inland salt lakes in the world. Today it measures fifty-one kilometers by six kilometers, matching historical sources that cite dimensions of seventy *li* by seven *li*. Others note dimensions of fifty *li* by seventy *li* and also

95

into them in a process called "planting the salt" (*zhongyan*); when the water evaporated, salt formed.[2] [The government] registered local residents as "section workers" (*qifu*).[3] It provided them with grain and exempted (*fu*) them from other taxes and the corvee (*yong*). It recruited one hundred men to serve as patrolmen, called "protecting treasure guards" (*hubaodu*). On the first day of the second month of the year, preparation of the sections was begun; in the fourth month, the "planting" started; by the eighth month, all work was completed.[4] Every year each producer family at Anyi Pond seeded 1,000 "mats" (*xi*) of salt, while families at Xie Pond seeded 20 mats fewer.[5]

---

sixty-four *li* by seventy *li*, which would make the lake rectangular: see, respectively, *Yunlu manchao* [*YLMC*] 2.25; note to Zuo Si, "Weidu fu" (Song of the Wei capital) in *WX* 6.4a. The product of the lake is now referred to as Hedong salt. Additionally, at least ten other elements and minerals are extracted from its waters nowadays. The lake's production of sulfides and sulfuric acid makes up about 40 percent of China's annual production and is exported globally. See Qi Wuchang 祁武昌, "Gulao yancheng yizhan xinzi: Shanxi Yuncheng jishi" 古老鹽城一展新姿: 山西運城紀事 (New look for an ancient salt town: An account of Shanxi's Yuncheng). *Renmin ribao* 人民日報, overseas edition. July 27, 1991.

[2] One *xi* was equal to fifty *mu* of land (*SWJZ* 13 *xia*.13a). An agricultural metaphor was used because every spring the lake's salt fields required plowing, tilling, irrigation, and sun; see Wang Leiming 1985, 325–26n1. The water was let successively into a series of fields; by the time the water reached the last field, it was uniformly one to two inches deep and ready for evaporation. Plowing enabled the water drawn into the fields to sink into the ground easily, leaving the dense salty portion on top. It also buried the previous year's waste and made for higher-quality salt (Qian Gongbo 1964, 160). Warm sun and winds were critical to this process: "If the southern wind does not rise, the tax revenues will fall" (*STKS* 57.820–25). The south wind thus became synonymous with "salt wind" (*yanfeng*).

[3] In pond salt prefectures resident families were called "section households" (*qihu*), after the pond salt sections they worked year after year. From each household the state drafted two adult males (*qifu*) to engage in production.

[4] This was in the third month (*WXTK* 15.7b). In the five months' slack time from the ninth to the first month of the year, salters leveled fields, repaired houses and storage, and so on (*HDYFZ* 2.1b–3b).

[5] The first *sui* (year) should probably read *hu* (household, family), as in *WXTK* 15.7b. According to a note in the *SS*, this should read "every year, each *household*" produced this amount (*SS* 181.4413n4).

    The mat became a unit of measure for Xie salt because reed mats were used in the drying process: earth was hoed loose, matting laid on the ground, and wet salt spread on top, so the water drained into the soft ground. Since all harvesting was

This salt supplied [revenue for Xie] prefecture itself and the three capitals as well as the following: Jizhou[b], *[p. 4414]* Yanzhou[a], Caozhou [also Jiyin], Puzhou, Shanzhou[a], Yunzhou[a], and Guangjijun (all in Jingdong [dong and xi], Map 4); Huazhou[b], Zhengzhou, Chenzhou[b], Yingzhou[b], Ruzhou, Xuzhou[b], and Mengzhou[b] (all in Jingxi [bei and nan], Maps 5 and 6); Hezhongfu, Shanzhou[b], Guozhou, and Qingchengjun (in Shaanxi); Jinzhou[b], Jiangzhou[b], Cizhou[a], and Xizhou (in Hedong, Map 7); Suzhou[b] and Bozhou[b] (Huainan [dong and xi], Map 8); and Hebei's (Map 7) counties south of the Yellow River, in Huaizhou and Chanzhou.[6] The government

---

done at one time, weighing by scales was not as efficient as measuring by mats. See Li Xuezhi, "Shumian yijian," cited in Qian Gongbo 1964, 164. There were basically two sizes of mats. Small mats, which seem to have been the standard when unspecified, weighed 116 to 116.5 catties (*SS* 181.4414–15). Large mats have been variously recorded at 200 or 220 catties (*SHY* 36.7b, 10/1004; *WXTK* 16.1a).

If each salter household at Anyi produced an average 1,000 mats, and each at Xie County 980 mats, and one mat was equal to 116.5 catties, then each family at Anyi annually produced 116,500 catties and at Xie County, over 114,000 catties. These levels of productivity are noted in Qian Gongbo 1964, 161.

For charts and graphs of Northern Song Xie salt production, distribution, and revenues, see Qian Gongbo 1974, 395, 397–98, 399–400, 404. For a chart of Northern Song Xie production and sources for these figures, see Qian Gongbo 1964, 161. Also see a more complete and detailed table in Guo 1984b, 83, which includes average production quotas per salter household and mat–catty equivalents.

[6] The "three capitals" often mentioned in the text probably refer to Bianliang (Kaifeng), also called the Eastern Capital (Dongjing); Henanfu (Luoyang), also called the Western Capital (Xijing); and Yingtianfu (Songzhou, present-day Shangqiu, Henan), also called the Southern Capital (Nanjing[a]). By 1042 Damingfu (present Daming County, Hebei) was known as the Northern Capital. In the Southern Song, Lin'an was known as the Provisional Capital (Xingzai) (*SS* 85.2105–106). Transport routes to Kaifeng were the most developed: at least three land routes and eight waterways began or merged there (Aoyama 1963).

Caozhou was equivalent to Chengshi in Xingrenfu in the Northern Song and was known as Caozhou in Nanjing[a] Circuit, under Jin control during the Southern Song. Xuzhou[b] is another anachronism; it was Yingchangfu in the Northern Song, and in Nanjing[a] Circuit under the Jin during the Southern Song. After Shaanxi's Shanzhou[a], Xiezhou was also listed (*WXTK* 16.1a). In the mid-Dazhongxiangfu reign (1008–1016) Qingchengjun was the name of Ronghe (present-day Shanxi, northwest of Xie Pond), a county in Hezhongfu, Yongxingjun Circuit. The name was abolished in 1068 (*SS* 87.2144–5). After Huaizhou, the *SS* seems to have omitted Hebei's Weizhou[c] (*XCB* 109.2544, 10/renchen/1030). Here, *henan* refers marked all restricted monopoly areas with signs to make this clear to the people.[7] The merchant trade areas included the following: Caizhou, Xiangzhou[b], Dengzhou[b], Suizhou[a], Tangzhou, Jinzhou[a], Fangzhou[a], Junzhou[a], Yingzhou[c], Guanghuajun, and Xinyangjun [all in Jingxi]; Shaanxi's Jingzhaofu, Fengxiangfu, Tongzhou[a], Huazhou[a], Yaozhou, Qianzhou[b], Shangzhou, Jingzhou, Yuanzhou[a], Binzhou[a], Ningzhou, Yizhou[c], Weizhou[b], Fuzhou[a], Fangzhou[b], Danzhou[a], Yanzhou[b], Huanzhou, Qingzhou, Qinzhou[b], Longzhou, Fengzhou, Jiezhou, Chengzhou, Baoanjun, Zhenrongjun, and Chanzhou counties north of the [Yellow] River.[8] Five catties (*jin*) of either kernel or powder salt equaled one peck. Kernel salt was priced from thirty-four to forty-four cash per catty and divided into three grades.[9] In 996 (Zhidao 2) the two ponds produced 373,545 mats of salt, each mat equal to 116.5 catties.[10] In 997 (Zhidao 3) sales revenues reached over 728,000 strings (*min*).[11]

---

to the southern bank of the Yellow River. These, then, are the twenty-eight prefectures to which the text frequently refers.

[7] This was the case for other types of salt as well. In 1980 a Chinese survey team discovered a stone inscription on a mountainside dated 1194 and signed by the Tea and Horse Agency of Baocheng in Lizhou[a] Circuit, present-day Shaanxi, near the Sichuan border. It warned: "Monopoly salt must not exit this boundary (northward into Jin territory). If there is any violation, local authorities are permitted to make an arrest. The offender shall be sent to the local government office, sentenced immediately, and fined fifty strings, which shall be rewarded to the one who made the capture" (Ou Delu 1989, 62).

[8] After Jinzhou[a], Shangzhou is listed in *XCB*. Here, *hebei* refers to the northern bank of the Yellow River. This made for a total of thirty-seven prefectures (*XCB* 109.2545, 10/renchen/1030).

[9] On 7/wuchen/976 it was noted that prefectures were instructed to reduce the selling price from sixty to fifty cash per catty, and that which was priced at forty cash was to be cut to thirty; pond salt was cut to forty-four cash, later to forty (*XCB* 17.374).

[10] Guo 1984 (p. 83) worked from previous secondary scholarship to compile a comprehensive table of pond salt production in the Northern Song. He provides specific sources for each figure, here presented in Table 2:

The editors now begin to excerpt memorials to the throne. The Xie monopoly may be divided into three stages: from 960 to 1047, a period of frequent shifts between government and merchant sales with gradual expansion of merchant sales; from 1048 to 1067, the "golden age" of Xie salt policy under Fan Xiang; and from 1068 to 1127, ushered in by Wang Anshi's reforms, a period of increasing government manipulation of vouchers. The first policy issue at the end of the 990s concerned the direction the state should take regarding distribution in the region.

During the Xianping period (998–1003) [Zhenzong's] commissioner of revenue (*duzhishi*), Liang Ding, stated:

Period	In Mats (large/small)	In Catties	Salter Household Annual Quotas (in small mats)	Source
996	373,545 (small)	43,517,992.5	983	*SS* 183; *WXTK* 15
1005	Increase	Increase		*XCB* 87
1006	Decrease	Decrease		*XCB* 87
1016	387,220 (small)	45,111,130	1019	*SHY* 23.30
1020-1021	376,200 (small)	43,827,300	990	*XCB* 97; *SS* 181
1030	655,120 (small)	76,321,480	1724	*XCB* 109; *Yuhai* 181
1031-1033	7,893 (small)	919,533		*XCB* 114; *SHY* 23.37
1034-1036	Shut down	Shut down		*XCB* 114, 115
1048-1049	375,000 (large)	82,500,000		*XCB* 165; *SS* 181
1061	Decrease	Decrease		*SS* 181
1070-1076	360,000 (large)	79,200,000		*XCB* 312; *SHY* 24.21
1073	428,601 (large)	94,292,220		*XCB* 254
1075-1076	350,000 (large)	77,000,000		*XCB* 280; *SHY* 24.14
1077-1080	391,666 (large)	86,166,520		*SHY* 24.21
1086	366,972 (large)	80,733,825		*SHY* 24.26, 24.28; *WXTK* 16
1094-1098	346,915 (large)	76,321,480		*Changbian shibu* 28; *Changbian benmo* 137
1098-1100	Shutdown	Shutdown		*SS* 181
1102	15,302 (small)	1,782,700		*SS* 181, *WXTK* 16
1105	Recovery	Recovery		*Changbian shibu* 28; *Changbian benmo* 137
1108	381,588 (large)	83,949,382		*Changbian shibu* 28; *Changbian benmo* 137
1109	350,394 (large)	77,086,856		*Changbian shibu* 28; *Changbian benmo* 137
1112	693,831 (large)	152,642,960		*Changbian shibu* 28; *Changbian benmo* 137

[11] For a breakdown of revenue quotas in Yongxingjun Circuit by prefecture, county, market town, and hamlet, likely compiled around 1078, see *SHY* 22.1a–2b, 23.8b. For Qinfeng Circuit, see *SHY* 22.2b–4a.

I request that in Shaanxi's border areas, Xie salt be traded not by merchants but by the government.[12]

A large portion of the salt produced by nomadic empires bordering the Song was smuggled across the border; it was one of the few goods they could exchange for

---

[12] On 1/12/1003 Liang Ding spoke at greater length on the merits of government transport and sales than this cryptic statement reveals. He explained the price of salt relative to that of grain and fodder under the merchant provisioning system and how the price of white rice in Han prefectures was consequently higher than in the tribal regions of Qinfeng and Yongxingjun circuits. He predicted dire consequences if government sales of Xie salt and convoys were not implemented and recommended where tax revenues of border prefectures were to go. Few merchants had come to sell in those in distant prefectures so locals had difficulty obtaining salt, which, in turn, drove them to traffic in blue salt. The *SS* quote is merely Liang Ding's conclusion after a considered analysis (*SHY* 23.27a–28b; *XCB* 54.1175–77).

Back in 8/993 the Xixia trade in blue and white salts, both major competitors to Xie pond salt, was addressed at length. The emperor decreed that tribesmen be prohibited from trading on pain of death and that merchants distribute Xie salt [along the border]. Since the Xixia used their salt to purchase grain, this directive was aimed at making life difficult for them as well as generating profits for the Song state. However, violations continued unabated and tribesmen short of salt took to pillaging along the border. Merchants, finding little profit there, went elsewhere (*SHY* 23.22b–23a).

Blue salt came primarily from Black Pond (Wuchi), and white salt from White Pond (Baichi). Both fell under the jurisdiction of Lingzhou in Xixia territory near Yongxingjun. Back in 1000, when Liang Ding headed the Shaanxi salt administration, he pushed for government sale of Xie salt at the border, but met with opposition. Three years later he again suggested this. He was censured and dismissed from office in connection with other offences (*SHY* 23.28b–29a; Zhang and Liu 1996, 355-56.

When blue salt became an important part of the trade between the Song and the Xixia, the Song attempted to use the product for political leverage. On 12/yimao/1001 Li Jihe, commissioner of the Luoyang imperial gardens (*Luoyuan shi*), spoke on the necessity of not relaxing prohibitions on blue salt (*XCB* 50.1093). The garden, stocked with animals, was maintained in Luoyang for imperial hunting pleasure. The administrator in charge of the sanctuary and his deputy were military officials (*SS* 169.4056–57). For more on blue and white salts as competition and on proponents and opponents within the Song camp and their political and economic arguments, see Ma Shuqin 1989, 71–76. Other salt lakes in the region included Tile Pond (Wachi), Hot Spring Pond (Wenquanchi), Long-tailed Pond (Changweichi), and Red Peach Pond (Hongtaochi) (Ma Shuqin 1989, 71).

Chinese luxury crafts.[13] Blue and white salt produced by the Tanguts competed with Xiezhou salt and precipitated frequent conflicts between the Northern Song and the Xixia in the eleventh century. In the early 990s the Shaanxi fiscal intendant proposed allowing merchant sales in Shaanxi as a way of resisting the intrusion of Xixia salt and thereby stemming the further loss of revenues, which had already become insufficient to cover county expenses.

Supplementary sources indicate that when the market was allowed to follow its own course, some places went without salt because merchants did not find it profitable to sell there. The government resorted to gerrymandering the trade areas in an attempt to get salt better distributed and to reduce the overwhelming violations in the areas where it was not. The Songshi seems to gloss over these considerations and gives the argument for government sales short shrift. Although the authors were clearly aware of the role of salt in interstate relations, they focused on revenue losses to the state engendered by smuggling. Government versus merchant sales were debated again.

The emperor decreed for [Liang] Ding to act as the Shaanxi military regulator (*zhizhishi*) and further appointed him, together with the imperial warder of the Inner Hall (*neidian chongban*), Du Chengrui, co-regulator of Shaanxi blue salt (*qingyan*) and white salt (*baiyan*) matters.[14] [Du] Chengrui stated:

> After the prefectures of Fuzhou[a], Yanzhou[b], Huanzhou, Qingzhou, Yizhou[c], and Weizhou[b] began observing the prohibition on blue salt, merchants were ordered to bring in fodder and grain, then to transport Xie salt to the border to sell. Its price was to be comparable to that of blue salt, so people would eat the cheaper salt [and not smuggle]. It is necessary to make them fear the law, so the blue salt of the tribal regions will be hard to sell. Now I have heard that Xie salt transported to the border has been priced the same as [more expensive] salt in the interior. [I am afraid that this will surely encourage] the people living along the border to flout the law in pursuit of profit and enter tribal territories to trade blue salt illegally. This will fuel illicit trade while creating resentment among the common people.[15]

---

[13] On 12/jimao/1005 gifts presented to the Song court by the Khitan included ten bowls of white salt and ten cases of blue salt (*XCB* 61.1375).

[14] This was decreed after Liang Ding memorialized on 1/12/1003 (*SHY* 23.27a–29a; *XCB* 54.1175–77).

[15] Whether these were actually Du Chengrui's words is debatable. Liang Ding's biography in *SS* does not indicate the name Du Chengrui. See also Liang and Bao 1994, 585.

Others memorialized that [government trade] was not feasible.[16] [Yet Liang] Ding asked to wait for arrangements (*woyun*) to be made at the border and for [an imperial] courier (*shengzhuan*) to be sent to Xie pond to [announce a] ban of the merchant trade.[17] Subsequently, salt was transported to the border, but at burdensome expense, and the border people suddenly were without provisions.

There was heated dissatisfaction. Consequently, the supervisor (*gouyuan*) of the Salt and Iron Office, Lin Te, and the Yongxingjun prefect (*cishi*), Zhang Yong, were ordered to deliberate. They felt [the monopoly] was helpful neither to the government nor the people so they petitioned for restoration of the merchant trade policy. [The emperor] severely rebuked [Liang] Ding and dismissed him from the post of commissioner of funds.[18]

A second policy debate followed in the first decade of 1000. With the partial restoration of merchant sales, prices for merchant-provisioned goods were jacked up and it became impossible to maintain military stockpiles. So the new Shaanxi fiscal intendant, Zhu Taifu, proposed resorting to government sales once more. He was opposed by another ranking Shaanxi official. In the end, the emperor dismissed both of them after a censor looked into their mutual charges of impropriety. The third major debate of the first twenty years of Zhenzong's reign follows below.

In 1016 (Dazhongxiangfu 9) the Shaanxi fiscal intendant (*zhuanyunshi*), Zhang Xiangzhong, stated:

[As of now] the two ponds have stored 21,761,080 strings worth of salt. I calculate we may be able to increase our surpluses even further, *[p. 4415]* and I hope that we may carry out the [old monopoly] regulations [wherein households must purchase salt based on their property assets, so we reap an

---

[16] In response to a request by the fiscal intendant, Zhu Taifu, it was decreed on 9/jihai/1004 that Tongzhou[a], Huazhou, and Yaozhou (all in Yongxingjun) become subject to merchant sales (*XCB* 57.1258).

[17] *Woyun* refers to the effort to work out a solution (Wang Leiming 1985, 327n4). *Shengzhuan* refers to government postal carriages in which imperial orders were carried and, by extension, imperial orders for dispatch. A direct overland route ran from Kaifeng to Xiezhou; for details see *QYSL* 10.3b–4b, 11.12a. For postal systems, see Ma Chujian 1997.

[18] Liang Ding was dismissed on 5/22/1003.

estimated 20 million strings, equivalent to more than twenty times the Xie salt revenues of twenty years ago].[19]

Zhenzong decreed:

The maximum bounty of the land has no doubt already been reached. To be overzealous in seeking revenues, I am afraid, may lead to periodic shortages.

And so he did not allow it.

A flashback to fifty years before recounts the easing of punishments for illegal trading over time. But the penalties were to no avail in any case, since they addressed neither the proximate nor the ultimate causes of smuggling.

Long before this, during the Five Dynasties period, the salt policy was too harsh.[20] In 961 (Jianlong 2) a policy on the illegal trade (*lanru*) of government salt was first instituted. In restricted areas, trading up to ten catties or boiling up to three catties of brine meant a sentence of death; in cases where over thirty catties of "silkworm salt" were brought into the city, the superior offices were to be petitioned regarding punishment.[21] In 962

---

[19] The post may actually have been assistant fiscal intendant (*zhuanyun fushi*) instead, as in 4/dinghai/1016 (*XCB* 86.1982; *SHY* 23.30a). On 4/dinghai/1016 Zhang Xiangzhong memorialized on this first major glut of Xie salt, which lasted from 1008 to 1016. He stated that the Anyi and Xie ponds had accumulated 388,808,928 catties of salt with a value of 21,761,080 strings. He thought even greater yields could be realized. The emperor, however, felt that revenues were quite large already and that more would be excessive (*SHY* 23.30a–b; *XCB* 86.1982).

[20] The Later Jin's (936–947) salt policy was the harshest of the Five Dynasties; the Later Zhou eased it, but still resorted to the death penalty (Wang Leiming 1985, 327n1).

[21] Decreed on 4/jiwei/961 (*XCB* 2.44; *SHY* 23.18a). The latter notes that for bringing more than twenty catties into the city, the punishment was twenty strokes on the back and a year of labor in exile.

A distribution scheme referred to as "silkworm salt," practiced in the Later Tang (923–936) and Northern Song, was distorted from a form of aid into an onerous fee. It was originally designed to address the needs of silk-producing households in remote villages. In spring, when villagers were low on funds, the Song government gave them a quantity of salt; once the silk-producing season was over in autumn, they paid the value back in silk, according to the summer tax rate (*Taizong shilu* 977, cited in interstitial commentary of *XCB* 2.44 [4/jiwei/961] and *XCB* 18.398–99

(Jianlong 3) the death penalty was eased and applied to those who traded up to 30 catties or boiled up to 10 catties of brine. The emperor was petitioned regarding punishment for anyone who conveyed over 100 catties of silkworm salt into the city.[22] After 966 (Qiande 4) imperial decrees [further] eased prohibitions.[23] In 977 (Taipingxingguo 2) it was finally decreed that for illicit trade of more than 200 catties, for boiling brine, or instigating smuggling of over 100 catties, and for bringing into the city over 500 catties of silkworm salt, punishment was tattooing on the face and delivery to the palace gates.[24] In 994 (Chunhua 5) a change was made so that former offenders would be sent only as far as the local prefectural prison. For the residents of Daizhou's Baoxingjun [Hedong] who privately marketed Khitan salt from Guduidu and Taoshan, in 987 (Yongxi 4) the emperor decreed that anyone dealing in one catty or more would be punished accordingly; for 50 catties, military duty and banishment were imposed; for over 100 catties, one was escorted to the palace gates.[25]

The Songshi *next provides pond producer statistics for the first quarter of the eleventh century. The government registered 380 salter households at Xiezhou, set them an*

[2/dingwei/977]). This salt distribution method eventually became routine, then mandatory, and prefectures were assigned quotas to dispose of in this way. After 1041 the state discontinued actual distribution, yet still required payment. Fourteen years later this fee was reduced; households that did not want the salt still paid 60 percent of the full fee (*SHY* 26.8b, 1/29/1133).

[22] This was on 3/dinghai/962 (*XCB* 3.65).

[23] On 11/wuxu/966 it was decreed that the death penalty applied to illegal trade of 100 catties or illegally boiling of 50 catties, and that the corvee and banishment applied to bringing 300 catties of silkworm salt into the city or illegally selling it (*XCB* 7.182).

[24] To be "sent to the palace gates" indicates a probable death penalty, pending imperial decree. One such decree, announced by the Finance Commission on 2/18/977, elaborates on specific salt-related crimes and their punishments (*SHY* 23.19a–20a). The same penalties were discussed on 2/dingwei/977 by a bureau which prefaced its discussion with the rationale: if powerful families were not prevented from monopolizing the resources of mountain and marsh, then full revenues would not go to the government (*XCB* 18.398–99).

[25] Daizhou is present Daixian, Shanxi; Taoshan is at the Great Wall in present-day Hebei. In *SHY* (23.22b) residents south of Dashizhai are also included; instead of Khitan it reads "the northern border"; Taoshan is omitted.

annual quota, and gave them rations and payments. In the thirty-odd years from 996 to 1030 production rose dramatically from 373,000 mats to over 655,000. Production rose while the number of salters remained the same partly because saltern officials hired temporary labor to assist.[26] In the beginning, officials responsible for hiring did so at their own discretion; gradually they systematized the hiring of the temporaries and used them as regular labor while the old salters came to play a secondary role in production. Thus the system evolved from one that requisitioned salters to one that hired them, and the nature of the hiring itself evolved from a private basis to a public one, depending on the region.[27]

The Song inherited the distribution regions for pond, sea, earth, and well salts from the Five Dynasties. In turn, it divided pond salt distribution into three geographical areas: south of the ponds, in Jingxinan and Jingxibei, it sold "southern salt" via merchant sales; west of the ponds, in Yongxingjun Circuit, it sold "western salt" also via merchant sales; east of the ponds, including Jingdongxi, Hedong, Hebei, and parts of Huai, it sold "eastern salt" primarily via government sales.

From the Tiansheng period (1023–1031) on, the two ponds employed altogether 380 salter households who were natives of [Xie] prefecture or neighboring prefectures. Each household annually committed two laborers. Each laborer was provided with two pints (*sheng*) of rice a day, and each household was given 40,000 cash a year.[28] Annually, 1,526,429 piculs (*dan*) of salt were produced, with one picul being fifty catties. This was equivalent to 655,120 mats, with one mat being 116 catties.[29] In restricted monopoly regions, all service was performed by government workers appointed from among the villagers to act as service runners (*yaqian*) or hired hands who were termed "recorded heads" (*tietou*).[30] They transported government

---

[26] *SHY* 23.34a (1/1027).

[27] Kawakami 1974, 59–61, 66–67.

[28] *XCB* 97.2260 (12/wuzi/1021). According to Liang and Bao (1994, 587), these practices dated to the beginning of Song, not just from the Tiansheng period.

[29] Salt production at the two ponds doubled over the three intervening decades from 996. The *XCB* on 10/renchen/1030 notes 160 catties per mat (*XCB* 109.2544). Might this be a mistaken transposition of the characters "ten" and "six"?

[30] The restricted areas referred to the three capitals and twenty-eight prefectures. *Yaqian* was a service duty required of first-class village families for a two-year period; it entailed handling government goods, providing cart transport, and manning

tribute [taxes paid in kind] by water or overland routes. In prefectures with merchant trade, merchants also serviced the border districts of Qinzhou[b], Yanzhou[b], Huanzhou, Qingzhou, Weizhou[b], Yuanzhou[a], Baoanjun, Zhenrongjun, and Deshunjun. Traders were called upon to provide fodder and grain and were compensated with salt.[31]

The salt distributed and sold in merchant-sales prefectures in Jingxi was called southern salt; in Shaanxi it was called western salt; in monopoly areas it was called eastern salt. To prevent encroachment, boundary lines were drawn.[32] At the beginning of the Tiansheng period (1023–1031), after deliberating the pros and cons of the tea and salt monopolies, the offices in charge of budgets (*jizhisi*) stated the following:

> Merchants formerly recruited by the two ponds to sell southern salt pay cash [for salt] at the capital's Monopoly Goods Bureau. In 1022 (Qianxing 1) the annual revenues were only 230,000 strings, 140,000 less than the figure for 1019 (Tianxi 3). We request that all this be abolished. Instead, let the merchants provision fodder and grain at the border. To halt the abuse of private trade, we should *[p. 4416]* put greater effort into restrictions and publicize them.

Later, the emperor reversed the decree allowing cash payment [for salt] at the capital for the merchants' convenience.

---

salterns, storehouses, postal stations, river crossings, and flotilla transport (Dai Yixuan 1957, 59).

On intercalary 5/5/1026 the Shaanxi fiscal intendant relayed a plaint from one of the "recorded heads" concerning their hardships. Ministerial deliberation concluded that it would be difficult indeed to perpetuate such a system. The major transportation conduit at Xiezhou, the Yongfengqu or "Ever-bountiful" Canal, had been in a state of disrepair since the Northern Wei in the early 500s (*SHY* 23.33b–34a). On 10/renchen/1030 Sheng Du and Wang Sui differentiated pond salters from temporary hired laborers in the last of their five listed advantages of a policy of merchant sales (*SS* 181.4416; *XCB* 109.2545).

[31] *XCB* 109.2544–45 (10/renchen/1030).

[32] *XCB* 109.2545 (10/renchen/1030); interstitial commentary in *XCB* 146.3534 (2/yiwei/1044). Reorganization of distribution boundaries between salts, particularly pond and sea salt, is described in Guo Zhengzhong 1990a, 291–92.

For two years, from 1000 to 1002, the state relied on merchant interest in selling salt to encourage their provisioning border areas, but then reverted to government salt distribution.[33] *In 1030 an official vividly described the glut of pond salt so the court endorsed merchant sales once again. This prompted the disbanding of the government distribution apparatus and merchant sales of Xie salt resumed in sixty-four prefectures, marking the first time the merchant sales policy was so widely implemented.*

In the three capitals and twenty-eight prefectures, the government undertook transport of salt and burdened the common people by the consequent corvee. In 1030 (Tiansheng 8) a memorialist to the emperor argued:

> The government monopoly of salt has resulted in few benefits and a great deal of harm. The two ponds have accumulated such mounds of salt that innumerable trees have sprung up, so big that one can barely get one's arms around them. We ought to allow merchant sales but must stabilize the selling price to ease the people's pain.[34]

The emperor decreed that a Hanlin academician, Sheng Du, and the executive censor (*yushi zhongcheng*) Wang Sui should deliberate the reform

---

[33] The *SHY* includes the arguments of Sun Mian for merchant trade and Chen Shu for government sales; eventually Chen's ideas were adopted (*SHY* 23.24a–27b).

[34] *XCB* 109.2545 (10/renchen/1030). The meaning of the figure of the trees is obscure. This second major Xie salt glut occurred between 1028 and 1032. The memorialist, Wang Jing, was a civil service examination candidate who gave a firsthand report of the amount at stake. On another occasion he had memorialized in favor of tightening restrictions to what Taizong had imposed. People then had been afraid to boil illicitly and the government earned a great amount. Zhenzong, though, had softened penalties and illegal trade rose as revenues fell (*XCB* 109.2546; *SSJW* 4.38). Wang Jing recommended merchant trade, but the ministers disagreed. The empress dowager, however, sided with Wang. In an exchange of 10/bingshen/1030 she asked the ministers: "I have heard that the salt the people eat is bad. Is this true?" They replied: "Only imperial provisions and the court's salt are good. The people all eat salt with dirt in it." She retorted: "Not so! The imperial provisions also have dirt in them and are inedible. Why not discuss the recommendation for merchant trade?" The ministers explained that the locales would suffer [from lost revenue] if they took that course of action. The empress dowager said: "How can that be any worse, since millions of inedible catties are thrown away already?" The ministers dared not argue further (*XCB* 109.2546).

of the system.[35] They consequently drew up five advantages of merchant sales and submitted them:

> When merchant sales are prohibited, the tasks of felling wood and constructing boats and carriages [for salt transport] exhaust the soldiers and populace. Eliminating this burden would be the first advantage. Land transport presses "recorded heads" and cart owners into service. The poor flee in fear year after year. Abolishing this would be the second advantage. Boat transport entails the risk of capsizing as well as pilferage by flotilla workers who add foreign matter such as sand and saltpeter, which makes the salt taste terrible and leads to illness and swollen feet. Pure salt for all would be the third advantage. Currency is the state's source of trade; it ought to be circulated. Wealthy families, however, hoard silver ingots, leaving less in general circulation and making life difficult for the public. This year we have received more than 600,000 strings of cash from merchant sales to cover expenditures. This would be the fourth advantage. The annual cost of paying government inspectors, soldiers, pond salt producers, and hired labor will be saved. This would be the fifth advantage.[36]

In the tenth month [of 1030 (Tiansheng 8)] the emperor decreed to abolish the monopoly policy in the three capitals and twenty-eight prefectures. [He] allowed merchants to pay gold or silver at the capital Monopoly Goods Bureau, then to receive salt from the two ponds.[37] After one year of implementation, revenues rose by 150,000 strings of cash compared with

---

[35] After the previous exchange with his mother, the emperor decreed on 12/23/1032 for Sheng Du, Wang Sui, as well as Li Zi, the auxiliary academician of the Bureau of Military Affairs (*shumi zhixueshi*) and temporary finance commissioner, to look into the matter and in the end adopted Wang Jing's plan (*SHY* 23.37a; *XCB* 109.2546, 111.2597).

[36] This was part of a long discussion on Xie salt on 10/renchen/1030; the *XCB* notes *yanguan*, or salt officials, as opposed to the similar characters for *jianguan* (*XCB* 109.2545).

[37] On 10/16/1030 Sheng Du and others requested that the emperor abolish the Xie monopoly and implement merchant trade in conjunction with payment of gold, silver, and cash at the capital Monopoly Goods Bureau (*SHY* 23.35a). Probably following this recommendation as well as the delineation of five advantages of merchant sales, the emperor issued his decree. On 4/18/1031 Sheng Du spoke in detail on rewards to officials for informing on and apprehending contraband salt and on punishments for negligence. He also set out strict Xie salt boundaries and clear boundaries within which only merchant trade could operate (*SHY* 23.35b–36a).

1029 (Tiansheng 7).[38] After that, [however,] annual tax revenues declined, so the Hanlin academician, Song Xiang, and others were ordered to compare income of the period from 1031 (Tiansheng 9) up to 1039 (Baoyuan 2) with income of the period from 1022 (Qianxing) through 1030 (Tiansheng 8). They found that under the new policy, annual tax revenues had fallen by 2,360,000 strings.[39] So in 1040 (Kangding 1) it was decreed that the salt policy at the capital [Kaifeng], the Southern Capital, Jingdong prefectures, and Huainan's Suzhou[b] and Bozhou[b] would all revert to government distribution as before.[40] However, before long, the monopoly policy in the capital was again loosened. The emperor decreed that the finance commission should deliberate on the selling of Huainan salt in the eight prefectures of Jingdong. Thus, [Jingdong's] Yanzhou[a] and Yunzhou[a], and [Huaixi's] Suzhou[b] and Bozhou[b] all [came to] consume Huainan [rather than Xiezhou] salt.[41]

With conflict looming in the north, the salt trade again became strategically linked with provision of grain and fodder to the border where a massive standing army was stationed. After 1034 and the rebellion of the Xixia founder-to-be, the government urged merchants to deliver desperately needed supplies to the border, and Xie salt was the nearest available enticement to convince merchants to go to the risk, trouble, and expense. The state gave merchants vouchers for bringing north grain and fodder, which they could exchange for cash, gold, or silver at the capital or for salt at Xiezhou. Salt vouchers were called yan jiaoyin, yanyin, or yanchao. By the early 1040s, however,

---

[38] *XCB* 123.2909 (6/guiyou/1039).

[39] *XCB* 123.2910 (6/guiyou/1039). On 3/guiwei/1034 it was decreed to forgive half the 3,371,416 mats of salt that Xiezhou salt workers owed (*XCB* 114.2672). Concerning the third glut in 1034, it was memorialized on 2/1/1034 that ten years worth of salt had stockpiled. From this it may be extrapolated that 240 million catties had accumulated. The memorial requested that production stop for three years. According to the *SHY*, the emperor agreed to two years (*SHY* 23.37a); according to the *XCB*, he agreed to three years (*XCB* 114.2662, 2/renchen/1034; *XCB* 115.2688, 7/jichou/1034).

[40] This led to a fourth glut between 1039 to 1040. On 12/24/1040 Ouyang Xiu noted that Xie salt was piled mountain high and recommended a price cut for three years so that merchants would be enticed to trade; see Ouyang Xiu's "Tongjinsi shangshu" (A petition to the Tongjinsi) for details in *JSJ* 45.1021; *XCB* 129.3069–70.

[41] *XCB* 123.2910 (6/guiyou/1039).

merchants had raised the price of provisions while the government price of salt had not
kept up. The government had to produce many times more salt to collect the same amount
of revenue. In 1040 it reinstated government sales to stabilize the salt price but the
people were again burdened with additional corvee and receipts remained insufficient.

After the rebellion of [Li] Yuanhao, troops were assembled at the western border, but those who came to supply fodder and grain were few and far between.[42] The local governments grew anxious about military provisions. Because of insufficient distribution, merchants who were allowed to provision [the army] were given vouchers, to be cashed in for gold or silver at the capital Monopoly Goods Bureau. For the provisioning of other goods, vouchers (*quan*) could be redeemed with pond salt.[43] Hence, feathers, tendons and horns, glue and paint, iron and charcoal, *[p. 4417]* as well as roof tiles and lumber came to be exchanged for salt.[44] Unscrupulous merchants and avaricious clerks colluded to the point that for two wooden beams assessed

---

[42] Li Yuanhao (1002–1048), founder of the Xixia, was descended from the Toba who had established the Northern Wei (386–532) in the first period of division. The head of the Toba had paid obeisance to the Tang court and so was honored with the imperial surname, Li. Li Yuanhao's grandfather, Li Jiqian (963–1004), constantly harassed the Song border. Jiqian's cousin, Li Jipeng (962–1004), had accepted an office at the Song court in 980 and had the imperial surname, Zhao, bestowed upon him. Li Yuanhao himself was schooled in Chinese learning: he translated the *Classic of Filial Piety* (*Xiaojing*) and the *Erya* dictionary into the Xixia language. He also amassed much territory in the area of present-day Ningxia. Although the Song was unable to defeat him, years of warfare weakened his forces and he negotiated a peace. He was honored with the title "Master of the Xia State" (*Xia guozhu*) in 1044, then died not long after at age forty-six. His kingdom survived him by nearly 180 years, until it was demolished by the Mongols in 1226. Both Li Yuanhao and his son petitioned to have salterns established to legitimate their export of blue salt into China proper, but to no avail. For more on the Xia kingdom, see *SS* 485.13981–14033.

[43] *Quan* (commonly pronounced *juan*) refers to a written proof of a set price, also called *yaoquan*; here it refers to *jiaoyin*, on the basis of which cash, tea, salt, incense, and other goods could be obtained. Qian Gongbo compares *jiaoyin* to today's bill of lading (*tihuodan*). *Jiaoyin* can be distinguished from *jiaozi* because they could not be circulated as money. The use of such proofs to obtain cash and tea was begun in 985 (Wang Leiming 1985, 330n2).

[44] The government set up warehouses to handle leather, horns, saltpeter, and the like for the manufacture of fire arms, as well as saddles, carpets, and so on (*SHY* 23.39b, 52).

at 1,000 cash, a merchant was rewarded with one large salt mat of 220 catties. The waste of pond salt [as its value deflated] was incalculable. As the salt price continued to plummet, no traders came, so that neither the government nor private interests were benefited.[45] In 1042 (Qingli 2) the capital's monopoly policy was revived and all merchants who had received vouchers at an inflated price, as well as those who had already taken on salt but not yet sold it, were to have it recalculated or to refund the proceeds to the government. In the interior prefectures the government would procure all privately held salt and set up salterns to sell it at an increased price. Merchant sales of salt in the eleven prefectures of Yongxingjun, Tongzhou[a], Huazhou[a], Yaozhou, Hezhongfu, Shanzhou[a], Guozhou, Xiezhou, Jinzhou[b], Jiangzhou[b], and Qingchengjun were again prohibited; service runners managed transportation of government salt by cart. Further, no merchant salt was to privately enter Shu. Exchange Bureau offices (*zhebowu*) established in Yongxingjun and Fengxiangfu allowed [merchants] to pay in cash instead of Shu commodities, then gave them salt to sell in Shu.[46] After some time, the eastern and southern salt areas all reverted to the monopoly. The soldiers and civilians pressed into transport [service] were overwhelmed by their burden; and the prefectures fell into disarray. [Yet] the consequent salt profits were not sufficient to alleviate the urgent needs of the local governments. In addition, when the border counties attempted to induce merchants to trade in fodder and grain, voucher prices became inflated by several times. The capital's hard currency was greatly depleted and the treasury further diminished.

The second stage of the salt policy, characterized by stabilization of merchant sales, began in the mid-Northern Song when troop provisioning and government transport were in danger of collapse. In 1048 the official Fan Xiang proposed a salt voucher law for Shaanxi, which hearkened back to Liu Yan's system of merchant transport and trade in the Tang. Fan Xiang separated salt from provisioning and proposed cash payments from merchants to be used toward supplying the border. He instituted cash payments for vouchers of exchange with which merchants might obtain pond salt. This bypassed

---

[45] Taken verbatim from 1/dingsi/1042 (*XCB* 135.3215).

[46] This transaction would eliminate indiscriminate acceptance of goods in exchange for salt. It was proposed in a 1/dingsi/1042 memorial by the Xiezhou regulator and intendant of salt, Fan Zongjie, and also comes verbatim from *XCB* (135.3215).

the problem of inflated supply costs, spared locals the hardships of corvee transport,
ensured sufficient provisioning, and helped balance the budget. .

An erudite of imperial sacrifices (*taichang boshi*), Fan Xiang was a native
of Guanzhong [present Shaanxi].[47] Familiar with the problems of the salt
trade, he insisted that profit from the two ponds was great, and the reason it
could not finance border needs was the rampant pilferage in both the public
and private sectors. Should the policy be changed, the annual expenditure of
many millions of strings of cash could be saved. So he drew up a plan and
presented it. At this time Han Qi was assistant commissioner of military
affairs (*shumi fushi*), and he and the special drafting official of the Secretariat
(*zhizhigao*), Tian Kuang, petitioned that [Fan] Xiang's plan be adopted.[48] In

---

[47] Fan Xiang (?–1060), as pond salt administrator, is compared with Liu Yan in the
Tang. During Renzong's reign, when the Xixia exerted pressure on the border, the
court increased the price of grain to induce more merchants to supply the army and
buy into salt vouchers. Consequently, the state's salt stores were depleted as
merchants moved glut salt at a cheap price. Fan Xiang proposed replacing the
government distribution policy with the voucher salt law, which could save several
million strings a year [in transport and other costs]. Later, when he served in
Shaanxi, Fan concurrently managed Xie salt. In 1048 the voucher salt policy was
first implemented, and merchants paid 4,800 cash per voucher, with each voucher
good for 200 catties of salt. Merchants would sell this salt at a price determined by
the Salt Directorate at the capital. Shen Kuo notes that the range was between
thirty-five and forty cash per catty; if it went higher or lower, the government
would adjust the quota of salt distributed (*MBT* 11.25a; *SS* 303.10049). In 1053,
however, Fan was demoted, and the salt policy became riddled with abuses again.
He was restored to his post five years later but soon died.

[48] In 5/jiaxu/1041 Tian Kuang, executive assistant of the Court of Imperial Sacrifices
(*taichangcheng*), auxiliary in the Academy of Scholarly Worthies (*zhi jixianyuan*), and
signatory official (*qianshu*) of the Shaanxi Military Intendancy Supervisory Office
(*jinglue anfu panguan*), presented fourteen points of military policy. The fifth touched
on the blue and white salt prohibitions. Frontier inhabitants were often recruited as
guards, but they never received proper [supervision or background checks] unless
there was a problem. With the livelihood of border residents dependent upon the
trade of blue and white salt, a government monopoly would cut them off. During
Taizong's time when the monopoly was in force, border people had sided with Li
Jiqian against the Song. So the court reversed its position and pacified the tribes,
which was better than spending huge amounts on the military (*XCB* 132.3133–34).
On 2/16/1044 Han Qi and Tian Kuang spoke on the impact of importation of
blue salt into the border economy. Frequent dealings between border and western
tribal peoples meant that Xie salt sales were already feeling the effects of competition

1044 (Qingli 4) the emperor decreed that [Fan] Xiang should hasten to Shaanxi to discuss this with the circuit fiscal intendant-general (*du zhuanyunshi*), Cheng Kan.[49] [Cheng] Kan, however, disagreed with [Fan] Xiang, and shortly thereafter, [Fan] Xiang had to leave office due to mourning (*zaosang*).[50] In 1048 (Qingli 8) [Fan] Xiang again offered his opinion and was appointed Shaanxi judicial intendant, concurrent with being military regulator of Xie salt, so that he could implement his plan.

His system worked as follows. All formerly restricted areas were now to be placed under merchant sales and [merchant] salt was allowed to enter Shu. Provisioning of the nine prefectures with fodder and grain [under the old system] was abolished. [Merchants] were to pay for salt in hard cash and then receive the salt. The price varied according to the distance of the location where [the merchant] paid the cash [from his market] and his preference for eastern, western, or southern salt. For eastern and southern salt, [merchants] paid cash at Yongxingjun, Fengxiangfu, and Hezhongfu. Total annual cash paid was for 375,000 large mats worth of salt. [Merchants] were given the necessary vouchers, which were verified at the ponds themselves, where salt was supplied according to the numbers.[51] This practice completely eliminated drafting soldiers and common people for overland transport. In addition, because Yanzhou[b], Qingzhou, Huanzhou, Weizhou[b], Yuanzhou[a], Baoanjun, Zhenrongjun, and Deshunjun were located near the Black and White Ponds [in the Xixia salt-producing areas], rapacious individuals had been smuggling blue and white salt across the border, taking profits, and upsetting the system.[52] So [the government] hired

---

with the cheap, tasty blue salt. They clearly would suffer further if the blue salt trade was legalized. In addition, Shaanxi would be short of funds (*SHY* 23.38b–39a).

[49] Decreed 2/2/1044 (*SHY* 23.38b).

[50] *Sang* generally refers to a death in the family; *zaosang* refers specifically to the death of a parent. In the Song, mourning observances, which entailed withdrawal from official duties for a number of years, were particularly esteemed.

[51] One voucher for a large mat of salt might cost a merchant six strings, but he could then sell it for ten strings, a four-string profit. For the range of prices of eastern and western salt in Yongxingjun and Qinfeng, see Kawahara 1977, 11.

[52] In 11/jichou/1043 the executive censor Wang Gongchen requested that blue salt be traded only at Baoanjun on the Xixia border, from where it could be transported to Fuzhou[a] in central Yongxingjun. Merchants could sell it in Guangdong but not in

merchants to provision [the populace in the interior] with pond salt. They were given vouchers [purchased in the interior] at favorable *[p. 4418]* prices, then upon return [to the north] were compensated with pond salt [to transport back to the interior]. The government sold the salt brought in this way while prohibiting private sales and tightened restrictions on blue and white salts. In border districts the old policy that had allowed provisioning of iron, charcoal, tiles, lumber, and the like [in return for awards in salt] was reformulated. [Merchants] who had earlier received vouchers at an inflated price, as well as those who had received salt but not yet sold it, were to have the value [of their holdings] recalculated and pay the difference to the government. Further, it was ordered that the governments of the three capitals as well as Hezhongfu, Heyang, Shanzhou[a], Guozhou, Xiezhou, Jinzhou[b], Jiangzhou[b], Puzhou, Qingchengjun, and Guangjijun continue to sell [salt] until merchant sales were smoothly in place. Cash received was used to buy and transport fodder and grain to the nine border prefectures; the remainder was left at the Monopoly Goods Bureau to support the central treasury. After [this policy] had been in place for several years, avaricious merchants were out of luck and the people within the passes achieved a stable livelihood. So public and private both benefited.[53]

In 1049 (Huangyou 1) the censor of miscellaneous affairs (*shiyushi zhizashi*), He Tan, again raised the argument that the policy change had been ill-advised.[54] The following year the assistant commissioner (*fushi*) in

---

Shaanxi or Hedong. In the first place this would not affect salt policy; and in addition it would allow merchants to show profits and remove the necessity of government-organized transport (*XCB* 145.3506).

On 11/xinmao/1043 a policy criticism official, Sun Fu, memorialized against easing the monopoly on the flavorful Xie salt because he feared there would be no stopping its trade (*XCB* 145.3507–8). That same day Ouyang Xiu also memorialized, [but] against relaxing blue salt restrictions because the "bandits" of Li Yuanhao's Xixia would reap profits, use them to seduce the people, and in a few years the entire area would be under their control (*XCB* 145.3509).

[53] For the entire description of the plan, see *XCB* 165.3970–71, 10/dinghai/1048.

[54] He Tan argued on 10/renxu/1049 that merchants felt there was too little profit to be made since the increase in the government's salt price. This led to [a distribution slowdown, resulting in] decreased tax income amounting to millions of strings in Shaanxi. Other circuits, too, had seen declines. If a change was not positive, the former method ought to be reinstated (*XCB* 167.4016).

charge of the census, Bao Zheng, was dispatched to review the practice on the ground. Upon his return he spoke of the advantages of the current policy. When merchants were called upon to pay cash, the salt price in the eight prefectures, including Yanzhou[b] and Huanzhou, was lowered, then when merchants brought salt in, the selling price was increased [to encourage them].[55] The three capitals, Hezhongfu, and other regions did not allow government trade. The finance commission argued that if merchants rarely came to the capital to trade, the salt could become expensive. It petitioned for both public and private trade [in the capital] but prohibited government trade in all other places. Both requests were granted.[56]

The finance commissioner, Tian Kuang, petitioned to employ [Fan] Xiang for long-term management to concentrate on these affairs. So [Fan] Xiang was promoted to temporary Shaanxi fiscal intendant and given gold and purple robes.[57] [Fan] Xiang initially declared that [the government] could make 2,300,000 strings of cash annually.[58] By 1051 (Huangyou 3) income reached 2,210,000 strings, while in 1052 (Huangyou 4) it was 2,150,000. The figure for that year marked an increase of 680,000 [strings] compared with 1046 (Qingli 6) and an increase of 200,000 [strings] over 1047 (Qingli 7). Furthermore, in the past the Monopoly Goods Bureau had made annual outlays of 6,470,000 in cash in 1042 (Qingli 2) and 4,800,000 in 1046 (Qingli 6). Now it no longer had any funds. Even though the annual income of the Bureau was irregular, in 1045 (Qingli 5) it still reached 1,780,000 [strings,] while in 1054 (Zhihe 1) it flagged at only 1,690,000. At that time [Fan] Xiang had already been found guilty of some other offense and was

---

[55] Bao Zheng's review of salt operations probably occurred in 1049, as detailed in *XCB* (167.4016–18, 10/renxu/1049), and not in 1050, as also noted in *SHY* (23.39b). Bao assessed Fan's policy positively: during the ten years of its implementation, the Monopoly Goods Bureau had saved several million strings of cash annually. He also noted problems in the Shaanxi salt trade, including sly merchants who worked in collusion with government clerks, leading to revenue losses (*SHY* 23.39b–40a).

[56] *XCB* 167.4018 (10/renxu/1049).

[57] Fan was appointed deputy Shaanxi fiscal intendant (*XCB* 171.4120–21, 12/wuxu/1051; *SS* 303.10049).

[58] This was what he had promised but was unable to deliver (*XCB* 187.4517, 7/renchen/1058).

dismissed. The fiscal intendant Li Can was ordered to replace him.[59] In 1056 (Zhihe 3) taking the income level of 1054 as the annual tax quota, the government calculated [that annual tax income from salt distribution] could cover [as much as] 80 percent of border expenses.

Cash flow woes were directly linked to the value of salt vouchers. Originally, only the capital's Monopoly Goods Bureau issued salt vouchers; later other Monopoly Goods offices in Yongxingjun and Qinfeng circuits also issued them. In the 1050s with oversupply and inflation, the vouchers depreciated, were recalled, and were sent to Xiezhou to be destroyed. The price fluctuation was in part due to the seasonal character of salt production and so Fan Xiang built storehouses to hold salt when the price was too low. In 1058 he was recalled from forced retirement to deal with renewed problems. He then separated the value of the vouchers from the price of salt.

After some time provisioning of border areas in place of cash [payment for salt] was again allowed, but the problem of overvaluation of goods grew and with it the voucher value fell.[60] The annual loss in government revenues was no less than a million [strings]. *[p. 4419]* In 1058 (Jiayou 3) the finance commissioners Zhang Fangping and Bao Zheng petitioned to reinstate [Fan] Xiang again, so he returned to the management of salt affairs.[61] He petitioned again to stop the border provisioning. Those [merchants] who had received vouchers [probably for provisioning] from before 1058 had to pay another 1,000 cash for each voucher before they were given salt. [Fan Xiang] further noted that merchants who carried vouchers for salt to be sold in the capital had all lost money [due to depreciation]. [To give them relief] he petitioned [that the court] establish an office in the capital with 200,000 strings of cash in reserve to prepare for merchants who arrived [with salt vouchers]. If the voucher value was lower than the salt price, the government would [buy up salt to help] sell vouchers. A voucher was set at 6,000 [cash], a mat of salt at 10,000 [cash]. These figures were not to be increased or decreased so that the market price would stabilize; none could manipulate it. [The emperor] decreed for the director of salt (*duyanyuan*

---

[59] Fan Xiang was dismissed in 4/1053 (*XCB* 187.4517, 7/renchen/1058).

[60] *XCB* 187.4518 (7/renchen/1058).

[61] *XCB* 187.4517 (7/renchen/1058). At the time Bao Zheng was executive censor and head of the Censorate (*yushitai*).

jianguan) to concurrently head this office. From then on [vouchers] more or less recovered their former [value and merchants no longer suffered losses]. Shortly afterward, [Fan] Xiang died and the assistant fiscal intendant, Xue Xiang, succeeded him.[62] By 1065 (Zhiping 2) annual revenue was 1,670,000 [strings].

In 1061, a year after Fan Xiang's death, Xue Xiang became Shaanxi fiscal intendant, serving concurrently as Xie salt commissioner. He conducted the same basic policy as Fan Xiang but abolished voucher salt taxes in the west and lowered the Xie salt price so that it could compete with cheap smuggled Xixia blue salt. He annually directed salt workers to increase production, which resulted in a glut. Production was suspended for several years. In 1063 he cut the number of regular salters by half, replacing them with temporary workers.

Initially, fearing dwindling prefectural and county salt tax revenues under the policy of merchant trade, [Fan] Xiang calculated the losses [to the prefectures and counties] of government-sold salt money and so allowed them to tax voucher salt to make it up. So the prefectures and counties continued to tax as in the past. In 1061 (Jiayou 6) [Xue] Xiang abolished these charges [on merchants] and memorialized to reduce the selling price of salt in the eight prefectures. The two ponds' salters were annually pressed into performing services in Xiezhou, Hezhongfu, Shanzhou[a], Guozhou, and Qingchengjun; in addition, they suffered other forms of exploitation. So it was decreed to rotate salters [at these locations] every three years.[63]

---

[62] Fan died in the seventh month of 1060. In 1061 Xue Xiang succeeded him as Xie salt military regulator. During his eight-year tenure, Xue improved management, maintained tax collection, and relieved the burden of the salt households. Both Xue and Fan were considered ideal salt administrators (*SS* 328.10583–88). For more on Xue, see also Wang Leiming 1985, 334n4 and 362–63. The fifth and last major glut of Xie salt occurred between 1060 and 1063 under Xue Xiang, when an estimated 500 million catties accumulated (Guo Zhengzhong 1984a, 46). After this date, records are scarce. In the late 1090s the salt lakes flooded and were not repaired for four years, which doubtless relieved over-accumulation. For a largely positive assessment of Fan's policy, particularly its response to supply and demand, and its impact on Song paper money, see Qian Gongbo 1964, 163. For Bao Zheng's assessment, see *XCB* 171.4120 (12/wuxu/1051). For an analysis of Xue Xiang's eight-year Xie salt operation, see Guo Zhengzhong 1990a, 935–40.

[63] The triennial rotation at these locations was actually in practice by 1026 (Tiansheng 4) (*XCB* 104.2410).

Whenever the accumulated tax salt reached over 3,370,000 mats, half [of the normal annual amount] was forgiven. Then the government, seeing how much salt had accumulated, made special provisions to stop seeding salt for a period of one, two, or three years to give the workers relief. Later labor was also reduced, halving the number of pond salters and hiring [temporary] workers in their place. The people of the five prefectures finally had some peace [thanks to Xue Xiang].

In the eleventh century import bans on blue and white salt were to little avail. Xue Xiang was supported in his policies by Wang Anshi.

The Xiqiang tribe came to control profits from blue and white salt produced at the Black and White Ponds. From the time of Li Jiqian's rebellion these salts had not been allowed to cross the border.[64] Before long, however, the prohibition was abolished, then restored again. At the start of the Qianxing period (1022) the emperor decreed that those on the Hedong border who violated the blue and white salt prohibitions were to be sentenced according to Shaanxi policy [i.e., presumably severely]. During the Qingli period (1041–1048) Li Yuanhao submitted money and petitioned [for permission] to sell annually 100,000 piculs of blue and white salt to the local governments. Emperor Renzong felt that this would disrupt policy and rejected [the proposal]. From the time that Fan Xiang deliberated prohibitions on merchant trade in the eight prefectures and made the prohibitions on blue and white salt more severe, the price of government salt rose. Increasing numbers of natives and [Xixia] tribesmen traded blue and white salt, flouting the law and risking the death penalty; they were not willing to stop. During the Zhihe period (1054–1055) the emperor decreed that tribesmen who were sentenced to death for violating the blue and white salt policy instead be banished to an island in the ocean.[65] This was

---

[64] Li Jiqian's rebellion is addressed in the context of smuggled blue and white salt in 8/993 by the assistant fiscal intendant Zheng Wenbao, who supported merchant sales, which he said would reap returns and lead to the defeat of Li Jiqian without a battle (*SHY* 23.23a).

[65] This decree seems to have been prompted by the call of He Zhongli, auxiliary academician of the Longtu Pavilion (*longtuge zhi xueshi*), to ease punishments, on 7/19/1055 (*SHY* 24.1a).

prompted by people joining together to petition on behalf of the violators. A Jiayou period (1056–1063) amnesty permitted banishment to closer areas.[66] From then on, prohibitions were somewhat more lenient.

At the beginning of the Xining period (1068–1077) the emperor decreed that the Huainan fiscal intendant, Zhang Jing[a], should examine *[p. 4420]* the gains and losses of Shaanxi's salt and horse [policies].[67] [Zhang] Jing[a] accused [Xue] Xiang of deceitful reporting, but because Wang Anshi sided with [Xue] Xiang, it was [Zhang] Jing[a] who was punished while [Xue] Xiang was promoted to transport intendant (*fayunshi*) of Jiang, Huai, and other circuits.[68] A remonstrance official (*jianguan*), Fan Chunren,

---

[66] On 1/1/1056, when Renzong fell ill in the Daqing Hall, eunuchs turned to the chief councilor, Wen Yanbo, to help cover up his illness. The court narrowly avoided a number of crises as Wen Yanbo and other high ministers spent night and day in the Forbidden City working to forestall potential rebellion. When the emperor recovered, he issued general pardons and reduced penalties for trading blue and white salt (*SS* 313.10259). Also see McKnight 1981, 73–93, and on the fundamental purpose behind general amnesties, 112–27.

[67] The Song-Xixia salt and horse trade frequently led to tension. In 993 the Song restriction of salt delivery to the Xia provoked an attack by Li Jiqian on Huanzhou. When restrictions were lifted, relations thawed (*SS* 485.13987). When the Xixia occupied Black and White Ponds, Li Yuanhao requested permission to send salt to the Song border, but was refused. The Xia also often complained of being fleeced by horse merchants. When Li Jiqian's son Li Deming was in power, he was taken advantage of by merchants when trading horses and swore to kill them (*MBT* 9.33a).

On 12/guiwei/1070 the pacification commissioner, Han Jiang, memorialized on Shaanxi's Salt and Horse Intendancy, whose vouchers were becoming depreciated (*XCB* 218.5311). The Song was in dire need of army mounts. The northwest breeding pastures occupied 1,000 *qing* (about 15,000 acres) of land and cost 40 million strings annually to maintain, but only produced about 300 horses. In the tenth month of 1068 the emperor sold pearls to purchase horses. Xue Xiang used salt taxes to buy 10,000 head one year (*SS* 328.10586).

[68] Xue Xiang became intendant of Shaanxi horse purchases and inspector of pasture affairs, thanks to Wang Anshi's recommendation (*SS* 328.10588). Zhang Jing[a], who accused Xue Xiang of being out for recognition and profit, came up short with his evidence and so was himself punished (*SS* 328.10587). The office of transport intendant, charged with the flotilla transport of tribute grain, tea, and salt of Huai, Zhe, Jiang, and Hu circuits, was disbanded in 1132, and his duties taken over by fiscal intendants. For the evolution of this position, see *SS* 167.3963–64. The term *caochen* referred to fiscal intendants, and included *du zhuanyunshi*, *zhuanyunshi*, *fushi*, and *panguan*.

criticized these actions and delineated five offenses committed by [Xue] Xiang.[69] But [Xue] Xiang remained in his post. [Fan] then petitioned to establish a sales saltern in Yongxingjun, using 100,000 strings of cash meant for border expenses as a salt voucher fund to be stored at Yongxingjun. Subsequently, the voucher fund was increased to 200,000 strings.

In the 1070s under Shenzong, voucher inflation again occurred; one means to control this inflation was to restrict the number of vouchers issued.

In 1071 (Xining 4) the emperor decreed that Shaanxi follow the exchange note (*jiaozi*) policy of Shu and abolished the sale of vouchers (*chao*).[70] When [officials] pointed out the policy's unfeasibility, he restored the old one.[71] In 1074 (Xining 7) the Secretariat Department (*zhongshu*) deliberated over the many unbacked vouchers issued for Shaanxi salt, which had caused the price to fall. Then when vouchers were exchanged for grain and fodder [merchants again inflated] the prices of [these standard] border purchases. [The Secretariat-Chancellery] petitioned to assign the exchange notes a value equal to their cash value to relieve the emergency. The emperor decreed that Pi Gongbi, Xiong Ben, and Song Di should administer this,

---

[69] Renzong had established the position of remonstrance official, an imperial censor, to eradicate corruption (Wang Leiming 1985, 344n5). Fan Chunren opposed Wang Anshi's reforms. He believed that Xue Xiang's use of salt profits to purchase horses was no different than Sang Hongyang's policy of balanced distribution (*junshufa*), so he asked that the emperor dismiss Wang Anshi (*SS* 314.10281–292, particularly 10284).

[70] Decreed 1/24/1071 (*SHY* 24.5a; *XCB* 219.5329). *Jiaozi* were vouchers awarded for grain and fodder supplies, *chao* were vouchers paid for in cash.

[71] On 2/15/1071 the Secretariat-Chancellery pointed out that restricting merchants to certain destinations had an adverse effect on Xie salt sales, and so, on 3/14/1071 a decree ended the exchange notes program (*SHY* 24.5a–b and *XCB* 221.5381). The 1071 *jiaozi* system was in place for only two months; a second attempt at it in 1074 also ended before long (Guo Zhengzhong 1990a, 941).

On 4/renzi/1072 the emperor said that since the salt and wine monopolies were not to be lifted, they might as well be strictly enforced. Wang Anshi concurred: the benevolence of Tang and Yao could be attained without easing the monopolies. If the emperor wanted to benefit the people, agriculture should be emphasized. If inferior occupations such as trade were not prohibited, agriculture would be harmed (*XCB* 232.5628).

with Zhao Zhan to oversee [the work].[72] Further, 2 million strings of cash from the Inner Palace Treasury (*neizang*) were lent to the Finance Commission,[73] and a State Trade Bureau (*shiyi*) official was dispatched to the four circuits to buy up salt vouchers (*yin*). Qinfeng and Yongxing salt vouchers would continue to be issued at an annual quota of 1,800,000 [strings worth].[74] In 1075 (Xining 8) the Secretariat-Chancellery memorialized on the advantages and disadvantages of Shaanxi salt vouchers (*chao*), as well as [laying out] eight points of a new policy.[75] Basically it stated that capital for the purchase of vouchers was limited and too many vouchers were being issued. When the vouchers could not all be bought up, their value fell and grain became more expensive. Therefore, they should not be issued without limit. When merchants wanted to exchange [them] for cash, and the government would not purchase them, they fell into the hands of *jianbing* [individuals trying to corner the market; in today's parlance, we might call them speculators], and the voucher price dipped even further. When the border was in dire need, [the state] often overissued vouchers, so it was fitting that [sales] salterns be established to stabilize the market price.[76]

---

[72] For the change in responsibilities of these four men, see 6/renchen/1074 (*XCB* 254.6214–15, 6257, 6261–62, 6264–65). At this time, Shaanxi overissued vouchers so there was not enough salt to cover them, and the voucher price tumbled. The court proposed exchange notes to alleviate the situation. Zhao Zhan felt the notes had to be covered by a sufficient amount of capital: "If we overissue empty vouchers, we mislead the people." But since there was disagreement, he did not gain the position and was appointed prefect of Cangzhou instead (*SS* 341.10879).

[73] According to the *XCB* of 11/yisi/1074, the amount was 3 million strings (*XCB* 258.6290).

[74] *XCB* 258.6291 (11/bingwu/1074). In the first month of 1074 the Yongxingjun and Qinfeng investigation commissioner (*chafang*), Li Chengzhi, memorialized that in the 1040s people were allowed to trade Qinzhou[b] salt vouchers and Chuan exchange notes, but over 10,000 strings were still outstanding. He requested to have this pardoned to relieve the border peoples; it was so decreed (*XCB* 249.6072). On 6/jiaxu/1074 it was decreed that because Shaanxi's sales salterns had accumulated two years' worth of salt, they should temporarily halt procurement (*XCB* 254.6207).

[75] According to the *SHY*, intercalary 4/14/1075, it was the Finance Section (*hufang*) within the Secretariat Department that drafted the eight points (*SHY* 24.7a–9a).

[76] In other words, a voucher quota should be set because the funds used to buy them back were limited; this was the first of eight points covered at length on intercalary 4/14/1075 (*SHY* 24.7a and *XCB* 263.6437). The second point: sales salterns were

necessary to stabilize the salt price and prevent merchants from falling victim to speculators, who depressed the price. The succeeding points were not included in the *SS*:

(3) The money for military supplies came from the circuit, while that used to buy salt vouchers came from the court; should all vouchers be absorbed by the market, there would be no loss either for the central or local government.

(4) The voucher price had become depressed due to government neglect; since merchants had already delivered supplies to the border, the State Trade Bureau should buy vouchers back at the depressed market price.

(5) If procurement-sales salterns did not stabilize the voucher price, then military supplies for which vouchers paid would be worth less than face value. The normal value was one voucher per mat of salt. For every one voucher the government bought, merchants bought ten in private; 90 percent of the profits therefore went to merchants, and only 10 percent to the government. Hence, even though the Trade Bureau proposed to buy at the depressed price, it was inadvisable to discard the policy of purchasing at their normal value.

(6) Since procurement-sales salterns purchased vouchers at their normal price, the reduced-price sale at prefectures during emergencies did not cause much loss. The previous case of southeastern salt proved this: the state Trade Bureau bought vouchers at the depressed market price and did not make money; voucher price reflected maneuvers by speculators.

(7) Old vouchers were expected to exchange for the quota figure of 1.66 million strings at mid-year. Though annual sales of salt were estimated to reach 2.2 million strings, excluding Xihe Circuit, which had its own wells and so used little Xie salt, there was not likely to be a 500,000 to 600,000 string increase (by year's end) even with stringent monopoly prohibitions. In some areas there were gluts. Sales figures did not reflect actual salt use. Recently a new [annual] quota of 3 million strings had been set for circuits that also had tribute [tax rice, silk, etc.] to pay. Because Xihe Circuit's share was undetermined and exchange notes remained in circulation, it was deemed unnecessary to set another figure other than actual sales. If any location needed salt it could apply to the Trade Bureau's voucher trading centers by following the procedure for merchant exchange; then merchants could buy vouchers and sell salt at places in need so that smugglers would have no chance [to operate there].

(8) The mishandling of western salt vouchers created inflated prices. Now the state bought at a depressed price and so, too, did the people. If the trading centers at Yongxingjun bought up all the vouchers, it would waste government capital and might cause a lack of funds for new vouchers. This had to be stopped immediately. The actual salt sales money received from Yongxingjun and Qinfeng was 2.2 million strings, excluding Xihe Circuit. The 1.8 million strings worth of vouchers given them was insufficient. If the government also offered old vouchers (in addition to new), then what was the difference between that

Now it was necessary that a quota be established for the number of vouchers issued. The 2,200,000 strings worth of salt actually sold by the two circuits was to be the amount for vouchers: Yongxing Circuit was to issue 815,000 [strings] worth; Qinfeng Circuit, 1,385,000 [strings] worth, including Xihe Circuit's 537,000.[77] Yongxingjun was to dispatch an official to buy back [western Xie salt] vouchers and allocate 100,000 strings of cash annually to [its] Fiscal Intendancy for that buy-back.[78] It also was to persuade people to [come forward] to get credit for exchanging vouchers according to the State Trade Bureau's credit policy. Excess vouchers [now useless in merchant hands] were to be sent to the Xie ponds and destroyed. The emperor decreed that [officials] should act in accordance with this petition but the responsible offices [continued to] distribute vouchers beyond quota just as before. In 1076 (Xining 9) the emperor decreed that the censor (*yushi*) should impeach the [offending] Shaanxi officials. The Finance Commission was forbidden to issue vouchers beyond quota.[79]

A merchant distribution procedure was proposed in the face of abuses and the encroachment of government sales in merchant sales areas.

In 1077 (Xining 10) the Finance Commission stated:

> Abuses of the salt policy are due to Xihe Circuit overissuing vouchers, making the [voucher] price fall and the fodder and grain prices rise. Furthermore, in what are supposed to be merchant sales districts east, west, and south of the

---

and issuing new additional vouchers? Instead of charging extra fees, it was better to sell vouchers based on a monthly quota and to observe the "flying money" policy (*SHY* 24.7a–8b; *XCB* 263.6437–39).

[77] Xihe Circuit underwent numerous changes: at times it was not an administrative unit at all. It may have been located near Xizhou in Qinfeng Circuit (*SS* 87.2162).

[78] Western salt was Xie salt that had been transported to twelve prefectures in southern Henan and northern Hubei; merchants were allowed to provision the front, then transport [salt] to Shaanxi and Xixia. Eastern salt was sold in the three capitals and in Chenzhou, Yingzhou[b], Xuzhou[b], Ruzhou, Mengzhou[b], Zhengzhou, Huazhou, Caozhou, and Shanzhou[b] (Wang Leiming 1985, 335–36nn 2, 3).

[79] Decreed 2/6/1076 (*SHY* 24.9a). On 11/guihai/1076 the emperor decreed that the Finance Commission ministers, recently engaged in discussing the Shaanxi salt voucher policy, were to present its advantages and disadvantages as soon as possible (*XCB* 279.6821).

three circuits *[p. 4421]*, the government also sells, disrupting merchant participation. The salt policy should be changed now and government sales abolished. Old vouchers, collected and stamped, as well as old salt that has already been distributed [among merchants] must follow the rule of additional payments (*jia'na*): The government should buy up all old vouchers and merchants must report their sales of already distributed salt by a deadline. [At that point] a new price will be reckoned, the [number of] salt mats stamped, and a counterfoil given. Under the old policy, vouchers for one mat of eastern or southern salt cost 3,500 [cash]; vouchers for one mat of western salt ran 1,000 less than that. The government should buy up these vouchers completely. But first they must be checked and recorded by the proper officials at Xiezhou's salterns, and then merchants can proceed to sell. For salt that has already been requested, a deadline will be set according to the merchants' desired destination. For eastern and southern salt, add 2,500 cash per mat [worth of vouchers], while for western salt, add 3,000 cash per mat [worth of vouchers, for changing old vouchers to new]. Vouchers must be exchanged by the deadline. Government sales in the two regions [Qinfeng and Yongxingjun circuits] must be abolished. Salt sold by the Intendancy (*tijusi*) shall be marketed at the new price and cash received is to be used to purchase old vouchers. Merchants wishing to exchange [old vouchers for new] are allowed to do so. The government shall stamp and record according to the law. Merchant sales areas all have one official [in charge]. Mats of salt [in inventory] shall be reported within ten days, after that the extra [*jia'na*] fee [for old unsold salt] will be charged if necessary and the vouchers stamped [accordingly] and recorded. New vouchers are to be given and old vouchers can be used to pay the extra fee.

All of this was implemented. In other designated government sales areas, the State Trade Bureau also charged an extra fee for the purchase of salt.

Changes in the Xie salt administration in the eleventh century are recapitulated.

According to the old system, places north and south of the [Yellow] River, west of [Jingdongxi Circuit's] Puzhou and Caozhou, and east of [Qinfeng Circuit's] Qinzhou[b] and Fengzhou (Map 9) all consumed Xie salt.[80] From the reign of Renzong (1022–1063), Xie salt was sold by

---

[80] The Chengdufu Circuit tea official noted on 6/22/1078 that Xie salt was also imported into Sichuan. Merchant sales of Xie salt there, however, were adversely affected by the overissuing of vouchers (*SHY* 24.16b).

merchants; the government did not monopolize it. In the Xining period (1068–1077) the Trade Bureau began to impose the monopoly upon Kaifeng, Caozhou, and Puzhou prefectures.[81] In 1075 (Xining 8) the assistant minister of the high court of justice (*dali sicheng*), Zhang Jingwen, began government sales of Xie salt, and so the following all practiced such: Kaifengfu's Yangwu, Suanzao, Fengqiu, Kaocheng, Dongming, Baima, Zhongmou, Chenliu, Changyuan, Zuocheng, and Weicheng as well as [prefectures in other circuits, including] Caozhou, Puzhou, Chanzhou, Huaizhou, Jizhou[b], Shanzhou[a], Xiezhou, Hezhongfu, and so on. Before long, a proposal that merchant sales be instituted was once again adopted. So merchant sales were implemented in Tangzhou, Dengzhou[b], Xiangzhou[b], Junzhou[a], Fangzhou[a], Shangzhou, Caizhou, Yingzhou[c], Suizhou[a], Jinzhou[a], Jinzhou[b], Jiangzhou[b], Guozhou, Chenzhou[b], Xuzhou[b], Ruzhou, Yingzhou[b], Xizhou, Xijing, and Xinyangjun. As for the counties under the jurisdiction of the imperial capital (*jixian*), as well as Chanzhou, Caozhou, Puzhou, Huaizhou, Weizhou[c], Jizhou[b], Shanzhou[a], Xiezhou, Tongzhou[a], Huazhou[a], Shanzhou[b], Hezhongfu, the Southern Capital, and Heyang, the Xie Salt Intendancy was ordered to transport and sell there. It was also decreed that the Finance Commission should study the pros and cons [of government versus merchant sales].[82]

---

[81] By 4/jiashen/1074 it was decreed that since Minzhou in Qinfeng Circuit was short of grain because so few merchants had come to provision, the Finance Commission was to examine the southeastern salt voucher policy and the western salt policy for their long-term advantages and disadvantages (*XCB* 252.6159).

[82] See *XCB* 274.6717–18 (4/guichou/1076). Some idea of logistics of salt transport can be gained from a memorial by the Imperial Transport Intendancy (*nianyunsi*) of Sanmen (Yongxing) and Baipo (Jingxibei), both anachronistic Southern Song place names. This intendancy was charged with government convoy transport to the capital: On 2/xinhai/1083 the Imperial Intendancy requested a loan of 300 boats from the [Xie] Transport Intendancy to transport monopoly goods, including salt and tea, up the Si River (a tributary of the Luo River, in today's Henan), where the Imperial Intendancy's boats would take the goods on to Hebei. Later, however, the assistant transport intendant, Jiang Zhiqi, stated that Bian Canal convoy boats [presumably of the Xie Transport Intendancy] had had an annual construction target of 1,700 boats, which had recently been reduced to only 748; money saved on construction and materials was to go into reserves. The [Xie] Intendancy transported 6.2 million piculs but had at its disposal only 700-odd boats, so it asked that it be

The government forced the populace to purchase salt in order to dispose of it. Finance commissioner Shen Kuo initially supported the government distribution scheme endorsed by Wang Anshi, but expediently reversed his position after Wang lost his post in 1074.

When the salt price rose, people refused to buy it, so a quota was imposed whereby the people had to purchase [a certain amount] according to their wealth and property value. Informants were encouraged with a substantial reward from a violator's [confiscated] property. Those who bought government salt and did not consume it all, but held it for some time, were considered [violators] of the anti-smuggling regulations. [Because of these impositions] the people grew resentful. According to the old salt policy *[p. 4422]*, each mat was [priced at] six strings; by this time each was worth only a little over two strings. Hence merchants would not bring in grain and the border stores became depleted. The Shaanxi fiscal intendant, Pi Gongbi, was summoned to deliberate.[83] [Pi] Gongbi emphatically stated that government sales were not feasible, but Shen Kuo, then finance commissioner, was not to be swayed.[84] Wang Anshi supported [Zhang] Jingwen's policy.[85] To ingratiate himself with Wang, [Shen] Kuo argued that merchant sales annually cost the government over 200,000 strings of

---

pardoned from apportioning its boats to the Baipo Imperial Transport Intendancy; the emperor agreed (*XCB* 333.8016).

[83] *XCB* 280.6869 (2/wushen/1077).

[84] On 2/25/1077 the Finance Commission relayed the conclusions of Pi Gongbi, then also high commissioner of Xie salt (*zhizhi Xieyan shi*). Because Xihe Circuit's vouchers were overdistributed, their price had fallen, and that of grain and fodder had risen. Merchant-sales prefectures were also subject to government sales, so merchants were not very interested in the trade there. Government sales had to be cut back. An extensive passage on proposals for handling southeastern salt followed (*SHY* 24.13a–14a; *XCB* 280.6869–70).

Shen Kuo, as magistrate of Ningguo (in present-day Anhui), paid particular attention to water conservancy and agriculture. He participated in Wang Anshi's reforms and became deputy finance commissioner. He is also known for his wide-ranging scientific interests and studies.

[85] On 3/wuyin/1077 Zhou Yin, the attendant censor (*shiyushi*), memorialized that salt commissioner Zhang Jingwen had raised prices without authority and treated the populace harshly. Zhou Yin asked for his dismissal, but Zhang was still in office as of 10/13/1077 (*XCB* 281.6889).

cash.[86] When [Wang] Anshi left office, [Shen] Kuo was [still] finance commissioner; and he now claimed that government sales ought to be abolished.[87] So merchant sales were allowed in Heyang, Tongzhou[a], Huazhou[a], Xiezhou, Hezhong, Shanfu [likely Shanzhou[b]], Chenliu, Yongqiu, Xiangyi, Zhongmou, Guancheng, Weishi, Yanling, Fugou, Taikang, Xianping, and Xinzheng. In areas whose [merchant-generated] revenue fell below the level of official sales, the government would again undertake distribution. So Chanzhou, Puzhou, Jizhou[b], Shanzhou[a], Caozhou, Huaizhou, Nanjingfu, and the nine counties of Yangwu, Suanzao, Fengqiu, Kaocheng, Dongming, Baima, Changyuan, Zuocheng, and Weicheng all returned to government sales as before.[88] The emperor decreed that merchants should enter the capital and sell all their salt to the Trade Bureau. Each mat could be adjusted down in price by more than 1,000 [cash]. People were required to purchase their salt at the Trade Bureau; private transactions with merchants were to be reported and the salt confiscated.

---

[86] On 2/wushen/1077 Shen Kuo elaborated on abuses and remedies: (1) vouchers were being issued beyond what was needed, leading to their depreciation; (2) [expensive] eastern salt and the more competitive western salt should be priced equally to prevent manipulation by clerks and soldiers; (3) issuing of vouchers was to be assigned to the Finance Commission exclusively; (4) the price of vouchers sold by different departments was to be the same to prevent hoarding (*XCB* 280.6871–72). See also *XCB* 281.6885 (3/bingyin/1077).

[87] In 1074 Wang lost his position as chief councilor and became prefect of Jianningfu (Wang Leiming 1985, 337n4). He was recalled in 1078 but forced out of power again in 1085 by Sima Guang after the death of Shenzong. At that time Shaanxi salt profits had fallen by half.

On 5/bingwu/1082 Shen Kuo, now military intendant of Fu[zhou[a]] and Yan[zhou[b]]'s [Yongxingjun] Circuit, memorialized at length on a strategy for pacifying the nomads. [That pacification] might come to a desert battle, and then there would be dangers of overextended supply lines, and taking this initiative would be exhausting. As long as the regions south of the mountains were controlled, there would be grain for the troops, pastureland for the people, and salt ponds for the merchants. In Shen's view, if blue and white salt ponds fell under Song control, there would be no need for government sales of Xie salt, and salt taxes could be collected [from merchants to be directly applied to] frontier needs (*XCB* 326.7857–58). Shen Kuo here reversed his earlier position advocating government sales; he now insisted on their cancellation.

[88] *XCB* 281.6884–85 (3/bingyin/1077).

Pi Gongbi focused on merchant distribution to aid the defense effort.

Pi Gongbi's salt policy took into account the amount of salt distributed from the two ponds over time and set the [sales] quota at 2,300,000 strings annually.[89] There was also an order to establish seven sales salterns at the capital to buy back eastern and southern salt vouchers. The Trade Bureau calculated a need of 593,000 strings [to fund this program]. Since the Finance Commission was short on cash, it had [the seven sales salterns] sell vouchers [to merchants] for western salt. Purchasers would have to pay 30 percent [of the value of their old vouchers] in cash and the remaining 70 percent could be traded to get new [western salt] vouchers, according to the [new voucher] price set for the border. Consequently, [the government] could collect old vouchers circulating among the people and new vouchers could easily be sold [for cash]. The emperor decreed to adopt this proposal.[90] [Pi] Gongbi also petitioned to restore Fan Xiang's old policy [with the aim of] equalizing market prices. It was decreed that a loan of 300,000 strings be allotted to the Finance Commission to buy vouchers in the capital.

Before this, Xie salt [distribution] had been divided between eastern and western sales districts, with western salt sold in scattered points along the border. Because border prefectures took on so many vouchers in their efforts to procure [needed] fodder and grain, vouchers and salt prices there fell. Thus the prices for the eastern and western [sales] territories diverged. [Under Pi Gongbi] the price of western salt was now to be increased to be comparable to eastern salt and thus voucher values would be equalized. The annual income increase was approximately 120,000 strings. No longer did a price differential exist between east and west. The restrictions on western salt were abolished.[91] The fiscal intendant, Pi Gongbi, petitioned to increase the former quota for Xie pond salt vouchers (2,200,000 strings) by 100,000 to aid border purchases; then it was again bolstered to 2,420,000 [in the late

---

[89] The Finance Commission memorialized about this on 4/renyin/1077 (*XCB* 281.6894).

[90] The Finance Commission memorialized about this on 4/guimao/1077 (*XCB* 281.6895).

[91] This price stabilization policy of Pi Gongbi's was discussed on 2/bingchen/1079 (*XCB* 296.7211–12).

1070s]. Merchants who had already requested western salt were ordered to pay additional fees in adherence to the new [price equalization] policy.[92] In 1080 (Yuanfeng 3) the Finance Commission commended Zhang Jingwen for making Xie salt sales profitable, and he was promoted and awarded silk.[93]

[p. 4423] The next year (1081) the provisional (*quan*) Shaanxi fiscal intendant, Li Ji, stated:

> Before the new policy was implemented, voucher price depended on the number [of vouchers] the concerned office issued. That number was set with the implementation of the new policy. From the winter of 1077 (Xining 10) until the end of 1080 (Yuanfeng 3), [vouchers for] more than 1,770,000 mats were issued. The salt ponds, however, only produced 1,175,000 mats. Over 590,000 mats worth of extra vouchers remained in the hands of the public and private sectors. There could not but be a decline in [the voucher] price.[94]

So, the Finance Commission was ordered to stop issuing vouchers. In 1082 (Yuanfeng 5), because the Ministry of Finance still felt that there were too many vouchers in circulation, [the court] halved the annually budgeted 2 million [strings worth of] vouchers for Shaanxi's army. But in the end,

---

[92] This recounting appears in a decree of 2/17/1079 (*SHY* 24.17b–18a).

[93] Decreed 6/25/1080 (*SHY* 24.19b).

[94] This statement was made on 4/12/1081 by Li Ji, then concurrently Xie salt commissioner. He requested a small cut in the voucher quota to help stabilize prices (*SHY* 24.20b–21a). *XCB* (312.7562) gives a second date: the end of 1079 (Yuanfeng 2). On 1/bingshen/1080 the emperor referred to the problem of depreciating vouchers, noting that even an infusion of 5 million strings would be unable to ameliorate abuses. If profits were not 100 percent, the policy should not be changed. The emperor concurred that able men like Guan Zhong of Qi, Sang Hongyang in the Han, and Liu Yan in the Tang had barely maintained the policy of balanced distribution, and inferior policymakers had certainly not succeeded. Even though the younger generation might be unhappy about the change, they should wait and see (*XCB* 296.7202–3). On 1/guichou/1081 Li Ji, as Shaanxi fiscal intendant, memorialized on the poverty of the region. In the nearly three years that he administered Xie pond, not a bit was discarded so over 200,000 strings had been amassed for local use and the state was not burdened (*XCB* 311.7542). Back on 7/gengchen/1079 Li Ji had reported on inflation of voucher prices while wealthy merchants struck it rich. The emperor consequently decreed to set three deadlines per year for [the exchange] of Shaanxi vouchers (*XCB* 299.7271).

voucher oversupply [meant that the government] was unable to stabilize the price.[95]

In the late 1080s, under Zhezong, the Xie Salt Commission was able to establish its own turf; it required that all vouchers to be returned to it and not to the circuit Fiscal Intendancy.

In 1086 (Yuanyou 1) the Ministry of Finance and the Xie salt commissioner proposed the following:

Eight prefectures: Yanzhou[b], Qingzhou, Weizhou[b], Yuanzhou[a], Huanzhou, Zhenrongjun, Baoanjun, and Deshunjun—all government sales areas—have a quota of 15,500 mats [each]. Merchants shall deliver payment to these eight prefectures' Trade Bureaus, where they will be given vouchers, as was done under Fan Xiang's old policy. Any money the government owes the merchants will be paid from the Fiscal Intendancy's annual voucher fund. The money [made by the Trade Bureaus] will go to the Fiscal Intendancy for buy-back purposes. One official above the rank of gentleman-for-rendering service (*chenguulang*) is to manage offices in the capital in charge of trading salt vouchers for cash and deliver payments to the treasury of the Salt Directorate.[96] If any Xie salt vouchers are submitted, they are all to be turned over to our [Xie salt] office, not given to the Fiscal Intendancy. No other offices are permitted to engage in [Xie voucher] trade; even if there is a decree [allowing this, any such requests] must be repetitioned. Vouchers bought must be sent to our office. If vouchers circulating among the people are too few, the circuit's cash should be used to issue more. The Ministry of Finance should be petitioned for permission to sell them.[97]

The emperor approved, and subsequently 27,000 strings of cash in transaction charges were collected against Xie salt the merchants brought in.

---

[95] The ministry's statement was made 8/3/1082 (*SHY* 24.22b; *XCB* 329.7915). On 2/gengshen/1083 the Ministry of Personnel noted that Hao Zongchen, former sheriff (*wei*) of Anhua County in Qingzhou (Yongxingjun Circuit), had apprehended a salt smuggler, Li Ping, and captured twenty catties of blue salt. For this feat he was to be granted the first class of reward (*XCB* 333.8020).

[96] The *chenguulang* was a prestige title (*sanguan*), one of twenty-nine civil titles graded from 1b down to 9b, and used before 1080. For details, see Kracke 1978, ix–xiii, x–xii.

[97] This memorial was presented 10/3/1086 (*SHY* 24.27b–28a; *XCB* 389.9452–53).

These revenues were added to reserves for purchase of vouchers in the imperial city.[98] The price of salt distributed through the provisioning system increased or decreased depending on conditions, just as it had with the voucher system in Xihe. In Chanzhou, Huaizhou, Huazhou[b], and Yangwu, the salt price was set at 8,200 cash [per mat]. At the time many Shaanxi inhabitants were privately refining saltpeter into crystals in a process called "pouring the saltpeter" (*daoxiao*); the result closely resembled Xie salt. In 1096 (Shaosheng 3) the military regulator Sun Lu reported this. It was decreed that offenders be punished by a reduced degree of the smuggling law.[99]

Initially, under Shenzong (1068–1085) the government undertook the sale of Xie salt, but in Jingxi it instituted merchant sales. When Shen Xiyan was fiscal intendant, he reverted [Jingxi] to government distribution. He petitioned to borrow 200,000 strings from the ever-normal [granary] reserves (*changpingqian*) to buy Xie salt and sell it within [Jingxi] Circuit. Xie salt at that time in the hands of merchants was bought up by the central government at a profit. The merchants suffered from this. When Zhezong ascended the throne, a palace *[p. 4424]* censor, Huang Jiang, impeached [Shen] Xiyan. In 1086 (Yuanyou 1) Jingxi revived the old system of merchant sales, but the government also continued selling there.[100] In 1098

---

[98] The Shaanxi Circuit Xie salt commissioner stated this on 3/26/1087 (*SHY* 24.28a–b).

[99] This was reported by Sun Lu on 11/2/1096 and answered by the Chengdufu, Lizhou[a], and Shaanxi tea bureaus (*SHY* 24.32a–b). Penalties for smuggling depended upon the region and amount of salt involved. Illegal production was generally considered more serious than illegal sales. The amount of salt illegally produced which would incur the death penalty was gradually increased (i.e., the law relaxed); at about this time in the Northern Song, at least 100 catties or more would have been grounds for execution.

[100] See the Ministry of Finance statement of intercalary 2/bingwu/1086 (*XCB* 369.8905–6).
On 2/dingyou/1091 the Xie salt sales official, Sun Jiong, memorialized that counties under the jurisdiction of the Western Capital, Heyang, and Zhengzhou were not government sales areas. He requested that local governments there be ordered to try violators according to the regulations of his office (*XCB* 455.10906).
On 7/yichou/1091 the high commissioner of Xie salt and the Three Ministries stated that the Shaanxi High Commission of Xie Salt had been an independent organ but later the fiscal intendant took over its administration. They felt the lack of

(Yuanfu 1) government sales [in Jingxi] were finally banned.[101] In the counties of Yongxingjun north of the Wei River, including Gaoling, Liyang, and Jingyang, just as in the six prefectures including Tongzhou[a] and Huazhou[a], the government continued to sell salt, but offices were prohibited from buying Xie salt at the Exchange Bureau and trading it for gain.[102]

Between 1077 and 1080 production had reached 1.175 million mats, but under Huizong in 1098, after bad weather damaged the ponds, it took decades to reach this level again.

Soon after, floods damaged the Xie ponds, so the small-pond salt of Hezhongfu's Xiezhou, the earth salt of Tongzhou[a] and Huazhou[a], the rock salt (*shiyan*) of Jiezhou, and the government well salt of Tongyuanjun and Minzhou were allowed to be sold within their own circuits, while Jingdong and Hebei salt also circulated.[103] In 1100 (Yuanfu 3) the emperor

---

an independent administration would harm the salt policy and requested that a high commissioner of Xie salt be reappointed; this was approved (*XCB* 461.11024).

On 7/22/1091 the reviewing policy advisor, Fan Zuyu, argued that when Fan Zongjie was high commissioner of Xie salt and implemented government distribution, many abuses occurred. When Fan Xiang became Shaanxi judicial intendant, and concurrently high commissioner of Xie salt, he eradicated all of Fan Zongjie's abuses and revenues increased. In this debate Han Qi and Bao Zheng supported Fan Xiang. Subsequently Fan Xiang concurrently became Shaanxi fiscal intendant, but when Li Can replaced him, revenues fell. So Zhang Fangping and Bao Zheng requested that Fan be reappointed. Both Fan and his successor Xue Xiang were capable administrators and concurrently held the position of intendant. This showed that the success of salt matters depended on the man and not on the position. If a separate Intendancy were established, it would not have the clout to influence the prefectures if its power were weak. If it were too powerful, it would be another burden on the prefectures, compete for revenues, and seek to secure its own interests (*XCB* 461.11024–25).

On 7/dinghai/1091 the Ministry of Finance memorialized that 13,000 mats annually sold by the Xie Salt Intendancy could not be moved by the one-year deadline, so an extension of an additional year was granted (*XCB* 462.11046).

[101] 4/11/1098 (*SHY* 24.32b).

[102] This according to a decree of 8/bingshen/1088 (*XCB* 413.10041).

[103] Tongyuanjun was later known as Gongzhou[b] in Qinfeng Circuit (*SS* 87.2164). It neighbored on Minzhou and encompassed the "Salt Stream Stockade" (Yanchuanzhai). See the Three Ministries' statement of 10/1/1098 and decree of 10/17/1098 (*SHY* 24.32b). With the Xie ponds in ruins, pond salt from Hezhongfu and Xiezhou, earth salt of Shangzhou and Huazhou, rock salt of Jiezhou, and well salt of

decreed that Ma Cheng, the Shaanxi assistant fiscal intendant and military regulator of Xie salt, hasten the preparation of wooden rafts [for transport to locales] in Shaanxi and Hedong, and that Xue Sichang should repair the Xiezhou salt ponds.

In 1102 (Chongning 1) [workers] repaired, irrigated, and sowed sections (*qiyan*) of salt ponds north and south of Xiezhou's Jiawa, thereby producing over 1,782,700 catties of salt.[104] A large salt marsh east of Xieliang [near present-day Linyixian (Shanxi)], which stretched for over 100 *li,* generated hundreds of thousands [of catties] annually. From the beginning of the Yuanfu period (1098–1100), [however,] heavy rains had damaged the ponds. It was decided to repair them. In 1105 (Chongning 4) pond restoration was completed. Altogether over 2,400 sections were built and officialdom celebrated.[105] A eunuch, Wang Zhongqian, had managed the corvee work.[106] His aim was to achieve high tax revenues. Critics pointed out that the depth of brine in Xie Pond was [normally] just one foot. Under the scorching heat of the sun, fanned by the southern winds, it quickly became salt, and its profits were reliably plentiful. Should one aim for revenues [by producing even greater quantities of salt] beyond quota, one could disregard the timely winds and sun and add extra water, but the salt collected would be bitter and unpalatable.

Cai Jing attempted to consolidate salt affairs under the central government and extend the voucher system. He pushed a number of devices that filled the state coffers and would be imitated in the Southern Song. One was to require merchants to pay several cash surcharges before receiving a load of salt; another was to regularly issue new vouchers so the government could extract additional money from merchants who were forced to trade in their old vouchers at a loss.[107]

Tongyuanjun and Minzhou could be traded in Shaanxi (*XCB* 503.11969). On 1/jisi/1099 it was decreed that since the Xiezhou ponds had sustained rain damage, a professor of imperial sacrifices be dispatched there to conduct sacrifices (*XCB* 505.12044). On intercalary 9/gengchen/1099 the right policy chief memorialized for 100 guards and a supervisor to protect the ponds (*XCB* 516.12274–75).

[104] "Section eyes" (*qiyan*) likely refers to salt fields or irregularities on their surface.

[105] *SHY* 24.39b (6/11/1105).

[106] Wang was Shaanxi Xie salt intendant (*SHY* 24.39b, 10/19/1109).

[107] A major blow to Xie salt distribution was the natural disaster that befell the ponds at the end of the eleventh century. But even more critical was Cai Jing's policy to

From the beginning of Huizong's Chongning reign period (1102–1106) policymakers felt the constant changes in the voucher policy not only confused [merchant-distributors] and deprived the government of its ability to set prices, they also burdened merchants with the cost of travel. They begged to have Fan Xiang's old policy restored and not lightly changed. Even though this petition was authorized, before long [it changed when] Cai Jing proposed:

> Merchants who transport Hebei and Jingdong powder salt to the capital and Jingxi pay the government 6,000 cash per bag, but the [state's] investment [per bag] is less than 1,000. Thus, in a short time, returns collected have reached 2 million strings. Should salt be delivered to Shaanxi [at merchant expense], returns will definitely double.

It was suggested that Han Dunli and others be dispatched to carry out the program in the circuits. When pond production was restored, [Cai] Jing still wanted merchants to sell northeast powder salt in Xie salt territories. He anticipated that consequently the Monopoly Goods Bureau would take in tremendous amounts in cash payments, and then he could claim credit for [the surplus] himself. So he had new vouchers for Xie salt circulate only in Shaanxi. In 1106 (Chongning 5) it was so decreed:

> The voucher policy has long had the confidence of the people. "Flying money" bills of exchange (*feiqian*) have enriched the state [*p. 4425*] greatly. By comparing this with previous methods, we have learned clearly its advantages and disadvantages. Now we shall set identification numbers for verification and allow the exchange of new vouchers for Xie salt. First, 5 million strings [worth of these new vouchers] have been allocated to Shaanxi and Hedong only for purpose of letting merchants there buy them. Merchants may go to the Monopoly Goods Bureau to exchange [old Shaanxi (Xie) vouchers] for southeastern salt vouchers. Those paying a surcharge (*tieshu*) of 40 percent in cash [go before] those paying the old 30 percent; those paying 50 percent [go before] those paying 40 percent. Furthermore, they must also carry a number of old vouchers. Those who pay 40 percent in cash are to carry 50 percent [in old vouchers]; those paying 50 percent are to carry 60 percent. Those not

---

move sea salt into former pond salt distribution areas. The following text shows him pushing to attract merchants to deliver sea salt to the pond salt center, Shaanxi.

wishing to pay surcharges are to [be given] 20 percent less [cash] than the old voucher value.

The cash-for-vouchers rate for salt merchants differed greatly depending on the distance they traveled, and vouchers were priced more cheaply on the frontier than in the interior as an incentive to trade at the frontier. At the Shaanxi border in the early eleventh century, for instance, a mat of salt cost only 2,640 cash; somewhat to the interior it was 3,080 cash; at Xiezhou and other prefectures close to the production sites it ran at least 4,400 cash.[108] Such a policy, however, led to merchant profits exceeding government surpluses and a decline in state revenue.

Before this, because rich merchants had controlled profits by manipulating [prices] to their own advantage, [the court] reduced the value of vouchers, increasing the cost of buying salt at the border [i.e., more vouchers were necessary to get the same amount of salt]. In 1105 (Chongning 4), even though the price of vouchers had been reduced, prefectures with provisional needs further raised the price of salt to merchants. Merchants holding [the cheap] vouchers [chose this time to] exchange them [for now high-priced salt] and reaped great profits. Then the emperor decreed that southeastern powder salt was to be offered for old Shaanxi [i.e., Xie salt] vouchers. Every 100 strings [worth of vouchers for powder salt] would require a payment of 30 percent in cash and 70 percent in old vouchers. Later, he again decreed to reduce the Shaanxi voucher price, [but] anyone who lowered [the voucher price to less than] 5,000 [cash] was to be tried according to the law.

When Cai Jing's surcharge system developed problems, the new chief councilor proposed restoring the former policy, giving merchants a deadline for resolving payments and exchanging old vouchers.

By 1110 (Daguan 4), when Zhang Shangying was chief councilor (*xiang*), [he led] deliberations about reviving the Xie salt trade according to the old policy and no longer allowing northeastern salt into Xie areas.[109]

---

[108] Kawahara 1979, 343n16.

[109] In the fifth month of 1110 Cai Jing lost the chief councilorship; in the sixth month Zhang Shangying assumed Cai's post of right executive of the Department of Ministries. Concurrently he was executive of the Secretariat, and he changed Cai's salt policy.

Soon after, an official suggested that since the Xie ponds had been revived, the old voucher policy should be observed. Merchants who had bought northeastern salt should register and receive a government refund within three days. Evaders were to be dealt with according to the smuggling laws. Before the Xie salt became available, the government would distribute its stocks of northeastern salt but halt [that distribution] when the Xie salt arrived.[110] Paid vouchers for which [northeast] salt had been disbursed were to be destroyed; those for which salt had not yet been disbursed were to await a separate decision. [Xie salt vouchers] continued to be sold in the capital and also in Zhengzhou, Zhongmou, Kaifengfu's Xiangfu and Yangwuxian. In Jingxibei's Chenzhou[b], Yingzhou[b], Caizhou, and Xinyang-jun where Wang Zhongqian petitioned for circulation of pond salt, [sales of vouchers for sea salt] had been temporarily halted. Merchants who had paid for northeastern salt destined for the Eastern Capital [where Wang now blocked its sale] and who had not yet taken possession of product were to receive instructions [about how to proceed] wherever they had gotten to by the time their [northeastern salt] vouchers could no longer be exchanged. Those who had arrived in the capital but not yet traded [their salt] could sell the entire load to the Salt Directorate. Shop merchants were permitted to purchase salt for retail sales.

Whether the face value of vouchers would fluctuate according to need or be set by law was another bone of contention, particularly since Cai Jing repeatedly manipulated the voucher system, and the voucher price affected grain provisioning. The Preface to the Songshi's economic monograph alludes to ministers who looked only at the short term, trying out then abolishing policies; this may well have been a commentary on Cai Jing's actions.

In 1111 (Zhenghe 1) the emperor decreed that Shaanxi vouchers were to be bought at face value and that officials who raised or cut that price were to be judged as having transgressed regulations. Before long, vouchers were in wider circulation in Shaanxi. Although they had a set face value of 6,000 copper cash, when the voucher price was higher, grain provisioning increased; when the voucher price was level, grain provisioning decreased.

---

[110] Presented 8/2/1110. It included the office to which proceeds should go: the Fiscal Intendancy, the reserves, or some other office; see *SHY* 25.1b–2a.

[Since] Shaanxi only had iron cash in use, when [the voucher price] was limited to 6,000 cash, one salt voucher per mat brought in a mere bushel (*hudou*) of 6,000 iron coins. This significantly lessened the state's income, so price changes were allowed to accommodate changing needs.

In 1112 (Zhenghe 2) Cai Jing returned to power. He continued to [*p. 4426*] alter the policy, and useless vouchers [accumulated] like rotten pulp. In 1116 (Zhenghe 6) when salt production at the two ponds flourished, more workers were hired to redouble the harvest effort and given rewards. When they subsequently produced red salt (*hongyan*), all officialdom celebrated, and the Xie salt military regulator Li Bailu and others were bestowed rewards according to rank.[111]

In 1117 (Zhenghe 7) it was decided to circulate Xie salt again. At the time Tong Guan, the pacification commissioner (*xuanfu*) of Guan and He, was actually in charge of it.[112] The emperor decreed that the government

---

[111] "Red salt" may be what Shen Kuo in *Mengxi bitan* referred to as "deep red salt" (*jiangyan*), likely a salt-like crystal with iron content. Finding red salt was considered a lucky sign. On 7/bingyin/1099 the Jingyuan (later a part of Qinfeng Circuit) military intendant, Zhang Jie, memorialized that while inspecting for military camp sites, they had discovered a pond with a circumference of ten *li* near the river at Jianwei from which red and white salts were extracted (*XCB* 513.12202). Jingyuan Circuit for a time included Jingzhou, Yuanzhou[a], Weizhou[b], Huizhou[b], and Yizhou[c], but was finally eliminated (*SS* 87.2157, 2159). On 8/xinsi/1098 a Jingyuan Circuit official memorialized that the construction of Jianweizhai (a fort or encampment at Jianwei) had been completed; it was decreed to call it Dingshuzhai (*XCB* 514.12216).

The appearance of red salt noted in the *SS* took place in the sixth month of 1116 (Wang Leiming 1985, 342n1). Shen Kuo described mountain waters that collected in Xie Pond, which never overflowed, even when it rained continuously, and never dried up, even during drought. The pond water was red and commonly called "the blood of Chi You." Zhang Qiyun believed that the Yellow Emperor had fought against Chi You was for no other reason than the salt of Xie Pond. The red of the water reflected the density of the salt (Qian Gongbo 1964, 160). Under 8/8/1111 the *SHY* also records that production of red salt that year was double the average. Consequently, Li Bailu, the Jixian Library compiler (*jixiandian xiuzhuan*) as well as Shaanxi Xie salt commissioner, was promoted, and the Xiezhou prefect and prefectural vice-administrator earned a reduction of time to their next evaluation (*SHY* 25.5b).

[112] The *xuanfushi* was not a regular official position but a very powerful one; it was charged with announcing awesome occurrences, pacifying border areas, and leading

would collect and pay for northeastern salt currently circulating in Xie salt areas. It was to be exchanged for commodities of equal value in the capital, while outside the capital the State Trade Bureau would handle it. Northeastern salt was to be traded according to the previous Xie salt policy [i.e., such salt circulating within expanded Xie sales regions had to be surrendered to the government]. Those who did not come forth to report [their sea salt stocks] would be dealt with according to the salt smuggling law.

Then in 1118 (Chonghe 1) the emperor formally decreed to restore the old Xie salt distribution program. But within a year the Monopoly Goods Bureau's annual revenues had fallen by several million strings. In addition, the voucher price had dropped and the purchase [of provisions] was discontinued. The Three Ministries met to discuss the issue and [Tong] Guan subsequently petitioned to leave the Xie salt administration. Shortly thereafter, the Three Ministries memorialized:

> Formerly, in northeastern salt regions merchants trading Xie salt had to complete their sales within a certain time limit. Salt that had not been sold by the deadline was to be transported [back] to Xie salt regions. Those who disobeyed were sentenced according to the smuggling law.

The capital and Jingxi again established posts to supervise [the trade]. Initially, during the Chongning period (1102–1106), because salt trade benefited only the local region, Xie salt was only traded within its own circuit. But because surpluses [from sales of] southeastern sea salt were plentiful, it was traded in several circuits. Now, when Xie salt was once more distributed [in other areas], merchants suffered losses from the changes [in policy], so the old policy was revived.[113] Taking into account merchant

---

the military of one or more circuits. Usually the post was held by the assisting councilor of state (*zhizheng*), concurrently a commander.

[113] At this time the debate concerned whether to expand sea salt sales in Xie distribution areas or expand pond salt sales. With the expansion of pond salt sales, merchants engaged in sea salt sales were forced to follow complex and strict regulations, including processing at the capital's Monopoly Goods Bureau, then going on to sea salt distribution areas outside the capital; at times they even had to surrender all their goods to the government, which would then turn around and sell them. These changes caused a crisis of confidence. The "old policy" presumably

uncertainty, [the emperor] decreed to all circuits that the voucher policy would not be altered; any who created rumors to disrupt it would be tried according to the law, with doubled punishments.

In 1126 (Jingkang 1) the Xie salt voucher exchange took into consideration the policies of the pre-[Shenzong period] (1068–1085). The [sales] territories for Xie salt and for northeastern salt were changed once more. Merchants who did not wish [to trade] salt could request cash according to their vouchers' face value, just as with the old policy. Subsequently, a one-mat voucher was set at approximately eight strings, and vouchers were collected at their face value. Those who brought in grain and fodder were allowed to pass directly to the ponds to obtain salt, and thus were spared the trouble of again [traveling] to the capital to have the vouchers endorsed.

---

refers to the resumption of sea salt sales in the capital and other northern areas, around the year 1119.

Section 2
SEA SALT

The discussion of sea salt comprises forty-four pages, or two-thirds of the treatise. Sea salt was more expensive and of better quality than pond salt. Its manufacture involved a process of subjecting salt water to percolation, then boiling it down until crystallization took place. Boiling sea water for salt came to be termed aobo *or "simmering the waves."[1] There were six main production areas: Jingdong, Hebei, Liangzhe, Huainan, Fujian, and Guangnan circuits, which the* Songshi *addresses in order of proximity to the Northern Song capital. By the Southern Song, only the four southeastern circuits continued to produce sea salt for the state, thus sea salt was also commonly called "southeastern salt."*

The treatise begins with a brief overview of terms and prices at the outset of the dynasty. It treats producers cursorily, despite the fact that the government strictly regulated and, in the Southern Song, stratified them into a hierarchy based on the size of their operations. Other contemporary sources describe how the highest-ranking salters came to act as liaisons between lower-ranking salters and the lowest level of the salt bureaucracy and how, like other officials, they perpetrated abuses upon the lower-ranking salters.

[*p. 4426*] Sea water was boiled to produce salt in six circuits: Jingdong, Hebei, Liangzhe (Map 10), Huainan, Fujian (Map 11), and Guangnan (Map 12). The salt boiling site or saltern was called a "pavilion site" (*tingchang* or *chang*); the laborers were termed "pavilion households" (*tinghu*) or "stove households" (*zaohu*).[2] Household members (*yanding*) turned in an annual

---

[1] This process lent its name to the title of the fourteenth-century work *Aobo tu* [*ABT*], by Chen Chun, which dealt with the techniques of southeast salt production; see also *XXCY* 25b–26a, 47b–48a.

[2] The first source of labor in salt production was individuals who lived near salterns and whom the government "persuaded" (*quanyou*) to register as workers (*SHY* 26.1a, 27.3b, 28.29a). The second source was independent salt makers forced to work in government-established saltworks, where they were organized into *jia*,

quota of salt to the government and either received payment or thereby met their tax obligation. There were no set regulations. In Liangzhe, soldiers were also ordered to boil quota salt. *[p. 4427]* The establishment or closure of [production] salterns in the circuits depended on their revenues and price levels. There was also no set system for pricing. The price of a catty of powder salt varied from forty-seven to forty-eight cash; [the salt came in] twenty-one grades.[3] In 997 (Zhidao 3) total sales amounted to over 1,633,000 strings of cash.

Chapter 2: Jingdong

The section on Jingdong salt is only a page long and ends with over forty years to go in the Northern Song; this region of the Shandong peninsula was lost to the Southern Song. The text names prefectures to which the local salt was distributed and several types [merchant, silkworm, and household] of salt taxes.

Northern Song

In Jingdong (Map 4) the Taoluo saltern in Mizhou prefecture annually boiled more than 32,000 piculs and supplied Mizhou as well as

---

borrowed operating funds, and paid their taxes with the salt they produced. In Zhedong's Mingzhou[b], for example, over 460 originally free salter families were compelled to register for state service. Another group pressed into salt making were individuals previously convicted and then pardoned (*SHY* 26.11a). By the early Southern Song salters fell into a separate category of household registration, which was distinguished from other village households regarding taxes (*SHY* 26.1b–2a, 4/29/1131; *SHY* 26.5a, 3/26/1132). "Stove households" included miscellaneous workers who were not given any registration status, which meant no clear rules, protections or exemptions. "Preparation workers" (*beiding*) were temporary laborers, hired by other salters and, as such, equivalent to private servants (*HSRC* 78.7a–b). A category of households known as "small fires" (*xiaohuo*) had been independent, using little fuel, small stoves, and small cauldrons. They now were also part of the government's operations (*CYZJ jia* 14.6a–b). Others such as the "cauldron households" (*guohu*) are covered in the *SS*. Guo categorizes the many types of Song salters based on production techniques, status and origins (Guo Zhengzhong 1990a, 69–86, 146–53).

[3] Thirty-one grades of salt are on record for 12/wuzi/1021 (*XCB* 97.2261).

Yizhou[a] and Weizhou[a].[4] Only Dengzhou[a] and Laizhou [further north] observed merchant sales. Later four salterns were added at Dengzhou[a].[5] In the past the Southern Capital [Yingtianfu] and the seven prefectures of Caozhou, Puzhou, Jizhou[b], Yanzhou[a], Shanzhou[a], Yunzhou[a], and Guangjijun consumed pond salt; the others consumed the salt of two local prefectures [Mizhou and Dengzhou[a]] which the government sold. In the winter of 1041 (Qingli 1), because the eight prefectures of Zizhou, Weizhou[a], Qingzhou, Qizhou[a], Yizhou[a], Mizhou, Xuzhou[a], and Huaiyang were still suffering from a year of calamity, the emperor decreed to loosen the regulations.[6] Merchants were allowed to trade [sea salt] and the government collected taxes from them. While Mizhou and Dengzhou[a]'s annual taxes were abolished, [regular] households were ordered to pay rent. Afterwards, because Yanzhou[a] and Yunzhou[a] were contiguous [with sea salt sales territory], their consumption of pond salt was ended and [that supply] replaced by sea salt. Revenue [from those prefectures] was collected just as in Zizhou and Weizhou[a] prefectures.[7] From then on, [over ten] prefectural

---

[4] Jingdongdong and Jingdongxi quotas in cash string equivalencies from the *Guochao huiyao* are listed in *SHY* 23.12b. Mizhou was present-day Zhucheng, Shandong. It faces the sea, with mountains at its back, and produces large amounts of sea salt (Wang Leiming 1985, 343n2). At the time written about, Mizhou was located in Jingdongdong. One famine year when local people traded salt for food, officers pursued them, and violent confrontations ensued. Those caught were sentenced to death. On 1/jiawu/1018 the Mizhou prefect, Wang Bowen, requested that salt restrictions be eased until prosperity was restored (*XCB* 95.2182).

The first *SHY* entry for Jingdongxi is a 5/961 decree indicating that the region was also consuming sea salt, which, because transport was upstream, entailed greater expense than Xie salt. It was decreed that Xuzhou[a], Suzhou[b], Yunzhou[a], and Jizhou[b], which had formerly consumed sea salt, were now to be provided with Xie salt (*SHY* 23.18a; *XCB* 2.45). On 6/guisi/1034 the four seasonal salt and iron taxes at Yizhou[a] (Jingdongdong) were lifted for one year (*XCB* 114.2678).

[5] As of 11/bingyin/1041 Mizhou had one saltern, Dengzhou four (*XCB* 134.3199).

[6] The *XCB* of 11/bingyin/1041 does not include Mizhou in the list; it notes, rather, that merchants were levied a tax (*XCB* 134.3199). Back in 3/xinchou/1021, because Yunzhou[a] and Puzhou had suffered flooding, households lacked food. Zhang Dexiang requested that they be given loans and provided salt, excusing payment (*XCB* 97.2244).

[7] That Yanzhou[a] and Yunzhou[a] could circulate sea salt may have been the result of a petition by Zhang Guan (*XCB* 134.3199n, 11/bingyin/1041; *SS* 292.9766).

governments [in Jingdong and Huainan] no longer kept stockpiles of salt. They discontinued advances of annual "silkworm salt" to the common people, but continued to make the people pay [anyway].[8] During the Zhihe period (1054–1055) the emperor finally decreed that these cash payments from the common people be reduced by 30 percent.[9]

But by the early 1080s we see two circuit officials rewarded for generating surplus revenues. Of all the issues that could have been discussed here, the Songshi *editors chose to indicate only who was promoted, who succeeded whom, and who was to report to whom. This focus highlights (and so may have been intended as criticism of) the notorious relationship between fiscalist aims of the monopoly and personnel rewards during the reform period.*

In 1080 (Yuanfeng 3) the Jingdong assistant fiscal intendant (*zhuanyun fushi*), Li Cha, stated:

> The Southern Capital [Yingtianfu], Jizhou[b], Puzhou, Caozhou, and Shan-zhou[a] circulate Xie [pond] salt; the other twelve prefectures circulate sea salt. I petition that following the present tax policy [described below] [we] establish trade salterns.[10]

According to this policy, all salt boiled by "stove households" was to be sold by the government itself; prohibitions on private marketing were renewed. Annual revenues reached over 273,000 strings of cash, with half being surplus. When Wu Juhou was circuit fiscal supervisory official (*zhuanyun panguan*), he succeeded [Li] Cha in administering the salt policy and surpluses grew ever greater. In 1083 (Yuanfeng 6), comparing the income of Jingdong salterns with that of Hebei, in the year and a half from the change in salt policy to the present, 360,000 strings of cash in

---

[8] *XCB* 134.3199 (11/bingyin/1041). Similarly, see a 1/22/1072 decree in response to the fiscal intendant on the matter (*SHY* 24.5b–6a; *XCB* 229.5572). For the detailed changes to the "silkworm salt" policy see Guo Zhengzhong 1990a, 593–600.

[9] Originally Zizhou, Weizhou[a], Qingzhou, Qizhou, Yizhou[a], Mizhou, Xuzhou[a], and Huaiyangjun had monopoly restrictions eased; only Yanzhou[a] and Yunzhou[a] continued to trade sea salt (*XCB* 181.4389–90, 10/renzi/1055).

[10] Li Cha requested this on 6/25/1080, and the emperor agreed (*SHY* 24.19b).

surpluses were realized.[11] [Li] Cha and [Wu] Juhou were both promoted and [Wu] Juhou was further bestowed robes of the third rank (*sanpinfu*).[12] The emperor decreed that salt money be transported and stored in the Northern Capital [Taiyuanfu].[13] Hebei fiscal intendant-general Jian Zhoufu and a supervisory official, Li Nangong, were to receive instructions from [Wu] Juhou and put them into effect in Hebei.[14]

---

[11] The Jingdong fiscal intendant made the comparison between Jingdong and Hebei on 2/28/1083, and the emperor decreed rewards (*SHY* 24.22b–23a).

[12] Decreed 3/10/1083 (*SHY* 24.23a; *XCB* 334.8033).

[13] These were revenues from salt sales under the new policy based on Li Cha's ideas; decreed on 5/1/1083 (*SHY* 24.23a; *XCB* 335.8062). This move was made apparently to check Wu Juhou's possibly inflated statistics (*XCB* 335.8062).

[14] Decreed 6/15/1083 (*SHY* 24.23b; *XCB* 335.8083). [The next year] on 11/dingsi/1084, Wu Juhou reported to the court that 150,000 surplus strings of salt revenue used to purchase 136,606 bolts of silk had been delivered to Zezhou. He requested that 130,000 bolts of silk be purchased with the salt money annually; his request was approved (*XCB* 350.8388).

On 2/guiyou/1086 the general censor, Liu Zhi, memorialized that most intendants were not trustworthy. He requested that they be investigated now that a new emperor had taken the throne. In particular the Hebei vice-fiscal intendant, Li Nangong, was harsh and mean. The late emperor had disliked his personality and employed him only in minor offices, but Li had maintained his influence through his connections. When the circuit initiated monopoly restrictions on the salt trade, Li Nangong applied them so oppressively that the entire circuit suffered. The northern border was a strategic location, ill suited to his sort of administration. Li was subsequently transferred to Hedong (*XCB* 366.8777–78).

Chapter 3: Hebei

The Hebei section comprises four of the forty-four pages on sea salt and, due to geopolitics, covers only the Northern Song. It begins with a description of salterns and distribution points. Merchants within the circuit as well as in Jingdong, which bordered it to the east, distributed Hebei salt.

Northern Song

[p. 4428] In Hebei the Binzhou[b] saltern annually boiled over 21,000 piculs.[1] It provided [revenue] for its own prefecture and the miscellaneous needs of Dizhou and Qizhou[b] as well as Qingzhou, Zizhou, and Qizhou[a] in Jingdong. The following were [Hebeidong and Hebeixi, Map 6] merchant sales areas: Damingfu and Zhendingfu [highest level prefectures]; Beizhou, Jizhou[c], Xiangzhou[a], Weizhou[c], Xingzhou[b], Mingzhou[a], Shenzhou, Zhaozhou[b], Cangzhou, Cizhou[b], Dezhou, Bozhou[a], Binzhou[b], Dizhou, Qizhou[b], Dingzhou[b], Baozhou, Yingzhou[a] [also Hejianfu], Mozhou, Xiongzhou, and Bazhou[b] [common prefectures]; Deqingjun [in Liangzhe Circuit, Map 10]; Tonglijun [also Anlijun], Yongjingjun, Qianningjun [also Qingzhou], Dingyuanjun [in Huainanxi Circuit, Map 8], Baodingjun, Guangxinjun, Yongdingjun, and Ansujun [military prefectures].[2] Later [operations at] Binzhou[b] were divided into four small saltworks (*wu*), and Cangzhou added three small saltworks, producing annual [tax salt quantities of] 9,145 piculs, which funded the various expenditures of the circuit. After Jingdong's Zizhou, Qingzhou, and Qizhou[a] became merchant sales areas, Binzhou no longer supplied them with salt.

In the mid-eleventh century the advantages of merchant trade were defended in the face of a proposal for instituting government distribution.

---

[1] Hebeidong and Hebeixi quotas in cash equivalency, from the *Guochao huiyao*, are listed in *SHY* (23.12b–13a).

[2] Dingyuanjun was the Five Dynasties name for Yongjingjun, which is listed two names earlier, so is redundant (Wang Leiming 1985, 344n3).

From the Kaibao period (968–975) on, Hebei salt was allowed to be [merchant] traded and the government collected a surcharge.[3] The annual income quota was 150,000 strings of cash. A petitioner suggested putting into effect government distribution so [the state] could realize extra income. The remonstrance official at the time, Yu Jing, emphatically stated:

> In past years, because of war, Hebei has had to draft able-bodied men and tax the populace in many ways. For several years they have had no respite. I am pained that the people of Yan and Ji, having lived under Khitan control for nearly a hundred years, have forgotten their southern identity. This is largely because of the simplicity of Khitan laws, the cheapness of [their] salt and wine, and the lightness of their taxes and service duty. In the past, Taizu extended his grace to Hebei Circuit and so allowed merchant sales; if we now monopolize the trade, the price will definitely jump and the people will harbor resentment. Then what use will regrets be? In the region north of the Yellow River [*heshuo*] the soil is mainly salty brine, and the taxed land of commoners cannot grow any grain. The only way for them to pay the Double Tax is to scrape the briny earth and boil salt.[4] A monopoly will definitely cause them to flee, and if the salt price is high, many will break the law. It will not be a good thing for the state if the border people maintain grievances. I thus beg to maintain the old policy of merchant sales.[5]

---

[3] This was decreed on 4/970. In the early 960s, in six prefectures—Xingzhou[b], Mingzhou[a], Cizhou[b], Zhenzhou[b], Zhaozhou[b] (all in Hebeixi) and Jizhou[c] (Hebeidong)—the government allowed merchant sales only twenty *li* outside the city; later it lifted all prohibitions (*XCB* 11.246, 4/jiawu/970). On every catty merchants were to pay a customs tax of one cash and a stationary sales tax of two cash, on pain of confiscation. Half of the goods would be given as a reward to the person who made the arrest. Tax bureaus were to be set up in prefectural towns, and corrupt officials dismissed (*SHY* 23.18b).

[4] Scraping the briny or salty earth in Hebei was likely to be distinguished from earth salt production exclusive to Hedong. The Hebei procedure to extract salt along the shore seems to have been one of several techniques used to produce sea salt. It entailed cultivating the barren soil and sand that the tides had continually infused with high salt content, leaving "white flowers" or "salt frost" in their wake. This salty substance was then scraped off into mounds to be filtered and finally boiled down.

[5] *XCB* 159.3851–52 (11/wuzi/1046). On the same date the investigating censor, He Tan, described a paradox: if the government did not restrict people from producing salt in small quantities, government sales would fail, but if it prohibited them from doing so, the people would suffer. Because many Hebei prefectures

The deliberation [over implementing the monopoly] was thus put to rest.

Another proposal for government sales was countered by a convincing argument against it, the context being competition posed by Khitan salt. No mention is made of tensions between the Song and Xia. Revenue generation was the overriding concern.

In 1046 (Qingli 6) the finance commissioner, Wang Gongchen, again proposed the government sale of salt from [the Binzhou and Cang-zhou salterns] so that revenues could be consolidated. The fiscal intendant-general, Yu Zhouxun, felt this to be inadvisable and argued:

> When merchants sell salt, they collude with local officials through whose territories they must pass. They pay less than 20 to 30 percent [of the duties owed]. I petition to have prefectures and counties calculate the full duties and require merchants to pay all charges together at the destination where they sell. There will thereby be a gain of over 700,000 strings of cash annually.[6]

The Finance Commission petitioned to adopt this plan, to which Renzong responded:

> To cause the people to suddenly have to consume expensive salt—can this be my intention?

So the Finance Commission settled on the monopoly. Before the policy was enacted, Zhang Fangping had an audience with the emperor and asked:

---

had briny earth, plants would not grow, and so boiling salt was the only available occupation. Salt paid for the people's food, clothing, and taxes. If prevented from making any salt on their own, the people would immediately become impoverished and turn into bandits. The Fiscal Intendancy had called for deliberation on the issue, so the people were already concerned. He Tan advocated that merchant sales continue as before, because they allowed for a set tax quota and sizable revenues; with the monopoly, merchants might be too apprehensive to trade, and then tax income would not increase (*XCB* 159.3853–54). Back on 8/jiayin/1032 the court had forgiven the salt money due from temporary residents of Anlijun in Hebeixi (*XCB* 111.2586).

[6] *XCB* 159.3852 (11/wuzi/1046).

Why is the salt monopoly to be restored in Hebei?

The emperor replied:

> [p. 4429] We have only considered a policy, not necessarily restored the monopoly.

[Zhang] Fangping said:

> When the [Later] Zhou dynasty's Emperor Shizong ran a monopoly in Hebei salt, offenders were promptly sentenced to death.[7] Once, when he was on a northern expedition, elders came in droves to tell him tales of woe. They desired that the salt tax be replaced by the Double Tax and for salt monopoly restrictions to be loosened. This was allowed, so now the Double Tax is in place. How can we possibly impose the monopoly again? Furthermore, even before the monopoly is even in place, Khitan smuggling is already rampant. If we implement it and the salt price rises, the Khitan will sell even more. This will lead to resentment towards us, and good fortune for them. As they bring in ever more salt, we will be unable to stem [the trade] without resorting to troops. And once a border war begins, will salt revenues be able to cover the costs of the military?

The emperor, who had his eyes greatly opened, replied:

> I will tell the chief councilor to abolish the policy.

[Zhang] Fangping then pointed out:

> Even though the policy has not yet been handed down, every household already knows of it. It is fitting that it be abolished by an edict written by yourself; this cannot be handled by a subordinate.

---

[7] Since Shizong of the Later Zhou reigned from 944 to 959, his name may be a mistake for Song Taizu, and this scribal error may have originated in Su Shi's obituary on Zhang Fangping upon which later works were based. See "Zhang Wending gong muzhiming" (Epitaph for Zhang) in *SSJ* 88.3592. The correct monarch is named in the line "In the Kaibao reign of (Song) Taizu (968–975), it was decreed that the monopoly of salt in Hebei be abolished and merchant sales carried out"; see Zhang Fangping, "Lun Hebei queyan zou," (Memorial on the Hebei salt monopoly) in *GCZY* 108.3636–38.

The emperor was pleased and ordered [Zhang] Fangping to compose an imperial edict in secret and issued it. Elders in the region north of the Yellow River welcomed the edict and celebrated with Buddhist and Taoist ceremonies in Chanzhou for seven days to repay the emperor's benevolence. Then they had the edict carved in stone and installed in the Northern Capital. Later, whenever the elders passed by the inscription, they could not help but kowtow and weep.[8]

Debate over merchant versus government sales continued.

As time passed, salt revenues declined. During the Huangyou reign period (1049–1053), they fell to nearly half the old quota.[9] When the Shanzhou[b] executive inspector of prefectures (*lushi canjun*), Wang Boyu, supervised the Yanshan saltern in Cangzhou, he suggested that merchants receive salt in bags from the prefectures of Cangzhou and Binzhou[b]. Each bag was not to exceed three piculs and three pecks, with one peck being six catties. Apart from the three pecks counted as wastage and not calculated, the rest was to be reckoned at half. Documents were to be issued as certification, then after prefectural and county officials verified them, merchants were allowed to go to their sales prefectures where they paid cash [as a duty]. Any who stored or received an amount in excess of that for which they had certification were to be punished; merchants who privately carried additional salt with them were to have their goods confiscated. At the time the prefect of Cangzhou, Tian Jing, and [Wang] Boyu deliberated jointly and presented this to the emperor, who decreed that it be tested. When, after a year, annual tax revenues increased over 30,000 strings, this became a set policy.[10] In 1075 (Xining 8) when the

---

[8] This episode was recorded 11/wuzi/1046 (*XCB* 159.3852–53). Words attributed to Zhang Fangping may not be accurate (Wang Leiming 1985, 345n2).

[9] On 3/wuchen/1054 the Kaifengfu staff supervisor, Wang Ding, was sent to Cangzhou to investigate the pros and cons of the salt policy there (*XCB* 176.4254).

[10] Here let me insert other issues chronologically. In 9/bingzi/1061 the prefect of Xiongzhou, Hebeidong, Zhao Zi, was promoted to commander of local armies. He had previously caught and killed a Khitan who had been transporting salt down the Jie ("Border") River, the line between Hebeidong and Khitan territory. Though the Khitans complained, the court considered Zhao's action to be outstanding and promoted him (*XCB* 195.4720).

finance commissioner, Zhang Dun, again petitioned for government distribution of Hebei salt, the salt tax intendant of Hebei and Jingdong, Zhou Ge, was summoned for input. The monopoly was about to be implemented when Wen Yanbo argued that this was not appropriate.[11] The emperor decreed to retain the old policy.[12]

In the mid-1080s two impassioned memorials to Shenzong criticized a policy shift to government sales and its effect upon Hebei residents. They used the example of Renzong, portrayed as modest, frugal, and not allowing the tax policy to become oppressive.[13]

The Hebei Jie River inspector and chief military inspector (*xunjian dujian*), Zhao Yong, noted for his ability and knowledge of border conditions, would slit open the belly of any enemy caught violating salt prohibitions and drown him. The enemy feared Zhao Yong so much that they called his boats, which boasted a tiger head at the prow, "Tiger-Head Zhao" (*XCB* 200.4852, 2/xinwei/1064). The military inspector, a position often found on the frontier, was responsible for the militia and maintained order in the locale. The position was generally a low one, but in the Northern Song it was also filled by officials with higher office. Their jurisdiction ranged from market towns to counties up to ten prefectures. There were also ad hoc permutations of the title, including "bandit-catching military inspector of the Yangzi River, Yellow River, Huai River, and the Sea" (*Jiang He Huai Hai zhuozei xunjian*) and "arresting agent for tea and salt smugglers" (*xunzhuo sichayan*), and so on.

On 12/gengchen/1066 Ouyang Xiu memorialized on the taxation system. Nonarable areas of Hebei were expected to produce salt: boilers had to pay both a salt tax and a land tax, and even in areas where salt production was prohibited, people were required to submit taxes. With what were they to pay? (*XCB* 192.4656).

[11] Zhang Dun argued on 6/wushe/1075 that Hebei and Jingdong, the only circuits without government distribution, had lost great amounts of government money (*XCB* 265.6490). The Preface to the *SS* "Monograph on the Economy" (Shihuozhi) notes that sometime between 1094 and 1097, during Zhezong's reign, Zhang Dun reintroduced the New Reforms (*SS* 173.4156). Wen Yanbo (1006–1097), chief councilor from 1041 to 1048, would later oppose Wang Anshi's reforms (Wang Leiming 1985, 346n4).

[12] Decreed on 8/1/1076 (*SHY* 24.11a; *XCB* 277.6772).

[13] The jump from page 4429 to 4433 is caused by the start of a new chapter: Chapter 182, Monograph 135, Political Economy Part 2, No. 4, "Salt" (Part II).

[p. 4433] In 1084 (Yuanfeng 7) the prefect of Cangzhou, Zhao Zhan, petitioned to have Damingfu, Chanzhou, Enzhou, Xin'anjun, Xiongzhou, Bazhou[b], Yingzhou[a], Mozhou, Jizhou[c], and so on, implement monopoly sales in order to increase revenues. Within only half a year this earned [the government] 167,000 strings. When Zhezong ascended, the investigating censor (*jiancha yushi*), Wang Yansou, stated:

> For two years now Hebei has implemented the new salt policy. The price of salt has doubled, which has not only robbed merchants of their profits but also forced the people to pay more for the sake of government returns. I have heard that poor families compare salt to medicine [in its preciousness]. Since the land north of the Yellow River is the foundation of the empire, our ancestors considered [the benefits from it, such as salt] and extended these to the people with their grace. I hope Your Majesty also will see benefiting the people, rather than harming them, as advantageous. To restore the former salt policy will mean bestowing infinite good upon all the living souls of Hebei.[14]

It happened that the Hebei fiscal intendant, Fan Ziqi, memorialized that the salt tax should be collected in full. Fan E was dispatched to deliberate this. [Wang] Yansou again stated:

> When I was in Hebei, I also heard that merchants petitioned for the abolition of the monopoly and were willing to pay more taxes if this were accomplished. Decisionmakers only thought about collecting an incredible amount of taxes from merchants as *[p. 4434]* [supposed] profit; they rarely thought about the damage done by price increases that the merchants then imposed on the common folk. In 1046 (Qingli 6) not only was the Finance Commission's monopoly policy not acted on, neither was the petition of the Fiscal Intendancy to increase taxes. Renzong merely said that he was concerned about the people's paying a higher price for salt, so the old policy was retained. At that time annual revenues were estimated to increase by 600,000 strings. Did Renzong not know how to benefit the state? It is that he believed hoarding by the people to be better than hoarding by the state. Now that Your Majesty has just ascended the throne, it is befitting to enact

---

[14] As investigating censor, an honorary title, Wang Yansou memorialized on 10/jimao/1085 (*XCB* 360.8611–12).

the intent of Renzong and not lose the hearts of the people for the sake of small profit.[15]

The following year, Hebei's monopoly policy was lifted and merchant sales were continued.[16] In 1091 (Yuanyu 6) the Hebei Salt Tax Intendancy petitioned to allow merchants to sell salt, paying a tax at the salterns, and required, depending on their class of household, that they enlist a guarantor. They were given "small vouchers" priced variously according to the distance the merchant would travel to sell, and they had to be used within a certain time limit.[17] Merchants could trade in non-government-supervised market-town shops.[18] [The Hebei Salt Tax Intendancy proposed] to raise the old 50 percent tax on the salt to 70 percent.[19] By then the [whole system of] salt tax was probably already in place.

Later in the 1090s another flip-flop was precipitated by anticipated border tensions in Hebei.

During the Shaosheng reign period (1094–1097) the Hebei government again [began to] sell salt; then later it was decreed to once more follow the

---

[15] This continued Wang Yansou's discussion of 10/jimao/1085. He specified the amount of 592,800-odd strings of surplus and went on to discuss severe problems of the Jiangxi and Hunan salt policies. The people expected the emperor to rescue them as they looked northward (towards the capital) and believed that the court understood their suffering (*XCB* 360.8612–14).

[16] *XCB* 364.8732, 1/dingsi/1086. The context to this passage is the major new direction taken under Zhezong's initial reign period (1086–1093). During this time, the reforms of Shenzong had been largely negated, and in Hebei and other circuits, government distribution of pond salt was replaced by merchant distribution.

In a lengthy memorial of 11/jiachen/1088 the executive of the Ministry of Finance, Su Che, discussed construction on the Yellow River dikes, especially the corvee involved and the use of salt money, which represented the people's sweat and blood (*XCB* 416.10118–20).

[17] During the Song, vouchers were categorized by the size of the mat they were good for, either large or small. Other Song measurements for sea salt included "pockets" (*nang*) of a variable 500 catties and "bags" (*dai*); see Wang Leiming 1985, 348n4.

[18] Requested on 2/6/1091 (*SHY* 24.29b; *XCB* 455.10904).

[19] This memorial was presented by the Hebei Salt Tax Intendancy on 5/jiaxu/1091 (*XCB* 458.10963).

Jingdong [merchant trade] policy.[20] In 1100 (Yuanfu 3) the commissioner for fostering propriety (*chongyishi*), Lin Yu, stated:

> The Hebei monopoly salt will not necessarily bring in taxes at previous levels. Moreover, the Khitan are selling more and more salt. I am afraid there will be border conflicts.[21]

The following year (1101) the reviewing policy advisor (*jishizhong*), Shangguan Jun, also backed up [the assertion that government sales would not succeed and nomads would move into the salt market], but none of it came to pass.[22]

---

[20] The context to this statement is yet another policy swing in the middle of Zhezong's reign, when Shenzong's government distribution was restored.

On 5/xinsi/1097 Zhang Dun argued for a monopoly of Hebei salt and asked why Hebei alone was exempted from restrictions. Councilors repeated the events of Renzong's time and pointed to the stone inscription in the Northern Capital as an argument against it (*XCB* 488.11593). On 11/jisi/1097 the Hebei Fiscal Intendancy memorialized that Hebei should observe government sales, as did Jingxi Circuit (*XCB* 493.11700). On 7/wuchen/1098 the minister of finance, Wu Juhou, memorialized that since Hebei and Jingdong owed several years of salt taxes, an official be dispatched to collect them (*XCB* 500.11916).

[21] Lin Yu memorialized on 10/28/1100 at some length against government distribution. He recounted a previous ban on it at the end of Renzong's reign in the late 1050s, which had been greeted gratefully by the elders of Chanzhou, the site of the Song-Liao treaty (*SHY* 24.33a–b). Lin's post, commissioner for fostering propriety (*chongyishi*), was a Song military title. In the Tang the post had been called the commissioner for the palace corrals and stables (*xianjiushi*). Usually there were no duties, only a rank. In 1112 it was changed to grand master for military strategy (*wulue dafu*) (*SS* 169.4056).

[22] Shangguan Jun was a *jinshi* in Shenzong's time and died during Huizong's; see *SS* 355.11178–81. He pointed out on 10/1/1101 that Hebei had not been a monopoly area in the past. Renzong had declared that he would not allow a Hebei monopoly, nor have the people eat expensive salt. Yet this was what was put in place in 1097—government revenues were down, famine had devastated the populace for successive years, and commoners had difficulty meeting their labor duty. Shangguan recalled the memory of Renzong to abolish the monopoly (*SHY* 24.33b–34a). For Shangguan Jun's complete memorial, see Shangguan Jun, "Shang Huizong qi ba Hebei queyan" (Memorial to Huizong in support of lifting the monopoly in Hebei) in *GCZY* 108.3647–49.

In 1119 (Xuanhe 1) the capital, the regions around the capital (*sifu*), and the briny areas of Huazhou[b] and Heyang were all converted to cultivated fields, thus halting illegal production of salt.[23] The prefect of Heyang, Wang Xu, was rewarded because of his encouragement of the change.

In 1121 (Xuanhe 3) the salt policy was significantly altered: salt [on which the government had previously charged merchants a] tax was [made available to merchants] in a new voucher program.

Any tax-salt vouchers that had not yet been sold [i.e., in the government's hands], as well as those already paid for and those either submitted or not submitted to the storehouse [i.e., in merchant hands] had to be taken to the Monopoly Goods Bureau and exchanged for new policy vouchers, which could then be used for trading. Those who had traded [their vouchers in for salt] under the old tax-salt policy had to report [their inventory], buy additional new vouchers, and sell the additional salt (*daimai*). Where the salt taken on against (old) vouchers had already been sold, merchants did not have to buy an additional quantity.

At first the new policy requiring the exchange of old tea and salt vouchers for new ones at a loss created discontent among the populace as well as merchants, but it did not extend to Hebei. At this point [1121], however, Hebei and Jingdong both had to follow it.[24]

---

[23] The "four territories," all in present-day Henan, were established between 1102 and 1106 and between 1111 and 1117: they included Chanzhou in the north, Yingchangfu to the south, Gongzhou[c] to the east, and Zhengzhou to the west (Wang Leiming 1985, 300n1 and 348–49n4).

[24] On 3/1/1124, in one of the last *SHY* entries for Jingdong and Hebei, the Secretariat and Department of Ministries noted that Hebei and Jingdong were successfully carrying out merchant sales with vouchers; they decreed that the officials responsible should be rewarded (*SHY* 25.22b–23a).

Chapter 4: Liangzhe

The Liangzhe section is three pages long. It begins eighty years into the dynasty and covers only up to the second-to-last Northern Song emperor, with eight years to go to the end of the Northern Song; there is no coverage for the Southern Song. Of southeastern producers Liangzhe was second only to Huai. The account first enumerates salt-producing prefectures in Liangzhe, their salterns, and production capacity. While reorganization of salt regions in the Southern Song that combined Zhe and Huai into one unit may explain why the Songshi account is so sparse, a significant portion of the Song huiyao and other material addressing Liangzhe was never used. It is logical that the northern areas no longer part of the Southern Song might not be addressed, but one would imagine that the circuit including the new capital would be covered to some degree. Furthermore the greatest smuggling problems seemed to occur in this region.

Liangzhe, which corresponds to present-day Zhejiang Province, was bisected from northeast to southwest by the Qiantang River, the final section of the Zhe River, which fed into Hangzhou Bay. In the Southern Song, it was divided in two. Liangzhe Xilu (or Zhexi), meaning "Western Zhe Circuit," lay to the north and west of the river from present-day Shanghai to Zhenjiang. It was a deltaic plain with interconnected waterways, which made for smooth boat transport; its markets were also much more developed. Liangzhe Donglu (or Zhedong), meaning "Eastern Zhe Circuit," which lay to the south and east of the river, was rugged, broken by mountains, and less developed. This topography not unexpectedly had an adverse effect on distribution.

Northern Song

[p. 4434] In Liangzhe (Map 10) the Hangzhou saltern annually produced over 77,000 piculs; in Mingzhou[b], the eastern and western Changguo directorates (*jian*) produced over 201,000 piculs; Xiuzhou's saltworks (*chang*) *[p. 4435]* produced over 208,000 piculs; Wenzhou['s] northern and southern Tianfu directorates and two salterns at Miying and Yongjia produced over 74,000 piculs; and Taizhou[a]'s Huangyan directorate produced over 15,000 piculs [annually]. All provided [revenue for] the prefecture and Yuezhou[a], Chuzhou[a], Quzhou, and Wuzhou[b]. During the Tiansheng reign period (1023–1031), Hangzhou, Xiuzhou, Wenzhou[a], Taizhou[a], and Mingzhou[b] each had one directorate, while Wenzhou[a] had three saltworks. Still, the circuit's annual tax [salt] resources dropped by

68,000 piculs compared with before.[1] They provided income for the circuit and Shezhou (Jiang[nan]dong, Map 10).[2]

The earliest Songshi entry on Liangzhe dates to the 1040s.[3] It addresses the difficulties of government transport and the need to raise the salt price to cover this. Unfortunately, the high salt price aggravated smuggling.

---

[1] On 11/jiazi/1026, when Li Yuqing was Xiuzhou prefectural vice-administrator, he requested that salterns be set up in Haiyan and Huating (*XCB* 104.2426). On 5/renwu/1032 salterns at Hangzhou and Xiuzhou were dismantled (*XCB* 111.2581). By 2/gengxu/1036 they had been restored (*XCB* 118.2775). The *SS* omits Linpingjian in Hangzhou, which was later called Yanguan (Liang and Bao 1994, 615).

[2] The start of the *SHY* section on salt provides a lengthy list of revenue figures, probably compiled before the Zhiping period (1064–1067) of Yingzong. The Liangzhe revenue list (*SHY* 22.13b–17b) is broken down by prefecture (Hangzhou, Yuezhou[a], Suzhou[a], Runzhou, Huzhou, Wuzhou[b], Mingzhou[b], Changzhou[b], Wenzhou[a], Taizhou[a], Quzhou, and Muzhou), then by county, market town, and saltern. Guo Zhengzhong (1983, 91) provides a table of aggregate Liangzhe salt production from 978 to 1231: Table 3.

Period	In Catties	In Piculs	Source
978-1022	28,750,000	575,000	*SS* 182
978-1022	33,900,000	678.000	*WXTK* 15
1026-1029	25,500,000	510,000	*SS* 182
1026-1029	30,500,000	610,000	*WXTK* 15
1111-1118	Increase	Increase	*SS* 182
1129-1132	Decrease	Decrease	*SHY* 26.9
1159	100,052,400	2,001,048	*SHY* 23.13-15, 26.43
1162	99,271,400	1,985,428	*SHY* 23.13, *CYZJ jia* 14
1165-1173	94,368,900	1,887,378	*SHY* 23.17
1165-1173	98,500,000	1,970,000	*SHY* 27.33
1170	151,650,000	3,033,000	*SHY* 27.33
1171-1173	101,078,850	2,021,577	*SHY* 23.17, 28.1
1174-1177	94,638,900	1,892,777	*SHY* 28.1, *CYZJ jia* 14
1174-1177	94,368,900	1,887,378	*SHY* 23.17, 28.1
1230-1231	97,200,000	1,944,000	*SS* 182, *WXTK* 15

Note that the trough (not mentioned in *SS*) occurred in 1026–1029 at 25.5 million catties, the peak in 1170 at 151.6 million catties.

[3] *SHY* coverage of Liangzhe begins sixty years earlier. One of the earliest records, dated 6/985, concerns a proposed change from government to merchant sales in Zhe. The Finance Commission petitioned for this, but when the prefectures complained [probably about loss of revenue], the old system was restored (*SHY* 23.21b–22a). Smuggling was a problem from the outset. On 11/985 the emperor decreed punishments in Liangzhe: for a violation of one ounce to 100 catties,

At the beginning of the Qingli period (1041–1048) the military regulator's office stated:

> For successive years, rivers have run shallow so that transport of government goods by water has been obstructed and expenses have grown ever greater. We request consideration of an increase of the salt price for the six circuits of Jiangnan[dong and xi], Huainan[dong and xi], Liangzhe, and Jinghu.

This was handed down to the Finance Commission to deliberate. The Finance Commission memorialized that Jinghu had already been mandated an increase, but as to the other four circuits' thirty-eight prefectures, the price should be increased by two or four cash per catty. The emperor decreed that when the rivers' flow was restored, the former price policy would be reverted to.

Later, storage depots (*zhuanbancang*) were established in Jiangzhou[a] and the number of [government] transport boats and merchant rental boats for moving the salt was increased. [To cover these extra expenses] the military regulator's office petitioned for an increase of the salt price by five cash per catty in the six circuits' fifty-one prefectures. Suffering under the high price of government salt, people even went without, and so all the circuits complained.[4] After some time Han Jiang, returning from a

---

exile; above this, tattooing on the face and delivery to the palace gates (*SHY* 23.22a).

[4] Even in Liangzhe, a major producer, salt was not necessarily available to all. The record for 4/bingzi/999 notes that Zhang Yong, the executive censor appointed prefect of Hangzhou, saw many people engaged in private sales to support themselves. When several hundred were arrested for smuggling, he exhibited lenience. When subordinates asked him to be stricter, Zhang explained that Qiantang had 100,000 families, 80 to 90 percent of whom made a living by selling salt. Severity might cause them to become outlaws (*XCB* 44.941). In a poem of the late 1050s Ouyang Xiu wrote: "The stoves look busy as beehives as they boil sea water for salt. Who knows how many people dressed in white go to their graves for want of salt." See Ouyang Xiu, "Song Zhu Zhifang tiju yunyan" (Sending off Zhu Baochen, salt transport intendant) in *JSJ* 7.837. Su Shi noted in the late 1060s to 1070s, "The poor and timid lack any salt. When I lived in Zhezhong, I saw the inhabitants of the valleys go several months without." Su Shi, "Shang Wen shizhong lun queyan shu" (Letter to the chief councilor, Wen Yanbo, on the government salt monopoly) in *SSJ* 73.3451. For more on Su Shi, see his biography (*SS* 338.10801–818).

military inspection tour in Jiangnan, also spoke on the suffering of the people.[5] Afterwards the Liangzhe fiscal intendants, Shen Li and Li Suzhi, memorialized:

> This circuit's salt taxes amount to 790,000 strings annually; in 1058 (Jiayou 3), they fell to 530,000. In one year 3,099 persons were convicted of smuggling.[6] The problem lies in the high price of government salt; smuggling cannot be halted and the government's tax revenues continue to decline. We request that you cut the government price, abolish the salt convoys, and let shop owners (*puhu*) and service runners go to salterns for salt; this way [the salt] will be of good quality and the price equitable.[7] The people will be unwilling to flout the law and the government's revenues will certainly increase.

The transport intendant disagreed, but [Shen] Li and [Li] Suzhi pressed for a trial period of two to three years, after which the results would be weighed. The emperor agreed.

The Liangzhe fiscal intendant described the plight of salters and transporters. Despite the emperor's insistence on fair support of salters in the mid-1000s, bureaucrats did not necessarily follow through. The salters had no means of livelihood other than working salt and were totally dependent on the government, which provided them with the support necessary to live, in the form of cash, paper money, cloth, or grain.

---

[5] During Wang Anshi's reform period, Han Jiang was assisting civil councilor of state (*canzhi zhengshi*) and later replaced Wang Anshi as chief councilor. Before this, when Han was supervisor of the census (*hubu panguan*), he dealt with famine in Jiangnan by enacting measures to aid the populace and was made sympathetic military intendant (*tiliang anfushi*) in charge of disaster relief (Wang Leiming 1985, 349n1).

[6] A dozen years earlier Fan Zhongyan had noted that 1,000 persons had been convicted of smuggling in a year in his "Zou zaiyihou hexing sishi" (Four necessary rehabilitation steps in the aftermath of a catastrophe), in *Fan Wenzhenggong zouyi* [*FWZY*], 197–98.

[7] Government sea salt was transported by boat convoys, each carrying some 5,000 bags; at 300 catties a bag, each convoy carried about 1.5 million catties (*SHY* 27.38a; *SHY* 27.41a).

[Shen] Li had previously discussed the advantages and disadvantages of the eastern salt [program] and delineated the problems of the salters, storehouses, and transport:

> We must care for the laborers so that they do not become impoverished, rest transport workers to allow them a means of livelihood, manage storehouses well so that there will be no rapacious exactions, halt smuggling, and reduce the price of government salt. If these five actions can be implemented, annual revenues can be increased by 1 to 2 million strings of cash.

He compiled and presented a work, *The Salt Policy (Yance)*, of twenty chapters in which he especially emphasized the extreme hardship of salt producing families.[8] From the Huangyou reign period (1049–1053) on,

---

[8] Out of the 10,000 strings the state designated for salters, 3,000 were absorbed by officials as clerical fees (*aodi yanqian*) and 2,000 by clerks for other uses; of the 5,000 that arrived at the saltern, further appropriations meant that only a pittance remained for the salters (*SP*, 2240). Wang Anshi, who served for three years in Liangzhe at Yinxian in Mingzhou, captured the plight of producers in a poem, "Shou yan" (Collecting salt):

> ... *While salters resign themselves to their shabby huts,*
> *Soldiers in patrol boats raid them again and again.*
> *The sea islands became wastelands long ago,*
> *Their inhabitants today are even more hard-pressed.*
> *Starvation is assured for those who do not boil salt;*
> *Who among them should wait for the raids on their place?*
> ... *One man's trifle is another man's livelihood,*
> *Why do we tread on the poor salters so?*

(*Wang Anshi ji* [*WASJ*], 2186. Another local salt official in Northern Song Liangzhe wrote that this was not the life one hoped to give one's wife and children. Here are excerpts from Liu Yong's "Zhu hai ge" [ZHG] (Song of the sea-brine boilers):

> *How do the sea boiler families make a living?*
> *The wife raises no silkworms, the husband farms no land.*
> *Their daily income is a pittance.*
> *As soon as they make a pan of salt, it all goes for taxes.*
> ... *Before they know how salty the brine*
> *They must gather fuel from the hills.*
> *Braving leopards and tigers,*
> *Leaving in the morning, returning at night*
> *On boats or with shoulder poles, they work without respite,*
> *So that the great stoves can be kept fiery hot.*

repeated decrees ordered that government support to salters was to be given in cash, that those who produced above-quota salt were to be given quality grain and fabric, and that those who owed previous annual taxes were to be forgiven them. But however great the emperor's *[p. 4436]* compassion, bureaucrats rarely carried out [his orders].

In the 1060s Wang Anshi opposed a merchant's proposal for franchising. Termed "merchant shop-sold salt" (puhu shangfanyan), "gambled salt" (puyan, pumaiyan), or "merchant-sold salt" (shangfanyan), this form of trade nevertheless apparently caught on like wildfire.[9] Zhao Bian advocated this policy since revenues from it were already on the rise. With the increase of both merchant and illegal salt trading, government salt sales generally declined.

From the Xining period (1068–1077) on, the five prefectures of Hangzhou, Xiuzhou, Wenzhou[a], Taizhou[a], and Mingzhou[b] together had under their administration six [production] directorates and fourteen [procurement] salterns. But because the salt price remained so high, smugglers abounded, and eventually turned to banditry. Thus great amounts of tax revenue were lost.[10] In 1069 (Xining 2) a certain Wan Qi put forward his desire to buy the right to sell (*pu*) Liangzhe salt to the

---

In the process from briny mix to flying snow,
    They just manage to get by on loans.
Weighed in for the minimum price,
    The salt costs ten times that to produce.
... Wife and children are pressed into the work,
    Each one taking on a sickly green hue.
... When our military needs are resolved and our treasury full,
    The salt and iron monopolies should be abolished.

Su Shi and Ouyang Xiu also wrote poems describing the hardships of salters; see Guo Zhengzhong 1996, 37–60.

[9] Yuki 1984, 45.

[10] Much of the illegal salt in Liangzhe was actually conveyed by government convoys that were commandeered by official personnel (*SHY* 24.2a). Because of this, Liangzhe smuggling was described as parasitic and hidden, as opposed to the more open and violent activity in Jiangnanxi and Fujian (Yuki 1984, 50). As many as 17,000 persons were convicted of smuggling in Liangzhe in one year (Su Shi, "Shang Wen Shizhong lun queyan shu" (A memo to Wen, director of the Chancellery, on the salt monopoly) in *SSJ* 73.3451. Huang Zhen misquotes Su Shi when he says 170,000 had been charged (*HSRC* 71.17b).

populace.[11] [Wan] Qi was sent to the transport intendant, Xue Xiang, to determine the advantages and disadvantages [of his proposal].[12] Shenzong consulted Wang Anshi, who replied:

> Zhao Bian has said that Quzhou practiced the selling of salt rights (*puyan*) to merchants and thus brought in tax revenues equal to that of Liangzhe Circuit as a whole.[13] He only looked, however, at what Quzhou and Huzhou could sell and was not aware that Quzhou salt encroached on Raozhou and Xinzhou[b], and that Huzhou salt encroached on Guangdejun and Shengzhou, and this is why Quzhou and Huzhou revenues were able to rise. The situation of Suzhou[a] and Changzhou[b] is hardly comparable to that of Quzhou and Huzhou. What is to be done now is to establish salt-boiling households, apprehend smugglers, transport [product] in a timely fashion, and enforce the inspection of salt quality. When this is all done, the salt policy will take care of itself. There is no need to alter it.

In the 1070s the judicial and salt intendant, Lu Bing, pressed for reimbursement of salters. Administrators rated the salt content of salterns, most of those in Liangzhe were concentrated around Hangzhou Bay and along the sea where the soil is most alkaline. The materials from which drying pans were made lent color to the processed salt. The government organized stoves and workers into units. It also resorted to requiring wine shop owners to sell salt and forward the tax receipts therefrom.

In 1072 (Xining 5) Lu Bing was temporarily appointed Liangzhe judicial intendant while continuing as [the region's] sole salt intendant. Previously [Lu] Bing, along with the assistant staff writer (*zhuzuo zuolang*),

---

[11] *Maipu* and *pumai* were synonymous measures undertaken to contract out the collection of salt taxes. Wan Qi was a major merchant who was often mentioned in connection with salt policy.

[12] For more on Xue Xiang and his tenure in Shaanxi as fiscal intendant as well as transport intendant of Jiangnan, Huainan, and Liangzhe, see *SS* 3/19/1069; also see his biography in *SS* 328.10585–88. Xue Xiang's merit as fiscal intendant in Shaanxi was debated at court (*SHY* 24.3a–4a).

[13] Zhao Bian, a native of Quzhouxian, was an esteemed local and central government official. He disagreed, however, with Wang Anshi's reform policies and thus incurred Wang's dislike (*SS* 316.10321–25). Quzhou, or Xin'anjun, is present-day Quxian (Zhejiang). Huzhou or Wuxingjun, is present-day Wuxing County, also in Zhejiang (Wang Leiming 1985, 350n2).

Zeng Mo,[14] toured Huainan and Liangzhe to investigate the situation. At that time salters [turned their product over] directly to the salterns, which did not pay them in a timely fashion. So salters suffered additional burdens. [Lu] Bing first petitioned for the cash saved at the Transport Intendancy and other cash in amount of 1 million strings to serve as compensation.[15] Salterns had their yield rated and the rating system reflected the amount of salt that could be extracted from a standard quantity of brine. The Yangcun saltern in Qiantang County, with Muzhou and Shezhou to its north, and the Qianqing saltern in Yuezhou[a] both had low brine content and were rated at 60 percent.[16] South of Yangcun was Renhe's Tangcun, rated at 70 percent. Yanguan saltern was rated at 80 percent. Eastward along the seacoast were the Shiyan saltern in Yuezhou[a]'s Yuyao County as well as the Minghe saltern in Mingzhou[b]'s Cixi County, both rated at 90 percent. The Daishan and Changguo salterns, the Shuangsui saltern to their southeast, and the South and North Tianfu salterns of Wenzhou[a] were rated at 100 percent.[17] From Daishan to the two Tianfu salterns the seawater yield was greatest. From Minghe southwest to Tangcun, where saliferous earth was processed, the yield was 60 to 70 percent. At Yanguan and Tangcun, iron pans were used, which gave the salt a bluish tinge. At Yangcun and Qianqing salterns, trays of woven bamboo lined with lime were used, which gave the salt a yellowish tinge. To the east of Shiyan the seawater was relatively salty. Although [salters there] also used bamboo

---

[14] The *XCB* of 2/wuchen/1072 notes the name Zeng Dian instead of Zeng Mo (*XCB* 230.5602–3, interstitial comment).

[15] *XCB* 230.5602 (2/wuchen/1072); but *XCB* 247.6027 (10/gengyin/1073) cites 1071 from the *SHY*.

[16] In addition to the water's salt concentration, rainfall also affected production. According to present climatic patterns, Zhedong's Wenzhou[a] and Taizhou[a], for instance, are in a high precipitation isohyet of seventy inches per year; north of Mingzhou[b] it averages fifty inches per year (*People's Republic of China Atlas*, 55). The Liangzhe coast was at times also plagued by severe typhoons; such climatic conditions halted manufacture.

[17] *XXCY shang* 15. For more on the ten-point rating system of sea water set up by the Liangzhe judicial intendant, see *Yinxian tongzhi* [*YXTZ*] 5.44b–45a.

trays, the salt was very white.[18] Lu Bing limited the number of trays of salt to be processed at one firing to prevent private boiling. He organized three to ten stoves into one *jia* unit. In salt-producing regions he grouped families into units of five (*wu*) and ten (*shi*) for mutual surveillance.[19] In addition, *[p. 4437]* [Lu] called upon wine shop owners to buy a certain amount of salt. They were to obtain the salt from the government and sell it. Each month they had to forward tax payments to officials and were not to transgress their wine sales area. He cracked down on smugglers severely. Even if the punishment were less than the beating, tattooing, and exiling to hard labor (*pei*), offenders were punished by beating (*zhang*) and exiled 500 *li* along with their wives and children.[20] In both Kaifengfu and Jingdong Circuit, 500 soldiers were added to make arrests.[21]

---

[18] This section on yields was taken from the *Bozhai bian* [*BZB*] 3.14; *XCB* 230.5603, interstitial comment, 2/wuchen/1072. Zhexi's iron cauldrons were heavy and had to be supported by bricks, but the salt produced in them was considered superior. Zhedong's bamboo pans could only withstand a few days of use (*XXCY shang* 44, item 65). Workers wore wooden shoes and used large pieces of wood to stir the bubbling mixture, which emitted noxious fumes that sickened them (*YLMC* 2.25).

[19] After 1071 in the Northern Song, Liangzhe administrators began to apply the *baojia* system to sea salters (*HSRC* 80.7a–b). Based on village *baojia*, salt producer *jia* units were also for mutual assistance and surveillance. Verification of people, furnaces, and pans was essential to curbing illegal activity (*SHY* 26.31b). Usually one *jia* group of approximately twenty households was attached to one boiler furnace (*CYZJ jia* 14.6b). During the first ten years of Xiaozong's reign (1163–1189) the organizational and surveillance functions of the *jia* were emphasized. Households took turns ensuring delivery. The *jia* head, a position that rotated among *jia* members, had a significant role in advising the saltern official (*HSRC* 80.7b, 9a). In the early period, household registration and military units were based on the fives (*wu*), comprised of five soldiers or families, and the tens (*shi*), comprised of ten soldiers or families.

[20] *XCB* 230.5602–3 (2/wuchen/1072). For more on regulations on beatings, see McKnight 1981, 46, 82–83, and 93. McKnight has studied the periodic "acts of grace" from the Han through Song, general amnesties that regularly freed offenders or reduced their sentences. He suggests that this malfunctioning of the judicial system was a way to solve a bureaucratic crisis brought about by a huge population and a small number of judges.

[21] Lu Bing had been hoping for twice as many troops; the responding decree was issued 10/18/1073 (*SHY* 24.6a).

Lu Bing was depicted as overly zealous in prosecuting those who failed to pay taxes and lost his office despite revenue increases. The emperor pardoned the Liangzhe salters as a solution to the repayment crisis, but again subordinate officials did not necessarily observe this.

At the time only Hangzhou, Yuezhou[a], and Huzhou prefectures did not implement [Wang Anshi's] New Policies.[22] The Transport Intendancy prosecuted and punished them for falling behind in tax revenues.[23] Wang Anshi said to Shenzong that since the arrest law was strict, penalties could be lessened. After a time the emperor consequently decreed to the Liangzhe Salt Intendancy that prefectures experiencing declining revenues were not to be penalized but should be divided into three grades according to amount of shortfall and seriousness of violations, which [the prefectures] were to report.[24] In 1074 (Xining 7), though salt revenues had increased under Lu Bing's management, criminal cases overwhelmed [the judicial system]. Concerned about the numbers of the wrongly convicted, [the emperor] demoted Lu Bing to Huainan and filled his vacancy with the Jiangdong fiscal intendant, Zhang Jing[b], who was to handle [the crisis] as he saw fit.[25] [Zhang] Jing[b] reported that under [Lu] Bing's administration, officials at the Yuezhou[a] directorate so pressured workers for salt payments [whether in cash or in salt is unstated] that [they fell deeply into debt, and] a mother was driven to kill her own son [as a result of family conflict over the matter].[26] A decree called for an investigation of Lu Bing's crimes, but he escaped prosecution.[27] For having increased tax revenues, he was actually appointed erudite of imperial sacrifices and promoted one grade. After a

---

[22] Yuezhou[a] was changed to Shaoxingfu in 1131, when Shaoxing became Gaozong's new reign name. Its seat was Kuaiji, present-day Shaoxing County (Zhejiang) (Wang Leiming 1985, 351–52n1).

[23] On 11/dingsi/1072 the Liangzhe Salt Intendancy stated that the Yuezhou[a] prefect, Kong Yanzhi, had "obstructed [implementation of] the policy" and caused a drop in revenues (*XCB* 240.5826).

[24] Decreed 2/28/1073 (*SHY* 24.6a; *XCB* 242.5907).

[25] *XCB* 253.6197 (5/bingchen/1074).

[26] *XCB* 256.6265 (9/1074).

[27] He was meant to receive sixty strokes of the heavy bamboo but was pardoned on 9/guihai/1074 (*XCB* 256.6265).

year the Finance Commission stated that because of the laxness of the Liangzhe Fiscal Intendancy (*caosi*), salt revenues had greatly declined, so the emperor ordered the assistant staff writer, Weng Zhongtong, to deliberate [and come up with a new strategy].[28] At the beginning of the Yuanyou period (1086–1093) there was discussion concerning [Lu] Bing's implementation of the Zhexi salt policy.[29] He so zealously strove to increase tax revenues that the number of offenders sentenced to exile reached over 12,000 persons. For this [Lu] Bing was finally tried and lost his office.[30] The Liangzhe salters were required to submit an amount of

---

[28] *XCB* 264.6479 (5/dinghai/1075). For the twelve-year gap in *SS* coverage from 1074 to 1086, see the 12/9/1081 record on the compilation of a salt code; 181 articles were divided into *chi*, *ling*, and *ge*. It was in four chapters with two additional chapters of contents, and was to be named the Yuanfeng Salt Code of Jiang, Huai, Hu, and Zhe. Its woodblock printing and distribution were formally requested and the project directors rewarded (*SHY* 24.21b–22a).

Salt revenue for fourteen Liangzhe prefectures in 1076 (Xining 9) was recorded at 1,113,138-odd strings; in the first year of the Yuanfeng period (1078–1085), 871,884-odd strings. See *SHY* 23.11a–b and Yuki 1982, 31 for a table of southeastern revenues between 1074–1078. Two other lists, presumably for Southern Song production, also exist. One is from the *Zhongxing huiyao* (specified on *SHY* 23.17a). It shows for Zhexi, (including Xiuzhou, Pingjiangfu, and Lin'anfu, with saltern breakdown) 1,137,145-odd piculs (*SHY* 23.13a–14a); and for Zhedong (including Shaoxingfu, Mingzhou[b], Taizhou[a], and Wenzhou[a], and their respective salterns), 848,283-odd piculs, (*SHY* 23.14a–15a). The other list is from *Qiandao huiyao* (specified on *SHY* 23.18a). For Zhexi it shows, 1,144,177-odd piculs and for Zhedong, 743,201-odd piculs, with the same prefectures listed (*SHY* 23.13a–18a).

[29] Zhexi should read Liangzhe. The criticism of Lu Bing's misbehavior occurred when he was out of office in Yuanyou 3 (4/renyin/1088), not at the beginning of Yuanyou in 1086 (*XCB* 409.9978).

[30] During Wang Anshi's reforms, Lu Bing was in charge of Liangzhe salt. A harsh stickler for the law, he did not exempt older people, women, or children. In one year thousands were convicted. In the Yuanyou period (1086–1093), however, he was found guilty of torture in his zealous enforcement of salt policy and lost his post. Lu Bing's policy had also been extended to Huainan, thus his impact was significant (*SS* 331.10670–71). For the damage done by Lu Bing, see Lü Tao's memorial on 8/jiachen/1087 (*XCB* 404.9849). After mourning his father, Lu Bing retired to a temple appointment. Only then was he was criticized for having enforced the Liangzhe salt policy too vigorously. On 4/renyin/1088 the right policy monitor, Liu Anshi, memorialized on Lu's extremes and recommended that since Lu's crime was no less than Wu Juhou's, the precedent for Wu should

salt according to the number of adult males, but their debts grew ever greater. In 1087 (Yuanyou 2) the emperor decreed that those debts be forgiven.[31] Later, more debts accumulated without hope of repayment, and at the beginning of the Yuanfu reign (1098–1100) an investigation commissioner reported this situation. But the responsible parties replied that it was because the imperial decree had not been implemented, despite the fact that the right policy monitor (*you zhengyan*), Zou Hao, had emphatically expounded upon the problem [of salters falling into debt].[32]

Here follows a twenty-year gap in the Songshi *record from 1098 to 1119.*

*   *   *   *   *

On 9/14/1103 a decree was handed down for 100,000 strings to be given Liangzhe from reserve (fengzhuang) *money as salt funds. The following month, on 10/28/1103, a proposal was put forward to increase the salt given to merchants servicing Zhedong and Zhexi to compensate for the difficulties of transport in those mountainous regions.[33] On intercalary 8/12/1110 a Salt Code of 130 items was completed. The southeast followed the Yuanfeng policy of government sales, while*

---

be followed for heavier sentencing (*XCB* 409.9978). Liu Anshi, on 5/xinhai/1088, protested that Lu Bing's sentence of two additional years' official review was not in keeping with the nature of his crimes. Anything short of execution would be too light. And inappropriate punishment would reflect poorly on His Majesty (*XCB* 410.9990–92).

The gentleman-for-discussion (*chengyilang*), Zhang Yuanfang, reported on 2/dingmao/1086 that Liangzhe's annual fund for salt production, formerly 300,000 strings, was now 400,000. Even though the figure had increased, profits were lower because of expenses in carrying out the law, including various sorts of rewards. He requested that procurement salterns be closed and salters be allowed to boil and trade but pay a monthly charge (*XCB* 365.8764).

[31] Decreed 8/12/1087. The "salters of Liangzhe" actually refers to those of Qiantang, Renhe, Yanguan, and Changguo (*SHY* 24.28b–29a; *XCB* 404.9836).

[32] The Song adopted the Tang titles of left and right completioner (*zuo shiyi, you shiyi*), but changed them to left and right policy monitor (*zuo zhengyan, you zhengyan*) in 988. From the Yuanfeng period (1078–1085) these positions were charged with judicial criticism of policies and official conduct. The left office was under the Chancellery Department (*menxia sheng*); the right office was under the Secretariat Department (*zhongshu sheng*).

[33] *SHY* 24.37a.

other areas permitted merchant sales. Two weeks later, on intercalary 8/25/1110, a decree stressed the importance of observing the Salt Code, *since profits from southeastern salt were the basis of paper currency for the three southeastern circuits. This was picked up again on 12/20/1110 with a line about future restoration of government sales. On 12/26/1110 the six southeast circuits were to be studied to determine the advisability of this. By 12/29/1110 the go-ahead for merchant sales using new vouchers was given.[34] On 1/12/1111 additional voucher regulations for Liangzhe and Huai were described. On 1/23/1111 the emperor decreed how evaluations were to be conducted for Huai and Zhe officials in response to concern about the behavior of storehouse and saltern officials. On 3/21/1111 setting salt prices, and the pros and cons of raising the price, were discussed.[35] On 3/25/1112 a decree touched on the importance of salt funds and the timing of payments to salters. On 5/22/1112 the Department of Ministries responded that there was insufficient capital to compensate the salters; the emperor answered that it would be paid from the circuits' tribute funds.[36] On 2/1/1113 distribution problems were raised. On 9/4/1113 it was decreed that Huai would take up Liangzhe's silkworm salt policy.[37]*

*   *   *   *   *

When salt tax revenues at the Minghe saltern in Mingzhou[b] did not increase, it was assigned to Yuezhou[a]'s jurisdiction.[38] In 1119 (Xuanhe 1) Lou Yi, in charge of Mingzhou[b], petitioned to have Minghe returned. He also asked for 570,000 bags of salt from nearby Taizhou[a]. The emperor decreed:

> Mingzhou[b] had three salterns. Because of maladministration, the Minghe saltern was placed under Yuezhou[a], and merchants have begun to congregate [there to buy]. The other two salterns have accumulated vast quantities of salt about which nothing has yet been done. Yet instead of working on that, you ask eastward from Yuezhou[a] and westward from Taizhou[a] for gains. A policy change will harm the law and shake the people's trust.

[Lou Yi] was ordered to make a detailed report on his management.

---

[34] *SHY* 25.2b–4a.

[35] *SHY* 25.4a–5b.

[36] *SHY* 25.5b–6b.

[37] *SHY* 25.7a–8b.

[38] Minghe was near the boundary between Mingzhou[b] and Yuezhou[a].

It is unfortunate that the Songshi *coverage of Liangzhe concludes here, for the significance of salt from this area for Southern Song revenues cannot be overstated. While Fujian and Guang sea salt and Sichuan well salt were produced primarily for local consumption, Zhe salt, together with that of Huai, was distributed across nine circuits and eighty prefectures south of the Huai River.[39] In 1223 this amounted to over 7,500,000 households, or nearly 60 percent of the empire's population.[40] In this vast area twelve to sixteen burgeoning cities included the preeminent Lin'an, with a population over one million in the late thirteenth century. Because of the size and wealth of the marketing region, the monopoly in Liangzhe and Huai severely tested the state's organizational capabilities.*

The Songshi's *Liangzhe account leaves off abruptly for the next 140 years, suggesting that the editors were not composing a new account and simply left off their copying here. This highlights the drawbacks of the* Songshi *account. My reconstruction below carries the story from 1119 through 1260 and employs a partly chronological, partly topical organization.*

✻   ✻   ✻   ✻   ✻

Regarding official evaluation and personnel, on 7/13/1119 rewards were decreed for Hangzhou and Yuezhou[a] storehouse officials, while fines and penalties were ordered for Taizhou[a] and Mingzhou[b] officials. On 2/13/1120 the Liangzhe Salt Intendancy reported to the court on the best (Hangzhou, Yuezhou[a]) and worst (Taizhou[a], Mingzhou[b]) records for distribution at warehouses, compared with previous years. On 4/9/1120 the Secretariat Department relayed a Monopoly Goods Bureau's report of negligence, tardiness, and laxness on the part of salt officers and patrols on the seaboard, which had allowed the rise of smuggling. All responsible officials were to be demoted.[41] On 5/29/1121 the Department of Ministries, concerned that a fee of 20 strings on each voucher worth 100 strings was too low, suggested that 5 strings be added to fund the salters' capital.[42] On 3/22/1122 the Liangzhe salt, incense, tea, and alum intendant, Li Yuquan, memorialized on the need to crack down on the irregular behavior of officials and clerks.[43]

On 4/8/1123 a decree called for policies to facilitate merchant trade, including reduction of fees and new vouchers, because of the overstock of salt at storehouses.[44]

---

[39] *HSZLS* 51.11b, 4/end of month/1172.

[40] *WXTK* 11.116.

[41] *SHY* 25.11a–b, 12a–b.

[42] *SHY* 25.13b.

[43] *SHY* 25.16b–17b.

[44] *SHY* 25.19b–20a.

On 3/2/1124 the Department of Ministries relayed to the court the Monopoly Goods Bureau's report on Liangzhe salt intendant Li Biru's instructions, which highlighted the problem of salt goods not moving. Prefectural and county officials were held accountable for insufficient sales and had to make up any shortfalls before being transferred. On 11/27/1124 a memorial from the Monopoly Goods Bureau supervisor Wei Bochu stated that since Liangzhe's eastern and western circuits now each had its own intendant and administrators, they no longer accepted vouchers from each other's merchants. Wei feared the competition between the two would ultimately derail the voucher system. He hoped that the court would rule that Zhedong and Zhexi must allow the exchange of merchant vouchers between them, compare their annual tax income differences, and conduct inspection rounds to support united action in boosting revenues.[45]

In Zhexi the production process was referred to as "sunning the ashes" (shaihui). Ashes (hui) from the reeds used as fuel were spread on a raised bed (tanchang) rigged with dikes and gates near the sea. The ashes' dark color increased the rate of evaporation. The drying beds then were flooded with sea water, which was pumped up hydraulically and allowed to dry overnight. In summer it took one day for a bed to dry; in winter, several days.[46] The beds were surrounded by ditches into which water was fed. The salty solution was swept into a percolating vat and filtered with sea water through further layers of ashes. When the brine was sufficiently concentrated to be ready for boiling, it was channeled into an underground storage well via a bamboo pipe.[47] In Zhedong, the ash stage was skipped, but the batch of brine took somewhat longer to process. The water channeled into the raised beds was allowed to evaporate in the sun all day and by evening, crystals from the alkaline soil could be scraped off (guajian, guatu) and covered with grass. This irrigation and exposure procedure was repeated for five to six days until the brine was strong enough and a full vat had been collected.[48]

In Zhexi the unit of production was the furnace (zao). From two to ten furnaces formed a saltern or saltworks.[49] At the beginning of the Song only three or four

---

[45] For the two dates in 1124, see *SHY* 23b–24a, 25.23a.

[46] *ABT*, plate 23; Yoshida 1993, 7.

[47] *ABT*, plates 1, 5; Yoshida 1993, 115, 117–18. See a similar description in *YLMC* 2.25.

[48] "Yan" in *Kuaiji zhi* [*KJZ*] 17.52b–53b. Also, 1926 photo reprint of the *Qing Jiaqing* ed. 17.44a–45a, cited in Worthy 1975 (115n32). Worthy notes this process was characteristic of the Shaoxing area and not necessarily of the entire circuit. For discussion of differences in production between Zhedong and Zhexi, see Yoshida 1963, 38–43.

[49] *ABT*, plate 1; Yoshida 1993, 115; *CYZJ jia* 14.6a–b. Four to five furnaces at one Baolang saltern are described in *Haiyan Ganshui zhi* [*HYGSZ*], *juan shang*.

saltworks operated in Liangzhe. After 1085 there were fourteen; by 1162, forty-two. In Zhexi between 1131 and 1162, twenty-four saltworks operated over three prefectures: four in Pingjiangfu (Northern Song Suzhou), ten in Lin'anfu, and ten in Xiuzhou. In Zhedong, eighteen were distributed among four prefectures: three in Taizhou[a], four in Shaoxingfu, five in Wenzhou[a], and six in Mingzhou[b].[50] Numbers fluctuated depending on productivity or exigency; sometimes saltworks were shut down as soon as the quota was filled. At the beginning of the Yuan, salt production was stopped in the tenth month of the year for that reason.[51]

In the section on 1/19/1163 the Song huiyao describes how the government set up a daily schedule specifying the time salt workers were to start and stop boiling; this regimen was duly registered and reported. When the fire was set, the supervisor had to give orders for bringing on the brine solution. When the fire was doused, he was to collect and store the brine.[52] Processed salt was temporarily kept in a guarded unit (tuan) with several furnaces, which usually had five to seven storage rooms, so that workers did not have to transport the salt to distant depots. When the storage rooms were full, the salt was sent on to where it was to be sold under the seal of the household and measured again upon arrival.[53] The final production procedure was this weighing. The salt bags were only to be manufactured by the government. They were filled only once, sealed, and stamped. In the Zhe and Huai regions large bags generally held 300 catties and small bags held 60 catties; other sea salt regions used different sized bags. Large bags made up for salt's lack of firmness and tendency to spill; small bags were more popular with merchants, but they could not go beyond prefectural boundaries.[54]

Due to the disruption of production in Zhedong during the early Southern Song, salt from other circuits was temporarily distributed there. Fujian salt was imported into the Huai-Zhe trading area for four months, as reported on 1/29/1130. Guang salt was imported beginning the same year for five years.[55] There were at least two attempts by a Sichuan official, Zhang Chun, to have well salt sold in Huai-Zhe: the first attempt was prohibited by the chief councilor, Qin Kuai, in 1132, and the second was rejected by the emperor on 5/dinghai/1132.[56] On 8/25/1131 the Zhexi tea and

---

[50] *YH* 181.36a. For production prefectures in the Northern Song by 12/wuzi/1021, see *XCB* 97.2260–61; *WXTK* 15.8a; *BZB* 3.14.

[51] *Caomuzi* [*CMZ*] 67.

[52] *SHY* 27.11b–12a.

[53] *ABT*, plates 4, 47; Yoshida 1993, 117, 149.

[54] Bag size may have been tied to vouchers; the "small" vouchers were for use only within the prefecture where the salt was produced. See Liu Jun 1973, 272–73.

[55] *SHY* 25.34a–b, 36a–b.

[56] *XNYL* 54.23a–b, 54.15a, respectively.

salt intendant, Liang Rujia, recommended rewards, including silk and a reduction of reviews, for all subordinates for their role in restoring production to 1.4 million strings after the defeat of the Jin. According to a 3/2/1132 memorial by the Zhexi tea and salt intendant, Xia Zhiwen, procurement had already increased by 8.77 million catties.[57]

On 12/17/1131 and 2/5/1132 the Zhedong and Zhexi Intendancies requested more severe punishments, including demotion, for negligent salt officials.[58] *At monopoly bureaus, administrators often committed graft, mishandling merchant vouchers and funds. It was suggested that such officials be punished according to regulations relating to middlemen.*[59] *Tax officials of the prefectures, counties, and market towns along the Yangzi River were prone to halting salt merchant boats, seizing documents, and making exactions. Soldiers, too, made illegal demands. They were to be punished by three years' banishment.*[60]

Regarding Liangzhe salt transport, passage from places of production to storehouses or selling places was accomplished predominantly via water routes up the Huai and Yangzi Rivers or to the lower and mid-Yangzi and from there to northern and southern markets.[61] *Canals connected the Yangzi to the Huai. It was noted on 2/5/1132 that another route followed the Qiantang River, which connected Lin'an at its mouth, to Quzhou and Wuzhou*[b] *to the west, and other prefectures further upstream. As noted on 10/19/1131 each saltern was to hand over its cashed vouchers on the same day to the supervising office (zhuguan si). The supervisor was to gather all records and await the arrival of the registering official (haobu guan), who would deliver the books to the proper office for inspection.*[62]

Regarding salt and the military, imperial army soldiers as well as prefectural troops flouted the law by trading salt. Military personnel who did not report offenses or who acted illegally in collusion with others were punished according to military law, as noted on 9/10/1129.[63] *Destitute commoners turned to banditry and smuggling, as did soldiers. Commoners also traded illegally under the protection of soldiers, as was memorialized on 10/11/1133. Military and civilians banded together through networks to trade salt. Inside the city, if 100 catties was involved, the punishment followed earlier regulations and a reward of 200 strings would go to the informant. For a deal struck outside the city, penalties seem to have been somewhat*

---

[57] *SHY* 26.2a–3b, 9a.

[58] *SHY* 26.3a–b, 4a–5a.

[59] *SHY* 27.38b.

[60] *SHY* 26.3b–4a.

[61] Liang Gengyao 1988, part 2, 14–30.

[62] *SHY* 26.4a, 26.3a, respectively.

[63] *SHY* 32.21b–22a.

lighter, as stated on intercalary 4/3/1132. Any army commander-general (tongzhiguan) who ignored violations would be punished, according to a 4/7/1132 decree.[64] *When high-ranking military officials smuggled, however, the court dared not investigate. Thus the army caused disorder and a slump in salt tax revenues, as noted on 12/jiawu/1132.*[65] *Although it was illegal, local military and administrative units turned to salt transport and sale to resolve their financial difficulties. The punishment for military men illegally trading government salt was two years' banishment, as noted on 9/13/1176.*[66] *In 1180 however, officials were permitted to transport and sell salt in locations where few merchants had come. On 10/15/1204 the Zhexi tea and salt intendant, Shi Miyuan, reported that archers, local militia, and salters were in league to cover up illicit boiling and sales. He asked that patrols found guilty be punished to the same degree as saltern officials.*[67]

Zhe salters from the beginning of Southern Song were ranked into upper, middle, and lower households based on the size of their operations; they were funded and taxed accordingly.[68] *On 3/26/1132 the Department of Ministries and Ministry of Finance responded to Zhexi's tea and salt intendant, Liang Rujia, that salters were not to be placed in the same category as regular village households for taxes and the corvée. The more salt they produced, the more their obligations were cut. Upper households that submitted 10,000 piculs of salt annually had their tax duty cut 30 percent; middle and lower households that produced twice as much as the previous year's quota had taxes reduced 30 percent. The upper class was further subdivided into "highest" and "second highest."*[69] *From the ranks of upper-class households was chosen the head of eighty households (lizheng); from middle households was chosen the huzhang. Both were responsible for ensuring that their members paid their taxes.*[70]

Upper households felt it beneath them to register as salters; only middle- and lower-class households were so counted. Upper households enjoyed the privilege of employing others and usually did not deal personally with lower households, but sent servants or proxies instead.[71] *Upper households expedited salt collection on behalf of officials and came to employ other households (beiding) to leach and boil. When a household completed these tasks, the household chief (zhuhu) measured, collected,*

---

[64] *SHY* 26.17a–18b, 26.5b–6a, respectively.

[65] *XNYL* 61.9a–b.

[66] *SHY* 28.6b–7a.

[67] *SHY* 28.11a–b, 49b.

[68] *HSRC* 80.6b–7a.

[69] *SHY* 26.5a–b.

[70] *HXZ* 10.1019.

[71] *HSRC* 80.7b.

and placed the salt into the unit's storehouse.[72] *On the basis of this accounting the all-critical salter funding was reckoned. The inevitable collusion between upper households and government supervisors led to upper households themselves serving as superintendents* (duzhang) *and collector-generals* (tongcui), *prime positions from which to embezzle salter funds and abuse lower-ranked families.*[73] *By the 1260s rich households no longer engaged in boiling.*

But even the rich could be bankrupted by their responsibilities. A service duty assigned to upper and then middle households required them to host county administrators and saltern officials, cover their carriage fees, and provide rice and drink for their porters (jiaozi).[74] *As time went on the state ceased to distinguish between rich and poor households and levies became regressive, with the poor paying a higher rate. By the last quarter of the dynasty all three levels of household were consolidated without distinction.*[75]

The numbers of salters in Liangzhe generally rose through the late imperial period. In late Southern Song, Liangzhe had 10,000 to 20,000 households or 30,000 to 40,000 salters.[76] *At the beginning of the Yuan in Liangzhe, only 9,600 salter households remained.*[77] *Their numbers later grew to more than 17,000 households, then declined again to only 7,000 due to disasters, plague, absconding, and death. The old quotas fell on the shoulders of the remaining households.*[78] *At the beginning of the Ming Liangzhe again had 30,000 active salters; by the Qing there were over 180,000.*[79]

To curb the transfer of property and workforce mobility, salters could not by law pawn, mortgage, or sell property. Frequent exhortations to comply with this regulation suggest that it was often violated. One official at the end of the Song confiscated large amounts of salter land without apparent justification.[80] *In the early 1300s Qu Tingfa of the Xiasha saltworks in Huating (Zhexi), who was part of an upper salter household and known as the "Old Master of Numerous Fields," actually acquired control of 10,000 hectares* (qing) *of land, including rented official fields.*

Because salters were meant to concentrate on manufacture and were not permitted to move freely, they were exempted from the corvee and had their Double

---

[72] *ABT*, plate 46; Yoshida 1993, 148–49.

[73] *HSRC* 80.2a–4.

[74] *HSRC* 80.8b–9a.

[75] *HSRC* 80.6b.

[76] Guo Zhengzhong 1990a, 106.

[77] Chen Chun, "Ti *Aobo tu*" [TABT] 16.96a.

[78] *YS* 97.2496.

[79] *Liangzhe yanfa zhi* [LZYF] 7.1b–20b.

[80] *HSRC* 80.12a–b.

Taxes commuted (zhe'na) *to salt. From 1163 they were allowed to pay taxes with their above-quota salt. Every three years their tax was recalculated according to available manpower, output, and quality. If salters concealed information, they were sentenced to two years of banishment. On 1/19/1163 literati reported to the court that because of the corvee exemption, unscrupulous well-to-do persons posed as salters, taking on the names of individuals who had fled. They thus encroached on the rights of the poor and also the government's income.*[81]

Procurement in 1132 had increased by over 8,770,000 catties (175,400 piculs). Revenue from voucher sales increased by over 514,300 strings, while the total amount of salt sold in shops at the prefectural and county level increased by over 5,820,000 catties (116,400 piculs). As a consequence the Zhexi tea and salt intendant, subordinate officials, and clerks were rewarded.[82] Sometimes requests came for a saltern to be set up: on intercalary 4/25/1132 a Mingzhou[b] magistrate pointed out that the soil of his area was brackish. Since residents were already boiling salt and selling it illegally, it would be profitable to open up a saltern there. On 3/7/1133 the Monopoly Goods Bureau recommended that a Mingzhou[b] saltworks allow salters to borrow thirty strings of cash in three installments and set a procurement price of seventeen cash per catty for the additional quota salt produced.[83]

Salter violations occurred across the region. Zhang Yuan called for a schedule of disciplinary actions to be taken against those who were tardy in forwarding their quotas, failed to repay loans, joined the military, or fled to other stoves. From the outset, such offenses were punishable by eighty strokes under the Southern Song. After military labor, salters were sent back to their saltworks and counted once again responsible for their quotas. Far from sympathizing with salters, Zhang labeled them "stubborn and slippery types."[84]

An investigating official, Zhu Yi[a], memorialized on 1/29/1133 that it was impossible to contain long-distance smuggling if both ends had to be investigated; therefore, cases were to be closed at one end, cleared up at the other.[85] On 9/5/1133 a Zhedong prefectural official reiterated a decree of 12/8/1132 calling for salters who privately sold any amount of salt to be beaten and exiled to Guangnan without leniency.[86] It was noted on 10/28/1142 that for three repeat offenses an offender received a certain number of strokes according to the severity of the case, regardless any imperial pardons in effect. In cases where information had been concealed,

---

[81] *SHY* 27.10b–11a, 12b.

[82] *SHY* 26.9a–b.

[83] *SHY* 26.6a–b, 9b–10a.

[84] *SHY* 26.13a–b.

[85] I.e., who was doing the illegal selling, and who the illegal buying (*SHY* 26.8a–b).

[86] *SHY* 26.15b, 18b–19a; *XNYL* 69.4a–5b.

punishments became more severe by one grade. The same held true for officials and clerks involved in illegal trading.[87] One downside of these regulations was noted on 7/6/1166, with the comment that when salters were banished, the number of production personnel fell. On 6/17/1171 Ye Heng proposed that any salt produced above quota amounts be collected in a timely manner to help curb smuggling.[88] The most desperate salters turned to banditry and piracy. They killed large numbers of commoners in Zhedong and in turn were killed by troopers.[89]

On 8/10/1133 the Zhexi tea and salt intendant, Zhang Yuan, described how when salt officials were concurrently county administrators, they kept insufficient records and did not properly monitor salt production. He suggested that salterns forward records to the county monthly and that the officials involved be punished if irregularities were discovered.[90] If a local administrator was concurrently a saltern official, he was required to get his saltworks records cleared before transferring to a new post, as Ye Heng had suggested.[91] According to a Ministry of Justice memorial of 10/15/1133, if a magistrate did not monitor salt collection, his punishment was eighty strokes. If he was guilty of outright abuses, his punishment was doubled. If a saltern head refused to release workers who had fled from another saltern, 100 strokes was to be meted out.[92]

Abuses by patrols and soldiers were rampant. The record for 11/23/1134 reports that soldiers at Lin'anfu designated to guard the gates picked fights, damaged baggage, seized possessions, herded family members off boats, planted packages of salt on boats, then blackmailed travelers for it. So a request for additional soldiers to guard the water gate at Pingjiangfu was shelved. On 8/12/1135 ministers petitioned that the court should adhere to the law and care for salters. They opposed wasting time trying to apprehend smugglers by posting patrols day and night on riverbanks, on the borders, and along paths.[93] In late 1161 in Shaoxing (Zhedong), bandits were said to be at work where merchant boats gathered. Two hundred navy men from neighboring Mingzhou[b] camped in the area and were rotated every three months, which brought some stability. In mid-1160 an order was given to magistrates to record the names of all smugglers; any apprehended twice were to be exiled.[94]

---

[87] *SHY* 26.29b.

[88] *SHY* 27.22a–b, 34a.

[89] *HSRC* 77.1a–b, 2a.

[90] *SHY* 26.13a–b.

[91] *SHY* 27.41b.

[92] *SHY* 26.20b.

[93] *SHY* 26.24a–25a.

[94] *SHY* 27.8a–b, 27.4b–5a, respectively.

The court reiterated in 1166 that salt officials were to be chosen on the basis of their ability and reliability.[95] While patrolmen were entrusted with apprehending offenders, it was apparently unusual for them to do so. However, on 1/19/1171 a Mingzhou[b] military inspector (xunjian), Gong Wei, confiscated 5,000 catties of salt and was injured while leading soldiers in an attack on some smugglers. The emperor was at a loss to determine a reward for this rare initiative. In the end, Gong was granted a three-year appointment free of review, in accordance with the regulation on officials who had confiscated 5,000 catties of contraband.[96]

Income more than doubled at the three major branches of the Monopoly Goods Bureau, from approximately 6 million strings in 1130 to 13 million in 1136, with 80 percent of the 1136 income derived from salt itself.[97]

The state levied various taxes on producers. In some cases in early Southern Song Zhexi, fees that lower salter households now had to pay for transport of their product had to be paid in lengths of silk. A magistrate on 2/18/1138 noted that this silk was worth seven times the money owed, which the salters already had no means to pay.[98] The illegal but widespread practice of local governments forcing households and the local militia to buy set quantities of salt was widespread in Shaoxing, as noted 4/6/1158 and 1/25/1159.[99]

Regarding finances at the saltern, on 10/18/1128 the associate tea and salt intendant for the Provisional Capital, Xu Gongyu, argued that funds for salt production ought not be used for other purposes (mobilizing the militias and army, soldiers' cash wages and grain, and so on) lest it wreak havoc on the voucher policy. Instead, those monies ought to be irrevocably designated for saltworks.[100] On 6/1/1143 ministers stated that the shortage of operating funds at salterns was due to officials issuing too many types of loans without keeping records of them. Since salt officials disliked the strictness of the ever-normal regulations on loans, they used salt funds instead, which siphoned off state investment in the industry. The Ministry of Finance then deliberated with the Monopoly Goods Bureau and petitioned that salter loans be provided out of ever-normal funds.[101]

On 2/24/1160 the temporary executive of the Ministry of Finance, Shao Dashou, proposed measures to deal with the shortage of salt funding. In Zhe and Huai this money came from various fees charged by storehouses, but because smuggling

---

[95] *SHY* 27.20b.

[96] *SHY* 27.28b.

[97] *CYZJ jia* 17.8b.

[98] *SHY* 26.25a–b.

[99] *SHY* 26.38b–39a, 42b.

[100] *SHY* 25.33a–b.

[101] *SHY* 26.31a.

meant that government salt moved slowly and because saltworks officials engaged in graft, revenues were short. Shao proposed that the complete payment of funds owed salters be made possible by setting aside 300 cash from the regular fee of 5,000 cash paid by merchants on each bag of salt. Although Shaoxing was a producer and one of the most populated areas of Zhedong, only 160,000 catties of salt were sold there annually, compared with more than the 3 million and 5 million catties sold in nonproducing Quzhou and Wuzhou[b], respectively. This was because Shaoxing residents preferred to buy smuggled salt. Shao also proposed disciplinary action for prefectural administrators who doled out extra catties as favors. Investigations found an extra 67 catties in one bag and an extra 79 in two others at a Tongzhou[b] storehouse.[102] In another case, one bag held 100 extra catties, making it a total of 400 catties. In an extreme case described on 11/1/1172, merchants came away with as much as 1,000 catties more than they were supposed to have.[103] On 5/23/1165 the salter funding process was described by the Zhexi tea and salt intendant, Yao Xian: 50 percent of the funds were granted to each boiler at the saltworks; they received the remaining 50 percent at the procurement saltern once their product had been submitted for weighing. Unfortunately, most poor salters could not last until weighing time, so they fled and their salterns fell into disrepair.[104]

On 9/9/1159 the Zhedong salt intendant, Du Jie, stated that Wenzhou[a] annually produced over 35,000 bags, yet distributed only 15,000 to 16,000 bags. The resulting glut was due to the rough terrain, which discouraged merchants. He proposed giving one extra bag for every ten bags to those who would sell within the circuit and two extra bags for every ten to those who would sell in other circuits.[105] Time limits applying to both officials (who distributed to merchants) and merchants (who sold to consumers) were made flexible to ensure that the salt moved. On 5/30/1163 it was decreed that Wenzhou[a] salterns could extend the time in which they had to distribute accumulated salt by another half year; in addition, they gave bonus salt to encourage buyers. Merchants and shopkeepers were originally given two months to deliver Huai and Zhe salt to the interior; when this deadline came and went, it was extended by another month, as indicated on intercalary 11/22/1164 and 1/23/1165.[106] Difficult terrain continued to pose an expensive obstacle. Some locations were inaccessible and even for those with access, waterways often ran shallow or dried up during drought. The water routes in Wenzhou[a] and Taizhou[a] were mainly via the sea, while land

---

[102] *SHY* 27.2a–3b.

[103] *SHY* 28.48a, 27.41a, respectively.

[104] *SHY* 27.18b–19a.

[105] *SHY* 26.43b–44a. These bonuses involved extra salt offered for a restricted period to attract merchants to localities where a backlog of undistributed salt had accumulated.

[106] *SHY* 27.13b, 16a–b, 16b–17a.

routes had to cross mountains, as was noted on 9/9/1159.[107] *Land transport in general was more difficult, and countless draft animals died in the effort.*[108]

The practice of forced purchases continued in the Southern Song. Local officials in Zhedong made commoners purchase certain amounts, a practice that had been outlawed in 1159.[109] Inflation took its toll on consumers: the salt price rose from 60 cash per catty in 1112 to 700–800 cash in 1131.[110] Supplementary trade taxes (touzi) intended for the circuit and prefectural office (gongshiku), with funds earmarked for official expenses such as receptions, travel to the court, and dismissal, sometimes went into the purses of Huai and Zhe intendants, friends, and relatives. According to the censor on 5/13/1156, tens of thousands of strings were used by the Huaidong intendant for shopping sprees, entertainment, and so on.[111] Saltern officials allowed underlings to lend salters money at high interest, then deducted the amount loaned from the salter's rightful state funds; punishment for this, ordinarily two years' banishment, was to follow regulations for usury committed by investigating commissioners (jianlinguan). For accepting up to eight bolts of goods (presumably as "interest"), the punishment was banishment for one year; the next eight bolts got the official an additional degree of punishment; for fifty bolts, offenders were sentenced to banishment 2,000 miles away, as noted for 1160.[112]

On 9/15/1165 ministers detailed the enforcement of extra charges on merchants. In the past the three Monopoly Goods Bureaus had annually charged a seventeen-string surtax per bag when merchants turned in their vouchers for salt; they now proposed adding three more strings to the fee. The Ministry of Finance would inform the Monopoly Goods Bureaus to carry out the order the day the directive arrived. Merchants who had processed their vouchers but not yet gone to the warehouse for salt might pay the extra charge at any of the three office locations. Those who paid were given salt first. Those who had already received salt had to report to the issuing office within three days and pay the surcharge within ten days before they could sell. To buy vouchers, merchants had to pay twenty-two cash of "regular" supplementary tax, ten cash of "return" supplementary tax, and one cash of "hiring" money. Inspection officials were not to open sealed salt bags, on pain of punishment.[113]

---

[107] *SHY* 26.43b–44a.

[108] *MBT* 11.16–18.

[109] *SHY* 26.42b.

[110] *XNYL* 50.10a.

[111] *SHY* 26.33b–34a.

[112] *SHY* 27.5a.

[113] *SHY* 27.19b–20b.

On 6/11/1166 the Ministry of Finance presented three measures dealing with the ratios between paper currency, cash, bills, silver and gold, and other monetary instruments. Other discussions of currency ratios occurred on 12/29/1172 and 5/2/1173.[114] When the government took over the printing of bills in 1160, it based their value on that of copper currency. Various correctives were employed to slow devaluation due to overprinting, including government purchase of above-quota salt, using money to cover the costs of printing salt vouchers, as well as using salt profits from merchant sales to buy up paper money, as decreed on 3/28/1174.[115] On 2/14/1212 a decree detailed the forms of money that each of the three Monopoly Goods Bureaus and the voucher sales offices could use and their exchange rates.[116]

The point of distribution became a significant bone of contention. On 8/17/1168, as a follow-up to a petition of 8/1165, the Wenzhou[a] prefect petitioned that salterns were more efficient than prefectural storehouses in distributing salt. He observed that the bulk of the money collected from merchants at storehouses was intended to go towards funding the salters; but because of a variety of abuses, the money was never available in sufficient amounts. When the quantities of salt distributed at storehouses turned out to be significantly less than those distributed at salterns, saltern distribution was mandated again and again. The prefect listed eight advantages of saltern distribution for the government; it would eliminate superfluous personnel, covert extra weight awards, transport disturbances, foreign matter added en route, and the hardship on salters delivering to prefectural storehouses.[117] Zhedong, disadvantaged with respect to geography, markets, and wealth, retained its storehouses to cultivate merchant interest. Zhexi, which was more developed and had better transport arrangements, restored saltern distribution.[118]

Extraneous staffing had become a major problem. Huang Zhen asked, "Do ten sheep need nine shepherds?" He listed off the staff of one branch office to illustrate: eight wine and tea servers, sixty fanners, thirty hangers-on, their one hundred and fifty relatives, four or five hundred members of the lower echelon, in addition to two procurement officials, one sales agent, and their followers in the countryside, for a total of over one thousand members.[119] Many officials at warehouses had not passed the examinations, but had came to their positions by appointment, and some were

---

[114] *SHY* 27.21b–22a, 42a.

[115] *SHY* 28.1a–b.

[116] *SHY* 28.53b–55a.

[117] *SHY* 27.24b–25b.

[118] Liang Gengyao 1988, part 2, 18; *HNZG*, 19.11a–12a, "Song nanlu yancang ji" (Salt storehouses in southern circuits in the Song). For the differences in the salt monopoly structure in Zhedong and Zhexi, see Zhang Jiaju 1935, 24.

[119] *HSRC* 71.7a.

military men with no knowledge of civilian affairs, as reported on 12/13/1163.[120] *On 4/23/1213 the Zhedong Intendancy proposed to eliminate two out of five bag inspectors at the Wenzhou[a] salterns, one of two market-inspectors at the Wenzhou[a] storehouses, and one staff position. The emperor decreed further cuts.*[121]

A number of factors cut into optimal production. Overcast weather slowed evaporation, and rain diluted the cauldron solution. Work halted altogether in the winter months.[122] *The marsh reed season ended by the eighth or ninth month, so fuel supplies constrained furnace firings. By the early 1170s, due to drought, Wenzhou[a] quotas were temporarily exempted from review.*[123] *But at other times salt was produced beyond the quota. The only legal manner in which quota and above-quota, or "floating," salt could be disposed of was through government procurement. In establishing quotas officials took the highest production record as the norm. The producers had to reach quota without raising expectations further. Quotas were set on a monthly basis, to be delivered in three installments, on, say, the tenth, twentieth, and thirtieth of the month. Sometimes, however, a special envoy would demand that bags be presented days early, advancing the deadline and creating an excuse to charge late fees.*[124]

Huang Zhen blamed falling production on excessive staff and corruption at branch salt administration offices. A salter was theoretically paid fifteen strings of cash for each bushel of salt he produced, but because clerks and supervisors each demanded extra amounts and the salters did not have it to submit, salters were actually charged as much as eighty strings per bushel.[125] *In the 1270s an "investigate and clear out" procedure (tuipai) was instituted whereby every three years the state reassessed production quotas as well as the resources of boiler households.*[126] *On his visits to Zhexi salterns, Huang Zhen reported on all manner of official abuses, including harassment, destruction of property, beating of debtors, extortion, and kidnapping women for ransom.*[127] *In 1213 regulations stated that saltern and warehouse officials had to resolve any outstanding debts in their records at the end of their term.*[128]

---

[120] *SHY* 27.14a–b.

[121] *SHY* 28.55b–56b.

[122] *ABT*, plate 44; Yoshida 1993, 147.

[123] *SHY* 27.36b–37a.

[124] *HSRC* 71.14b–15b.

[125] *HSRC* 71.7a.

[126] *Jinhua Huang xiansheng wenji* [*JHH*] 31.11b.

[127] *HSRC* 71.5b–6a; *HXZ* 9.14a–15a; *SJFZc* 29.2a–2b.

[128] *SHY* 28.56b–57a.

Massive amounts of funding did manage to reach salters periodically through the assistance of a few humane officials. In 1260 Huang Zhen, as head of Huating County, Jiaxingfu, in Zhexi, concurrently the temporary procurement official of its saltern, forgave all salter debts.[129] *Moreover, he turned over 600,000 strings of designated state funds to the salters. His predecessor, Sun Zixiu, had distributed 500,000 strings. Before that Yan Shilu had turned over even greater amounts.*[130]

*The Zhedong Salt Intendancy memorialized on 4/7/1174, during a major glut, that less than a third of the regular salt procured at Taizhou*ᵃ *and Wenzhou*ᵃ *could be distributed annually. The two prefectures were not easily accessible. They bordered on Fujian, through which smuggled salt was brought in. Thus their quotas were temporarily reduced. This also marked an attempt in Liangzhe to reduce the boiling facilities: eight salterns in Taizhou*ᵃ *and Wenzhou*ᵃ *cut nearly 170 stoves, about a third of the circuit's total.*[131] *Between 1184 to 1187 another glut occurred in Zhe, this time of 2.75 million piculs (137.5 million catties).*[132] *After the 1190s less data survives on such accumulations, though they certainly continued. In later Southern Song, only a fraction of the quota for the Huai-Zhe region—sometimes 600,000 or even as few as 100,000 bags—was actually distributed out of an annual quota of 900,000 bags.*[133] *On 9/22/1195 the Zhedong and Zhexi intendants as well as the Lin'anfu tea and salt official once again raised the issue of bagged salt. In the past they had permitted subordinates to add extra product to attract merchants, but this put a heavy burden on salters. Clerks who added the largest number of extra catties were to be punished as a lesson to all.*[134]

---

[129] *HXZ* 9.14a.

[130] *HSRC* 77.1a–b; *SS* 389.11932, 424.12664.

[131] *SHY* 28.1b–2b.

[132] *SHY* 28.23b.

[133] *QZCG* 1.81a–b.

[134] *SHY* 28.47b–48a.

Chapter 5: Huainan

The Huainan section is the longest of the sea salt sections at twenty pages, or nearly a third of the Songshi text. Huainan, or Huai, corresponded to today's Jiangsu and Anhui provinces. The northeastern half was called Huainandong or Huaidong; the southwestern half was called Huainanxi or Huaixi. The text begins with a list of production sites, annual production quotas, and distribution destinations.

Northern Song

[p. 4438] In Huainan Circuit (Map 8), Chuzhou[b]'s Yancheng directorate annually boiled over 417,000 piculs; Tongzhou[b]'s Lifeng directorate produced over 489,000 piculs; and Taizhou[b]'s Hailing directorate and Rugao (county) stored over 656,000 piculs produced by the Xiaohai saltern.[1] Each supplied its own prefecture and also the

---

[1] *SHY* coverage of Huai begins with a detailed breakdown of the strings of cash earned by Huai prefectures and counties: for Huaidong, see *SHY* 22.8b–11a; for Huaixi, *SHY* 22.11a–13b. For specific salterns and their figures, see *SHY* 23.15a–16a. As of 11/996 Huainan had eighteen prefectures, nine of which were government sales areas (*SHY* 23.23a–b). The *XCB* of 11/dingmao/996 notes that merchants traded by sea routes and because their salt was relatively cheap, many took up the trade. Some even armed themselves and became bandits (*XCB* 40.855). Guo Zhengzhong (1983, 79–80) presents aggregate Huai production and stove number (Table 4):

Period	In Bags	In Piculs	In Catties	Source
976-997		1,347,905	67,395,250	*Huanyuji* 130; *Jisheng* 39; *SS* 182; *WXTK* 15
998-1022		2,154,000	107,700,000	*SS* 182, *WXTK* 15
1023		1,942,000	97,100,000	*SHY* 23.32
1026-1029		1,456,460	72,823,000	*SS* 182
1029-1033		Increase	Increase	*XCB* 113
1073-1086		3,200,000	160,000,000	*Mozhuang manlu* 4
1113-1117		Increase	Increase	*SS* 182
1111-1127		3,692,310	184,615,500	*CYZJ jia* 14
1129-1132		Decrease	Decrease	*XCB* 103-111
1132-1135		<2,140,688	<107,034,400	*SHY* 28.20, 26.29
1147-1158		3,800,000-3,900,000	190,000,000-195,000,000	*SHY* 26.39

following: Luzhou[a], Hezhou, Shuzhou, Qizhou[c], Huangzhou, Wuweijun (all in Huainan); Jiangningfu, Xuanzhou, Hongzhou, Yuanzhou[b], Jizhou[a], Yunzhou[b], Jiangzhou[a], Chizhou, Taipingzhou, Raozhou, Xinzhou[b],

Period	In Bags	In Piculs	In Catties	Source
1158		3,300,000	165,000,000	*SHY* 26.41
1162	447,285	2,683,711	134,185,550	*SHY* 23.15
1165-1166	447,285	2,683,711	134,185,550	*SHY* 23.17
1169	510,832		153,249,600	*SHY* 27.33, 34
1170	672,300	4,033,800	201,690,000	*SHY* 27.33
1171-1173	650,000	3,900,000	195,000,000	*SS* 304; *Xu tongkao* 19
1174-1176	728,000	4,368,000	218,400,000	*SHY* 28.20-21
1187		3,400,000	170,000,000	*SHY* 28.24
1225		Decrease	Decrease	*SS* 182; *WXTK* 15
1230-1231	650,000	3,900,000	195,000,000	*SS* 182; *WXTK* 15
1235-1236	465,500	2,793,000	139,650,000	*SS* 182; *WXTK* 15
1241-1257	<650,000		<195,000,000	*SS* 182

Note: Guo's tables all incorporate other scholars' figures but there is no acknowledgement of who, no exact page numbers, and no Bib to help with determining the full titles of some of the works.

Peak production occurred from 1174 to 1176 at 218.4 million catties; the trough was from 976 to 997 at 67.4 million catties. Also covered in the *SHY* Huai section are Jiangnandong (*SHY* 22.17b–20a); Jiangnanxi (*SHY* 22.20a–22a); Jinghunan (*SHY* 22.22a–23b); Jinghubei (*SHY* 22.23b–26b).

From the beginning of the Song those given the death penalty and then pardoned were often sent to perform labor under guard either on Haimen Island in Tongzhou[b], Huaidong (present Jiangsu), or on Shamen island in Dengzhou, Jingdongdong (present Shandong). Salterns in Chongmingzhen and Dongbeizhou in Tongzhou[b], as of 12/xinmao/980, registered those sentenced to labor as salters (*XCB* 21.485). A 10/yimao/972 report indicated that a salter named Pang Chong and others at Haimen industrial center rebelled but were later subdued by the guard Zhao Lingrong; 300 were beheaded (*XCB* 13.290). On 2/guisi/974 it was reported that the prefect of Qizhou (Huaixi Circuit), as well as the prefect of Bozhou (Hedong Circuit), had been tried for graft of above-quota salt moneys. They were sentenced to beating with the heavy bamboo and stripped of their civil service privileges (*XCB* 15.318). The administrator of the Lifeng industrial center, site of the first glut of Huai salt, between 979 and 980, memorialized that, like tea, which had piled up in mounds so high that it had to be burned, salt was also accumulating as officials sat helplessly by (*Gongshiji* [*GSJ*] 51.2a–b).

Shezhou, Fuzhou[d], Guangdejun, and Linjiangjun (all in Jiangnan, Maps 10 and 13); Changzhou[b], Runzhou, Huzhou, and Muzhou (all in Liangzhe, Map 10); Jianglingfu, Anzhou, Fuzhou[e], Tanzhou, Dingzhou[a], Ezhou, Yuezhou[b], Hengzhou[a], Yongzhou[b], and Hanyangjun (all in Jinghu, Map 14).[2]

Haizhou's three salterns at Banpu, Huize, and Luoyao annually boiled over 477,000 piculs, while Lianshuijun's Haikou saltern boiled over 115,000 piculs. Each supplied its own prefecture as well as Xuzhou[a] (Jingdong, Map 4); Guangzhou[a], Sizhou, Haozhou, and Shouzhou (all in Huainan); and Hangzhou, Suzhou[a], Huzhou, Changzhou[b], Runzhou, and Jiangyinjun (all in Liangzhe).[3] In the mid-Tiansheng period (1023–1031), Tongzhou[b] and Chuzhou[b] each had seven salterns, Taizhou[b] had eight, Haizhou had two, and Lianshuijun had one. The amount boiled had fallen to 697,540 piculs fewer than previous years; these facilities supplied the circuit and the four circuits of Jiangnandong, Jiangnanxi, Jinghubei, and Jinghunan. In the past, Huainan salt also supplied Liangzhe Circuit, but this ceased in 1029 (Tiansheng 7).

The procurement price varied across the southeast. Because salterns handled several functions (including boiling, procurement, voucher collection, and distribution), which encouraged irregularities, storehouses were established along the distribution routes to separate the processes. They were known by different names, such as "military storehouse" (juncang), "city storehouse" (duyancang), "hut storehouse" (ancang) around the Xie ponds, and "sea storage" (haicang) on the coast. When abuses also arose at the storehouse sites, policymakers questioned their merit.

Storehouses were set up to house all salt procured.[4] Tongzhou[b] and Chuzhou[b] each had one, while Taizhou[b] had three; they stored salt of

---

[2] Luzhou[a] is present-day Hefei (Anhui). Jiangningfu is present-day Nanjing.

[3] Jiangyinjun is the Southern Song name; the Northern Song name was Jiangyin (Tan Qixiang 1982, Maps 24–25 and Maps 59–60).

[4] *HSRC* 71.16a–b; *Su Shunqin ji* [*SSQJ*] 5.61; *Yunjian zhi* [*YJZ*], *juan shang*, "Cangku" (Storehouses); *SMZ* 3.23b–25a. An important Huai transfer station was at Yangzhou[a], where ten-*li*-long salt convoys streamed past (*Ru Tang qiufa xunli xingji* [*RTQF*] 1.7, 7/21/838). The depot at Zhenzhou[a] became a major rival: "All came from here, left from here, was collected here, dispersed here, inexhaustibly coming and going" (*Bizhou gaolue* [*BG*] 4.12a). Zhenzhou[a] collected

those three prefectures. Two transfer depots were also set up: one in Zhenzhou[a], to receive salt from the five storehouses at Tongzhou[b], Taizhou[b], and Chuzhou[b]; and one in Lianshuijun, to receive salt from Haizhou's Lianshui. Jiangnan and Jinghu annually shipped grain to Huainan, then returned with salt. Southeastern salt revenues were the greatest of all the empire. The government paid four cash per catty in Huainan, Fujian, and Liangzhe's Wenzhou[a], Taizhou[a], and Mingzhou[b]; six cash in Hangzhou and Xiuzhou; and five cash in Guangnan. The selling price was determined by the distance the salt traveled; in some cases [the state] sold it for ten times the [procurement] cost.[5]

At the turn of the eleventh century under Zhenzong officials debated whether Huai salt should be sold by merchants or the government: merchant sales were key to provisioning the border but government sales curbed smuggling. The latter point won out, for the moment.

In 1001 (Xianping 4) the executive assistant of the Palace Library (*bishucheng*) and auxiliary official of the Historiographical Office (*zhishiguan*), Sun Mian, petitioned:

If we let Jiangnan and Jinghu conduct merchant sales of salt and have merchants engage in "equitable exchange" at the border, trading grain and fodder [as well as] paying gold, silver, or silk at the capital, then both state and people will benefit and profits will indeed be plentiful. To those concerned that Huainan will see a drop in its annual revenue [from government-distributed salt] because Jiangnan and Jinghu will be opened up to merchant sales, [I say, with those merchant sales] the state's provisioning of grain and fodder will remain sufficient to the needs of border troops, and

---

salt from Tongzhou[b], Taizhou[b], and Chuzhou[b] and forwarded it to Jiangnan, Hubei, Huaixi, and Jingxi (*SHY* 27.17a–b).

[5] In Jinghunan and Jinghubei, Huai salt sold for sixty-four cash per catty; it cost commoners three pecks of rice to purchase one catty. In 12/jiyou/983, after a memorial by the Jinghu fiscal intendant, Li Weiqing, it was decreed that the price be reduced by ten cash (*XCB* 24.567). In 8/996 the Jiang and Huai transport intendant, Yang Yungong, apprehended thirty-nine salt smugglers and sent them to the palace gates, where they were pardoned. Since they had long been unemployed, the emperor thought it better to put them to work at river transport (*XCB* 40.850).

[merchant] payments of gold and silver will fill the government treasury. Moreover, this will spare [us, the state] from hiring carts, drafting commoners, and making them brave the elements over great distances. If Jinghu has to transport [*p. 4439*] tens of thousands of strings of cash, if Huainan has to transport thousands of piculs of grain, and laborers have to be drafted to deliver them to distant border areas [rather than enlisting merchants to do such work], then government expenses and the suffering of the people will no doubt be multiplied.[6]

The emperor decreed for the executive of the Ministry of Personnel (*libu shilang*), Chen Shu, and others to deliberate. [Chen] Shu stated:

The reason that the government monopolizes salt sales in Jiang and Hu is to halt illegal boiling in sea-salt-producing areas. If we now allow merchant sales and end government sales, [local governments] immediately face losing a year's tax income.[7]

---

[6] The *SS* completely omits Sun Mian's impassioned request of 11/jimao/1001, which was recorded at great length in the *SHY* and *XCB*. He delineated ten advantages and refuted three doubts concerning merchant trade. The advantages included filling markets with goods and circulating money, benefiting the tea trade, sparing the government boat transport costs, and allowing even remote areas to enjoy salt (*SHY* 23.24a–27a and *XCB* 50.1084–85). Sun Mian's post of *bishucheng* was charged with collection and, at times, compilation of records, including imperial documents, classic canons, dynastic histories, astronomical observations, and calendars (*SS* 164.3873, 3878).

[7] The *SS* also abbreviates Chen Shu's opposition to merchant trade in 1001, when he argued that it would lead to an immediate shortage of cash. After a policy analysis, Chen Shu criticized Sun Mian, saying that he lacked understanding of the big picture and was unsuited for his position (*SHY* 23.26a–27a). Previously Chen had been vehemently opposed to government distribution in Jiang and Huai and would have been expected to support Sun. He may have been reluctant to do so after the Censorate called him to account for his persistent pro-merchant views. On 10/18/1011 the emperor asked rhetorically how he could put annual revenues first when the people's welfare was at stake (*SHY* 23.30a). On intercalary 6/bingxu/1015 it was related that when the salt monopoly was first instituted in Huainan, small merchants experienced hardship. Now it was even worse. In the prior three or four years offices had set time limits on bringing vouchers; merchants had to claim goods within a hundred days or pay a surcharge of two cash for every ten cash worth. Small merchants either did not know of the fee or were unable to pay. Those in charge paid scant attention to merchants but only to their own convenience and changed rules at will. Suspicious, the merchants stopped trading (*XCB* 85.1937).

So [Sun] Mian's proposal [for merchant trade] was put to rest. Not until the beginning of the Tianxi period (1017–1021) were merchants called on to pay cash, grain, and silk [for vouchers] at the capital and go to Huai, Zhe, Jiangnan, and Jinghu prefectures to exchange them for salt.[8] In 1022 (Qianxing 1) cash and goods brought to the capital [for salt vouchers] totaled 1,140,000 strings of cash. At that time salt boiled at Tongzhou[b] and Taizhou[b] showed annual losses and very few reserves remained, so payment in grain and silk was abolished and only cash payment was accepted. After some time the stores of salt recovered.[9]

In the 1030s when government transport led to revenue losses, merchant sales were again proposed.

In 1033 (Mingdao 2) the assistant executive of the Secretariat-Chancellery, Wang Sui, proposed:

Huainan salt starts out being of excellent quality. From Tongzhou[b], Taizhou[b], and Chuzhou[b] it is transported to Zhenzhou[a], then on to Jiang, Zhe, and Jinghu. Flotilla clerks and boatmen steal and sell the salt, replacing it with

---

[8] The Finance Commission memorialized on 9/jiachen/1017, adding that these circuits ought to follow Xiezhou's precedent (*XCB* 90.2079).

[9] On 6/renchen/1018, due to (some unspecified) disaster and lack of food, it was decreed to give salters of Tongzhou[b], Taizhou[b], and Chuzhou[b] advances of cash and grain and to forgive their debts (*XCB* 95.2195, 107.2505–506, 3/jiashen/1029). On 6/14/1023 the Finance Commission's salt and iron supervisory official, Yu Xianqing, spoke on eight pros and cons of salterns in Tongzhou[b], Taizhou[b], and Chuzhou[b], including the need to relocate wine shops at least ten *li* away from production sites to prevent salters from getting drunk (*SHY* 23.31a–32b). In 12/wuwu/1024 the prefect of Qizhou in Huaixi, Li Yigeng, was reprimanded for requiring payment in silk without authority. The people were so poor they were unable to pay (*XCB* 102.2369). On 2/bingxu/1028 it was decreed that Jiang-Huai salt and grain convoy workers be given a month's relief in the eleventh month of every year and told to report back in spring (*XCB* 106.2466). When Zhang Lun first became vice-fiscal intendant in the early 1020s, [Huai] salt revenue had fallen for ten years. He memorialized to excuse Tongzhou[b], Taizhou[b], and Chuzhou[b] salter debts, help them with equipment costs, and offer a good procurement price. Thus annual revenues increased by several hundreds of thousands. Salterns were established in Hangzhou, Xiuzhou, and Haizhou; their output added 3.5 million strings of revenue. After Zhang's three-year term, tribute rice also increased (*XCB* 106.2479, 8/jiaxu/1028).

sand and dirt [to maintain net weight]. The greater the distance the salt travels, the more foreign matter is added until it becomes virtually inedible. Even sentencing violators to beatings with the whip, stick, or bamboo followed by hard labor and exile has not stopped these crimes. When for several years the Grand Canal ran shallow and transport was obstructed, villagers in distant prefectures immediately were stranded with no table salt. At the same time in Huainan 15 million piculs of salt had accumulated, to the point that there was no more storage space, so it was piled open to the elements with only straw for cover.[10] Every year there is loss and waste. Furthermore, upon presenting their salt, salters are to receive funding, but the government has none to give, so the impoverished often turn to banditry. Such is the seriousness of the problem. I propose [that we] temporarily promote merchant sales for a period of three to five years and have merchants forward cash to the capital; also [we should] establish a Trade Bureau in Yangzhou* to which merchants can forward cash, grain, and silk. Salt will be given according to the value of those goods. The first advantage [to this scheme] is that if a picul of salt sells for approximately 2,000 cash [two strings], 15 million piculs can bring in 30 million strings to provide for the state's expenditures. The second advantage is that [people] everywhere in Jiang and Hu will be able to consume white salt of high quality. The third advantage is that we can reduce the annual costs of water transport, the possibility of boats sinking, and offenses committed by boatmen. The fourth advantage is that boats formerly used for salt transport may now be used for grain transport. The fifth advantage is that payments of cash from merchants can be used to pay salters.[11]

Merchants were allowed to trade inside cities or in market towns.

At the time Fan Zhongyan, military intendant (*anfu*) of Jiang and Huai, also spoke of the benefits of merchant salt sales, so the emperor decreed that the special drafting official of the Secretariat (*zhizhigao*), Ding Du, and others deliberate with the finance commissioner and Jiang and

---

[10] This marked the second major glut of Huai salt. Fifteen million piculs multiplied by 50 catties per picul was equal to 750 million catties, valued at approximately 30 million strings, equal to all revenues for the entire year (*XCB* 113.2655, 12/wushen/1033).

[11] On 5/xinsi/1033 Wang Sui presented a work, *Huainan yunhe tu* (Maps of Huainan canals), to the emperor. He had probably been commissioned to do this, and in all likelihood his commission was the result of his proposal concerning the five benefits of merchant sales (*XCB* 112.2618).

Huai military regulators. All feared that allowing merchant sales would lead to rampant private trading that would encroach upon local government [revenues]. They thus petitioned for an order to the military regulator's office to increase boat transport to the circuits to enable them to have stores of two to three years. *[p. 4440]* The system of 1017 (Tianxi 1), which permitted merchants to bring cash and grain to the capital and to the Huai, Zhe, Jiangnan, and Jinghu salterns, was revived. Traders in Tongzhou[b], Chuzhou[b], Taizhou[b], Haizhou, Zhenzhou[a], Yangzhou[a], Lianshuijun, and Gaoyoujun were not to trade outside those cities, while in other prefectures they could trade in market towns but not in the villages. Those who brought cash to the capital would be given extra salt, and by imperial order the Fiscal Intendancy was to allocate cash to be paid to salters. The emperor decreed that all this be implemented. In 1035 (Jingyou 2) the circuits' trade did not yield any surpluses, so [cash payments to local governments] were disallowed, while cash payments to the capital continued as before.[12]

In the 1040s the emperor decided to employ the Three Items and Four Items Policies to attract merchants, who could make a profit several times over (i.e., several hundred percent) by transporting goods to the border and bringing salt back from the Xie ponds. They also gained by using Liangzhe vouchers to get Huaidong salt and exploiting the difference between the government's selling price and the price in local markets.

In 1040 (Kangding 1) the emperor decreed that merchants who transported fodder and grain to the Shaanxi border and wished to receive southeast salt would be given an extra amount. At this time Hebei grain was cheap, so the Finance Commission, having already petitioned for the implementation of the Three Items Policy (*sanshuofa*) in the interior prefectures [in the northwest], now also had [the state temporarily] purchase [from merchants] up to a maximum of 200,000 piculs of grain.

---

[12] On 7/guiwei/1033 Jiangdong's head salt tax was also waived (*XCB* 112.2623). On 9/guichou/1034 the Suzhou[b] homeless were pardoned their salt tax (*XCB* 115.2702).

[This grain was] paid for in [southeast sea] salt instead of cash from the capital.[13] In 1042 (Qingli 2) the emperor again decreed:

Those who engage in provisioning Shaanxi and Hedong and bring vouchers to the capital shall be paid half in cash and half in gold and silk. Those who do not wish to receive gold and silk shall be given tea, salt, or incense, whichever they prefer.[14]

Since the profits to be had from southeastern salt were considerable, merchants all wanted salt. So in 1048 (Qingli 8) Hebei enacted the Four Items Policy (*sishuofa*), salt [now formally] being one of the [standard] "items."[15] Prices charged for fodder and grain for the border quickly became inflated several times [compared to before the policy change]. When vouchers arrived in the capital, calculating merchants manipulated them to keep the salt price low. One hundred and eight catties of salt that before were worth 100,000 cash were now valued at 60,000 [cash worth]

---

[13] These were considered highly generous terms. Following the example of the Shaanxi policy, which gave merchants greater amounts of southeastern salt in exchange for provisioning, Hebei's provisioning system became more liberalized. At this point, salt was offered for grain outside the formal Three Items Policy.

[14] In 1042 the court for a second time decreed to give southeastern salt to merchants in exchange for up to another 200,000 piculs of grain.

A third glut occurred at this time, between 1041 and 1043. In Taizhou[b] alone, over 3 million piculs piled up (*XCB* 141.3388, 6/jiachen/1043).

[15] In the late 1010s northwestern circuits experienced urgent military needs so the state devised a means to transport supplies there. The price of grain and fodder was calculated according to the distance merchants had traveled, and they were given voucher certificates that they could redeem for three items: tea, cash, and incense or ivory. In 11/1048 Hebei was short of grain. To attract merchants to the provisioning policy, salt was added, which brought the program to four items. At the capital, for every 100 strings worth of provisions for the northwest, merchants were given thirty strings in cash and fifteen strings worth in ivory or incense. From outside the capital, they received ten strings in salt and forty in tea. (Due to an undetermined recording error, this does not total 100 strings) (*XCB* 165.3976, 170.4081; Wang Leiming 1985, 354n2; also 355n2). In 1038 when the Xixia suddenly arose the Song refocused on the northwest. The Three and Four Items policies, giving favorable terms to those willing to trade sea salt in regions categorized as pond salt areas such as Jingdong and Huainan, were part of the war effort against the Xixia.

in vouchers.[16] Since merchants could exchange their vouchers for under-priced salt, they no longer brought cash to the capital and the treasury's hard currency stores shrank further. In 1050 (Huangyou 2) the policy of requiring cash payments at the capital was restored, and slightly larger amounts of salt were awarded for such payments. Merchants who provisioned Hedong and Shaanxi for vouchers valued at 100,000 cash were given only 70,000 cash worth of salt; in Hebei this amount was reduced further to 65,000. Furthermore, merchants were ordered to pay a sum of 100,000 cash at the capital before goods could change hands; this was called "direct subsidization" (*duitie*). From this time, cash flow in the capital recovered somewhat.

Early on, in 1031 (Tiansheng 9), the Finance Commission requested that the Monopoly Goods Bureau have merchants pay cash to sell southeast salt. Revenue [from southeast powder salt vouchers purchased in the capital] was 1,803,000 strings of cash; this later increased to 4 million strings. During the Jiayou reign period (1056–1063) [funds for the] water transport [of salt] in various circuits were insufficient, so the Monopoly Goods Bureau's tax revenues dipped. The Transport Intendancy (*fayunsi*) was then ordered to assign an official to take sole charge of salt transport. During the Zhiping period (1064–1067) 2,270,000 strings of cash were paid at the capital. The six circuits of Huainan, Liangzhe, Fujian, Jiangnan, Jinghu, and Guangnan in 1050 (Huangyu 2) *[p. 4441]* [together] earned 2,730,000 strings, while in the Zhiping period (1064–1067), [they earned] 3,290,000 strings.

The Songshi *editors address Jiangnan and Jinghu within the Huai section, evidently because they were major recipients of Huai salt. Due to high government prices in these circuits, smuggling was commonplace and often led to violence, which spread to Fujian and Guangnan. Government sales were slow.*

Because salt transported to Jiang[nan] and [Jing]Hu accumulated so much foreign matter and the government priced it so high, people preferred to eat illegal salt. Those who lived by the sea made a livelihood either by fishing or from salt, which required little labor and earned great

---

[16] *XCB* 168.4032, 4050 (1/renzi/1050). According to the *SS Jiaokanji*, "108 catties" should read "800 catties" (*SS* 182.4458n6).

profits. Inordinate numbers of hooligans thus became smugglers and the pressure of arrests only forced them into banditry.[17] In Jiang and Huai even literati were attracted to [salt's] lucrative profits, and some sold salt for a living.

Qianzhou[a] (Jiangxi) bordered on Guangnan and also on Fujian's Tingzhou. Qianzhou[a] salt was not of good quality, while Tingzhou did not produce any at all, so many people in these two prefectures illegally traded Guangnan salt for gain. Every fall and winter after the harvest they banded together in the tens and hundreds, wielding weapons, banners, and drums, and roamed the eight prefectures of Qianzhou[a], Tingzhou, Zhangzhou, Chaozhou, Xunzhou[a], Meizhou, Huizhou[a], and Guang-zhou[b]. Wherever they went, they plundered grain and cloth, kidnapped women, and assaulted guards and soldiers. Once they had killed or injured a guard or soldier, they turned bandit and set up strongholds in strategic locations. They could not be caught so sometimes they were pardoned to coax them back home. As time went on, annual Qianzhou[a] government sales reached only 1 million catties.

In the 1040s and 1050s the importation of Guang and Fujian salt into Jiangnan and Jinghu was rejected in favor of the traditional supplier, Huai, under government distribution.

During the Qingli period (1041–1048) Guangdong fiscal intendants Li Fu and Wang Yao petitioned that Guangzhou[b] salt be transported to Nanxiongzhou to supply Qianzhou[a] and Jizhou[a]. Before a reply had arrived, over 4 million catties were shipped to Nanxiong, but the Jiangxi

---

[17] On 9/yichou/1043 the Hunan fiscal intendant memorialized on banditry carried out by the Yao tribesmen at the Guiyang directorate in Jinghunan. The Yao dwelt in valleys spanning Hengzhou[a], Guiyangjian, and Chenzhou in Jinghunan as well as Lianzhou[a] and Shaozhou[a] in Guangdong, and Huozhou in Guangxi, a region of over 1,000 *li*. They paid no taxes and performed no corvee. In Jizhou[a] (Jiangxi), a shaman named Huang Zhuogui ("the Ghost Catcher"), along with his brothers, learned the ways of the tribal people. They went to Hengzhou[a], lured several hundred tribesmen into salt smuggling, killed officers, then fled into the mountains. Huang was later captured and killed, but his followers amassed a group of 5,000 men to attack the local officers. Troops had to be dispatched to disperse them (*XCB* 143.3430).

Fiscal Intendancy did not feel this to be advantageous and would not accept the salt. Afterward the Finance Commission's supervisor of the census, Zhou Zhan, and seven others again petitioned for Guang salt to be transported to Qianzhou[a], while Jiangxi itself also petitioned for Guang salt for which they had already set payment aside. The emperor decreed for the vice-director (*yuanwailang*) of agricultural colonies (*tuntian*), Shi Yuanchang, and others to deliberate. They petitioned along the same lines as [Zhou] Zhan. But since the transport intendant, Xu Yuan, felt that shipment on to Qianzhou was ill advised, it was put to rest.

From the Jiayou reign period (1056–1063) [officials] petitioned for merchant trade of Guangnan salt to be instituted in Qianzhou[a] and Tingzhou, and for the prefectures and counties through which it passed to collect a customs tax. Others petitioned to have salt of the seven prefectures of Qianzhou[a], Tingzhou, Zhangzhou, Xunzhou[a], Meizhou, Chaozhou, and Huizhou[a] made available for merchant sales. They petitioned to have 7 million catties of Huainan salt transported to Qianzhou[a] and 2 million catties transported to Tingzhou in succeeding years. When people had sufficient salt, the banditry would cease of itself.[18] Still others petitioned *[p. 4442]* for the government to have salt shippers (*puyi*) and soldiers transport Guangnan and Fujian salt to Qianzhou[a] and Tingzhou.[19] No consensus could be reached.

First the vice-director of the Bureau of Operations (*zhifang*), Huang Bing, was dispatched to meet with subordinate salt administrators, prefects,

---

[18] Banditry became a major problem. In 6/1059 the assistant division chief, Zhu Chuyue, led Jiangxi troops against a Qianzhou[a] gang, led by a salt bandit named Dai Xiaoba, who had killed the magistrate of Qianhua County, Zhao Shu (*XCB* 189.4569). By 10/guihai/1059 the Qianzhou[a] inspector, Wang Xianfu, was dismissed and sentenced to Guangnan for not apprehending Dai (*XCB* 190.4595). On intercalary 8/dingwei/1061 Sima Guang alluded to the problem of Jiang and Huai salt bandits (*XCB* 195.4719).

[19] A *pu* station set up every ten *li* comprised the Song postal system, but here the text probably refers to stations which facilitated salt shipping. In Dongjing patrol posts stood every three hundred paces: five courier soldiers (*pubing*) at each post were responsible for neighborhood night patrol, fire watch, and other public affairs. *Puyi* were probably similarly employed servicemen (*Dongjing menghua lu* [*DML*] 3.24).

and prefectural vice-administrators (*tongpan*) to discuss the matter.[20] [Huang] concluded that Qianzhou[a] had long consumed Huainan salt and this could not be changed. But they [the court] could lower the price [of the forced-purchase salt residents were required to buy], which in recent years had increased to 40 cash per catty. Five household grades in ten counties were to pay [for the forced-purchase salt] according to the rate of their summer tax: for every 100 cash [owed], they had to buy two catties of salt, and this payment was to be submitted when the summer tax came due. Subsequently the mint intendant (*tidian zhuqianshi*), Shen Fu, was ordered to reexamine the feasibility of this [and he basically agreed with Huang, only fine-tuning his program]. [Shen] Fu and others petitioned to organize Jiangxi [tribute] transport boats into ten flotillas (*gang*), [to be] overseen by commissioners of the three ranks (*sanban shichen*), and to convey salt directly obtained from storage in Tongzhou[b], Taizhou[b] and Chuzhou[b] [in an effort to improve the salt quality]. The emperor decreed to carry out the plan of [Huang] Bing and associates, but in one year, sales had increased by only 600,000-odd catties [and the Huang and Shen plan was overturned by another official assigned to review its results].

The Jiangxi intendant tried to curb smuggling and abuses in the government transport system.

The Jiangxi judicial intendant, Cai Ting, was to supervise salt matters.[21] He ordered [smuggling] band leaders to relinquish their weapons to the patrol officers and soldiers. Any who [illegally] sold less than twenty catties of salt in "yellowfish baskets" (*huangyu longxieyan*), had less than five accomplices, or did not carry any arms were only charged the [merchant]

---

[20] The Tang and Song *zhifang yuanwailang*, a post in the Ministry of War (*bingbu*), was charged with drawing maps; recording boundaries of towns, villages, and military outposts; noting local products and customs, and so on. It presented new maps to the emperor every intercalary year (*SS* 163.3856).

[21] When the number of armed smugglers grew, Cai Ting had Huai salt transported to Qianzhou[a] and Tingzhou and confiscated weapons. His policy increased the salt sold by 400,000 catties annually (*SS* 328.10575–77). When in charge of sales in Qianzhou[a], Cai Ting noted that Jiangxi had relied on inedible Huai salt, so residents began smuggling Guangnan salt. They banded together and wreaked havoc, as in 4/1064 (*SHY* 24.1a–2a).

tax, and not taken into custody. After Huainan had organized new flotillas to transport salt, [Cai] Ting increased their number to twelve, each consisting of twenty-five boats that were sealed until arriving at their destination [to prevent losses en route]. Only on arrival did they distribute the salt. If any salt remained after official deliveries were completed, it was given to the transport crews. The government then offered them half price to buy it back. Thus the problem of smuggling was reduced, and the salt quality improved. Then the selling price was again cut, and annual salt revenues [from government distribution] increased to over 3 million catties, so the policy advocated by [Huang] Bing and others to collect tax [on forced-purchase] salt was cancelled. Previously, Tingzhou natives wishing to smuggle salt often first beat drums in the valleys to summon followers. On appointed days they assembled tens or hundreds of people to act in concert. Now prefectural and county officials exhorted neighborhood heads to capture the drummers, which intimidated the smugglers somewhat. The court recognized [Cai] Ting's capabilities and retained him in Jiangxi, where he remained for many years before he was transferred. After some time all salt bound for Jiangxi came from Huainan by flotilla, just as [the salt for] Qianzhou² did.

Jinghu Circuit had similar transport problems.

At first Jinghu Circuit also suffered from tainted salt and the amount annually transported to it was often insufficient. In 1065 (Zhiping 2) only about 250,000 catties [had arrived in the circuit]. In 1066 (Zhiping 3) Huaixi's twenty-four flotillas of hired civilian boats were dispatched [to Jinghu]; that year 400,000 catties arrived safely. In 1067 (Zhiping 4) the salt transported [to Jinghu] reached over 530,000 catties.

Back in the first quarter of the 1000s the emperor had lowered the price of salt in Jinghu; in the 1040s he agreed to increase it to generate more revenue.

At the beginning of the Qingli period (1041–1048) the Ministry of Finance's supervisory comptroller (*pan hubu gouyuan*), Wang Qi, stated:

> At the beginning of the Tianxi period (1017–1021) Jinghu's salt price was high, and the emperor decreed a cut of two or three cash per catty; but after

this, income *[p. 4443]* declined. I petition that the old price be restored so annual cash [income] will increase by 40,000.

[The emperor] agreed to this. During the Zhiping reign period (1064–1067) the Huainan fiscal intendants, Li Fugui, Zhang Chu, and Su Song, as well as the Finance Commission's supervisor of funds (*duzhi panguan*), Han Zhen, repeatedly petitioned for a reduction of the price of Huainan salt, but this did not occur.

Corruption and dangerous transport conditions prevented Huai salt from arriving in Jinghu and yet Guang salt was prohibited, which again stimulated illegal trade.

At the beginning of the Xining period (1068–1077) Jiangxi's salt revenues were stagnant. In 1070 (Xining 3) the judicial intendant, Zhang Jie, stated [in a recounting]:

Qianzhou[a]'s government salt was wet and full of extraneous matter; a catty was not full weight, but the price was as much as forty-seven cash. Smuggled salt from Lingnan entering Qianzhou[a] sold at a catty and a half for every catty, was pure and white, and was priced at only twenty cash. Thus the people of Qianzhou[a] took to Lingnan salt.[22] So it was suggested that we reduce the Qianzhou[a] salt price, select good boats, group them into ten flotillas, and have officers guard them. Later Cai Ting, feeling that the Gan River route was difficult, proposed to replace [the management of] salt boats every three years and to employ flotilla officers and boatmen based on the quality and quantity of the salt they delivered [retaining those who were most effective]. In this way the salt tax income became ample and smuggling declined.[23] After [Cai] Ting left office, the bulk of his policy was ignored. We request that it be restored.

---

[22] Qianzhou[a] (Jiangxi) was connected with Tingzhou (Fujian) because the people of both prefectures smuggled Guangnan salt. So the prefect of Lianzhou[a] in northern Guangdong memorialized to have merchants trade Guangnan salt in Tingzhou and Qianzhou[a], while the prefect of Tingzhou also petitioned to open up seven prefectures to merchant trade. The Zhenzhou[a] prefectural vice-administrator petitioned against the import of Guangnan salt to Qianzhou[a], favoring the import of Huai salt. In the end the court opted to transport Huai salt, but annual sales increased by only 600,000 catties (*XCB* 196.4739–40, 2/xinsi/1062).

[23] The Gan River originates near Qianzhou[a] and flows through Jizhou[a] (Linjiangjun) and Hongzhou in Jiangnanxi Circuit.

The emperor agreed to this. Twelve flotillas of Huai salt were to go annually to Qianzhou*. When Zhang Dun was investigation commissioner of Hunan, he ordered the circuit judicial intendant, Zhu Chuping, to administer boat transport of Guang salt and to sell an amount above the quota, but [his order] never was carried out.[24] In 1080 (Yuanfeng 3), when [Zhang] Dun was in power [at court], a certain devious Jia Dan managed to favorably impress [Zhang] Dun. Jia obsequiously recommended transport of Guang salt to Jiangxi, following Hunan policy. Jian Zhoufu was sent to Jiangxi to observe the situation.[25] [Jian] Zhoufu, [also] fawning on Zhang Dun, memorialized:[26]

> The transport routes to Qianzhou* are dangerous and distant so that little Huai salt arrives, and the people must endure the lack of it. Guangdong salt is not available [through regular government distribution], so smuggling occurs openly. [Whereas] Huai salt is priced at nine cash per catty by officials, if Guang salt is shipped in, after expenses, its cost will still be one cash cheaper than the Huai salt price, the product better, and transport routes safer. I petition to abolish the transport of Huai salt [to Qianzhou]. Instead, have boats deliver 10 million catties of Guang salt to Jiangxi's Qianzhou* and Nan'anjun, and divert the 6,160,000 catties of Huai salt to Hongzhou,

---

[24] Back in 1072 Zhang Dun, a Wang Anshi supporter, was the Secretariat's examiner (*jianzheng guan*) and Hubei investigation commissioner (*chafang*) responsible for investigating local implementation of the "green sprouts" (*qingmiao fa*, a system of farm credit), militia, and field and irrigation policies. As such he handled a regional conflict involving minority peoples in western Hunan; this is what is meant by the statement that he was investigation commissioner of Hunan. He was dismissed from his capacity as compiler of regulations for the Ministry of Finance (*bianxiu sansi tiaoliguan*) when Sima Guang restored the conservative policies, but by 1094, when he was left executive of the Department of Ministries (*shangshu zuo puye*), he restored the reforms (Wang Leiming 1985, 358–9n3).

[25] Decreed 9/28/1080 (*SHY* 24.19b–20a). The text is highly critical of Jia Dan, but he was known for his expertise in irrigation and water conservancy. A Suzhou* native, he wrote *Wumen shuili shu* (Irrigation works of Suzhou), which earned Wang Anshi's praise. In 1072 Jia was made executive assistant in the Court of Agricultural Supervision and managed the Liangzhe waterworks. Later he became a fiscal supervisory official in Jiangdong.

[26] The section concerning Jian Zhoufu and Zhang Dun was probably taken from Lü Tao's memorial to impeach Zhang Dun (*XCB* 370.8962–63, 2/1086).

Jizhou[a], Junzhou[b], Yuanzhou[b], Fuzhou[d], Linjiangjun, Jianchangjun, and Xingguojun so they can meet their old [government distribution] quotas.

It was decreed that [Jian] Zhoufu draw up the policy and present it to the emperor. He did so, with detailed rules. The policy was for the most part hard on the common people, and they suffered under it. Previously, Jiangxi people had been allowed to buy the right to trade salt *(maipu)* at salterns, but [Jian] Zhoufu switched this entirely to government sales.[27] [Because of the increased income generated, Jian] Zhoufu was appointed remote controller *(yaoling)* salt intendant of Jiangxi and Guangdong, and he set up his office in the Office of Agricultural Supervision.

The Jiangdong judicial intendant investigated salt operations in the 1070s, but due to personnel changes and politics, abuses remained undiscovered.

[p. 4444] In 1071 (Xining 4) [Jian] Zhoufu was transferred to manage the transport of Hebei salt.[28] The following year the intendant of ever-normal granaries, tea, and salt, Liu Yi, declared that the routes [from Guangnan to Jiangxi] were so treacherous that salt sales were adversely affected.[29] The emperor decreed that the Jiangdong judicial intendant, Fan

---

[27] Jian Zhoufu made a similar statement on 3/1/1081, noting that Jiangxi transported Huai salt, but now that there was a shortage and although Guangdong salt was not permitted, undesirable elements were flouting the prohibitions. He proposed allowing Guang salt in at an annual quota of 7 million catties, along with 6.16 million catties of Huai salt, to be distributed in salt-deficient prefectures. The emperor gave Jian one month to draft a plan (*SHY* 24.20a–b and *XCB* 311.7548). A few days later, on 3/4/1081, Jian Zhoufu again petitioned to ban franchising and impose a salt quota in Jiangnanxi Circuit. Profits from monopoly sales were to be used to pay those places where franchising had been abolished (*SHY* 24.20b).

[28] That year Jian Zhoufu was simultaneously Jixian Library compiler, Hebei fiscal intendant-general, and had responsibility for grain purchases from merchants, for which he paid them with vouchers *(dibian)* (*XCB* 319.7713, 11/9/1071).

[29] According to the *XCB*, Liu Yi memorialized on 3/yiyou/1082, not 1072, which makes more sense in the chronology to this point (*XCB* 324.7795). The Ever-normal Granary Intendancy *(tiju changpingsi)* was in charge of ever-normal storehouses, corvee exemptions, markets, wards, rivers and crossings, and water conservancy. It was supposed to adjust policy to benefit the peasants: if goods were moving slowly, the state bought them up and resold them to stabilize prices (*SS* 167.3968). It was decreed on 10/xinhai/1075 for Hou Shuxian to channel water

Xun, should investigate in person. Before Fan Xun had time to report, [Liu] Yi was tried and dismissed for [his outspokenness on] the corvee labor law.[30] By the time [Fan] Xun's memorial arrived, no further

---

from the Gou River into the Tongzhou[b] and Taizhou[b] waterways because 400 salt convoy boats were backed up (*XCB* 269.6604). Months later, on 4/wuzi/1076, it was noted that the former Jiang-Huai transport intendant, Zhang Jie, had neglected to repair the waterways and had willfully ignored a request to channel Chengongtang water into them, thus leading to salt shortages in the circuits. He was eventually cashiered (*XCB* 274.6702).

[30] Liu Yi had attacked the New Policies, citing ten oppressive abuses: (1) worst was the corvee labor law: not only did people have to pay the two seasonal taxes, but also fees for salt, tea, and the corvee-free tax—money owed the state in place of a household member capable of supplying corvee labor. This was a tax law without a sound reason; (2) tax rates were based on household registers: when registers were incorrect, people paid an unreasonable amount. This was a law with an inaccurate base; (3) the corvee-free tax was collected regardless of income level: originally only families without a corvee laborer paid to support the system, but the New Policies taxed everyone, including those in service. This was a law with no discrimination; (4) clerks who handled legal cases were paid many times the income of a magistrate or mayor. Overpayment was the fault of this law; (5) to support those overpayments, people were forced into labor service, the most onerous being salt- and wine-making; even wealthy families now paid seven times more than before. The people's heavy burden was the fault of this law; (6) the *kuanshengqian* tax was first imposed for emergencies but now, even with money strings rotting away in storage, the court has invented new charges. This was a faulty policy of charging excess emergency tax; (7) the court has neglected its responsibilities. Since His Majesty wished to make changes, ministers like Wang Anshi presented [the Reform] programs. Policymakers came and went, but the damage done would last for years. This was the fault of shortsighted policy initiatives; (8) high ministers with an eye out for their own well-being seldom contradicted the throne. This was the fault of irresponsibility; (9) the Liangzhe salt policy had been changed many times, yet the people never saw any benefits. This was the fault of reducing services while retaining charges; (10) heavy-handed government pricing oppressed the people. In Huainan each Yellow River corvee laborer was paid 15,000 cash a year so that a large household might have to contribute as many as sixty men with skimpy returns. In Hunan bow-purchasing agents set the purchase price at 20 cash, even though a bowmaker spent 2,000 [on production costs]. In Jiangxi the official price for a soldier's winter jacket was 800, when it had cost the maker 3,000. Liu concluded that great ministers had only one thing in mind: making money. They ignored the people completely. Since [the implementation of] Jian Zhoufu's salt policy, the people lamented and were on the verge of banditry. What was to be done? The emperor replied that Liu Yi's place was to follow orders. How dare he use these isolated instances to criticize the New

development had taken place, since prefectures and counties had willfully ignored orders. Before long [Jian] Zhoufu memorialized:

> [While I have been in charge,] Qianzhou[a] and Nan'anjun have executed the salt policy for just half a year and have already collected 140,000 strings in surplus revenue.[31]

He considered this his achievement. The emperor ordered the assistant intendant of transport (*fayun fushi*), Li Cong, to personally investigate the pros and cons. Knowing that [Jian] Zhoufu had just been shown favor by the emperor, [Li] Cong stated only that the salt policy ought to be adjusted according to conditions, but dared not point to any abuses.[32] In 1073 (Xining 6) [Jian] Zhoufu became executive of the office of the census (*hubu shilang*) and again memorialized that since Hunan's Chenzhou[a] and Daozhou bordered on [Guangdong's] Shaozhou[a] and Lianzhou[a], a few million [catties] of Guang salt could be imported there. He wanted to divert sales of Huai salt to [Jinghunan's] Tanzhou, Hengzhou[a], Yongzhou[b], Quanzhou[a], Shaozhou[b], and other prefectures. Based on the current policy for Jiangxi and Guangdong [to partially replace Huai salt in Jiangxi with that from Guang], he recommended Jia Dan's original proposal that the three prefectures of Chenzhou[a], Quanzhou[a], and Daozhou also be allowed to sell Guang salt. The emperor delegated the ever-normal intendant, Zhang Shicheng, and the fiscal intendant, Chen Si, to administer [the program]. The following year [Zhang] Shicheng and others delineated a[nother] proposal to the emperor.[33] When it was implemented, profits increased, but the people arose in indignation. Then Huaixi also adopted [Jian] Zhoufu's salt policy. The transport intendant, Jiang Zhiqi, memorialized to establish rewards and punishments for

---

Policies?! Liu was purposely hoodwinking his superiors and confusing inferiors! He was cashiered as an example to others (*XCB* 324.7796–801, 3/yiyou/1082).

[31] Jian Zhoufu memorialized on 7/gengzi/1082 as Hebei fiscal intendant (*XCB* 328.7905).

[32] Li Cong memorialized as Jiangxi and Huai assistant transport intendant on 10/gengshen/1082 (*XCB* 330.7951).

[33] Recorded 9/12/1084 (*SHY* 24.25b).

prefects, prefectural vice-administrators, and salt administration officials, which were written into law by the Ministry of Finance as decreed.[34]

---

[34] On 7/9/1083 the Department of Ministries and Ministry of Finance recounted the memorial of Jiang Zhiqi, the Jiang and Huai transport intendant: prefectural heads who were concurrently saltern administrators had no rules regarding their rewards and punishments; their sales performance was to be compared with that of their predecessors. In Jiang, Huai, Hu, and Zhe, officials were to report sales annually to the Transport Intendancy for comparison, and the best and worst records were to be presented to the Ministry of Finance for reference (*SHY* 24.24a; *XCB* 337.8117). On the same occasion Jiang Zhiqi went on to say that these circuits owed the Transport Intendancy 2 million strings of cash but would not pay unless forced by decree. He requested that these debts be treated in the same manner as debts owed the court. He also requested that the Fiscal Intendancy not assign an annual grain tribute that year to Chuzhou[c] or Tianchang County, and that it ensure that salt capital, transport fees, rice rations, and materials for shipyards of the Transport Intendancy not be assigned to other purposes. It was decreed that debt offenders would be sentenced to one year of labor (*XCB* 337.8117). Huainan prefectures had a old quota of 1,157,616 strings; during the Yuanfeng period (1078–1085) 1,166,040 were collected (*SHY* 23.10b–11a).

Back in 1073 the Finance Commission had memorialized that the Huainan Transport Intendancy took advantage of the north wind every winter to transport salt down the Bian River to Hubei, and then in spring used the south wind to send tribute grain back upriver to the capital. That particular winter and spring, however, the winds had not been favorable and of 120 convoys, 500 boats sank and many soldiers and workers drowned. After investigation, Jiang Zhiqi reported that more boats had sunk in this one year than previously (*XCB* 246.5992, 8/bingxu/1073).

On 9/jiayin/1091 the Jiang and Huai Fiscal Intendancies memorialized that stockpiled salt had been reduced one to two years' worth, but because the circuits had cut the sales price [and the salt went fast] they had been ordered to accumulate more salt (*XCB* 466.11141). On the same day, 9/jiayin/1091, the vice-director of the Ministry of Justice, Wang Di, memorialized concerning the Fiscal Intendancy's finances. The Intendancy was to use reserves of one area to remedy the needs of another and to spread out the work of the ever-normal warehouses. In 1091, when floods occurred in Liangzhe, the Fiscal Intendancy had to get supplies not only from Jiang and Huai but also from Jinghu because its own reserves were insufficient. The year before there had been no calamities in Huai, yet its Fiscal Intendancy sent messages to the throne complaining of a lack of military supplies and borrowed 200,000 piculs of rice for the armies. Supposing at the same time there had been natural calamities a thousand *li* around, then what? When the Fiscal Intendancy did not deliver tribute on time, its officials were punished; therefore they sought ways to save their own skins instead of developing a long-term method of improving revenue. The reason for the Fiscal Intendancy's

The transport intendant requested that the government turn over to producers the funds owed them.

In 1096 (Shaosheng 3) the Transport Intendancy reported on the poverty of Huainan salters. It normally fell to the circuits to provide the 640,000 strings of government funds [supposed to be given to salters to cover operations], and the funds rarely materialized. The people, receiving nothing, had to borrow at multiple interest. [The Transport Intendancy] requested that 100,000 strings of procurement funds be delivered to the salters. If funds were insufficient, they should be given certificates (*pingyou*), which they could "mortgage" to the government and for which they would receive 70 percent of the value interest free. When the salt funds

---

insufficient income: increased expenses of the circuit governments and greater demands of the treasury. Government had expanded and added more employees, military personnel, emissaries, and inspectors. This was perhaps unavoidable, but it had not been in ancestral times (the time of the Song founders). Since various sources of income, such as the *kuansheng* emergency fund tax from selling salt, money from applicants seeking a position in the palace guard, and savings from shipbuilding were now taken over by the Emergency Reserves Storehouse (*fengzhuangku*), what could the Fiscal Intendancy do? Though Emergency Reserves would not waste money on pleasure, but would prepare for military exigency, savings came only after normal expenses had been covered. But how could there be savings when the collection agency had no money to pay for its operations! Wang Di asked that the moneys the ancestors had not sent to the imperial treasury be returned to the Fiscal Intendancy (*XCB* 466.11141–42).

On 5/renzi/1092 Su Shi, prefect of Yangzhou*, memorialized about the harsh treatment that exhausted the populace. He identified six items in one memorial, four in another, and then repeated them when there was no imperial response (*XCB* 473.11292–93). On 7/gengxu/1092 Su Shi memorialized on the faults of the convoy system. He proposed enforcement of Yuanyou period laws that forbade customs inspection of convoys to allow shippers privacy and speed up transport. When shippers were happy, business would increase, and the economy would flourish (*XCB* 475.11324–33). On 1/jihai/1093 the vice-director of the Office of Funds (*duzhi yuanwailang*) memorialized on complaints about the newly set salt price in the southeastern circuits and requested directions on action (*XCB* 480.11424–25). The Transport Intendancy stated on 1/9/1096 that salters were sometimes forced to sell their certificates (*pingyou*), for which they did not receive even half the fair value (*SHY* 24.31a).

arrived, the salters would be given the remaining 30 percent and the notes destroyed.[35]

At the turn of the twelfth century, the chief councilor, Cai Jing, proposed a seven-point merchant trade policy for the southeast.

In 1102 (Chongning 1) Cai Jing proposed changing the salt policy. He stated that the want of salt funding for the southeast was due to the lack of merchant trade. He petitioned to increase the number of Buddhist ordination certificates (*dudie*) and the amount in the Emergency Reserves Storehouse (*fengzhuang* [*ku*])—also referred to as "shops and yards" money (*fangchangqian*)—for a total amount of 300,000 strings. He delineated seven articles:

> (1) allow merchants to use their own boats to transport but still strictly prohibit them from crossing boundaries and carrying extra loads of private salt; (2) exile those saltern officials and clerks who use nonstandard weights and measures or who do not distribute salt in a regular manner; (3) punish violators according to the above rule if those in posts at salterns, dikes and sluice gates, fords and river crossings, and so on harass salt merchants as they pass; (4) prohibit court-appointed officials, families enjoying the "shadow privilege" (*yin*),[36] nominees for office (*gongshi*), and clerks from obtaining salt bound for merchant sales districts;[37] (5) consider loans to salters; (6) consider an increase in the salt price if it is too low *[p. 4445]*; (7) let managing officials thoroughly delve into the advantages and disadvantages [of merchant trade] and make them known.

---

[35] The Intendancy's statement was made on 1/9/1096 and approved (*SHY* 24.31a–b). *Pingyou*, also called *gongping*, were issued by the government as proof of identity or ownership. Counties gave out household *pingyou*, on which were noted the taxes due as a sort of tax notification called *youzi* or *danzi*.

[36] As mentioned briefly in the Introduction, "shadow privilege" allowed middle- and high-ranking officials to secure a post in the civil service for their relatives (usually their own sons) and thereby perpetuate office-holding without going through the examination system. In other words, the sons enjoyed the "shadow" (or protection) of their fathers' government service.

[37] Offenders were condemned to two years in exile. Anyone cognizant who concealed information was punished to the same degree as the primary offender and informants were rewarded with 100 strings of cash, as noted 9/11/1119 (*SHY* 25.15a–b).

The following year the emperor decreed to abolish the tax on salt boats so as to forestall any abuses.[38] Salt boats were to be allowed to pass others to ensure speedy arrival.[39] Government flotilla officials who prevented them from doing so were to be punished.

Later the voucher law (*chaofa*) was changed. A voucher purchase office was established at the Monopoly Goods Bureau [in the capital]. Those who brought pond salt vouchers were given powder salt [in other words, Huai or Zhe sea salt], incense, or tea vouchers in exchange, plus 10 percent northeastern salt, office certificates (*guan'gao*), Buddhist ordination certificates, and miscellaneous goods.[40] Half the voucher value was given in powder salt and the rest in miscellaneous goods, while [devalued] old vouchers [for northwest pond salt] could only be exchanged for powder salt and office certificates. Thirty percent [of the old vouchers' value] was to be given according to the holder's preference, while 70 percent had to be in new vouchers.[41] The purchase price of vouchers for the people was set, to prevent the rich and powerful [from manipulating their value] and to stabilize the cost of supplies at the border. For every 100 strings worth of vouchers bought in Hebei, at least 5,000 [catties of salt] had to be provided; for the same value in southeast powder

---

[38] *Lishengqian* or *lishengshui* was a tax on merchant boats based on weight; only grain and foodstuffs were exempted. During Shenzong's reign (1068–1085), however, prefectures began to charge grain boats, calling this "five grains *lishengqian*"; not until 1102 was this taxing halted. Toward the end of Northern Song many locales began charging *lishengqian* even on nonmerchant boats.

[39] The order of passage stipulated that ordinary boats stop when government boats came down the river; merchant boats were now allowed to pass to gain time (Wang Leiming 1985, 360n4).

[40] This was the period when the salt ponds had been devastated by weather and Cai Jing promoted moving sea salt into former pond salt distribution areas. The *guan'gao*, also called *gaoshen* or *gaochi*, was a certificate conferring office; it was written on colored silk paper and enclosed in a silk bag. *Gao* were for high officials; "imperial orders" (*chi*) were for lesser ones; later the term *gao* was used for both cases. For details and a description of the agency in charge of issuing such appointment certificates, see *SS* 163.3841–46.

[41] This was the voucher "transfer ways" (*zhuanlang*) method, part of the *duidai* policy of 1103, by which merchants could exchange old pond salt vouchers to obtain vouchers for southeast salt. Normally, the old pond salt vouchers could not be exchanged for more than half their face value.

salt vouchers, at least 10,000 [catties]; for Shaanxi salt vouchers, at least 5,500 [catties]. Any who tried to shortchange [merchants] were sentenced to exile. There were provisions for dealing with harassment by government officials and clerks, and for extending voucher deadlines.

The proportion of government- to merchant-distributed salt can be tracked through the sales of vouchers, for which various surcharges were extracted upon exchange. We find the state devising increasingly complex calculations of voucher value to maximize revenue.

In 1105 (Chongning 4) because the price at which [merchants] bought salt differed widely, [the court] deliberated over the six circuits' salt [voucher] prices. [It] proportionately added ten cash to [voucher] prices at every increment above twenty cash [up to forty-five cash], but those at forty-five cash [or above] were kept the same. Anyone who came for southeastern powder salt might pay in gold, silver, silk, or other goods. The 20 percent interest formerly charged against loans to producer households was abolished. In 1106 (Chongning 5) the emperor decreed that [when merchants received sea salt] those who had not paid the cash surcharge should only be given [an amount of salt] no more than 20 percent [of the total face value of the sea salt voucher]. In 1107 (Daguan 1) those who [wanted to] receive southeastern powder salt were to pay an exchange fee [in cash] and submit a number of old vouchers, in accord with current policy: they were to pay 30 percent in cash [for that southeastern salt and 70 percent in old Xie salt vouchers]. Those who paid 40 percent [of their total voucher value] in cash were [to be allowed] to pay 20 percent [in old vouchers]; those who paid 50 percent in cash were [allowed] to pay 30 percent [in old vouchers]. This was later changed to those paying 40 percent [in cash] being [allowed to pay] 30 percent [in old vouchers] and those paying 50 percent [in cash could pay] 40 percent [in old vouchers]. Those who wanted southeastern salt by cash payment for new vouchers were to pay the surcharge according to the above rule for a 40 or 50 percent [cash] exchange. If those who wished to obtain new southeastern salt vouchers with cash did not carry [any of the] six grades of old vouchers, they would be given salt first. If they carried only five grades of old vouchers, their salt was given before those who held old vouchers for which they had not paid a surcharge and which had been issued before the tenth month of 1105 (Chongning 4). The six grades referred to the ratios of the surcharges, namely, vouchers paid for at 30, 40, or 50 percent [cash], those paid for with an instrument known as "equal to ten vouchers" (*dangshichao*), Hebei deeds (*gongju*), and exemptions.

Lack of consistency prompted the general censor to memorialize on the good old days of the voucher policy twenty years earlier, under Shenzong. Now problems were engendered by the evaluation system, forced purchases, the breakdown of provisioning, the high salt price, and depreciated vouchers.

At this time the voucher policy was not uniform, and public and private were confused. In 1110 (Daguan 4) an attendant censor, Mao Zhu, stated:

> During the Chongning period (1102–1106) the old salt policy [also known as the Yuanfeng policy of 1078–1085] was suddenly changed. The *[p. 4446]* circuits are [now] not allowed the use of government flotillas on the return trip to make income for their Fiscal Intendancies, but the government allows people to use vouchers to obtain salt, then transport it to designated prefectures and counties for trade. The selling prefectures and counties collect a tax from the merchants. The Salt Intendancy blames local governments for evaluating the performance of subordinates by the quantity of salt sold. If one cares for the people and does not bleed them dry, one is labeled an obstructionist and is subject to demotion. Which hard-pressed prefectures and counties do not compete to squeeze the populace? Thus in every county in the southeastern prefectures, households classified above the third class are coerced into purchasing a certain amount of salt according to the value of their property. This annual salt duty on upper-class households amounts to 1,000 strings, and even for the third and lowest class of households it comes to at least 30 to 50 strings worth. These are set figures and must be collected to meet the annual quota [presumably for salt sales]. Delays incur whipping. A county's annual [sales/distribution] quota is anywhere from 30,000 to 50,000 strings, which, [if] used as the standard from now on, [would] certainly lead to major problems.

He further stated:

> The court previously had only three circuits maintain stockpiles, yet this was plenty. The secret was simply the smooth operation of the voucher system

and mutual trust between superior and inferior. Revenues from southeastern powder salt provided for Hebei's needs; that from northeastern salt provided for Hedong's needs; and that from Xie ponds salt provided for Shaanxi's needs. All funds were kept in the capital and, according to amounts collected, an equal value of vouchers were given the three circuits. For example, when [merchants brought] Hebei's grain and fodder vouchers to the capital, where they exchanged them for cash—this was termed the "flying money" policy. When Hedong's three circuits' [grain and fodder vouchers] were brought to the capital, half the payment [to merchants] was in cash and half in silver or silks. With Shaanxi Xie salt vouchers, Xie salt was given [to the merchants], and any extra vouchers were folded back into the capital's funds. Cash amassed in the capital and vouchers circulated in the three circuits. When vouchers were brought to the capital, cash was paid out. There were no delays. So merchants were happy and anxious to transport grain and fodder to the border commanderies. When merchant trade flowed, commodity prices stabilized. There was one uniform price: a peck of rice was only 100-odd cash, and a bundle of fodder was no more than 30. Border storehouses were full to overflowing.

Yet, from the Chongning period (1102–1106) on, the voucher law has been changed so frequently the people have no confidence. The capital no longer has cash reserves, yet it has issued several times more vouchers than in past years. When vouchers are brought to the capital, *[p. 4447]* there is no money to pay for them, which has led to prices falling to less than a tenth of their value. No one is provisioning the border commanderies, so the government has to buy. When there are insufficient funds for the purchase of grain, then silver, silk, and cash mixed with vouchers make up the payment. The purchase of grain from the people is no longer calculated by vouchers but by silver, silk, and ready cash. The price for grain and fodder is elevated and inflated figures result. This has led to prices the government pays being several times the average price among the people: a peck of rice sometimes costs as much as 400 [cash]; a bundle of fodder, at least 130 cash or more. Military stockpiles cannot but be short, and revenues cannot but be insufficient. For instance, a Xie salt voucher issued for 6,000 [strings] is now only worth 3,000. Southeastern powder salt vouchers that merchants turn over bring 40 percent in ready cash, 60 percent in salt vouchers. The Monopoly Goods Bureau receives 70,000 [strings] in income, while the true worth [of the salt that the government has distributed to merchants] is 100,000 [strings]. Thus the salt capital dwindles imperceptibly.

I believe that if we do not follow the salt policy of the Xining (1068–1077) and Yuanfeng (1078–1085) periods, then commodity prices cannot be stabilized and border stockpiles will not amass. At present there is no other matter more urgent. Xue Xiang in the past elaborated [on this policy] during the Jiayou period (1056–1063). Before it had been implemented for very long, the price of grain quickly dropped and border provisions became plentiful. But the policy was not fully developed until the Xining and Yuanfeng periods. In recent years the Monopoly Goods Bureau, disregarding implications of frequent changes to the salt policy and the consequent effect on border provisioning, has hoped only to impose surcharges and purchase southeastern salt vouchers to increase receipts, so as to be rewarded. One set of vouchers has just barely been put in circulation when a new set is issued. These new ones are given priority for receipt of salt, so the earlier vouchers become so much waste paper. None profit from them, so merchants become resentful. I hope for Your Majesty's enlightened decree to the great ministers [requiring them] to select capable functionaries and successfully carry out the voucher policy. Let the people know that the present policy is not meant to be an obstruction and what has been done is not irreversible. A policy such as Xue Xiang's, which proved effective in the past, may be recommended and implemented.

Nowadays there is no lack of able men either in administration or in handling the voucher policy; nor do the capital's three warehouses lack any income from the commanderies and counties for emergency needs. If we have 3 to 4 million strings set in reserve (*zhuangliu*) in the capital and give out vouchers of exchange according to the amount of reserves, then when a voucher is brought in, cash can be paid without difficulty. When government and masses trust each other, vouchers will be considered worth trading because of their convenience.[42] If the amount [merchants wish to] cash is large, [the state] can give southeastern powder salt vouchers or Buddhist ordination certificates and the like. Apart from giving [merchants] southeastern powder salt vouchers or Buddhist ordination certificates and office certification (*chidie*) in exchange for old pond salt vouchers, it is decreed that other items should be exchanged for cash at the capital, which will be kept as the funds against which additional vouchers may be issued.[43] Those who receive [cash] are also to be tracked. [*p. 4448*] As for previously issued vouchers (*wenchao*), there ought to be a program in place to calculate the amount and reimburse in salt. In the past, establishing such a program was difficult; fixing a broken policy, however, is not easy either. For the sake of long-term income

---

[42] Literally, their light weight.

[43] *Chidie* was a document issued by the Department of Ministries and used by magistrates or *jinshi* degree holders when appointed to be examination proctors, envoys abroad, or delegates to receive foreign officials; these documents were also used by Buddhist priests when they were appointed head priest and for tablets bestowed on monasteries as an imperial favor.

we should overlook small problems at the moment. [I hope this suggestion] may be carefully considered for possible implementation.

Thus the administration attempted to restore Shenzong's policy and resolve voucher abuses by means of surcharges.

Not long afterward, when Zhang Shangying became chief councilor, deliberations began, aimed at restoring the old policy of merchant trade from the Xi[ning and Yuan]feng reign periods (1068–1085).[44] Fifteen million strings of the Palace Treasury's (*neifu*) cash were to be placed in special reserve, while the remainder was to be used in eradicating abuses of either cash, voucher, or commodity exchanges. Shaanxi was given 5 million strings worth of vouchers, while the Jiang and Huai Transport Intendancies were given 3 million strings worth of cash certificates [i.e., proofs of cash payment] and tribute money. The left assistant division chief in the Department of Ministries, Zhang Cha, handled southeastern salt affairs, while the ever-normal intendant of Jiangxi, Zhang Gen, managed the transport of Huai salt to Jiangxi.[45] The Salt and Incense Intendancy was abolished, and the salt matters of all circuits were reassigned to the Judicial Intendancy (*tixingsi*). It was decided to institute [a system of] five grades of old vouchers. Merchants who had already obtained new [salt] vouchers or vouchers for which they had paid a cash surcharge, and who did not have to pay extra surcharges, were the first to be given southeastern powder salt to trade. Huai and Zhe salterns were ordered to put 50 percent of their salt in reserve to await its transport by government flotillas to the three circuits' distribution points where merchants would come to obtain it. The other 50 percent was first to be given to those with new [salt] or cash vouchers and not carrying old vouchers.[46] So the old policy was reinstated

---

[44] Cai Jing was demoted in 1110. When Zhang Shangying became right executive of the Department of Ministries, and concurrently executive of the Secretariat, the salt administration received a boost in efficiency (Wang Leiming 1985, 363–364n1). Zhang and the emperor accepted the censor Mao Zhu's analysis and created a new salt policy along the lines of that under Shenzong and Wang Anshi.

[45] Decreed 12/26/1110. Zhang Cha was given two months to research the pros and cons (*SHY* 25.3b).

[46] Decreed 8/15/1110 (*SHY* 25.2b).

whereby merchants holding five kinds of old [devalued] vouchers were only given salt if they exchanged them for new vouchers. But because of concern that after months and years there would be no [salt] left to give out [due to miscorrelation with vouchers], a policy of added payments was established. Those holding vouchers for which they paid a 30 percent cash surcharge were to pay an additional 70 percent in cash at the Monopoly Goods Bureau; those with vouchers bought at the 40 percent cash surcharge were to pay an additional 60 percent cash; those who paid 50 percent or who had "equal to ten vouchers" were to pay an additional 70 percent; those who held Hebei cash payment documents had payments calculated at the 50 percent surcharge rate.

One office reported that the three circuits' voucher law followed the precedent of the Xining and Yuanfeng periods (1068–1085), entirely relying on southeastern powder salt for capital. If old vouchers were to be collected as a surcharge, this would be completely contrary to promotion of the Xining and Yuanfeng period voucher policy. But if this were not allowed, then the vouchers could not be collected [to be destroyed]. It was decided to cut the submission of Hebei cash payment documents as well as additional charges by 20 percent. The surcharges paid with imperial certificates of appointment, Buddhist ordination certificates, incense, miscellaneous goods, as well as southeastern salt were also to be cut 20 percent. The emperor decreed:

> Annual salt sales of the six southeastern circuits in the Yuanfeng period (1078–1085) were no less than several hundred thousand [strings of cash] for each circuit. Since initiation of salt vouchers [to cover government] transport, income has been deficient. Just take Jiangxi, where the prepurchase of salt and silk (*yumai*) by the government gives the people too low a price.[47] How can *[p. 4449]* this be called benevolence?

---

[47] *Yumai* or *hemai* referred to government loans made in return for eventual payment in silk, beginning in the last quarter of the 900s. Later the funds lent were also repaid in salt and other items. Gradually this exchange evolved into a tax for which prefectures set quotas based on property value. By the Southern Song "prepurchase" had been transformed into a regular, continually increasing cash tax. In Sichuan and Guangxi there were prepurchase markets for silks and such (Wang Leiming 1985, 364n3).

He ordered the southeastern circuits' Fiscal Intendancies to cooperate in administering transport.

Officials paid more for salt and stockpiled the product for the merchant trade.

In 1111 (Zhenghe 1) the emperor decreed that merchants who wished to follow the Xining and Yuanfeng policy of "transfer ways" (*zhuanlang*) could obtain salt by first using the three circuits' new vouchers, then going to whatever location and selling at a set price.[48] To collect more above-quota salt from Liangzhe producers to put into storage, the procurement price per catty was to be increased by three cash. Later Zhang Cha, in an attempt to equalize salt prices [across the southeastern circuits], increased it by two more cash per catty than the Shaosheng [period policy of 1094–1097]. The emperor agreed with his argument but approved only a one-cash increase.

Then critics argued:

> Previously salt merchants made payments to the Monopoly Goods Bureau to trade according to the "transfer ways" policy. The number of traders participating depended on the quantity of salt in reserve. In the southeast there were great amounts of salt, and since many purchased vouchers to obtain it, revenues multiplied. Merchants, however, are unwilling to go to places that lack salt. During the Yuanfeng period (1078–1085) distant locations had to stockpile two to three years' worth [through government transport]; less distant locations had to stockpile one to two years' worth; the closest locations still had to stockpile half a year to a year's worth. This was called "preparatory salt" (*zhunbeiyan*). With this salt the voucher policy could be executed. During the Shaosheng period (1094–1097) the old [government distribution] policy was observed and there were widespread stockpiles. Thus, after prices had been standardized, tax revenues increased by many times. The Fiscal Intendancy should not only strictly enforce transport of stockpiled salt but also maintain the number of Yuanfeng period stockpiles. Then the voucher policy will operate effectively and tax revenues will be abundant. The amount of salt boiled by salters and sold by the government is much greater now than in the past. Adopting the old prices of Yuanfeng would be enough [to create cash surpluses], let alone if we set new [higher] prices. We also have prepared production funds and money for loans [to

---

[48] Decreed 1/12/1111 (*SHY* 25.4a).

salters]. What worries can there be about revenue increases? If a catty is increased by one cash, it will be too expensive.

The emperor decreed to implement this. Salt intendants [were appointed] for all six circuits; an office was also established in Yangzhou[a] but closed not long after.

Policymakers again debated merchant trade of salt in exchange for cash, vouchers, or other commodities and manipulated the ratio of exchanges.

Critics again stated:

There used to be two ways in which merchants could buy southeastern powder salt at the capital's Monopoly Goods Bureau: the first was by ready cash payment; the second was according to the "transfer ways" voucher trade. Since the three circuits' [Jiang, Huai, Jinghu] vouchers may be traded [for salt] in the second way, we should revert to the old policy of also allowing ready cash payment. Then the merchants' money will go to the Monopoly Goods Bureau and not to speculators (*jianbing*), cash will remain in the capital, and merchants will head for the southeast.

The emperor decreed to adopt this plan. There were other proposals:

The old policy allowed commodities and government vouchers to be exchanged for salt so that the voucher price was maintained and did not fall much. The recent prohibition [of this combined exchange] was wrong. When the old salt vouchers were sold in the southeast, the Fiscal Intendancy allowed only ready cash payment so that [not many were sold] and there was much accumulation [of salt].

Thus vouchers were again to be used [as part of] salt payments as before. For powder salt there was a limit of 80 percent payment in powder [salt] vouchers and 20 percent in *[p. 4450]* cash, which was later increased to 30 percent.

Cai Jing ended government distribution; salt policy now called for merchants to be served in order, according to the type of payment they brought in.

In 1112 (Zhenghe 2) in Jiangningfu, Guangdejun, and Taipingzhou, the price of a catty was increased by two cash, while in Xuanzhou,

Shezhou, Raozhou, and Xinzhou[b] it was increased by three cash, and in Chizhou, Jiangzhou[a], and Nankangjun, by four cash, all based upon the distance from production areas [to the point of sales]. That year Cai Jing was again in power and significantly changed the salt policy. In the fifth month government transport and sales were abolished; merchants were to go to salterns to obtain salt. [Product] to be transported was placed in reserve storehouses. Merchants applied for salt at the Monopoly Goods Bureau [in the capital]; those first to arrive were given bonus salt as encouragement. Those who had bought "transfer ways" vouchers but not yet received their distribution had to pay [an additional] 30 percent in cash for every 100 strings worth. New vouchers had to be accompanied by 30 percent in old vouchers. Those who already had vouchers cleared had to pay additional fees according to the above formulas. Calculations were all in strings of cash. As for the order in which salt was given out, those who paid entirely in cash and did not carry old stock went first, those who still had old inventory went next, and those who carried [only] old vouchers went last. As for the purchase of vouchers in three circuits [Jiang, Huai, Jinghu], merchants who applied to pay 70 percent [of the value] of the southeastern powder salt in vouchers were allowed to pay 20 percent in ready cash. The same held true for northeastern salt. As for other types of vouchers, there was no uniform means of calculation. Again an intendancy was established in each circuit. Then the emperor praised [Cai] Jing's achievements.[49] Since merchants mistrusted the policy's vagaries, however, not many came to trade, so the emperor decreed that talk discouraging others from participating be punished and that the reward [for any informer] be increased to 500 strings.

The sixteen articles Cai Jing proposed in 1113 exceeded his measures at the beginning of the reign in breadth and depth, and included details on managing everything from the salters to merchants and officials.

In 1113 (Zhenghe 3) merchants following past practice first applied to the circuit then obtained salt from the saltern. Delays, however, led to this being abolished. If great amounts of extra salt were to be added,

---

[49] For details of the decree, see *Song dazhaoling ji* [*SDZJ*] 184.669.

officials checked the weight and gave vouchers when the merchants paid cash. Policy changed many times. Since Cai Jing wanted to net all merchant profits, he presented sixteen measures. It was decided that the purchase price of government salt would be 10,000 cash per bag of 300 catties. Those who wanted to sell might decide the quantity on their own. The old salt bonuses (*jiarao*) and allowances for the cost of hiring porters were abolished.[50] Merchant salt in the past had been transported by and stored in boats; this was changed to the northeastern salt method of using bags manufactured and sold by the government. Just as stipulated in the policy governing monopoly tea containers, tampering with the seals on salt shipments or engaging in forgery were punishable offenses, and reusing bags was prohibited. Salt collection and distribution were handled separately by two different offices: one collected product at the saltern and was charged with weighing pans and sealing bags; the other received the salt at the storehouse and was charged with inspection of documents and matching [a merchant's receipt] with the government's registration [of the sale]. [Officials] opened one in every twenty bags for inspection, then issued a tally agreement. Southeastern powder salterns also issued vouchers and a registration book. [Saltern officials] had to authorize any merchants who wished to change the saltern [from where they obtained salt], cancelling their registration books and vouchers and *[p. 4451]* turning over the tally agreement [indicating quantity to be issued] to the new designated location where the salt was to be dispensed. After having salt distributed to them, merchants then had to register at their new [purchase] locale.

Those who changed their destination en route also followed this procedure [that is, registering at their new purchase locale]. They had to submit vouchers within one year; in certain cases this time period might be extended for up to half a year. If by the time the deadline had passed they had not yet entirely sold the salt, their vouchers were destroyed and the salt registered with the government, to be sold only in the same sales locale. In general this followed the tea policy, but there were more provisos, which robbed the people of profits. In the name of discouraging

---

[50] This is the first mention of the term *jiarao* in the *SS* salt treatise, yet bonuses in salt given to merchants were awarded in regions outside Huai as well.

smuggling, illegal boiling, and overloading [merchants with more than the proper amount of salt], the policy of voucher exchange at a stipulated proportion and discount was imposed. When merchants presented vouchers for salt, it was often not given promptly, and they were forced to purchase new vouchers based on the original amount before being allowed to carry [only] half the amount of the original vouchers. Due to concern that directives were not being carried out, prohibitions on avoiding [the regulations] were strictly enforced, obstruction of the law denounced, and criticism of the policy severely punished. Every quarter [officials had to go through] an evaluation, and harsh admonishments sought to increase collection.

The government gave preferential treatment to those merchants bearing vouchers issued far from the point of production in hopes of attracting them to remote areas needing salt. Certainly the bureaucracy needed merchants for their role in distribution, yet with the constant manipulation of voucher policy, officials at times forced merchants into bankruptcy.

In 1114 (Zhenghe 4) few merchants traded in remote locales, and so salt storehouses distributed salt according to distance, giving it first to merchants from faraway locales. Subsequently, there was a mandate that [any merchant] carrying regular quota salt who did not purchase new vouchers within a month would have the quota salt confiscated, and any leftover salt as well. In 1115 (Zhenghe 5) voucher counterfeiters were sentenced according to law on [forging] Sichuan money vouchers.[51] In 1116 (Zhenghe 6), because big merchants in salt-producing prefectures were unwilling to deal, shopkeepers who sold small bags could pay twenty cash for vouchers, but were not to sell outside prefectural boundaries.

In 1120 (Xuanhe 2) the emperor decreed that the over 100 million [catties] of salt accumulated in the six [southeast] circuits be transported and sold by merchants. Just like at Huai and Zhe salt storehouses, amounts

---

[51] Money vouchers (*qianyin*) were Song period certificates that could be converted into cash. Sichuan money vouchers, commonly called *chuanyin*, were based on an iron standard, and printed with the year, face value, and a design. Their face value ranged from five hundred cash to one string; they were issued once every several years, but even so lost value from overprinting.

were to be calculated in current salt vouchers. In 1122 (Xuanhe 4) the Monopoly Goods Bureau proposed:

> In the past there was a saying that a peck of rice cost the same as a catty of salt: before the Xining and Yuanfeng reign periods (1068–1085) a picul of rice was no more than 600 or 700 cash [60–70 per peck], while the price of salt was 60 to 70 cash per catty. Now the price of rice is 2,500–3,000 cash per picul [250 cash per peck], while salt is still 60 [cash]. During the Chongning period (1102–1106) salt commanded a set price. When vouchers changed hands, a median price of 40 cash per catty was settled on. Now it is 37 cash per catty, so the government loses a bit more. We wish to increase the purchase price to 13,000 cash per bag. The going price for the salters' salt will also increase so that they can support themselves and smuggling will abate and cease.

Thus, old salt [bought with old vouchers] was entirely prohibited from sale in stores and the directive to register merchants and require additional cash payments and "carrying sales" (*daimai*) [the government giving extra salt to disperse gluts] was reapplied.

The Xie voucher program was raised as a model to adopt; Cai Jing's dizzying policy changes, aimed at sending more revenue to the capital, backfired in the cases of both Xie and sea salt.

When the salt voucher policy was initially implemented, salt amassed at the Xie ponds, cash amassed at the capital's Monopoly Goods Bureau, and vouchers amassed in border commanderies at ˙Shaanxi. Merchants provisioned the border with goods and grain, then received vouchers and returned. For goods and grain brought to the border, they could profit several times over; the only worry was having no goods to bring back, thus they strove to get vouchers and go straightaway to obtain salt from the Xie ponds. *[p. 4452]* The distribution area of Xie salt was exceptionally wide. Some [merchants] immediately received cash from the capital at 6,200 [cash] per voucher, then had to pay an agricultural surtax, but that was only several tens of cash.[52] Due to this [lenient policy],

---

[52] *Touzi qian* was an agricultural surtax charged whenever the government collected or paid out cash. In 973 the Sichuan Double Tax required an extra seven cash for every string of 1,000 cash; six cash for every bolt of silk; one cash for

many merchants [were willing to] trade in the prefectures and counties. During the Chongning reign period (1102–1106) Cai Jing initiated policy changes: merchants were first to tender cash to obtain vouchers, then go to salt-producing prefectures to receive salt. His idea was to gather the money of all regions into the capital so as to gain the favor of the emperor. So the voucher policy lost its effectiveness; merchants did not circulate, and the border no longer had supplies. When southeastern salt prohibitions were made more severe, the numbers of those convicted for breaking the law increased, and the people's table salt became full of dust and dirt. The Xie ponds' naturally pure product and profits were forsaken like excrement. As soon as a new policy had taken effect, it was suddenly altered again. First it was changed to the voucher exchange policy, the next year, to the voucher "rotation" policy. Rotation involved merchants changing more vouchers upon having already sold vouchers but not yet having received salt; then, after changing vouchers but still not having received salt, they had to pay additional cash. Altogether three cash payments had to be made before one could receive one voucher's worth of goods. The merchants had nothing left with which to buy vouchers; the money they already paid had completely disappeared. Within a day several tens of thousands of vouchers might be rendered worthless. Overnight rich merchants could become beggars, and some committed suicide by drowning or hanging themselves.

Concerted efforts at revenue procurement consumed Cai Jing's subordinates, but even they complained of the harm done by constant policy changes.

At the time a certain Wei Bochu, the [Three] Ministries chief clerk (*daxu*), was entrusted by Cai Jing to take charge of the Monopoly Goods Bureau.[53] In 1116 (Zhenghe 6) salt tax revenues reached 40 million strings, and [the responsible] officials were promoted. In 1117 (Zhenghe

---

every ounce of silk thread, catty of tea, and bundle of fodder. Gaozong increased this to forty-three cash per 1,000; Xiaozong increased it to fifty-six per 1,000. Here, Xie merchants had to pay this and other fees (Wang Leiming 1985, 367n1).

[53] Government clerks and subofficial functionaries were commonly called *xu*; those with more authority were termed *daxu*. This is the status Wei Bochu had; the third of the "Three Ministries" is missing (*WXTK* 16.5b).

7) due to another surplus in revenues, officials again had rewards bestowed upon them. [Wei] Bochu was promoted every year, gaining such high titles as grand master for thorough counsel (*tongyi dafu*) and edict attendant of the Huiyou Palace Hall (*huiyouge daizhi*).[54] Thereafter he became part of a faction with Wang Fu; however, [Cai] Jing became resentful and so dismissed him. [Wei] Bochu had no special talents, but he clandestinely colluded with those who dealt in vouchers to embezzle 40 percent of the merchant voucher payment funds [rightly government revenue]. [Cai Jing] aimed to bring in substantial revenue so he could pull the wool over the emperor's eyes. When the salt policy was changed once more during the Zhenghe period (1111–1117), [Wei] Bochu, who then enjoyed Cai Jing's trust, proposed:

> The court embarks on ways to gather revenue and impel merchants to trade without issuing directives. Hundreds of thousands in revenue arrive by the cartload. With these, after the court's needs, bureaucracy's expenses, and annual costs are met, there is still a surplus. This is indeed due to income from the salt monopoly. In recent years no stable salt policy was in place; it was changed at will to accommodate the convenience of public and private. Changes were not well planned, and abuses abounded. [But] after the establishment of a policy in the Zhenghe period (1111–1117) the source of abuses was cut off and both government and people have benefited. Before daily revenues did not exceed 20,000 strings and already people were surprised at the profusion. Nowadays, revenues are regularly as much as 40,000 to 50,000 strings. In one year, in one commandery, Chuzhou[a], merchant voucher revenues reached over 500,000 strings; *[p. 4453]* at the storehouses of one prefecture, Taizhou[b], merchants requested as many as 400,000 bags of salt. The new policy has been in effect for only two years, but revenues have already reached 40 million strings. Though past records have noted that wealth accumulated to the point of the money strings wearing out, that cannot be compared with the situation today. I beg to have the record of 40 million strings of income announced to the Historiography Office in order to manifest governance that enriches the state and benefits the people.

---

[54] The Huiyou Palace Hall was constructed in 1108 as the library for Zhezong's books and writings. All Song palace halls had an edict attendant (*daizhi*), who acted as caretaker in attendance on the emperor and advisor to officials (Wang Leiming 1985, 368n3).

When a small man is in favor, he is totally unscrupulous, bringing things to a head this way.

As court expenses rose, efforts to squeeze income from salt increased, including regulation of virtually anything that could be used to produce more revenue, including fish scales, seaweed, and even the grains that might be gleaned from used packaging. Piecemeal extensions of distribution deadlines were issued as a solution to bureaucratic difficulties in distribution.

By then, as expenditures of the court grew ever greater, the desire to increase tax revenues followed. Annual and seasonal evaluations were again announced: officials temporarily on leave were not to be paid for their time off; law violators even with shadow privilege were to receive extreme penalties. Detailed prohibitions covered minute matters such as [salt recovered from used] salt bags and dried saltfish (*xiang*).[55] Prefectures and counties focused entirely on increasing annual revenues so they would not be penalized, and all levels of regulation and oversight became increasingly harsh. In 1117 (Zhenghe 7) the emperor decreed:

> The recent change in salt policy has resulted in extreme rewards and punishments. Salt taxes are far too many. They are imposed by head count, covering even infants and domestic animals. Decent people are victimized and every household is wracked by worry. [I desire that the policy] return to its original form to benefit the commoners. Ministries are to enforce this decree to circulate new vouchers.

Offices in charge, however, were incapable of consistent implementation. Periodic performance evaluations (*bijiao*), which had been abolished, were again resorted to. Orders for surcharges at one point annulled were again

---

[55] This may simply have meant that salt smuggling might occur when salted fish were being transported (*SHY* 25.23b). The *xiang* were dried fish commonly made from *leyü*, related to herring or shad (*shiyü*), which entered rivers from the sea in the spring to breed. Once dried, a small amount of salt could be obtained from the skin. As to salt bags, grains of powder salt could be gleaned from collected bags (Wang Leiming 1985, 369n2). Another unusual method of salt extraction was from the burned ashes of the bog bean plant (*shuibo*), *Menianthus trifoliata*, a swamp weed. A similar method of burning seaweed was used in ninth-century Japan to refine *mo-shio* salt (Twitchett 1970, 56n59).

restored. The number of salt bags at one time increased [to a certain quota] was rolled back. The price of a bag once reduced to 11,000 [cash] was restored to 13,000. The people were thus exhausted, and smuggling flourished.

In 1126 (Jingkang 1) the emperor decreed that certificates paid for before the initiation of the new voucher system be returned to merchants to demonstrate the government's sincerity. Salt was given for the new vouchers, but "carrying sales" distribution of old salt would still be observed to a certain deadline.[56] Discussants stated:

> When Wang Fu was in office, he followed Cai Jing's corrupt policy by adopting the use of new vouchers. Additional fees and extra payments were required [on old voucher salt] before it could be sold, with a time limit at first of two months, then with an extension of one month. While in power, [Wang] Fu concentrated on taking advantage of the people and oppressing the lowly to benefit the mighty. The changing voucher policies had an effect worse than bandits. Today, however, not only has his precedent not been corrected, but the extension is cut to half a month, which is even worse than in Wang Fu's time. How can merchants not complain?[57]

The emperor decreed to extend the deadline.

Southern Song

At the beginning of the Southern Song under Gaozong the government continued the same types of revenue-generating strategies: taxing salters, charging fees of

---

[56] Glut salt was sold with regular salt at a certain ratio, such as two to five bags of glut salt to thirty bags of regular salt.

[57] Wang Fu, a close confidante of Cai Jing, succeeded Cai when public pressure forced him to step down. Since Wang Fu eliminated many fees and charges, he was regarded as an able statesman. But he was also allied with the eunuch Liang Shicheng and engaged in nefarious activities. When this became known, Wang Fu was disgraced as one of the "Six Bandits," along with Cai Jing, Zhu Mian, Li Yan, and the eunuchs Tong Guan and Liang Shicheng. When Qinzong ascended in 1126, Cai died en route to banishment, Zhu was dismissed, Li was ordered to commit suicide, Tong had his head displayed in the capital, and Wang and Liang were banished, then killed (*SS* 23.421–38; 468.13658–59, 13662–63; 470.13681–84, 13684–86; 472.13721–28).

merchants, and the proportional exchange of vouchers. It altered its policy five times in as many years.

After the move south, the government gave salt producers of Huai and Zhe production funds (*benqian*).[58] The prefectures built storehouses and had merchants purchase vouchers: fifty catties made one picul and six piculs made one bag [so one bag was three hundred catties], for which they paid [*p. 4454*] 18,000 in cash. In 1131 (Shaoxing 1) the emperor decreed that the Double Tax charged to salters of Lin'anfu and Xiuzhou be paid in salt, according to the policy of the Huangyou period (1049–1053). [Disciplinary] guidelines were also established for inspectors (*jianguan*) who neglected to investigate private boiling by salters or arrest smugglers.[59] In the ninth month of 1132 (Shaoxing 2) the emperor decreed that merchants were to pay a commercial tax of 3,000 [cash] per bag for Huai and Zhe salt. Those who had gotten salt but not sold it were also to follow this regulation; if within ten days they had not come forth to report [any remaining stock], they would be dealt with according to the smuggling law. At this time Lü Yihao adopted the proposal of the controller (*tixia*), Zhang Chun, to drastically change the salt policy. In the eleventh month the emperor decreed that 40 percent of Huai and Zhe salt be paid in vouchers issued after the present decree and 40 percent in vouchers issued after the move south in the Jianyan period (1127–1130).[60]

---

[58] The first entry on Huai salt in the Southern Song in the *SHY* is dated 11/21/1127. Because not many merchants were trading northeastern salt in the Eastern Capital, the minister of finance, Huang Qianhou, proposed allowing Huai salt into the northeast if merchants were willing to pay a "road usage" fee (*jieluqian*) per bag. The emperor decreed a two-string fee until the northeastern trade was restored (*SHY* 25.31a).

[59] It was noted on 12/17/1131 that not only [civilian] inspectors but military inspectors as well were to be punished by law, should they evade their duties (*SHY* 26.3a–b).

[60] After the phrase "paid in vouchers issued after the present decree," another should read: "20 percent to be paid in vouchers issued after the ninth month, *jiashen* day of this year" (Wang Leiming 1985, 370n1). Merchants with vouchers were served in a certain order at the salterns and this way avoided irregularities, an official noted on 4/14/1130 (*SHY* 25.36a). It seems that later this distribution to merchants may have been made on a first-come, first-served basis. The order of service was crucial because between submission of vouchers and actual

At first, feeling that the policy of voucher exchange at the stipulated rations was not feasible, Lü Yihao ordered merchants to pay additional cash. By this time not only were additional cash payments in practice, but the exchange policy was also added, so the situation worsened. In 1133 (Shaoxing 3) the silkworm salt charge on the people was reduced.[61] In the

---

distribution, there might be a delay of months, during which new vouchers might be issued and old ones devalued. See Kusano 1961, 123–54.

According to a 10/19/1131 memorial, salterns submitted vouchers to Intendancy bookkeepers daily (*SHY* 26.3a). In the event a merchant lost his vouchers due to flood, fire, or banditry, he could obtain a guarantor and repurchase them, a central ministry stated on 4/22/1132 (*SHY* 26.5b). In 1132 the proposal was made to allow merchants to choose the saltern and quantity of salt (*SHY* 26.20a–b). By 1165 merchants apparently were allowed to go to any of the three circuits to fetch salt (*SHY* 27.19b–20a). When merchants brought in a mix of new and old vouchers, these were figured according to a stipulated ratio. By 1132 the ratio was based on the date of issue of new vouchers, as compared with the two types already in circulation. Merchants with old Jianyan period vouchers, for example, had to buy new Shaoxing second-year, ninth-month vouchers. Those who already held ninth-month vouchers had to buy eleventh-month vouchers, so they held a ratio of 40:20:40 of eleventh-month to ninth-month to Jianyan vouchers (*XNYL* 60.14a–b). In 1132 submission of old vouchers had to be accomplished within ten days (*XNYL* 58.15b). In 1134 it was observed that this policy was alternately rescinded and restored (*XNYL* 80.2b–3a).

In Tongzhou[b] (Huaidong), along the river, two military leaders allowed subordinates to collect and trade salt privately by boat. On 12/8/1132 ministers recommended that the two be interrogated and their supervisor reprimanded for robbing the court (*SHY* 26.19a–b). An intendant noted on 5/15/1133 that after checking vouchers at the salterns the sales officials were to sign and stamp them with a seal with large characters and the date to prevent tampering. The Monopoly Goods Bureau was to inspect and authorize them (*SHY* 26.12b–13a).

[61] The decree was issued on 1/29/1133 in response to a ministerial statement on the benefits of reducing silkworm salt distributions. Because some prefectures and counties still pressed for 100 percent of it to be paid instead of 60 percent, strict enforcement was called for (*SHY* 26.8b).

In the first years of the Southern Song, Huai production plummeted to 350,000 strings worth compared with a previous high of 8 million strings (*CYZJ jia* 14.5b). To encourage war-weary salters to return, on 1/30/1133 the Huaidong tea and salt intendant announced aid the circuit would provide to producers, including cash, stove repair money, oxen, and rice (*SHY* 26.9a; *SHY* 26.10a). On 3/22/1133, in response to a request made by the Huaidong tea and salt intendant, it was decreed that producers would be pardoned of crimes committed during the war, except treason and murder, if they confessed within one month and returned first month of 1134 (Shaoxing 4) the emperor decreed that the Huai and Zhe salt voucher fee be increased by three strings of cash per bag, which was shipped to the Provisional Capital.[62] Subsequently it was decreed that Guang salt should follow suit. In the ninth month, because merchants were slow in coming, the three string increase was dropped. From 1129 (Jianyan 3) [until 1134] the voucher policy was changed five times, including the present change.[63] Since old Jianyan vouchers had not yet been completely turned in, it was decreed that old vouchers be used together with new ones.

A gap of several decades follows in the Songshi *record, from the 1130s to 1170s, though plenty of coverage exists in other sources, as can be seen below. Here I again reconstruct the period more or less topically to complete the years 1132 to 1172. Most of the problems and policies represent continuations of those of the Northern Song, especially the problem of wayward officials.*

*   *   *   *   *

---

to their occupation. Families of the guilty would be exempt as well (*SHY* 26.10b–11b). In some areas of Huaidong, production skyrocketed. A Taizhou[b] official reported on 8/18/1133 that production had risen from about 131,000 piculs to nearly 260,000. All salt officials were rewarded (*SHY* 26.13b–14a).

On 10/11/1133 the Ministry of Justice memorialized on new punishments for smuggling, which moderated previous laws. These included forty strokes for one ounce, one year of banishment for 20 catties, and labor service for 300 catties. One ounce of illegally boiled contraband would be reckoned as two sold; for the sale of merchant salt in restricted areas, punishments were twenty strokes for 1 catty and 3,000 *li* banishment for 300 catties. For commoners the punishment seems to have been less severe than for traders and producers (*SHY* 26.19a; *XNYL* 69.6a–8a).

[62] In a 1/5/1134 decree the emperor noted that out of the twenty-one strings per bag, 600 cash in addition to storage fees were to be used as salt capital (*SHY* 26.21a).

[63] The five changes in as many years began in 1130, when salt from Fujian and Guang was allowed in the Huai-Zhe distribution area and charged a tax of three strings per bag; in 9/1132, when Huai-Zhe merchants were also charged three strings per bag; in 11/1132, when this tax was altered to the proportional voucher exchange system; in 1/1134, when the policy for surcharges was adopted; and in 9/1134, when this surcharge policy was abolished and proportional exchange restored; see Liang Gengyao 1988, part 1, 6–7.

On intercalary 4/25/1132, as reflected by the memorial of a magistrate in Mingzhou[b] (Zhedong), magistrates hoped, despite smuggling, to have salterns established in their territories where farming was not possible. On 10/15/1133, according to the Ministry of Justice, magistrates who were concurrently saltern officials were to check cash records with boiling and procurement heads. Alternatively, boiling and procurement heads had to forward records to the magistrate's office at the end of the month. If there were any abuses in collection and the magistrate did not investigate, he would be punished.[64] According to a 6/15/1136 decree, prefectural and county officials as well as patrols were proscribed from entering salterns when it was not within their authority. If they disturbed the peace or demanded salt, then the amount involved determined the punishment. If supervisors neglected their duties, salters could complain to a higher authority.[65] On 4/27/1153 the Monopoly Goods Bureau at the capital proposed to reduce by half the regulations on reward and punishment for concurrently serving officials. On 9/22/1156 the executive censor (zhongcheng) described how patrols were normally not allowed inside saltern premises, but since saltern officials were also expected to patrol, this defeated the purpose.[66]

Current officials, those on leave, those with shadow privilege, those who had passed the examinations, and prefecture and county employees were prohibited from becoming merchants or trading salt, as indicated on 9/11/1121. However, it was reported by a tea monopoly official on 7/4/1134 that many merchants were in fact of wealthy families with shadow privilege and that various officials were selling voucher [that is, merchant] salt.[67] On 10/28/1142 it was decreed that any official, whether a ranking bureaucrat, clerk, guard, or militiaman, who traded salt was to receive 100 strokes. Anyone who concealed information had a grade of punishment added; if a purchase was not confessed to, the same punishment applied.[68] Punishment for illegal trade above 30 catties of salt on the part of sheriffs, guards, magistrates, prefectural vice-administrators, and petty officials was demotion or replacement. For taking up arms or forming gangs, if the circumstances involved 500 catties, the sentence was handed down according to existing laws. For cases involving over 1,000 catties the Department of Ministries was to be consulted, according to decrees of 11/16/1132 and 7/1/1145.[69] A tea monopoly official of Zhe and Jinghu complained on 2/5/1132

---

[64] *SHY* 26.6a–b, 20b.

[65] *SHY* 26.25a.

[66] Here the issue of trying to separate the salt operations from the predations of policing units is undercut by empowering saltern officials to exercise policing powers. The same abuses would presumably follow. *SHY* 26.33b, 35a–b.

[67] *SHY* 25.15a, 26.23a–b.

[68] *SHY* 26.29b.

[69] *SHY* 26.7a–b, 32a.

that functionaries often demanded bribes when merchants with proper documentation went to receive the goods to which they were entitled.[70] *In Guangxi, officials used aliases to pass themselves off as merchants, then sold back the vouchers they had purchased to the central government. Or they might allow merchants to trade only if they made a "contribution" to the public finance, as noted in a 2/9/1182 decree.*[71] *One Tang Zhongyou offers a well-documented example of corrupt bureaucratic behavior in the Southern Song. He owned various retail shops, obtained tax-free status for his relatives in trading, sold government wine, used treasury money, diverted guild craftsmen for his own use, and adopted aliases.*[72] *Once in 1172, when a monopoly administrator was found to have embezzled voucher funds from a Monopoly Goods Bureau, no precedent could be found for punishment of such an offense. He was eventually sentenced according to the rules on middlemen as of 1/17/1172.*[73]

Reward money represented another strategy for stemming smuggling. On 1/11/1158 records of the right policy monitor and Ministry of Finance showed that officials who had apprehended 10,000 catties in one batch—a rare event implying a powerful offender—were to be rewarded with promotion. Those who had apprehended 10,000 catties over time—implying many small-time violators—received a reduction of the time to their next official review, with a special reward if they had captured the head offender. Also in 1158 the reward for those who had apprehended violators was increased from 100 to 150 strings, and a thorough investigation back to the original seller was to be conducted.[74]

In emergencies, the state used salt vouchers for lending at interest. Trade treasuries (huiyi [ku]) established around 1136 lent vouchers as well as cash, gold, silver, and silk. They were at times abolished due to abuses but served as a precedent for mid-Southern Song practice.[75] *In Huainan a relief fund was offered to salters, as indicated on 1/30/1133. The upper grade of household was paid forty strings, the middle grade, thirty-five strings, and the lower grade, thirty strings. A ministerial proposal was made on 9/2/1139 to determine the actual expenses of boiling, then to*

---

[70] *SHY* 26.3b.

[71] *SHY* 28.13a.

[72] Ju Qingyuan 1935, 37–39.

[73] *SHY* 27.38b.

[74] *SHY* 26.36b–38a.

[75] *XNYL* 106.26a–b, 11/dingchou/1136. See also *Shilin zouyi* [*SLZY*] 8.12a–15a, "Zouqi juanmian huiyiqian zhuang" (Memorial on pardoning *huiyi* money).

set reasonable procurement prices.[76] *When the cost of fuel and rice increased, an attempt was made to raise the salt procurement price in other circuits accordingly.*[77]

Polarizing debate over distribution at salterns versus storehouses can be seen in an edict of 12/25/1157 and a memorial of 12/27/1157. On 3/18/1158 and 3/25/1158 the Huaidong tea and salt intendant argued for reestablishing prefectural storehouses. It was difficult for merchants to reach distant salterns and distribution rates there were low. In addition, none of the weights at salterns were standard because salterns, desperate to get rid of their salt, "adjusted" them—up to tens of catties. Cost analyses were carried out regarding the construction of new warehouses in Huaidong; it was proposed that former storehouses be used to save on materials.[78] *Salterns were reassessed: On 8/9/1158 the Huaidong intendant detailed the circuit's nineteen salterns, 452 stoves, and quotas. He proposed absorbing several salterns that were unproductive, overproducing, or too close to others. This recommendation came during the fourth Huai glut, at which time 3.74 million piculs, or 187 million catties, sat unsold.*[79]

In an extended ministerial address on 1/25/1160 four abuses were analyzed: (1) officials required that producers submit their salt first and be paid later; the address proposed to give them half their funding before production and half afterward; (2) officials counted above-quota salt as part of the regular production target, shortchanging salters on their work and growing lax; the above-quota policy was to be enforced and officers rewarded for increasing production; (3) patrols collaborated with producers and traders since they were powerless to control them; a crackdown was proposed; (4) tardiness in collection and storage led to spoilage and contamination by boatmen; it was proposed that shipments be housed promptly.[80] *On 7/5/1160 the Huaidong military intendant's coercion of fishermen into purchasing voucher salt, or be branded a criminal, was decreed to be abolished.*[81]

Ministry of Finance executive Shao Dashou proposed on 2/24/1160 to address the shortage of salter production funds by charging merchants 300 cash from a trading fee of five strings per bag. Ministers noted on 1/6/1214 that when officials did actually pay the salters, it was sometimes only 10 or 20 percent of the amount due.[82] *Even with full payments, producers faced shortfalls: if they were paid 10,000 strings, 3,000 might be taken by the responsible official, 2,000 charged as fees for clerks and*

---

[76] *SHY* 26.9a, 26b–27b.

[77] See *JNTZ* 81.5a.

[78] *SHY* 26.36b, 38a–b.

[79] *SHY* 26.39a–42a.

[80] *SHY* 26.26b–27b, 27.1a–2b.

[81] *SHY* 27.5a–b.

[82] *SHY* 27.2a–3b, 28.57a.

other agents, and the remaining 5,000 taken by the saltern for other appropriations.[83] *Huang Zhen noted twenty-two "routine operating fees" levied on a share of capital.*[84] *One of the fees deducted was a "container fee". Another was the "certificate fee"* (wenpingqian) *used by officials to extort capital outright to cover expenses or curry favor.*[85] *A "waste" allowance* (haoyan) *was charged for wastage during boiling. On a picul of salt, for instance, one peck of wastage salt had to be paid, for which the government only gave 500 cash, equivalent to just over 3 cash per catty.*[86] *At times surcharges were demanded in salt, so that a salter ended up submitting twice as much as his original quota.*[87]

The problem of merchant disinterest spurred the state to require not just more salt per bag but more bags per load in the policy of adding bonus salt. On 4/22/1161 the temporary executive of the Ministry of Finance, Qian Duanli, proposed that the rate be one additional bag for every five bags distributed.[88] *Imbalance is reflected in the Monopoly Goods Bureau 10/7/1164 statement that because Huaidong had such tremendous stockpiles, merchants carrying Liangzhe vouchers were allowed to go to Huai for salt. The capital sold vouchers for Tongzhou[b], Taizhou[b], Gaoyoujun, Chuzhou, Xiuzhou, Wenzhou[a], Mingzhou[b], and Taizhou[a]; Zhenjiang sold vouchers for Lin'an, Pingjiang, and Shaoxingfu. Differing rates of payment were applied depending on the form of currency a merchant used.*[89]

An effort was made to ease distribution as well as to resolve an emergency on 8/13/1164 in a decree that allowed over 3 million piculs (or 150 million catties) of a major Huai glut to cross the Yangzi River and be distributed in Liangzhe. A Taizhou[b] official, however, opposed this: he argued that it would lead the Jin to believe that Song was giving up the Huai area; the populace itself would think the state was unable to defend Huai; transport costs would amount to 500,000 to 600,000 strings; it would take 3,000 to 4,000 storehouses to store all the salt; and it might create a glut of Zhe salt. This discussion occurred during the fifth Huai glut.[90] *The Huaidong tea and salt intendant, Yu Zhaohu, memorialized on 1/22/1170 that in 1169, during the sixth Huai glut, that out of a production quota of approximately 2.7 million piculs, Huaidong salterns had stockpiled over 1.6 million piculs, or 80 million catties [that were not being sold]. He proposed having 25,000 bags sent to the Monopoly Goods*

---

[83] *SP*, "Yanfa," 41–42.

[84] *HSRC* 71.5b–6a; *HXZ* 9.14a–15a; *SJFZc* 29.2a–b.

[85] *HSRC* 71.21a–b, 80.1b.

[86] Zhang Xiuping 1983, 58.

[87] *SJFZc* 29.3b–4a.

[88] *SHY* 27.7b, 16b, 20b.

[89] *SHY* 27.9a–9b.

[90] *SHY* 27.10a–b.

Bureaus at the capital and Jiankang.[91] *The minister of finance, however, noted that at least 26,000 bags had not been distributed in Huaidong so he felt this sale would aggravate the problem (since it simply moved a batch of salt around rather than dealing with the glutted salt on the spot). He proposed that the capital and Jiankang bureaus allow merchants to buy two bags of glut salt for every thirty bags of regular salt.*[92] *On 1/23/1171 it was decreed that since 26,000 bags of accumulated Huai salt had already been sold by the Jiankang Monopoly Goods Bureau, another 20,000 bags could be disposed of similarly. Proceeds from the sales were to be kept as reserves in Jiankang.*[93] *On 2/12/1178 an intendant noted that Jingxilu was within the Huai-Zhe salt sales area, yet because it sat in a corner on the Jin border, merchants were unwilling to go there. Thus its market was flooded by smuggled Xie pond salt.*[94]

On 1/19/1163 scholars listed saltern abuses in hopes that the Huai-Zhe intendant would investigate: (1) to escape the corvee, wealthy families used the names of salters who had fled; (2) patrol officers accepted bribes and smuggled; (3) distribution storehouses put pressure on salterns by giving out extra amounts of salt, so salterns, fearful of their salt not moving, would add 20 to 30 catties, which led to further loss in revenues; (4) saltern officials no longer controlled firing times nor did they monitor the order in which salters worked so that some never got their turn to boil. The amount of salt per pan had dropped from an average 500 catties down to only 200 or even 100, meaning that some of the shortfall had gone into illegal trade; (5) salters were supposed to be paid when the salt was weighed in, but numerous expenses were deducted and the funds lent to wealthy families; (6) there was inequity in compensation, and procurement officials with many responsibilities had become lax in their duties. The Provisional Capital Monopoly Goods Bureau thus called for a commutation of salter taxes, for informants to report on patrol malfeasance, for numbered bags, each a standard 300 catties, for punishments to be given to bribe-takers or favor-givers, for keeping track of firing schedules, for reimbursement of salter production outlays upon presentation of product, and so on.[95]

Officials manipulated units of measure as well. Each saltern had its own catties, pecks, and baskets (luo), and often used irregular scales. Huang Zhen proposed standardizing the weights and measures at salterns and storage depots as a check on pilferage en route as well as to ensure that producers received their due. Huang Zhen proposed that a hu equal 100 pecks (dou).[96] On 12/18/1165 saltern disturbances

---

[91] It is not clear whether this means 25,000 each or was the amount was to be divided between the two.

[92] *SHY* 27.25b–26a.

[93] *SHY* 27.28a.

[94] *SHY* 28.7a.

[95] *SHY* 27.10b–13b.

[96] *HSRC* 71.11a, 80.9b–10b.

occurring at Tongzhou[b] and Taizhou[b] were reported. The solution was temporarily to distribute 20 percent of their salt at Zhenzhou[a] and build 280 new storehouses there to accommodate it. Tongzhou[b] and Taizhou[b] storehouses charged merchants 600 to 800 cash per bag as a transport fee, while Zhenzhou[a] storehouses charged only 500.[97]

In an amnesty on 8/12/1165, on the appointment of the Heir Apparent, the emperor decreed that Huai and Zhe salters were to be paid the funds owed them. When clerks gave the money out tardily, stingily, or only upon receiving bribes, or where they spent funds for private purposes, production work was disrupted and revenues fell. Xiaozong recognized the Zhe and Huai boilers' suffering at the hands of corrupt officials, pardoned them, and encouraged them to sue.[98] Part of the reason for extensive corruption was the considerable discretion officials enjoyed in the use of salter funds. As long as they paid out at some point, they could first borrow against the funds for other purposes, including personal expenses, and accounting was so lax, in the end it was easy for the money never to be paid at all. Although salters could keep their register of receipts as evidence, recording was inconsistent.[99]

On 7/6/1166 ministers stated that blanket banishment of salters [most likely those who boiled illegally] had depleted their ranks and reduced revenues, so it was decided they should be sent under guard back to their salterns.[100] On 9/21/1166, in an attempt to prevent smuggling, the Huaidong ever-normal tea and salt intendant, Yu Zhaohu, memorialized to have salters form jia units for mutual surveillance. Residents were to report any who dared smuggle, or the entire unit would be punished. Individuals who confessed would be pardoned and rewarded.[101]

According to a 10/7/1164 memorial the Monopoly Goods Bureau at the capital sold vouchers for Zhe's Xiuzhou, Mingzhou[b], Taizhou[a], and Wenzhou[a] as well as Huaidong's Chuzhou, Gaoyoujun, Taizhou[b], and Tongzhou[b]. The Monopoly Goods Bureau at Jiankang sold vouchers for the same four Huaidong prefectures. The Monopoly Goods Bureau at Zhenjiang sold vouchers for Liangzhe's Lin'an, Pingjiang, and Shaoxing.[102] When in 1166 the emperor decreed for the Zhenjiang Bureau also to sell Huai vouchers, a Huaixi quartermaster on 5/2/1166 countered that for thirty-odd years, the Zhenjiang Bureau had sold only Zhe vouchers and the Jiankang Bureau had sold Huai vouchers. To make an overnight switch would not be beneficial to merchants. According to the Huaidong quartermaster on 8/29/1172, each month the

---

[97] *SHY* 27.17a–18a.

[98] *SHY* 27.19a–b.

[99] *HSRC* 80.1b, 10a–b.

[100] *SHY* 27.22a–b.

[101] *SHY* 27.23a.

[102] *SHY* 27.9a–b.

three Monopoly Goods Bureaus were to report receipts and expenditures so that figures might be verified.[103]

There were also procedural differences between the regional bureaus. For purchases of salt, the state set varying proportions of currencies to be tendered.[104] *In 1166 payments for tea, salt, and alum were 60 percent in* qingji *(lightweight or high value instruments for the convenience of those who had to travel, such as gold, silver, and exchange notes [guanzi])*[105] *and 40 percent in cash or paper money. For frankincense, the ratio was 80 percent* qingji *and 20 percent cash or paper money. When the Left Storehouse* (zuozang) *ran short of cash, however, these ratios were changed to 50 percent cash and 50 percent paper money.*[106] *Salt was also linked to rice. According to an assistant division chief of funds on 5/14/1132, merchants desiring salt vouchers brought rice to the Monopoly Bureaus at the capital and Jiankang. Its value was calculated according to the current procurement price.*[107] *The Zhenjiang Bureau accepted entire payments in* qingji, *which the merchants considered more convenient than copper cash, as stated in memorials of 10/7/1164 and 5/2/1173.*[108] *From 1169 on, Huainan officials attempted to promote iron cash. In Huaidong, salt merchants usually used copper cash, which was eventually prohibited from crossing the river north (although this was later relaxed). With the overminting of iron, that currency also became devalued in Huai as in other places. Salt merchants could earn tax exemptions for payments made in cash, silver, and gold.*[109]

*   *   *   *   *

When the Songshi *narrative resumes in the later twelfth century under Xiaozong, stove numbers and sales for Huai and Liangzhe, or Erzhe ("The Two Zhe"), were compared and contrasted. The discrepancy between them was due to the high rate of smuggling in Liangzhe. This problem could be traced to official supervision, or lack thereof, at the production stage. As it turned out, Huai salters could fill production quotas in a matter of months. They were still required to submit everything above-quota, for which they were paid a higher procurement price. Yet the potential for illegal sales was also increased by the excess production capacity.*

---

[103] *SHY* 27.21b, 40b.

[104] *SHY* 27.9a–10a. Also see Kusano 1961, 123–54.

[105] These were early Southern Song government-issued certificates that could be exchanged for cash or vouchers for tea, salt, incense, and the like, but which could not be redeemed later when the government was hard up.

[106] *SHY* 27.21b–22a.

[107] *SHY* 26.7a.

[108] *SHY* 27.9a, 42a.

[109] *SHY* 31.22b (6/16/1175).

In 1170 (Qiandao 6), the executive of the Office of the Census, Ye Heng, memorialized:

> Profits from boiling sea water comprise half of today's revenues. In recent years salt revenues have not increased and merchants are not circulating all because of the problem of smuggling. Take, for example, the volume of salt traded in Huaidong and Erzhe [Liangzhe]. Huaidong has 412 salt stoves, whose annual quota is over 2,683,000 piculs of salt; last year the two Monopoly Bureaus sold over 672,300 bags of Huai salt, which brought in over 21,963,000 strings of cash. The Erzhe quota is over 1,970,000 piculs; but last year the two Monopoly Bureaus sold [only] 202,000-odd bags of Zhe salt, bringing in 5,012,000-odd strings of cash, even though [Erzhe operates] over 2,400 salt stoves. Huaidong's salt quota exceeds that of Erzhe by [only] one-fifth; in salt sales figures for last year, Huaidong exceeds Erzhe by two-thirds. However, Liangzhe actually has three-fourths again as many stoves as Huaidong. This discrepancy is due simply to smuggling in Erzhe. I wish to have officials sent to each circuit to take measures.[110]

---

[110] The *SS* abbreviates Ye Heng's memorial and is also off by one year from the *SHY* date of 6/17/1171. Ye Heng stated that if boiling were properly observed, if salters were paid on time, and if honest clerks were selected, smuggling would dissipate of itself. The problem began with control over production. Liangzhe, with over 2,400 furnaces, had six times as many as Huaidong, which had 411 (the *SS* quotes 412), yet the Liangzhe production quota between 1165 and 1173 was set much lower. The only way to eliminate smuggling was to ensure that salters received adequate food and clothing. He recommended appointing one official each to Huainan, Zhedong, and Zhexi. Each would lead fifteen guards and one secretary to inspect salterns, confirm the number of stoves and trays, oversee patrolmen and archers, and inform the Intendancy of violators. All accompanying personnel, including officials, clerks, and soldiers, were to receive an extra stipend to cover costs. He also pointed out that although an increase in sales of 100 percent was to be rewarded, it would be much more difficult for Huai to attain such an increase since Huai had already sold 18 million strings worth, compared with only 5 million strings for Zhe. Thus Huai should be eligible for reward with an increase of 25 percent. In the past local officials had been more lenient than salt officials when it came to salter violations; now local administrators would receive the same punishments [as salt officials], with no pardons for serious violations, gluts, or obstruction. By the same token, local and salt officials were to receive equal rewards for revenue increases (*SHY* 27.33a–35a).

The actual time it took to reach the circuit's quota was a factor that contributed to smuggling. Liangzhe's 2,400 furnaces decocted an average of six cauldrons of salt per day. At 300 catties per cauldron, this amounted to 1,800 catties, or 36 piculs daily per furnace. In one day all the furnaces in Liangzhe could

The Songshi *alludes to the "stone lotus test"[111] breakthrough in hydrometric testing, which spread to Liangzhe and other areas with significant implications for output. This efficiency vis-a-vis government production quotas was to have implications for illegal trade as well.*

[p. 4455] In 1181 (Chunxi 8) the emperor decreed to halt the "carrying sales" [aimed at] disbursing glut salt. The court had promoted such sales, but never fully realized [the anticipated revenue], because the

---

optimally produce 4.32 million catties, or 86,400 piculs. The annual quota of 1.89 million piculs thus took only twenty-two days to produce. Furthermore, after adoption of the stone lotus test, each furnace nearly doubled its capacity to 3,000 catties daily (*SHY* 28.20b). This works out to only a dozen days needed to meet the annual quota. By contrast, Huai's 412 furnaces had to operate an average of 181 days a year to fill its quota of 2.68 million piculs. Even after the stone lotus test was adopted, it still took 108 days. The potential for smuggling was enhanced by the large amounts of above-quota salt that could be produced.

On 12/16/1171 ministers complaining of a glut in Huaidong requested that the salt be transported to Zhenzhou[a] storehouses and then to Ezhou, Hubei, for sale. Each convoy was to transport 5,000 bags (*SHY* 27.37b–38a). By 5/7/1172 the transport program to Ezhou was cancelled due to mismanagement by Liu Bi (*SHY* 27.38b). Though Huaidong was a producing center, Huaixi often experienced scarcity. On 3/15/1180 natives of Zhongli and Dingyuan counties in Haozhou (Huaixi) complained that because their prefecture had no merchant trade, they went without salt. On that day the chief councilor presented a memorial from the Huaixi fiscal intendant: government salt was not sold in Haozhou, nor were there merchant sales. It was decreed to restore government sales, but without forced quotas (*SHY* 28.11a–b).

[111] Around 1174 Huai salters devised an ingenious test based on a pre-Southern Song technique to ascertain the salinity of the brine before it was boiled. According to the *Aobo tu*, if a solution were too dilute, not as much salt would result and fuel would be wasted. The test involved tossing ten dried lotus seed cases that had been cured in brine of different strengths into the solution. Each seed case had a specific gravity that caused it to float in a solution of equal or greater strength. A similar test was to toss ten seed cases in: if all floated immediately, the solution was good and ready; if seven floated, it was 70 percent saline; if three or more sank, it was less than 70 percent saline and the mixture was dug up again and re-percolated (*ABT*, plate 25). This citation also notes a five-seed test carried out in a small bamboo tube. For the test used in Liangzhe, see *XXCY* 47a–b, which also notes Fujian variants using peach kernels and chicken eggs. For a short description of the dried lotus seed test, see *YLMC* 2.25. See also a memorial by the Hubei salt merchant Hu Wufu on 7/29/1183 in *SHY* 28.20b.

central salt offices inevitably appropriated any income they produced. In 1183 (Chunxi 10) the Hubei salt merchant, Wu Chuan, stated:

> Of the state's profits from boiling sea water, Huaidong brings in two-thirds. Under the jurisdiction of Tongzhou[b], Taizhou[b], and Chuzhou[b] there are sixteen procurement salterns, twelve production-supervisory salterns, and 412 stoves.[112] At the beginning of the Shaoxing period (1131–1162) a stove could handle only 11 firings (*chou*) at most, with each firing producing 100 catties of salt. At the beginning of the Chunxi period (1174–1189) salters succeeded in testing [the salinity of] the brine, from which time each stove has been able to handle from 25 to 30 firings, an increase of 50 percent over the old practice. For this reason when salterns procure the producers' salt, the increase of 20 to 30 catties is called "floating [above-quota] salt." Over 10,000 firings worth of salt are procured daily. If each firing produces 20 catties of above-quota salt, then [10,000 firings a day means] 200,000 catties of floating salt, which equals 2,000 regular firings.[113] If each firing earns 1,830 cash, less 200 cash for boat and foot transport fees, this leaves [the actual price of] 1,630 cash. This [floating] salt, if delivered to the central reserves, will bring in over 4,517,500 strings in voucher sales. To boot, flotillas charge other fees for each bag of salt. When the salt is sold [by the salters to government agents, the government asks for] extra volume so that [the producers] suffer from hunger and cold and cannot avoid engaging in private sales. Should the court take this seriously and actually pay the salters [the production funds owed them], illegal sales can be eliminated.

So the emperor decreed to turn over 1,100,000 strings of production funding that Tongzhou[b], Taizhou[b], and other prefectures' salterns owed the salters.[114]

---

[112] Taizhou[b], with annual production of 1.61 million piculs, and Tongzhou[b], with 780,000 piculs, were the most productive Huai areas (*CYZJ jia* 14.6a).

[113] The Huai-Zhe directorates boiled day and night. In the late 1180s producers assigned to be foremen (*zongxia*) appropriated salter funds, then so the workers would not report them, allowed them to boil illegally. Ten rainy days might be reported as thirty; during the extra twenty days, at the rate of six trays per furnace per day and 300 catties per tray or 1,800 catties per day per furnace or 18,000 catties per day per center, 360,000 catties could be produced (*CYZJ jia* 14.6a–b). As of 9/16/1186 it was decreed that the Huai and Zhe Salt Intendancies abolish the post of furnace foreman (*SHY* 28.26a).

[114] Decreed 7/29/1183. In a Ministry of Finance memorial dated 5/1/1184 the Huaidong intendant, Zhao Buliu, reported a glut of 2.75 million piculs, or 137.5

The government under Ningzong devised new schemes by which merchants were to dispose of old vouchers, in order to maintain revenues. This concluded the overall account of Huai salt.

At the beginning of the Qingyuan reign period (1195–1200) the emperor decreed to abolish the rotational exchange of salt vouchers. Instead, officials were to calculate the number of leftover vouchers [still in circulation], which were called regular distribution vouchers, and supply salt to merchants in order of issuance along with those who had already submitted [old] vouchers to storehouses. This decree came about due to the Huaidong intendant, Chen Sunzhi's, description of the many abuses arising from the rotational exchange system, which led to rich and great merchants suddenly becoming paupers.[115] In 1206 (Kaixi 2) the emperor decreed that from then on, for every bag supplied for new vouchers, an equal amount for old vouchers would be attached. Those who had more new vouchers than old, or those who wished to only turn in new vouchers for their salt, as well as those who had no old vouchers and who wished to buy all new vouchers, were allowed to do so. The new vouchers became the standard for accounting.[116] In 1209 (Jiading 2) the emperor decreed that salt fees for Huaidong would have a portion paid in paper money cut by 20 percent, and cash and paper money could be used half and half.[117] In 1210 (Jiading 3) the emperor decreed:

---

million catties (*SHY* 28.23b). This was the last glut of Huai salt for which we have clear data.

[115] Decreed 2/7/1195. Chen Sunzhi described merchants attempting to keep up with voucher rotations and manipulative families hoarding and selling vouchers, all of which led to income loss. He called for the end of the rotational system (*SHY* 28.46a–b).

[116] Decreed 1/2/1206 (*SHY* 28.50b).

[117] The *SHY* records this for the Jiatai period, or 1202 (*SHY* 28.49a). Attempts to use salt profits to buy them up were aimed at propping up their value (*Mianzhaiji* [*MZJ*], 6). Around 1260 a catty of salt was priced at 200 "old" paper money, worth only eleven cash (*SJFZc* 29.3b). On the problem of inflation, see Quan Hansheng 1948, 193–222. Taking into account the fees levied, 200 cash per catty ended up earning only five cash; in effect, boilers were paying just to sell (*HSRC* 71.19b–20a; *HXZ* 9.16a; *SJFZc* 29.4b–5a).

Those who have amassed vouchers will see an increase in the value of [these] old vouchers. [At present] they can be exchanged [at the rate of] 100 strings worth of paper currency per bag. From the day this order is received, an additional twenty strings worth of paper money must be collected per bag. The three Monopoly Goods Bureaus must stamp a vermilion seal on the voucher face, write "new voucher of such and such month and year" until one million bags worth have been sold, then discontinue the additional collection. *[p. 4456]* Any vouchers for which salt has not yet been distributed are to be regarded as old vouchers and must be brought to storehouses to be exchanged for salt [with an additional fee] within one year. This additional charge will be ten strings worth of paper money per bag. After the time limit, the vouchers are void.[118]

This is a general summary of the Huai and Zhe salt administration.

By way of an apparent epilogue, the Songshi *compares salt revenues, particularly at a site in Huai in the Southern Song, with those of the Tang in order to show the tremendous increase in and importance of salt revenues for the state.*

At the beginning of the Qianyuan period (758–759) under the Tang [emperor Suzong], Diwu Qi as salt and iron commissioner reformed the salt policy, then was succeeded by Liu Yan. Total salt profits of the empire then annually reached only 400,000 strings. By the Dali period (766–779) [of emperor Daizong, Tang revenues] had increased to over 6 million strings [annually], salt revenues making up one-half of the empire's tax income. During the [Song] Yuanyou period (1086–1093) the salt of Huai, the Xie ponds, and so on, annually reached 4 million strings, and already represented two-thirds of [annual] revenues in the Tang. During the final years of the Shaoxing period (1131–1162), Hailing directorate in Taizhou[b] [in Huainandong Circuit] alone distributed over 300,000 mats of salt for 6 to 7 million strings of cash. This single prefecture surpassed the [annual] earnings of the entire Tang empire![119]

---

[118] Decreed 8/27/1210 (*SHY* 28.51b).

[119] On 5/28/1160 rewards mentioned for twenty-one officials and clerks at a Taizhou[b] saltern for procuring over 40,000 catties annually were as follows: a three-year reduction until the next review for one upper grade official; a two-year reduction for five middle-rank officials; a one-year reduction for four lower-rank officials; and eleven to be feted (*SHY* 27.3b–4a).

By the thirteenth century under Lizong revenues fell, due in part to overtaxation of merchants. The treatise reviews the best and worst official records, then addresses Huai, Zhe, and at times Jiangxi, collectively. There is progressively less documentation from other sources from this point on.

In 1226 (Baoqing 2) the investigating censor in the Bureau of Investigation, Zhao Zhidao, stated:

> Salt production relies on salters; the salt trade relies on salt merchants. Hence, salters should be cared for, and salt merchants ought to be allowed their profits. At the beginning of the Qingyuan period (1195–1200) annual [salt] revenues stood at 9,908,000-odd [strings of] cash; in 1225 (Baoqing 1) they reached only 7,499,000-odd [strings]. It is known that the fall in salt revenues is due to merchants not making any profits. To bolster today's revenues, there is no other way than to relieve merchants and reduce taxes so that the bountiful salt tax revenues of the Qingyuan period can again be realized.

The emperor approved this. In 1228 (Shaoding 1), based on the statement of the general censor, Li Zhixiao, the establishment of salt stoves in [Zhedong Circuit's] Shangyu and Yuyao sea brine areas was cancelled. In 1235 (Duanping 2) the Department of Ministries *(dusheng)* stated:

> Huai and Zhe's annual quota salt is normally over 974,000 bags, but there has been a cumulative loss of more than 1 million bags over the past two to three years. Thus the population must consume expensive salt, and both government and the people are adversely affected.

An imperial decree stated that the Tea and Salt Intendancies of the three circuits should each establish a subordinate post in charge of ensuring that quotas were met, to take charge of reviving the salt quota and procuring loose salt. At the end of the year the Department of Ministries should evaluate their records. In 1241 (Chunyou 1) the ministers memorialized:

> After the move south, the founding of the state relied solely upon salt vouchers; the Shaoxing and Chunxi reigns all enjoyed profits from salt. From the Jiading period (1208–1224), over the past twenty to thirty years, the voucher policy has alternately been in effect or annulled, while the notion of "floating salt" [being the key factor in the downturn in salt revenues, rather than the unstable voucher policy] has never been eradicated.

The harm [this argument] has caused is indescribable. It is hoped that the responsible offices will meet to deliberate what should be implemented and what should be abolished. If the resources of Heaven and Earth are shared by official and commoner alike, will that not be a great achievement?

The emperor approved this. In 1245 (Chunyou 5) prohibitions against private sales and harsh taxation were sternly pronounced.

[p. 4457] In 1253 (Baoyou 1) the chief councilor stated:

The Provisional Capital's Monopoly Goods Bureau and Tea Office (*duchachang*) presented to this [Salt] Monopoly Goods Bureau its 118,156,833-odd strings of tea, salt, and other money which had been collected in 1252 (Chunyou 12).[120] This is well over 100 percent above today's new quota of 40 million strings. It is appropriate to follow the precedents of 1249, 1250, 1251 (Chunyou 9, 10, 11) and reward [the bureaucrats involved] as encouragement to newcomers.

An imperial decree followed the recommended rewards. In the fifth month of 1256 (Baoyou 4) the Provisional Capital's Monopoly Goods Bureau and Tea Office showed an increase of 91,735,912-odd strings over the new quota. Those in the Monopoly Goods Bureau, the Three Ministries, the Ministry of Finance, the Court of the Imperial Treasury, and the voucher treasury who had charge of the three circuits' [Huainan, Liangzhe, Jiangxi] relevant offices were rewarded according to regulation. This later became standard practice. In the twelfth month the palace censor, Zhu Yi[b], stated:

Recently tax quotas have fallen suddenly and sink day by day. For example, the Zhenzhou[a] branch office alone has reported a shortfall of over 20 million [strings]. This is due to high civil and military officials engaging in trade for profit.

So strict prohibitions against private trade were again pronounced.

---

[120] The *duchachang*, established in 1128 to manage the sale of tea vouchers, was considered a separate organ from the Monopoly Goods Bureau, with offices in Jiankang, Zhenjiang, Jizhou[a], and so forth; it was administered under the Department of Ministries' left and right superintendents (*tiling*).

The government moved to pay more for above-quota salt in order to control it, but, as we have already seen, it had difficulty simply monitoring the regular salt supply.

In 1257 (Baoyou 5) Zhu Yi[b] again stated:

The surplus revenues from salt are great indeed. The combined figures for Shu, Guang, and Zhe circuits are not even half the Huai salt quota. This is because [in Huai] copious brine supplies boiling and luxuriant marsh reeds provide fuel.[121] Thus along the seacoast there are "pavilion households" and "cauldron households," regular quota salt and above-quota floating salt. Regular quota salt, produced by pavilion households, is delivered to the government. Floating salt, produced by cauldron households, is sold to merchants. Regular quota salt makes up about four-fifths of the total; floating salt is one-fifth. At the beginning of the Duanping period (1234–1236), not wishing to let the profits of floating salt dissipate, the court set up ten offices to procure it.[122] The annual amount was 27,930,000 catties. Over the past ten years or so, the voucher policy has changed repeatedly, causing both government and people to suffer. The 650,000 bags of regular quota salt from the four prefectures of Zhenzhou[a], Yangzhou[a], Tongzhou[b], and Taizhou[b] are less than that of previous years, so how can we possibly have time to worry about the above-quota floating salt! Greedy and shameless scholar-officials, knowing that the court has halted purchase of floating salt, attempt to move in on this source of income. Yet countless stove boilers live in sandy shoals, sustained by only a few ounces of salt daily. Now that merchants may not trade with them and the court *[p. 4458]* will not purchase from them, their source of livelihood has been eliminated. Today there can be nothing better than to adopt the old policy of the Duanping reign and buy up

---

[121] Marsh reeds supplied the fuel as well as the material from which salt bags were woven. The government controlled the use and disposal of marshlands, as reiterated on 1/19/1163 (*SHY* 27.12b). By the late Song, however, many marshes had deteriorated or had otherwise been reclaimed. On the difficulties of reed collection and trade, see *HSRC* 71.8b–9b; for the transport of reeds, see *ABT*, plates 32, 34; Yoshida 1993, 138–39. This shortage of open marshlands became so exacerbated that by the Yuan, despite prohibitions against mortgaging or renting such land, what remained had been commandeered by rich households, who forced poor families to purchase their tinder (*Da Yuan shengzheng guochao dianzhang* [*DYDZ*] 22.20a).

[122] When these offices were later disbanded, above-quota salt became the source of renewed illegal trading. So the government again procured it, then sold it at a ratio of 30 percent government sales, 70 percent merchant sales (*Lidai mingchen zouyi* [*LMZ*], Zhu Yi[b]'s memorial, 173.16b–17a.

the cauldron households' floating salt. Production funds [for floating salt] ought to be more than those for regular quota salt, so that producers will all trade with the government. Selling this salt in the upper reaches of the [Yangzi] River and directly forwarding consequent salt revenues to the court will first of all halt the craze for profits among military leaders and secondly will enable cauldron households to continue production.

An imperial decree approved this.

Chapter 6: Fujian

Fujian, covered in five and a half pages, was categorized as a government distribution region. Of its eight prefectures, the four "lower" (xia sizhou)—Fuzhou[b], Zhangzhou, Quanzhou[b], and Xinghuajun—were coastal and salt-producing, while the four "upper" prefectures (shang sizhou)—Jianzhou[a], Nanjianzhou, Tingzhou, and Shaowujun—were sales regions located in the rugged interior.

Northern Song

[p. 4461] In Fujian Circuit (Map 11) the Changqing saltern of Fuzhou[b] annually produced 100,300 piculs, which provided [revenue for] the circuit itself.[1] From the Tiansheng reign period (1023–1031) Fuzhou[b],

---

[1] For Fujian revenues by prefecture and county, see *SHY* 22.26b–29b, 23.16b–17a. Guo Zhengzhong (1983, 105) shows annual production in Fujian from 978 to 1172, here in Table 5:

Period	Location	Production/Sales (in catties)	Source
978-1022	6 counties (Fuzhou)	5,015,963	*SHY* 23.34
978-1022	Changqing (Fuzhou)	5,015,000	*WXTK* 15
1028	Changle, Fuqing (Fuzhou)	5,718,245	*SHY* 23.34
1023-1101	4 Lower Prefectures	7,460,400	*SS* 183
1077	4 Lower Prefectures	Increase	*SS* 183
1078-1080	Fuzhou, Xinghuajun	19,767,500	*SHY* 27.38
1104	8 Upper / Lower Prefectures	25,400,000	*SHY* 24.38
1119-1138	8 Upper / Lower Prefectures	11,000,000	*SHY* 25.36-37; *CYZJ jia* 14
1152	8 Upper / Lower Prefectures	22,530,000	*SHY* 22.30, 24.38
1153-1156	8 Upper / Lower Prefectures	30,000,000	*SHY* 24.38, 26.34
1157	8 Upper / Lower Prefectures	22,530,000	*SHY* 22.30, 24.38
1162	8 Upper / Lower Prefectures	16,569,415	*SHY* 23.16
1165-1167	8 Upper / Lower Prefectures	16,569,415	*SHY* 23.17
1168-1170	8 Upper / Lower Prefectures	19,767,500	*SHY* 27.38
1172	8 Upper / Lower Prefectures	8,000,000+	*SHY* 27.39-40

Note: Guo neglects to differentiate between production and distribution figures.

Note that the peak period was from 1153 to 1156, at 30 million catties; the trough occurred in 978 at 5 million catties. See also Yuki (1982, 31) for a table on southeastern circuit revenues between 1074 and 1078. Fujian experienced five or six gluts over the course of the Song.

On 3/983 a treasury official memorialized for Fujian to allow merchant trade and set a catty at twenty-five cash (*SHY* 23.21b). On 11/9/1028 the Fujian Fiscal

Zhangzhou, Quanzhou[b], and Xinghuajun all boiled salt; their annual production increased 48,908 piculs over the old quota.

A salt smuggler rebellion had wide repercussions, particularly in the "upper" prefectures where prices were higher and smuggling was more common. The state forced upper salter households to sell salt and imposed a crackdown on smuggling.

In 1077 (Xining 10) a certain Liao En had become a powerful bandit and gathered around him a band that plundered the prefectures and commanderies. When [Liao] En was subdued, the executive censor, Deng Runfu, stated:

> Minyue's [the Fujian region] mountainous and forested terrain is dangerous and difficult over a distance of several thousand *li*. The number of hooligans there is greater than in other circuits, and they engage mainly in salt smuggling. Since [Liao] En has been subdued, no preparations have been made [to forestall a recurrence]. How do we know that no one will follow in [Liao] En's footsteps and rebel again?

So the emperor decreed for Fujian Circuit's Jian Zhoufu to examine the pros and cons.[2] [Jian] Zhoufu concluded:

> The government salt price in Jianzhou[a], [Nan] Jianzhou[b], Tingzhou, and Shaowujun is overly high, while the price of traded salt in Zhangzhou, Quanzhou[b], Fuzhou[b], and Xinghuajun is low, thus most smugglers sell in areas where salt is expensive.[3] In the past, Jianzhou[a] used to calculate the population's property values to determine the [amount of] salt they had to purchase. Yet people were afraid to seek *[p. 4462]* redress from the local government; even when they paid, they did not always receive salt. I petition to abolish this tax so as to reduce the salt price in Jianzhou[a],

---

Intendancy memorialized to close salterns in Fuzhou[b]'s Lianjiang, Luoyuan, Ningde, and Changxi counties because they were far from the sea and transport was difficult. Gluts occurred every year. The state then gave [the salt] land to the people and required them to pay taxes (*SHY* 23.34b, *XCB* 106.2485).

[2] Jian Zhoufu, Huainan assistant fiscal intendant, was transferred to Fujian where he suppressed the rebellion and tightened the salt laws, but in 1086 he was dismissed for corrupt administration (Wang Leiming 1985, 375nn2, 3; *SS* 329.10604–5).

[3] In the Northern Song, Nanjianzhou was in central Fujian Circuit.

Jianzhou[b], Tingzhou, and Shaowujun. I propose to recruit upper households to set up shops. The government should give them vouchers, set the amount per month that they must sell, and have them buy at the salterns. Then the common folk will be able to obtain salt easily, and smugglers will be unable to capture massive profits. We should also restore old storehouses, select clerks, and increase the number of guards. We should establish a policy that if one has smuggled or if one is cognizant [of smuggling] but conceals that information, there shall be no pardon; after three offenses the punishment shall be flogging with the heavy bamboo and deportation under custody (*bianguan*) to a neighboring prefecture. Offenders who have already been thus exiled and repeat the offense are to be flogged with the heavy bamboo and remain under custody where the violation occurred.[4]

All was implemented, and annual sales increased to over 230,000 catties, not including the amount salt officials sold beyond the quota.

When tax revenues rose in the late 1070s, officials were rewarded.

In 1079 (Yuanfeng 2) the salt intendant, Jia Qing, petitioned to change prefectural policies and have quotas established based on the prefecture's average figures over [the past] three years.[5] He also petitioned to reward, on a basis not limited to the regular policy, those arresting officials who had confiscated large quantities of smuggled salt.[6] In 1080 (Yuanfeng 3) [Jia] Qing submitted a report of annual tax revenues collected by salt sales officials under his administration; these figures were greater than the old revenues. The emperor decreed:

---

[4] After Jian Zhoufu memorialized to this effect, on 6/29/1078 he was made Fujian fiscal intendant, and concurrently salt intendant (*SHY* 24.17a). *Bianguan* originally referred to sending convicts to distant prefectures under custody. Here it also applied to salt smugglers (Wang Leiming 1985, 376n4). The lightest Song exile allowed one to reside in the prefecture; more serious was detention (*anzhi*); and most severe was *bianguan*.

[5] Jia Qing, then temporary Fujian fiscal intendant, and concurrently salt intendant, made his petition on 7/2/1079 (*SHY* 24.18b).

[6] Jia Qing recommended this on 10/7/1079 (*SHY* 24.19a; *XCB* 300.7309). On 12/22/1079 he was promoted for his successful salt administration (*SHY* 24.19a; *XCB* 301.7332).

[Jian] Zhoufu undertook instructions to create a policy; [Jia] Qing continued to carry it out. One year later tax revenues have increased, and smuggling has been halted; the southeast region relies on this undertaking.

At the time [Jian] Zhoufu had already been promoted to assistant finance commissioner (*sansi fushi*). Twenty officials in the circuit intendancy (*jiansi*) were rewarded.[7]

Shenzong died in 1085. Under the new emperor, the salt policy was frequently reviewed, leading in the 1080s to the dismissal of certain officials for advocating proposals on the wrong side of the political fence.

When Zhezong (1086–1100) ascended the throne, the executive censor, Huang Lü, memorialized that in Fujian, people were often oppressed by the salt policy.[8] The emperor declared:

Last year the late emperor set up a policy of inspection whereby censors and vice-ministers (*langguan*) were separately dispatched to circuit intendancies.[9] The censor Huang Jiang was dispatched to Fujian, while the censor Chen Cisheng was dispatched to Jiangxi to look into things.

---

[7] Decreed on 4/27/1080 after Jia Qing had presented his report on 1079 revenues. According to the *Song huiyao*, two officials, not twenty, were rewarded (*SHY* 24.19a–b). According to the *Xu Zizhi tongjian changbian*, twenty officials were deemed deserving of reward (*XCB* 303.7389).

[8] The executive censor, Huang Lü, memorialized on 4/dingchou/1085 that Shaowujun and Tingzhou had received so much salt that it was hard to sell. So based on property, the common people had been forced to take on and sell a certain amount. This abuse also occurred in Jianning, Guangze, and other counties of Shaowujun, as well as in Tingzhou, Jianzhou[a], and Jianzhou[b]. The investigating censor, An Dun, stated that the Fujian vice-transport intendant, Wang Zijing, also forced tea sales upon the people. The emperor decreed that the court would punish officials who imposed unwarranted burdens on the populace (*XCB* 354.8477).

[9] This statement was followed by the words, "They may follow the decree of the late emperor" (*XCB* 354.8477, 4/dingchou/1085).

Subsequently he decreed that the Ministry of Personnel director (*libu langzhong*), Zhang Ruxian, should examine the salt policy established by [Jian] Zhoufu.[10] [Huang] Jiang said:

Fuzhou[b] has followed the old [policy] of Wang [Anshi] so that every one part of the value of the salt produced there has been treated like the full ten parts produced in the rest of the prefecture. It is by this ratio that tax payments are figured, and the rest follow this method. The salt quota is reckoned as five times greater [than the current level elsewhere], but in actuality [what is produced] is only half that amount. Recently Wang Zijing memorialized to establish a salt production policy, but he did not examine [all aspects of such a policy] closely enough so that he indiscriminately increased all quotas. The discrepancy [between the Fujian quota and actual production levels] is great. In distant regions inhabitants have for a long time had no means of lodging grievances.[11]

The emperor entrusted [Zhang] Ruxian [to look into this]. The following year the intendant-inspector (*anchasi*) reported in detail the results of his investigation. This led to the trial of the Fujian assistant fiscal intendants, Jia Qing and Wang Zijing, for exacting high taxes and to their demotion to Hunan to oversee salt and liquor taxes. The executive of the Ministry of Justice (*xingbu shilang*), Jian Zhoufu, was tried for his carrying out of the salt policy in Jiangxi and exacting exorbitant taxes. He was demoted to prefect of Hezhou.[12] Jia Dan was tried for supporting transport of Guang

---

[10] Decreed 5/4/1086 (*SHY* 24.27a; *XCB* 361.8651, 11/dingsi/1085).

[11] As palace censor, Huang Jiang memorialized on 7/gengxu/1085 (*XCB* 358.8568). Wang Zijing seems to have been making his best effort. On 3/jiayin/1084, as Fujian vice-fiscal intendant, he memorialized that salt prices in Fuzhou[b], Quanzhou[b], Zhangzhou, and Xinghuajun were different; he requested that they be made uniform (*XCB* 344.8260).

[12] On 11/wushen/1085 the general censor, Liu Zhi, criticized Jian Zhoufu and his son Jian Xuchen and recommended their dismissal (*XCB* 361.8647). The palace censor, Huang Jiang, memorialized on 11/dingsi/1085 that Jian Zhoufu and his son, who were awaiting sentencing, should be demoted to distant offices (*XCB* 361.8651). On 12/guihai/1085 Liu Zhi recounted the oppressive southeastern salt policies of Jian Zhoufu and Jian Xuchen; Liu Zhi claimed that the case of Jian and son was no different from those of Wu Juhou and Wang Zijing. While there may have been extenuating circumstances, for the sake of applying the law uniformly and gaining public trust, the two would have to be cashiered (*XCB* 362.8656). On

salt to Jiangxi. Zhang Shicheng was tried for allying with and promoting [Jian] Zhoufu's policy and willfully oppressing [the people]. He was also dismissed. The Minqing county magistrate, *[p. 4463]* Xu Shou, alone applied the original salt policy and held office with integrity so people were not overly taxed. He was recommended to the court for reward. [Zhang] Ruxian petitioned to set the Fujian salt production and sales quota, and the emperor agreed.[13] All those who coerced people to become salters or who did not allow them to retire were sentenced to one year of penal servitude. If the salt intendant knew of the offense but did not bring it up [for trial], he was punished likewise.[14]

Later, the palace censor, Lü Tao, memorialized:

> Because abuses of the salt policy in Fujian, Jiangxi, Hunan, and so on oppress the people, the court has dispatched officials to investigate and dismiss clerks who amass profits, and so to give solace to the suffering poor. This shows that public opinion is critical. However, the abuse of adding extra to the quota of Guang salt transported to and sold in Hunan and Jiangxi, as well as the monopoly sale of salt in Jingdong and Hebei were all promoted by Zhang Dun. I hope that the appropriate office will root out his mistakes in order to remind ministers who rob the people and misguide the emperor to take heed.[15]

The investigating censor, Sun Sheng, also observed:

12/renwu/1085 Liu Zhi renewed his request for dismissal of the two Jians. Their creation of a salt quota had led to insolvency for miles around; they sacrificed the public good for private favors (*XCB* 363.8682). On 2/xinsi/1086 the Jiangxi and Hunan intendant inspector and right policy monitor, Wang Di, recounted the offenses of Jian Zhoufu and his son. Zhu Yanbo succeeded them, but still did not investigate to the bottom of the matter. The emperor demoted Jian Zhoufu to become prefect of Hezhou; his son was made a notary of the administrative assistant (*qianpan*) of Luzhou[a]; and Zhu Yanbo was made head of Xingguojun (*XCB* 366.8799). For Wang Di's biography, see *SS* 344.10941–45.

[13] *XCB* 368.8865–66 (intercalary 2/renchen/1086).

[14] *XCB* 369.8916 (intercalary 2/gengxu/1086).

[15] Lü Tao's long memorial of intercalary 2/dingsi/1086 also probes interpersonal rivalries (*XCB* 370.8962–64).

The abuses of the salt policy in Jiangxi and Hunan have subjected the people of these two circuits to cruel misery. Their distress is worse than war and conflagration. Only the [Jiangnanxi ever-normal] intendant, Liu Yi, dared speak up about the extent of the situation, but he was sentenced and removed from office.

The emperor decreed to reinstate [Liu] Yi to administer Shaozhou[a].[16] After the Chongning period (1102–1106) Cai Jing held authority. The salt policy was changed repeatedly. Fujian salt alone increased seven cash per catty from the beginning of the Zhenghe period (1111–1117). Applying the Xining period (1068–1077) policy, merchants were allowed to pay by *zhuanlang* transfer. Calculating the six circuits' transactions of powder salt money, for every 100,000 cash worth, 10 percent was deducted and sent to salt areas to serve as production funding.

Southern Song

Fujian's upper prefectures had been under government sales, the lower paid their taxes in salt. The upper prefectures changed to a voucher system at the beginning of Southern Song.

During the Jianyan period (1127–1130) when there was no trading in Huai and Zhe, in Min [Fujian] and Guang a voucher system was implemented. Before long, when merchants [again] circulated in Huai and Zhe, the voucher system in Min and Guang was abolished. In the past Min's four upper prefectures of Jianzhou[a], Jianzhou[b], Tingzhou, and Shaozhou[b] observed the government sales policy, while Min's four lower prefectures of Fuzhou[b], Quanzhou[b], Zhangzhou, and Huazhou[c] [which produced their own salt] observed the salt production tax policy

---

[16] Sun Sheng memorialized on 3/yihai/1086 about the oppressiveness of administrators: after Zhu Yanbo and Chen Si there was Wei Lun, prefect of Jizhou[a], where the people suffered most, yet the transport intendant, Jiang Zhiqi, recommended Wei's return after he had observed a mourning period. Only Liu Yi, Jiangnanxi intendant, was courageous enough to memorialize on the problems, yet he was dismissed. Liu Shu, fiscal intendant of Jiangnanxi for five years, had not uttered a critical word, and he was now being promoted to a court position. Sun requested the reinstatement of Liu Yi and the censoring of the others (*XCB* 372.9017–18).

(*chanyanfa*).[17] When the government sales policy was abolished, the system of tax payment in salt also became corrupted. With a voucher system in place, abuses of the salt production tax policy could be eliminated; however, old ways were not easily changed. Thus at the time the Fiscal Intendancy and [Salt] Intendancy petitioned for the four upper prefectures to observe the voucher system, the four lower prefectures were to continue to observe the old [production tax] policy.[18] When the voucher policy was abolished, the fiscal intendant was ordered to annually send voucher money in amount of 200,000 strings to the Provisional Capital's Monopoly Goods Bureau. After that, the amount either increased or decreased. In the end it was made 220,000 strings.[19]

Other sources treat Fujian during the twenty years before the next Songshi *entry.*

*   *   *   *   *

On 2/5/1130 a memorial was presented concerning the price per catty and payments to salters in Fujian. On 2/19/1130 another concerned the over-accumulation of vouchers in Liangzhe, for which there was no salt to be distributed. As a consequence merchants were given certificates, which they brought to the capital Monopoly Goods Bureau. There for every hundred strings [worth of Liangzhe vouchers] they were given forty strings worth of Fujian salt vouchers and sixty strings worth of Guangnan salt vouchers. For each bag of Fujian salt, a surtax of three strings was charged. On 2/27/1130 Fuzhou^b salterns were to be administered by the local magistrates, as was the case in Huai and Zhe.[20] On 4/14/1130 merchants were allowed to turn in their vouchers and get salt at salterns and warehouses. On 4/21/1130 it was noted that the court had ordered the trade of Fujian salt in the Huai-Zhe area due to political exigency. Now that Huai and Zhe salterns were [again] in full production, the trade of Fujian salt there would be halted.[21]

---

[17] Though the voucher system was abolished in Min, Min was still obliged to forward salt proceeds to the center (*XNYL* 32.23a, 4/xinmou/1130). The *chanyanfa* entailed paying salt as a form of tax (*SS* 183.4463, interstitial comment).

[18] Described on 2/4/1130 by the executive of the Ministry of Finance, Ye Fen (*SHY* 25.34b–35a).

[19] The figure of 200,000 strings was decreed on 10/29/1135 (*SHY* 26.25a).

[20] *SHY* 25.35b–36a.

[21] *SHY* 25.36a–b.

On 11/1/1138 the disadvantages of implementing in Fujian a new "small voucher" program in addition to government distribution were noted. It was decreed that the "small voucher" policy should be studied further.[22] On 4/9/1152 a former Tingzhou official memorialized that while Fuzhou[b], Zhangzhou, Quanzhou[b], and Xinghuajun were production places, Jianzhou[a], Jianzhou[b], Tingzhou and Shaowujun were selling points. Tingzhou annually transported 2.5 million catties of Fujian salt in twenty-five convoys. Overland transport expenses were significant, and various charges were imposed en route; the official proposed that they be combined into a single salt tax. If officials kept accounts, and merchants paid for salt where they were resident, receiving a certificate with which they obtained salt and could sell freely, and further if tax households (local families of means who formed the basis for the government's flotilla transport) paid taxes where they were resident, then there would be no smuggling.[23] In 1152 officials were sent to Fujian to take a count of the clergy; some monks were hired and given daily food in exchange for distributing government salt. At the time it was said that aside from tax payments and monastery expenses, a year-end surplus of 240,000 strings was reaped this way. By decree this surplus was handed over to the Left Storehouse.[24]

On 5/13/1156 the palace censor memorialized that Fujian collected fees without standardization. In addition, prefectures disregarded how much salt residents actually used, forced purchases, raised prices, and reaped profits at the expense of the people. This was to be punished by law. On 7/25/1156 the executive censor discussed disruptions caused by convoys in Fujian. In Jianzhou[a], in the past, only five and a half convoys had been employed, while over the past three years corrupt clerks had moved over forty convoys and still complained that this was insufficient to cover expenses. They ingratiated themselves with those above and engaged in abuses, thus pressing the salters.[25]

*   *   *   *   *

The Songshi continues in the early Southern Song, noting the brief adoption of the voucher policy.

[p. 4464] In 1157 (Shaoxing 27) the ever-normal granary intendant, Zhang Ruji, again reported on the voucher policy. The emperor consulted with his councilors of state. Chen Chengzhi replied:

---

[22] *SHY* 25.36b–38a.

[23] *SHY* 26.32b–33b.

[24] Wang Leiming 1985, 379n6.

[25] *SHY* 26.34a–35a.

In the mountainous regions of Jianzhou[a] and Jianzhou[b] the common folk flout the law to trade illegally; even the government monopoly cannot stop them. If the people are allowed to trade, how can this circumvent smuggling? The more smuggling, the lower the voucher revenues.

The emperor said:

The voucher policy was employed briefly. If it could have been implemented, our ancestors would already have done so. In general a good law is one that follows popular custom; otherwise it cannot endure.[26]

In 1178 (Chunxi 5) the emperor decreed to abolish the order for people of the two counties of Taining and Youxi to purchase salt according to property value.

Back in 1172 (Qiandao 8) the Fujian maritime trade supervisor (*shibo*), Chen Xian, had stated:[27]

---

[26] This exchange occurred on 10/28/1157 (*SHY* 26.36a–b). On intercalary 6/12/1159 the general censor memorialized on Fujian land and taxes. In the Five Dynasties land had been rated in three categories: the best was given to Buddhist monasteries and Taoist temples; the average was given to natives and immigrants; the lowest grade was for trade. Later, forty temples were reserved, with the rest of the land leased to the wealthy, from whom a tax was collected to cover military needs. Under Shen Diao's rule, however, income from land went into his own purse. According to Fujian law, salters were to pay the Double Tax, but Shen Diao imposed an overwhelming number of other charges, including a rice sprouts tax, a floating salt tax, an "empty salt" tax, a document salt tax, a punishment salt tax, a consumption salt tax, and a Military Intendancy tax. The people were drained and turned to banditry (*SHY* 26.42b–43a).

On 4/8/1161 the general censor submitted a memorial on the salt industry in Zhangzhou. Prefectures had been temporarily allowed to trade to cover the expenses of the army encamped there, but even after the army moved away, this trade continued. Villages were divided into eighteen salterns; guards organized the people into *jia* units; and widows, orphans, and elders in remote areas were compelled to journey to salterns to purchase salt every month (*SHY* 27.7a–b). On 1/11/1168 the emperor forgave salter debts before 1163 in Fujian's upper prefectures, and was considering a pardon of the money owed after 1163. But he declared he was constrained from further relief measures by the costs of the military. The Liangzhe fiscal intendant predicted the rejoicing of the people (*SHY* 27.23b).

[27] The missing reign name was Qiandao (*SS* 183.4486n2).

In Fujian, from 1079 (Yuanfeng 2) when the fiscal intendant, Wang Zijing, proposed the salt transport policy, there inevitably arose abuses of theft and excessive taxation. Moreover all other regions of the empire observed the voucher policy; only Fujian had to endure the disadvantages of salt transport. At the beginning of the Shaoxing period (1131–1162) Zhao Buyi attempted to establish the voucher law, but it could not be carried out because the [circuit's] Fiscal Intendancy used the salt flotillas to increase revenue; prefectures and counties used them to cover their annual expenses; officials used them to charge salt sales fees and other consumption fees; and clerks used flotillas as an excuse to collect delivery fees (*changliqian*).[28] Public and personal interests were at odds with one another. It is no wonder that a voucher policy could not be implemented. If the flotilla transport system were suddenly abolished before the establishment of a voucher system, people would have no salt to eat. So [those engaged in] water transport took this as an excuse to argue the inconvenience of the voucher policy and petitioned to preserve payments in paper money (*yinqian*). Yet when vouchers are abolished and flotilla transport remains, then the government salt price is high and the illegal salt price low. When the majority of people consume illegal salt and the government is not be able to sell, abuses of harsh taxation will certainly arise.

The transition from government to voucher sales was difficult and debated.

---

[28] A complex relationship existed between the state and the "tax households" who were engaged in flotilla transport. These households had to meet minimal asset requirements before being considered for duty. The state might variably put out all funds required for transport, and the people provide the labor; or the people might both put out funds and labor; or the state might borrow funds, with the salt and fiscal intendancies providing vessels and the people providing labor and a portion of the funds. Fujian salt transport involved a variety of these arrangements, which changed over time. The government charged different types of fees to cover costs. Before 1173 the prefectures and counties often borrowed from the transport households to cover shipping costs, but from 1173 on this was evidently replaced by local governments borrowing from the circuit Fiscal Intendancy.

Households that actually put up money for the loans could, in exchange for receipts awarded them after transporting a shipment, get salt to sell on the side. These receipts were numbered in such a way that determined the order of salt retrieval, but there were many hurdles (deadlines, manpower requirements) households had to clear after being given receipts. One observer aptly remarked, "The law, with all its precautions and restrictions, truly takes into account every possible contingency that might arise!" (Guo Zhengzhong 1990a, 385).

So the emperor decreed for [Chen] Xian to enact measures. [Chen] Xian petitioned to allow the Monopoly Goods Bureau to print vouchers in five grades from 100 to 5,000 catties. In preparation for the sale of vouchers, funding was first given to the three storehouses for the purchase of salt in anticipation of merchants coming to trade.[29] In the first month of 1182 (Chunxi 9), because the government had always shipped Fujian salt, vouchers created great pressures on the people, so the emperor decreed for the Fujian Fiscal Intendancy to maintain the previous government distribution system. In the third month the emperor decreed for the fiscal intendants, Fu Zide and Yang Youyi, to investigate the problems of government sales of salt and to make measures known.[30]

In 1186 (Chunxi 13) the Sichuan military intendant Zhao Ruyu stated:

> Tingzhou's natives are poor, yet the government's forced salt purchases are even greater than those of other prefectures. I beg to have Tingzhou follow the merchant voucher policy.[31]

---

[29] Chen Xian memorialized on 1/25/1172, then according to decree he drew up the measures (*SHY* 27.38b–40b). In the *SHY*, "100" reads "500" and a footnote gives six rather than five grades of vouchers (*SHY* 27.40a). On 1/21/1173, when the Secretariat-Chancellery stated that voucher sales were insufficient, it was decreed that they be replaced by government sales. Sold and unsold vouchers, as well as salt, had to be disposed of within one hundred days (*SHY* 27.42a–b). On 3/2/1173 Fu Zide remarked that the 4/16 deadline was approaching. Government shipments would take a few months to reach selling points. Taking advantage of the lack of salt, merchants smuggled it off in large baskets and traded right under the noses of inspectors (*SHY* 27.42b–43a). On 3/14/1173 Fu Zide proposed six measures regarding payment for convoy transport, salt trading centers, monitoring salt purity at salterns, abolition of salt taxes, banishment of those detaining county convoys, and enforcement of smuggling laws (*SHY* 27.43a–44b).

[30] On 4/4/1185 the Fujian assistant fiscal intendant (*yunfu*), Zhao Yancao, memorialized on misallocation of salt funds by prefectures and counties because no one official was in charge. He suggested an aide be responsible for monthly accounting figures such as distribution and collection (*SHY* 28.24b–25a).

[31] In the first decade of the 1100s the population of mountainous Tingzhou numbered 81,450 households, the majority of which engaged in smuggling. The local government forced residents to purchase "poll consumption salt" (*koushiyan*), which even the poor could not avoid (Wang Leiming 1985, 379n1). During the

The matter was handed down to the intendant, Ying Mengming, and to a Tingzhou custodian (*shouchen*) to deliberate. [Ying] Mengming and his colleagues stated:

> Some areas of the four upper prefectures are far from salt-producing locales. When the government does not [*p. 4465*] sell salt, then illegal trade is impossible to control. When people eat illegal salt, merchant vouchers do not sell. When vouchers are unprofitable, fewer merchants trade. Thus the voucher policy has been repeatedly enacted and cancelled. Even in vast Sichuan, vouchers have not fared well, [so how] much less [so] in Tingzhou. Therefore, though the voucher policy may be a good one, it cannot be effected in Tingzhou. We can only reduce prefecture and county revenue payments and tighten prohibitions on tax salt rations. Then Tingzhou natives may be relieved.[32]

Again it was directed for the fiscal intendant, Zhao Yancao, and others to enact measures for reductions: for annual transport of 2,004,000 catties, a total of 39,038-odd strings of tax was to be cut. Tax money to subordinate offices was also reduced so that the people of Tingzhou's six counties saw tax relief to the tune of 39,000-odd strings annually and local government tribute was reduced by 10,000-odd strings, excluding the sum going toward needs of the prefecture.[33] Since the revenues of the four

---

Southern Song 50 to 60 percent of the natives of Fujian's four upper prefectures engaged in smuggling (*XNYL* 85.6a).

[32] This was preceded by a memorial of 12/8/1186 by the Fujian assistant fiscal intendant, Zhao Yancao, which had been prompted by Zhao Ruyu's memorial. Zhao Yancao quoted high salt prices; he proposed cutting charges to establish a fair price and thus dissuade smuggling and encourage sales (*SHY* 28.26a–27a). On 3/22/1192 the Ministry of Finance quoted a memorial from the Fujian fiscal intendant on the necessity of restraining convoys, which charged high fees. The same day the Ministry of Finance stated how convoys were to be administered (*SHY* 28.36a–37a). On 1/7/1201 the emperor decreed renewed regulations regarding convoys: counties were to pack salt into baskets with no foreign matter; there was to be no price increase, no disparities in color or taste, and no forced quotas or sales (*SHY* 28.48b–49a).

[33] Tingzhou's six counties—Changting, Ninghua, Shanghang, Wuping, Qingliu, and Liancheng—were established at the beginning of the Southern Song (Wang Leiming 1985, 379n2).

upper prefectures were miniscule, those areas basically relied on the income from government sales of salt.

In the lower prefectures the government made the cash purchase of salt according to household assets effectively a tax.

Also [Fujian] prefectures along the seacoast practiced the policy of [requiring ordinary households] to pay tax in currency according to property value, while the government provided salt for their consumption. Later this became a regular tax, and [merchants] no longer were interested in trading in salt. This was a corruption [of the taxation system] in the four lower prefectures. In 1213 (Jiading 6) ministers emphatically spoke on this, so the Fiscal Intendancy was directed to exempt all the families of Fujian's four lower prefectures who had property assets of under twenty cash and an annual purchasing quota of five catties of salt from paying. Likewise, those households whose property was assessed at barely twenty cash were exempted from the salt tax.[34]

Interoffice competition arose between the Fiscal and Ever-normal Intendancies.

In 1226 (Baoqing 2) the investigating censor, Liang Chengda, stated:

Half the administrative units of Fujian are on the salt-producing seacoast. Control is wielded by the fiscal intendant, as this is his responsibility. Salt produced in Fuzhou[b] and Xinghua is transported for popular consumption in the twenty-two counties of Jianzhou[b], Jianzhou[a], Tingzhou, and Shaozhou[b]. The Fujian Intendancy manages ever-normal [granary] and tea affairs but not salt. The Fiscal Intendancy openly contends [with the Ever-normal Intendancy] for revenues for its own use, but recently [the Ever-normal Intendancy] has overstepped its bounds to generate surpluses, often by assigning flotilla transport [of salt] to counties under its jurisdiction. The counties not only must manage salt taxes for the Fiscal Intendancy but now also have the added burden exacted by the [Ever-normal] Intendancy. In the end the burden will most definitely be foisted upon the people and that will be worse than the damage imposed by [Wang Anshi's] "green sprouts" policy. I hope that [income from] the transport of salt will accrue back to the Fiscal

---

[34] According to the *SHY*, this was memorialized on 3/9/1214, not 1213 (*SHY* 28.57b–58a).

Intendancy; the [Ever-normal] Intendancy should not be allowed to operate outside its area of responsibility. As soon as authority returns to one source, the people's suffering will be alleviated.

The emperor approved this.[35]

In the ninth month of 1260 (Jingding 1) a pardon was issued from the Imperial Ancestral Hall (*mingtang*):

Fujian's four upper prefectures and their counties rely on salt taxes. At times there have been delays in payment. All delays [*p. 4466*] before 1257 (Baoyou 5) shall be pardoned. Those in charge who dare to flout the law and impose taxes according to head count will be investigated and reported by the intendancies.

The Fiscal Intendancy's salt convoys competed with those of the upper prefectures.

In 1262 (Jingding 3) the ministers stated:

Fujian's four upper prefectures are craggy, with little arable land, and their tax revenues are insufficient. The money and silver submitted as tribute by the prefectures and counties to the court, and the services demanded by officials, imperial relatives, and troops are all maintained by salt sales. The Fiscal Intendancy controls salt flotillas but does not sell salt. In recent years it has taken upon itself the transport of two flotillas of salt; more recently, some years [it has transported] ten to twenty flotillas, the same annual amount as that of the upper four prefectures [and by so doing, transgressing its authority and encroaching on prefectural revenues]. This does not include the volume [of salt] that flotilla personnel carried on the side. This conflicts with the annual salt sales quota of the four upper prefectures and their counties. In the face of this [competition] prefectures and counties cannot distribute their salt. Since they are unable to manage forwarding tribute, salt inevitably becomes the burden of common households. The abuses therein are indescribable.

---

[35] Liang Chengda's memorial apparently had little effect. Three years later, in 1229, the Yan Mengbiao Uprising took place. When Tingzhou's troops rebelled and occupied the county town, the people of Shaowujun and Nanjianzhou joined in, spreading the conflict to Zhangzhou and Quanzhou[b] and eventually including over 10,000 men. Several thousand Huaixi crack troops finally suppressed the rebellion two years later (Wang Leiming 1985, 380n2).

An imperial decree stated:

Fujian's Fiscal Intendancy must observe the customary policy without fail. Jianningfu, Nanjianzhou, Tingzhou, and Shaowujun must also follow this policy.

Chapter 7: Guangnan

The section on Guangnan, or Liangguang (the "Two Guangs"), totals only three pages. Guang was divided into an eastern and a western circuit: Guangnandong (or Guangdong) and Guangnanxi (or Guangxi).

Northern Song

Northern Song coverage begins late and is only one paragraph long. It lists producing prefectures and distribution points, then the problem of tax evasion as salt taxes rose. Intendants and prefectural officials acted concurrently as salt administrators here. Several entries in other sources date from before the first entry in the Songshi *(that is, 1031) and here precede the* Songshi *text proper.*

*   *   *   *   *

On 4/jisi/971 the emperor decreed that Guang's commercial taxes and salt policy should follow those of Jinghu, but that wine would not be monopolized.[1] On 4/971 the Guangnan fiscal intendant stated that because the circuit allowed merchant sales and Guangzhou salt was cheap, smugglers took it to Jingzhou and [Liangzhe's] Huzhou and thereby undermined [state] revenues. Since northern Guangnan bordered on Jingzhou and Huzhou, it was decreed that salt there should be priced the same as Jingzhou and Huzhou salt, at sixty cash per catty; prefectures south should price the same as Guangzhou salt, at forty cash per catty.[2] On 1/25/987 a Chaozhou official complained that 33,000 piculs of the salt produced was annually added to its stocks of 640,000 piculs, for which they already needed more storage. The Finance Commission stated that all of Guangnan had stockpiled over 2.3 million piculs, enough to last thirty years. Furthermore, [the tax quota] had been increased by 100,000 piculs annually. It requested that production be halted for a few years.[3] The problem of salters absconding was reflected in a 3/gengshen/1017 decree pardoning 3.732 million catties of salt that Chaozhou had been unable to collect.[4]

*   *   *   *   *

[p. 4466] Guangzhou[b]'s thirteen salterns, including Dongguan and Jingkang, annually produced over 24,000 piculs. They supplied their own

---

[1] *XCB* 12.263.

[2] *SHY* 23.18b–19a.

[3] *SHY* 23.22a; *XCB* 28.631.

[4] *XCB* 89.2050.

[Guangdong] circuit, [Guang]xi Circuit's (both Map 12) Zhaozhou[a] and Guizhou[c], and Jiangnan[xi]'s Nan'anjun (Map 13). Lianzhou[b]'s two salterns, Baishi and Shikang, annually produced 30,000 piculs, which supplied the prefecture as well as Rongzhou[a], Baizhou, Qinzhou[a], Huazhou[c], Mengzhou[a], Gongzhou[a], Tengzhou, Xiangzhou[c], Yizhou[b], Liuzhou, Yongzhou[a], Xunzhou[b], Guizhou[b], Binzhou[c], Wuzhou[a], Hengzhou[b], Nanyi, and Yulinzhou [all in Guangnanxi]. Further, that produced by Gaozhou, Douzhou, Chunzhou, Leizhou, Rongzhou[b], Qiongzhou[a], Yazhou, Danzhou[b], and Wan'anjun [all in Guangnanxi] each provided [revenue for] its own prefecture, with no set quota.[5]

---

[5] Guangdong and Guangxi revenues are listed by prefecture and county in *SHY* 23.1a–8b. Quota figures by prefecture and saltern are listed in *SHY* 23.16a–b. Figures in piculs are listed by prefecture in *SHY* 23.17b. Again, Guo Zhengzhong (1983, 107–8) provides a table of aggregate Guangdong and Guangxi production from 987 to 1192, here in Table 6:

Period	Location	Amount	Source
987	Chaozhou	33,000 piculs	*SHY* 23.22
	Guangdong/xi	100,000 piculs / 5,000,000 catties	*SHY* 23.22
988-994		Production discontinued	*SHY* 23.22
998-1022	Guangzhou	24,000 piculs	*SS* 183
	Lianzhou(b)	30,000 piculs	*SS* 183
1017	Chaozhou	Decreased production	*SHY* 23.30
1023-1063	Guangzhou	513,686 piculs	*SS* 183
1068-1085	Guangdong/xi	Increased production	*SHY* 24.20, 23
1131	Nanenzhou	708,400 catties	*SHY* 26.1; CYZJ *jia* 14
1137	Qinzhou	300,000 catties	*SHY* 26.29, *Shengzheng* 28
1162	Guangdong	331,060 piculs / 16,553,000 catties	*SHY* 23.16
	Guangxi	231,689 piculs / 11,584,450 catties	*SHY* 23.16
	Guangdong/xi	562,749 piculs / 28,137,450 catties	*SHY* 23.16
1165-1173	Guangdong	331,060 piculs / 16,553,000 catties	*SHY* 23.17
	Guangxi	229,097 piculs / 11,454,850 catties	*SHY* 23.17
	Guangdong/xi	560,157 piculs / 28,007,850 catties	*SHY* 23.17
1174-1177	Guangxi	11,528,700 catties	*SHY* 28.14

After the Tiansheng period (1023–1031) the thirteen eastern and western coastal salterns were all administered by Guangzhou[b]; annually, 513,686 piculs were produced and this supplied both [Guang]dong and [Guang]xi circuits. In Qiongzhou[a], Yazhou, and other prefectures, though, because the landscape was barren and difficult, average households had no way to sell the salt [the government had disbursed to them and expected them to market], an activity imposed like other compulsory service duties. Officials came and went, some raising the quota salt amount without proper authority, which led to the bankruptcy of salt boiling households.[6] In 1080 (Yuanfeng 3) Zhu Chuping memorialized to

Period	Location	Amount	Source
1187-1189	Guangdong	7,500,000 catties	*Liangchao gangmu beiyao* 1
	Guangxi	10,377,500 catties	*Liangchao gangmu beiyao* 1
	Guangdong/xi	17,877,500 catties	*Liangchao gangmu beiyao* 1
1190-1192	Guangdong	6,500,000 catties	*Liangchao gangmu beiyao* 1
	Guangxi	8,597,500 catties	*Liangchao gangmu beiyao* 1
	Guangdong/xi	15,097,500 catties	*Liangchao gangmu beiyao* 1

The high point seems to have been in 1162, with 16.6 million catties for Guangdong and 11.6 million catties for Guangxi; the low point, in 987, at 5 million catties for the two together.

On 4/jisi/971 it was decreed that Guang's commercial taxes and salt policy should follow that of Jinghu, but that wine would not be monopolized (*XCB* 12.263). On 4/971 the Guangnan fiscal intendant stated that because the circuit allowed merchant sales and Guangzhou salt was cheap, smugglers took it to Jingzhou and (Liangzhe's) Huzhou and thereby undermined state income. It was decreed that since northern Guangnan bordered on Jingzhou and Huzhou, salt there should be priced the same as Jingzhou and Huzhou salt, at sixty cash per catty; prefectures south should price the same as Guangzhou salt, at forty cash per catty (*SHY* 23.18b–19a). On 1/25/987 a Chaozhou official complained that 33,000 piculs was annually added to its accumulated 640,000 piculs, which were already in need of storage. The Finance Commission stated that all of Guangnan had accumulated over 2.3 million piculs, enough to last thirty years. Furthermore, (the quota) was increased by 100,000 piculs annually. It requested to halt production for a few years (*SHY* 23.22a; *XCB* 28.631).

[6] On 3/6/1034 the official in charge of salt, wine, and commercial taxes in Wushatouzhen in Yuezhou[b] stated that the sale price of government salt in Guangnandong's Guangzhou, Huizhou[a], and Duanzhou was fifteen cash, while the Guangzhou procurement price was only six cash. No wonder everyone was trading privately! He requested that the government salt price be cut to ten cash,

forgive [regular households] salt stocks that had not been sold, and to establish a boiling quota based on sales figures in order to benefit inhabitants of remote areas.[7] After some time the Guangxi fiscal intendant memorialized on local evasion of salt taxes. Even if the district magistrate (*xianling*) and supervisory officials were to be replaced, they had to stay on until all [those taxes] were collected. The Guangdong fiscal intendant, on the other hand, again memorialized that areas south of the Nanling mountains should follow the policy of the six circuits: prefectural-level officials were to serve as salt officials and the judicial intendant should concurrently serve as salt intendant. Their evaluations, rewards, and punishments were to follow those given for salt officials and salt intendants.[8] *[p. 4467]* Qiongzhou[a], Yazhou, and other prefectures again petitioned to levy salt taxes on the people, with the number of catties dependent on the class of the household; as a result, the people were made miserable again.[9]

---

which would bring in many times the revenue [of past government sales] (*SHY* 23.37b; *XCB* 114.2671).

On 5/wuwu/1070 Zhao Kui, prefect of Yulinzhou (Guangxi), memorialized that workers hired to haul salt from Rongzhou[a]'s Beiliu County to sell in Rongzhou[a], Yongzhou[a], and other prefectures were initially provided with money to purchase oxen and carts, but when the oxen died and the carts fell apart, they had to cover the replacement cost themselves. During the months of salt transport, each was given 200 cash and one picul of grain; they were not allowed to carry personal belongings in the ox carts. Zhao requested that in the months when workers were not given cash and grain, they be allowed to be use the carts for private hauling (*XCB* 211.5139).

[7] On 12/2/1080 the emperor noted that government salt was not selling in Qiongzhou[a], and that when Hainan prefectures procured salt stocks, they either demanded extra or did not pay for the delivered product at all, so that salters were bankrupted and fled. He ordered the Guangxi Fiscal Intendancy to set an amount of salt to be purchased per head [to ensure more regular and equitable procurement] as a pacifying measure. On 3/1/1081 the Finance Commission's commissioner of funds, Jian Zhoufu, memorialized on shipping Guangdong salt to Qianzhou (Jiangxi). He later presented a salt policy for Jiangxi and Guangdong (*SHY* 24.20a–b).

[8] The Guangdong assistant fiscal intendant Gao Bo so memorialized on 11/wushen/1084 because sales were declining (*XCB* 350.8386).

[9] Back on 5/15/1083 the minister of finance noted that the prefect of Qiongzhou[a], Liu Wei, calculated that in Qiongzhou[a], Changhuajun, Wan'anjun, and

Southern Song

Guangdong's navigable rivers meant that trade was unconstrained; Guangxi's rocky rivers made trade difficult. In the mid 1100s a decree assigned Guangdong a ratio of 90 percent merchant sales to 10 percent government sales; in Guangxi the breakdown was 80 percent to 20 percent.

After crossing the river to the south [the beginning of the Southern Song], salt from the two Guangs fell to the Fiscal Intendancy; salt was awarded to the prefectures based on their annual expenses. Guangdong, being traditionally rich, readily took to merchant trade. Guangxi's terrain was vast and barren and its table salt consumption limited, so merchant trade there was [unattractive and] difficult to carry out. Embarking from Guangdong, one could take advantage of large rivers that had no rocks awash at low tide; navigation was easy. Embarking from Guangxi, on the other hand, the rivers were narrow and rocky, and navigation was difficult. At the end of the Jianyan period (1127–1130) vouchers were sold [for Guangnan] but before long they were discontinued.[10] Government transport and merchant vouchers were alternately restored and annulled. The [Guang]dong and [Guang]xi fiscal intendancies were repeatedly joined and separated.

In the third month of 1131 (Shaoxing 1) people were called upon to work the saliferous earth of Yangjiang County in Nanenzhou. Sixty-seven stoves were constructed, which produced 708,400 catties of salt. That salt

---

Zhuyajun, each adult in first- to third-rank households be required to purchase one catty of salt per month, while fourth- and fifth-rank, as well as guest households, monks, priests, and servants, were to purchase half a catty a month. But the minister felt that these amounts were too great and requested a reduction by half for both categories; this was so decreed (*SHY* 24.23a–b; *XCB* 335.8068–69). On 4/gengchen/1099 the Guangxi judicial intendant, Zhang Jingwen, memorialized that the circuit ought to follow the precedent of southeastern policy (*XCB* 508.12105–6).

[10] Guangnan salt vouchers were issued for an emergency fund to cover the expense of guarding six imperial family members, including the emperor's mother, who had newly arrived at Qianzhou and had no resources. See 1/8/1130 memorial by the Bureau of Military Affairs (*SHY* 25.34a–b).

generated a surplus of over 30,000 strings.[11] In the twelfth month the
Guangxi Tea and Salt Intendancy was also formed.[12] In 1138 (Shaoxing 8)

---

[11] On 3/15/1131 the Ministry of Works presented the Guangnan Tea and Salt
Intendancy's report to this effect. According to the *SHY*, however, net revenue for
one year was only 19,250 strings from sixty-seven stoves. Two years later income
was 12,000 strings (*SHY* 26.1a; *XNYL* 43.8a). On 7/26/1131 the executive of the
Ministry of Finance, Meng Yu, presented the petition of the Guangnan tea and salt
intendant, Li Chengmai: at year's end saltern officials' performance ought to follow
Liangzhe practice, with rewards halved (*SHY* 26.2a).

[12] After this, on 1/14/1133, the Guangdong tea and salt intendant petitioned for
independent officials to oversee salt rather than have prefectural officials concurrently administer the voucher program. Annual tax revenues for Guangzhou,
Chaozhou, Huizhou[a], and Nanenzhou, were, respectively, 300,000 strings;
100,000 strings; 50,000 strings; and 30,000 strings. Guangzhou was the only
location with a salt inspector (*SHY* 26.7b–8a).

On 3/19/1133 the Monopoly Goods Bureau stated that according to a Jinghu
and Guangnan official, Guangdong produced [only] a small amount of salt and was
plagued by smuggling. This was because salter funds were not being paid and there
were delays in weighing product (*SHY* 26.10b). On 3/23/1133 the Department
of Ministries advised that the Guangnan salt procurement price had been raised
from seven cash per catty to twelve cash, but in Liangzhe the price for quota salt
was fourteen cash and for above-quota salt, over seventeen cash. It was decreed to
follow Liangzhe's price of fourteen cash (*SHY* 26.11b). On 8/9/1133 the Guangxi
fiscal intendant reported that salt unaccompanied by vouchers was illegal. Officials
and commoners who bought salt from salters or from those without vouchers
were to be considered smugglers. On the other hand, search and seizure against
those carrying vouchers was inappropriate (*SHY* 26.15a–b). On 9/18/1133 the
Guangxi official memorialized that the salt price ought not be set by the court but
based on the market price of private salt, to be reported daily to the prefecture.
The prefecture ought to report to the transport intendant at ten-day intervals, then
set [the salt price] at one to two cash less [than the market price]. He also proposed
that selection of service runners be stricter and that they be recruited from upper
households after a check for any criminal record (*SHY* 26.16a–17a).

On 2/8/1134 the investigating censor and Guangnan pacification commissioner
(*xuanyu*), Ming Tuo, memorialized that bandit fleets in Guangdong were causing
disruptions. A large ship had thirty oars; a small one at least ten. They were
equipped with weapons, gongs, and drums. They began with salt smuggling, then
turned to piracy. The large boats cruised the coast, hiding in inlets; the small boats
menaced the rivers. Eastward on the Dongjiang they proceeded to Chaozhou and
Huizhou[a]; westward on the Xijiang they advanced to Wuzhou[a] and Hengzhou[b].
Some passed many prefectures; others remained within one to unload salt or moor
in hidden places. Archers and soldiers took bribes. Ming Tuo felt it was not the
fault of the law but of the personnel carrying out the law (*SHY* 26.21a–22a). On

the emperor decreed that of Guangxi's annual salt, 20 percent should be moved through government sales in the five prefectures of Qinzhou[a], Lianzhou[b], Leizhou, Huazhou[c], and Gaozhou, while the remaining 80 percent was to be sold through the voucher program.[13] Subsequently the emperor again decreed that 90 percent of Guangdong salt be sold via the voucher program, and 10 percent by salt-producing prefectures and counties.[14] Guangnan was far from the central government, its terrain desolate, and its people poor. Its tax revenues were insufficient to support the bureaucracy, so the [Guang] Fiscal Intendancy turned to selling salt. Of those revenues, 40 percent went for the needs of the prefecture, and this was roughly sufficient, so the people did not have their levies increased. Zhaozhou[a] annually procured 36,000 strings worth of salt. Of

---

2/17/1134 the Guangdong and Guangxi pacification commissioner, Ming Tuo, again memorialized that the two circuits boiled a good deal of salt, but delivered to government hands far less than what they sold illegally because salter expenses were so high, saltern supervisors expected bribes, and inspectors dared not investigate abuses. Ming Tuo requested that waste be reduced and the salt price raised. Inspectors were not to engage proxies (*SHY* 26.22a–b).

On 4/21/1134 ministers reported problems related to shipping tribute in Guangdong, whether in silver or cash. With the costs of transport, shipping, and hiring labor, none of the prefectures wanted to be responsible for presenting tribute (*SHY* 26.22b–23a). On 6/23/1134 the Ministry of Justice reported on a memorial from Xunzhou regarding the assistant military training commissioner (*tuanlian fushi*), Meng Kui, who had forged the name of a merchant, then bought government salt in Wuzhou[a]. Due to wartime chaos, the goods had not been sold. When the shipment arrived on the banks of Xunzhou, it was confiscated by the tax official there. Such an act [of forgery and purchase] merited banishment, demotion, and a fine (*SHY* 26.23a).

[13] Decreed 6/6/1138 (*SHY* 26.25b). The monopoly of salt in Qinzhou[a], however, began in 1134, not 1138 (*SHY* 26.28a–29a; *WXTK* 16.8b). On 12/4/1138 the former Wuzhou[a] magistrate memorialized on the burden posed by government transport. Salt shipped from Shikang County in Lianzhou[b] (Guangxi) to Hengshanzhai in Yongzhou[a] (Guangxi) traversed arduous overland and water routes. [Owners of] hired boats and carts were not compensated for [their vehicles] being requisitioned and the foot-transport reimbursement was so paltry that porters were impoverished. Yamen runners and clerks all tried to avoid engaging in transport. Thus all expenses ended up on the shoulders of the already poor Guangxi inhabitants. The former magistrate petitioned to increase funding for shipping (*SHY* 26.25b–26b).

[14] Decreed 12/25/1138 (*SHY* 26.26b).

this, 7,000 strings were assigned annually to the purchase of tribute horses from Xunzhou[b] and Guizhou[b], while the rest went for the needs of the prefecture. When government sales were abolished, 7,000 strings were levied on the people under the name of "expenditure fees" (mifei qian). In 1139 (Shaoxing 9) Guangdong's government sales were abolished and the merchant voucher law enacted; revenues were collected to help cover the expenses of [Jinghubei Circuit's] Ezhou troops.[15]

The following chronological ordering of non-Songshi material fills in the Songshi record between 1139 and 1168.

*　　　*　　　*　　　*　　　*

It was decreed on 7/21/1139 that Guangdong would adopt the voucher system. On 5/6/1142 the Ministry of Finance stated regulations for distribution at both storehouses and salterns under the new voucher system in Liangguang. The salt administration was to be assessed according to the Zhe and Huai examples.[16] On 9/8/1142 ministers reported on the continuing debate over government versus merchant sales in Guangxi. Sales in Qinzhou[a] dropped from over 900,000 catties in the three years under government sales (1134 to 1137) down to less than 60,000 catties by 1141 under merchant sales. Government salt had cost 47 cash per catty, while merchant salt spiked to over 120 cash per catty. The ministers requested that government sales be restored in Qinzhou[a]. On 10/22/1142 it was noted that Qinzhou[a]'s original name had been "white skin," since its earth was white from salt. The Ministry of Finance ordered Guangxi to follow the 1138 ruling, which specified 80 percent voucher sales, 20 percent government sales.[17]

In 1143 there was a major Guang salt glut. On 3/22/1143 the Ministry of Finance presented a report from the Guangxi salt intendant to the effect that since the Shikang storehouse had been giving extra salt and exempting merchants from a foot-transport charge, its salt moved quickly. It was requested that the Yulinzhou storehouse, which had amassed a great deal, be allowed to follow suit. On 4/1/1143 councilors presented a memorial from the Guangdong fiscal supervisory official proposing that profits from vouchers be applied to financing the circuit's military

---

[15] While a present-day Ezhou sits southeast of Wuhan (Hubei), the Song dynasty Ezhou seems to have been at present-day Wuhan.

[16] SHY 26.26b, 27b–28a.

[17] SHY 26.28a–29a.

expenses, such as supporting the army stationed in the circuit. The emperor, however, decreed that if the [current] policy was not problematic, it should not be altered.[18]

On 4/19/1160 the Guangxi salt intendant stated that the prefectural vice-administrator of Qinzhou[a] had confiscated over 26,000 catties of smuggled salt. Even though there was no regulation on rewards for such an act, if the official had not carried out the arrest, there would have been no capture. The intendant recommended granting two years' reduction before the official's next review. On 5/28/1160 the Guangdong salt intendant suggested that Guangzhou saltern supervisory officials be rewarded by comparing their records with those of Huaidong.[19]

On 9/2/1160 ministers memorialized on the horse trade and the glut of salt. Horse-breeding took place in Sichuan and Guang. The state purchased horses, but not at a regular quota; it might be 3,000 horses one year, 2,000 the next. For every 1,000 head, a fair price of no less than 100,000 strings was paid, using the circuit's tribute money. The silver conversion to cash was approximately three to four strings per ounce. For tribal peoples, however, it was only two strings. It was proposed to make use of glut salt at Lianzhou[b] by transporting it to Hengshanzhai for the horse trade. Lianzhou[b] had a sales quota of 6 million catties, but had accumulated tens of millions of catties due to Leizhou and various production sites sending their salt there.[20]

On 4/2/1161 ministers reported that the Guangxi fiscal intendant had allowed taxes to be commuted. In Huazhou, of the tax rice quota of 8,000 piculs, the value of 6,500 piculs was commuted at Rongzhou[a] at the rate of two strings 600 cash per picul. But out of Huazhou's rice distribution quota of 15,000 piculs, 10,000 were collected by government purchase (hedi) at a price of 400 cash a picul, which was charged to its residents. This was [necessary] because before the monopoly, costs had been paid from salt revenues, but now the prefecture had none. No circuit was more desolate and barren than Guangxi, whose inhabitants lived an impoverished life. It was requested that half of its salt revenues be used to pay its annual costs in order to spare the population.[21]

On 12/13/1163 the Ministry of Finance noted that Guangdong's salt was flavorful and sold easily, but Guangxi's salt was bland and difficult to move. In order that the trade go smoothly, Guangxi should first sell its vouchers before selling vouchers for Guangdong. On 1/9/1164 a Jiang-Huai official reported that the Liangguang procurement price in one place was twenty cash per catty, but the selling price was forty cash. In another location the procurement price was eighteen cash

---

[18] *SHY* 26.29b–30a, 30b–31a.

[19] *SHY* 27.3b–4a, 4b.

[20] *SHY* 27.5b–6a.

[21] *SHY* 27.6b–7a.

per catty, but the selling price about fifty cash.[22] On 11/15/1164 the Guangdong Tea and Salt Intendancy stated that four salterns in Guangzhou, Chaozhou, and Nanenzhou produced so little and generated such scant taxes that they could not cover the expenses of the supervising official. The Intendancy requested that these four salterns, along with their supervisors, be combined with neighboring salterns.[23]

*   *   *   *   *

The Songshi *resumes after a thirty-year gap. After Guangdong cannibalized Guangxi sales, it was proposed in the mid-1160s under Xiaozong to combine their salt administrations.*

In 1168 (Qiandao 4) salt vouchers were abolished and the Guangxi Fiscal Intendancy was ordered to pay 200,000 cash for [salt] transport (*caoqian*) from its coffers.[24] Moreover, Guangxi's salt was [now to be] sold by its Fiscal Intendancy. From 1165 (Qiandao 1), as Zeng Lian had petitioned to have it combined with that of Guangdong, the commissioner of revenue (*duzhi*), Tang Zhuo, stated:

> Guangxi's salt voucher income is short about 80 million strings.[25] The two Guangs' salt affairs were divided between eastern and western intendancies but [Guang]xi Circuit's salt was frequently encroached upon by [the salt of Guang]dong Circuit. When Guangxi had an intendancy of its own, salt tax revenues experienced no losses. *[p. 4468]* Now, abolishing the [Guang]xi intendancy and joining it with that of [Guang]dong Circuit has led to loss of control over the entry of Guangdong salt [to the west], and so Guangxi has lost all its revenues.

---

[22] *SHY* 27.13b–14a, 14b–15a.

[23] *SHY* 27.16a.

[24] *Caoqian* could be an error for *chao* (vouchers), as in *WXTK* 16.8b, or for *xi* (profit), as in *SHY* 27.23b–24b on 6/4/1168. Moreover, 200,000 cash reads "210,000 strings" in *HSRC* 67.11a–b.

[25] The *SHY* on 6/4/1168 reads Guangdong rather than Guangxi, and the character "thousand" reads "ten," thus the figure should probably be 800,000 strings (*SHY* 27.23b–24a). The *SS* figure of 80 million is doubtful since annual revenues from Huai-Zhe production were only 13 million strings and that was sizeable. Guangnan production was much less.

This is how the decree [on the Guangxi salt quota] came about.[26]

In the late 1160s tension over the allocation of salt proceeds led to giving a portion to the Fiscal Intendancy and a portion to the prefectures.

Then councilors of state presented Jiang Fei's memorial:

> Salt proceeds used to accrue to the Fiscal Intendancy and were given to the prefectures to cover their annual needs, but since the sale of voucher salt, the Fiscal Intendancy has had to resort to income from transporting tribute rice *(miaomi)* at a high price. If the court now changes and does not give out salt vouchers but only has the Fiscal Intendancy dole out an annual quota [to prefectures], then the Fiscal Intendancy can make salt profits for itself, which will eliminate the abuses of trading in rice.[27]

---

[26] Before the 6/4/1168 decree the director of the Office of Funds *(duzhi langzhong)*, Tang Zhuo, had memorialized to restore the monopoly in Guangxi. Guangdong salt was transported on rivers with no dangerous rocks at low tide, while Guangxi salterns had to make use of creeks with many sand banks (*SHY* 27.24a). On 6/4/1168 it was decreed that the Guangxi fiscal intendant was to manage Guangxi voucher salt without combining it with Guangdong's (*SHY* 27.23b–24a).

[27] It may have been Jiang Fei himself who presented the memorial since he was in office from the second to the seventh month of 1168 (*SS* 213.5575–76). The memorial was presented on 6/4/1168. On that day it was decreed that Guangxi no longer issue salt vouchers and that the entire region would be under government distribution. Of 210,000 strings [so earned], 30,000 were to be given to Jingzhou, 80,000 to cover the purchase of horses, and the remaining 100,000 to Ezhou, for the expenses of the imperial army (*SHY* 27.24a–b). On 2/15/1170 ministers requested that Guangdong and Guangxi observe the voucher law (again). They memorialized on merchant fees, time limits, voucher printing, fees, encouraging merchant business, ending government transport and sales, and so on (*SHY* 27.26a–27b). On 6/26/1171 a memorial on the two Guangs' policy fluctuations recounted a history of the voucher trade, including salt collected, fees charged per basket, insufficient payment to producers, rampant smuggling, unmet sales quotas, the shipping of Guangdong salt to Guangxi, the condition of the waterways from storehouses to salterns, what salt was transported to which prefectures for what purposes (such as the horse trade), the basis of official evaluations, and the unusual circumstances in Qinzhou, which bordered on Jiaozhi (Cochin China). Government transport was not recommended (*SHY* 27.30b–33a).

In 1173 (Qiandao 9) the emperor decreed for Guangzhou again to observe the policy of government transport and sales.[28]

In 1176 (Chunxi 3) the emperor decreed for 30 percent of government salt profits collected annually by the Guangxi Fiscal Intendancy to be allocated to the prefectures and 70 percent to pay for transport. This was according to the petition of the military intendant, Zhang Shi.[29] After [Zhang] Shi left, the fiscal intendant, Zhao Gonghuan, increased the salt price per catty from 100 cash to 160 and increased Qinzhou's annual salt sales quota of 1,000 *hu* measures by 50 percent. In 1179 (Chunxi 6) the general censor, Jiang Pu, reported on Zhao's increases, so the emperor dismissed [Zhao] Gonghuan. He decreed that the Min and Guang salt sales

---

[28] The emperor decreed this on 12/15/1173, hoping the fiscal intendant would observe all laws and not allow recurrence of forced quotas and monetary demands above what was correct (*SHY* 27.44b–45a). "Guangzhou" here should read Guangxi (*SS* 34.656; *HSRC* 67.11a–b). On 2/5/1174 a Guangxi official memorialized that Guangxi had reinstated government transport. When it had been abolished in 1172 and the voucher law implemented, no funds remained for capital, boats, and carts. He requested that the fiscal intendant be allowed to borrow the necessary money. The emperor decreed the Left Treasury should lend 100,000 strings, to be returned within one year (*SHY* 28.1a).

[29] The post of military intendant was established in 1002 to administer the military and civil affairs of a circuit; it was also called the *jinglue anfushi* or *anfushi*, except in Guangdong, Guangxi, and Jingnan; finally only the two Guangs maintained the title of *jinglüe* (*SS* 167.3960–62). Zhang Shi's memorial, which prompted the 2/28/1176 decree, states that revenues from the Guangxi government distribution had been apportioned 60 percent to the Fiscal Intendancy and 40 percent to the prefectures. From 1165 on, however, when government sales were reinstituted, the Fiscal Intendancy collected 80 percent and prefectures received only 20 percent. He feared that the prefectures would be short of funds and impose all manner of charges [to make up the shortfall] (*SHY* 28.3b). Zhang Shi again memorialized on the circuit's salt. Guangxi was infertile and its Double Tax income meager. It depended on salt. Zhang proposed borrowing 400,000 strings under the control of the fiscal intendant for capital and transport expenses, to be returned from sales of salt. He described in detail the salt quota, which the Fiscal Intendancy was not to increase, as well as the price, transport charge, and interest for every prefecture. The concerned offices considered his proposal beneficial. Zhan Yizhi was instructed to report the 400,000 strings to the Department of Ministries, including a detailed report on annual budgets for horse purchases, saltern production funds, transport expenses, and so on, but no final decision was reached (*SHY* 28.3b–6b).

price and volume should be based on the old figures and that from then on, there should be no overstepping of authority to increase the price.[30]

In the 1180s the court favored a voucher policy in the region and joined the two Guangs under one intendancy.

In 1882 (Chunxi 9) the emperor decreed to dispatch the Zhexi Military Intendancy staff member (*fugan*), Hu Tingzhi, to inquire into the pros and cons [of government versus merchant salt distribution], then to deliberate with the commander-in-chief, fiscal intendant and [salt] intendant, and report on it. On his return, [Hu] Tingzhi was subsequently made the [salt] intendant of Guangdong, and concurrently he managed Guangxi salt affairs.[31] In 1183 (Chunxi 10) the emperor decreed:

---

[30] Decreed 9/27/1179 (*SHY* 28.9b). On 4/25/1179 the Qiongzhou[a] prefect memorialized that the prefecture's 450,000 catty sales quota had been increased to 1 million catties, but sales had not been able to meet this, and forced buying had resulted. As a consequence people fled or banded together, attacked towns, and plundered villages. He requested that the old quota be restored; this was approved (*SHY* 28.8a–b).

On 1/11/1180 the Guangxi military intendant and judicial intendant memorialized on the domino effect typical in other southeastern circuits. Because the government salt price was high, the Fiscal Intendancy was unable to sell it and so forced it upon the prefectures. The prefectures, unable to sell the salt, forced it on the people. So whether the state employed government sales or merchant sales, the forced exactions could not be eliminated. When, starting in 1174, government transport was reinstituted, all had to pay regardless of household rank. The burden of the upper households' exactions was now placed upon lower households. This was all due to tax quotas being too heavy (*SHY* 28.10a–11a).

[31] On 2/9/1182 the emperor decreed that Hu Tingzhi study the Liangguang salt administration. Hu recommended merchant trade. Under the Guangxi voucher policy most officials in the prefectures forged names, traded vouchers, or sold merchant salt themselves. Or officials traded with merchants but invented special requests and levies to bolster the public treasury. Others concealed reserve salt, then sold it. Under the merchant policy the Liangguang tax quota was set at 900,000 strings: Guangdong sold 100,000 baskets for 500,000 strings; Guangxi sold 80,000 baskets for 400,000 strings. The quota could [also] be set at 90,000 baskets for Guangdong and 60,000 baskets for Guangxi, but since there were other handling expenses, the quota of 100,000 baskets for Guangdong and 80,000 for Guangxi should remain. Hu's suggestions were approved (*SHY* 28.12b–15b). *Fugan* was the abbreviation for the Military Intendancy's staff members and supervisors (*anfusi ganban gongshi*).

Being several thousand *li* away, Guangnan has difficulty informing me of its problems; I feel the utmost regret about this. As for salt, the people used to sell it for a living, then the government took over sales because of the income to be had. For a long time this has been a scourge on the public.[32] I want to change this for their sake, to adopt merchant sales and eliminate government sales, so that the populace assuredly will be benefited. Yet benefits for the people mean disadvantages for the government. Idle talk is spreading. But what I am concerned about is the welfare of the people; what matter idle talk? Further, the established intendancies and officials are to serve the people. How can my goodwill not only not be applied but sabotaged? From now on, whoever commits such acts shall be punished according to the law.[33]

On 12/21/1182 Hu Tingzhi was appointed Guangdong salt intendant (*SHY* 28.15b). On 1/14/1183 Hu reiterated the pros and cons of the Liangguang voucher system. Item: officials of the two circuits were to personally go to Wuzhou[a] and deliberate. Every half-month administrators were to report to each other on figures for merchant voucher payments. Item: Shikang County was foggy and malaria-ridden, so none volunteered to serve there and appointments were mostly temporary. Hu requested that the court select capable officials and offer them promotions of one rank when their term was up. Item: Guangxi prefects, prefectural vice-administrators, assistants, and patrol officials who were able to encourage merchants, prevent smuggling, and increase revenues would have their next review moved up one year. Those who presided over a drop of 30 percent in revenues would have one year added to the time until their next official review (*SHY* 28.15b–17a).

[32] At year's end in some areas of Jiangxi and Guangnan entire villages were deserted by their inhabitants, "salt people" (*yanzi*), who went afield to trade (*YSJ*, 458).

[33] Decreed 1/22/1183 in response to the memorial of the chancellery imperial recorder (*qijulang*), Zhan Yizhi, to issue a special order warning the two circuits' supervisory officials (*SHY* 28.17a–b). On 5/29/1183, in response to a memorial on smuggling at Daxishan, it was decreed that the state crack down on flagrant official violations and report violators to the Department of Ministries (*SHY* 28.19b).

On 10/26/1183 the Guangdong salt intendant, Han Bi, who had been posted to Guangxi for nine years, memorialized on salt policy. Item: in the office at Jingjiang, Guangxi, the number of staff was excessive and there were insufficient funds for salaries. Officials had not been paid for months. Item: Yongzhou[a], Yizhou[b], Qinzhou[a], and Rongzhou[a] had from the start maintained armies to defend the border and paid out of salt [revenues] when the policy stipulated government distribution. Now this policy had been abolished, but the costs continued. Han Bi requested that the Guangxi Fiscal Intendancy carry out

So he ordered Zhan Yizhi to become prefect of Jingjiangfu and combined Guangdong and Guangxi salt matters into one intendancy. The two circuits' annual salt sales quota was 165,000 baskets.[34] [Zhan] Yizhi and others stated:

> Let 100,000 baskets be the salt quota of the two circuits now.[35] Wait three years or so to see if there is any change, then increase it. Let all charges on merchant vouchers in [Guang]dong and [Guang]xi circuits be exempted to make merchant sales convenient.

[p. 4469] In 1189 (Chunxi 16) the military intendant, Ying Mengming, stated:

> In the five or six years since Guang has implemented the voucher policy, prefecture and county offices have imposed quota vouchers upon the people. The harm of this exceeds that of government transport.[36]

---

transport as in the past. Item: Starting in 1174 Guangdong circulated vouchers, including Guangxi's, but Guangdong merchants were not allowed to trade in Guangxi. The glut of Guangxi vouchers meant that officials forced them on merchants, but the time it took to dispense vouchers (and salt) could cause the merchant to lose their original residency. Yet if they were not allowed to cross to the west, distribution would remain a problem. Han Bi requested that the area be permitted to go back to the policy of the Qiandao reign (1165–1173), [which allowed ready access west] (*SHY* 28.21b–22b).

On 12/21/1183 the Guangdong and Guangxi salt officials, Han Bi and Hu Tingzhi, memorialized that under the Guangdong policy since the Shaoxing period, merchants paid silver for vouchers in Guangzhou. The exchange rate was one ounce to 3,050.98 cash. Now, under the Liangguang system, each prefecture had a different exchange rate, which made accounting difficult. They requested that an ounce of silver be set at 3,050.98 cash [across the board]. The Guangxi Fiscal Intendancy was to observe this standard when assigning budgets for each prefecture (*SHY* 28.22b–23a). For the characteristics, nature, and goals of accounting in late imperial and Republican China, including comparisons with Western and Japanese accounting practices, see Gardella 1992, 317–39.

[34] Decreed after the Guangxi military intendant, Zhan Yizhi, and Guangxi transport assistant and salt intendant Lin Jie memorialized on 12/15/1185, with the stipulation that Guangdong's quota be 95,000 baskets and Guangxi's, 70,000 (*SHY* 28.25a–b).

[35] In *SHY* on 9/22/1186 "100,000" reads "150,000" (*SHY* 28.25b).

[36] On 1/11/ 1? J the emperor stated that Hu Tingzhi, whom he had delegated to investigate   u°ng salt, had not been thorough and merely agreed with what Zhan

The emperor decreed for [Ying] Mengming, Zhu Xiyan, and the Guangnan salt intendant, Wang Guangzu, to consider long-term beneficial measures that would not lead to abuses of quota exactions again.[37] In 1225 (Baoqing 1), when the Guangzhou[b] Military Intendancy's

---

Yizhi said. He delegated Ying Mengming to make changes and reimburse households. The trust of the people must not be lost (*SHY* 28.27b–28a). After Guangxi's salt policy was changed to vouchers, there was not much merchant activity. For six years the government and the populace suffered. When Ying Mengming was sent to Guangxi, the emperor enjoined him to be attentive to reforms. Fan Chengda, who served in Jingjiangfu (present Guilin), also relied on salt tax revenues because Guangxi was so poor, but the Fiscal Intendancy raised the price and the people suffered, so he petitioned to have this prohibited (*SS* 386.11869).

[37] Decreed 1/25/1189, upon Ying Mengming's report, to abolish the voucher system. While touring Hengzhou[a], Jinghunan, Ying had learned that the Guangxi salt law was constantly being changed so merchants with means had left the region. When he went to Jingjiangfu via Xing'an County, he found that the prefect, vice-prefect, and magistrate had summoned people purportedly in order to meet merchants, but actually to coerce them into paying further exactions. They had producers pay in salt to the point that they [could pay no more and] had to surrender their belongings as collateral. Upper-, middle-, and lower-class households went bankrupt. He also heard that some individuals used boundary markers and waste land as mortgage collateral which, when confiscated, was useless to the government, so the officials would force those neighboring on the land to purchase it. Some prefectures and counties allowed clerks to pose as merchants to sell salt. There were numerous irregularities. Ying recommended official distribution, law enforcement, and prohibition of illegal charges. He warned that the state had lost the confidence of merchants; it must not lose the confidence of the people (*SHY* 28.28a–29a).

Major gluts of Guang salt occurring from 1187 to 1189 in Gaozhou, Leizhou, Huazhou, Qinzhou[a], and Lianzhou[b] led to prefectures and counties implementing forced purchases (*SHY* 28.30b–34a). In 1190 Guangdong vouchers accumulated and could not be distributed (*SHY* 28.33b–34a). From 1190 on, Guang gluts were continuous. On 8/27/1194 it was decreed that the annual Guangxi salt tax quota be cut by 100,000 strings to relieve the people. Then the Guangxi transport assistant (*yunpan*) reported on reductions in prefectural quotas due to the court's act of grace, which might allow locales to sell without resorting to further demands (*SHY* 28.40a–45b).

On 2/13/1212 the Guangdong Intendancy presented the memorial of a former Chaozhou prefect who complained about the unfairness of the prefecture's seven grades of tax salt. Each county had its quota arbitrarily decided according to the salt content of its soil and its economic potential. Everyone in the county then paid according to the grade that they were assigned. When the price of salt rose, they had to pay a large amount of money to cover their taxes (*SHY* 28.52b–53b).

navy engaged in [salt] trafficking, the commander-general (*tongling*), Yin Zhuang, and the supervisor-in-chief (*tongxia*), Huang Shou, were both demoted one level.[38]

---

[38] *Tongling* was a military designation in the Southern Song; it was less prestigious than supreme commandant (*dutongzhi*) or commander-general (*tongzhi*). An army usually had two *tongling* under one *tongzhi*.

Section 3
EARTH SALT

The discussion of earth salt comprises only three pages of text. Primarily produced in Hedong Circuit, earth salt was important only for the Northern Song. The section begins with a list of production and distribution sites.

Chapter 8: Hedong

Northern Song

[p. 4469] The processing of alkaline soil for salt took place in Bingzhou's Yongli directorate [Hedong Circuit, Map 7], where over 125,000 piculs were manufactured annually. This supplied the prefecture as well as Xinzhou[a], Daizhou, Shizhou[b], Lanzhou, Xianzhou, Liaozhou, Zezhou, Luzhou[c], Linzhou, Fuzhou[c], and the military prefectures of Weishengjun, Kelanjun, Huoshanjun, Pingdingjun, Ninghuajun, and Baodejun.[1] Merchants were allowed to sell but could not operate outside these borders. During Renzong's reign (1022–1063) Yongli was divided into eastern and western directorates: the eastern fell under the jurisdiction of Bingzhou, the western under Fenzhou. Inhabitants of the prefecture's areas with alkaline soil (*jiantu*) were registered as pan households. Each year these households forwarded tax salt to the government; for any production beyond that the government paid cash. This was called "sales to the central authority" (*zhongmai*), and this policy was the same as that

---

[1] The Yongli directorate, near present-day Taiyuan (Shanxi), ranked first. Earth salt was also produced in Hebei and Shaanxi. Absconding households from Jincheng County (Zezhou) were forgiven their tax salt on 7/renwu/1032 (*XCB* 111.2584). Luzhou[c] was the Southern Song name for Longdefu. Quota figures for Hedong are given in *SHY* (22.4a–8b).

for sea salt. Annual production was 3,437 piculs less than the quota before Renzong. In Hedong Circuit, only Jinzhou[b], Jiangzhou[b], Cizhou[a], and Xizhou consumed pond salt; the rest consumed Yongli's earth salt. The government procurement price was six to eight cash per catty, while the government sales price was thirty-six cash. Annual tax revenues were 189,000-odd strings of cash.

Like pond and sea salts, earth salt in the 1050s was part of the merchant provisioning triangle. The government also taxed producers based on the grade of their saliferous earth.

From the Xianping period (998–1003) merchants were allowed to cart salt into Linzhou, Fuzhou[c], and Zhuolunzhai, all in the [north]west [corner] of Hedong to trade. The government sold the salt to them at a lower price [than it sold for via government distribution]. Later, when surplus salt piled up in 1040 in the Kangding period, production in the eastern directorate was halted for three years.[2] During the Huangyou period (1049–1053) the western directorate's salt production was temporarily halted until the stockpiles of salt had been reduced. At that time discussants petitioned to recruit merchants to provision Linzhou, Fuzhou[c], and Huoshanjun with fodder and grain and give them vouchers to be exchanged for salt. This the emperor approved. Then the price of fodder and grain became inflated, and vouchers worth 1,000 cash were undervalued by salt merchants and bought up at only a 400-odd cash value while the government still had to dole out fifty catties of salt per voucher. This meant a loss for local governments. [Officials] petitioned to abolish the provisioning [program] and [have merchants] bring in cash instead. The Fiscal Intendancy argued that this was inconvenient, so the

---

[2] A few years before, on 11/yiwei/1035, 77,700 piculs owed by salters of the Yongli directorate was forgiven (*XCB* 117.2763). Hedong produced a small quantity of earth salt; in southwestern prefectures near Yongxingjun, including Jinzhou[b], Jiangzhou, Cizhou, Xie salt had to be brought in. From 998 to 1003, however, Yongli's salt sold poorly so the government lowered its price and allowed merchants to ship it across the Yellow River westward. When this did not solve the salt glut, it was decreed that boiling be halted for two years, according to the *SHY*, as opposed to three, as stated in this *SS* entry. This was in response to a 2/15/1040 memorial from the Hedong fiscal intendant (*SHY* 23.38a–b).

petition was denied. The salt content of saliferous earth might be either strong or weak. If weak, revenues were low and producers became insolvent and unable to meet their tax quota. At the beginning of the Zhihe period (1054–1055) Han Qi petitioned that pan households report in after three years when the earth *[p. 4470]* in their area was exhausted, so that other salters could be chosen to replace them. The next year the emperor again decreed for salters to meet an annual tax quota [calculated] according to the grade of saliferous earth [they worked]. Discrepancies were pardoned and if a flood occurred, [the ruined salters] were replaced by other salters. The common people benefited from this [relief]. Hebei and Shaanxi also had those who boiled briny earth into salt, but their revenues were few. At the beginning of the Mingdao period (1032–1033) the emperor disbanded the briny-earth salterns of Hezhongfu and Qingchengjun and prohibited people from boiling salt because it undermined state revenues from pond salt.

By the mid 1070s, due to frequent losses, the government separated border provisioning from salt sales, required cash payments instead, and assumed responsibility for transport and sales.

In 1075 (Xining 8) the finance commissioner (*sansishi*), Zhang Dun, stated:

The two salt directorates' old annual quota of tax revenue was over 250,000 strings worth. Ever since merchants have been allowed to provision the border with grain and fodder, the numbers of vouchers given for salt have increased. Merchants have received vouchers of 1,000 cash worth, paying only half that price. County officials sustain hidden losses and shop merchants make incredible profits. Furthermore, since smuggling has not been prevented, tax revenues fall daily. Now they amount to only 104,000-odd strings. If the inflation of grain and fodder prices is taken into account, then the government receives in actuality only some 50,000 strings, which represents a loss of 80 percent from earlier revenue levels. I petition that the Xie salt [program] be taken as precedent and call on merchants to bring in cash to purchase [salt]. As an alternative, the government can [itself] transport and sell within the circuit. By tightening prohibitions against illegal sales, annual tax revenues will significantly rise. [The government can] use that cash to purchase grain and fodder for the border.

The emperor issued a decree along the lines of this memorial, and the government [began to] transport and sell salt within the circuit.[3]

In 1078 (Yuanfeng 1) the vice-commissioner of the Office of the Census (*hubu fushi*) in the Finance Commission, Chen Anshi, stated:

> I request that the precedent from before the Qingli period (1041–1048) be followed for salt produced at the eastern and western directorates in Yongli. Merchants should pay cash at Linzhou, Fuzhou[c], Fengzhou, Daizhou, Lanzhou, Xianzhou, Xinzhou[a], Kelanjun, Ninghuajun, Baodejun, Huoshanjun, and other prefectural offices, which will give them vouchers for that Yongli salt. This is to eradicate the abuse of adding bonus salt [in exchange for provisions whose price the merchants had inflated]. As before, merchants can choose their own sales site. They shall purchase salt already transported to sales salterns, paying the cost of transport. If this occurs, then the price of government salt will stabilize, and merchant sales will flow.

Subsequently this was carried out, and [Chen] Anshi was made Hedong fiscal intendant. [Chen] Anshi petitioned that those who violated the northeast's blue and white salts policy be punished according to the Huangyou period (1049–1053) decree: the leader and followers [of a smuggling band] were all to be exiled under surveillance (*bianpei*).[4]

---

[3] There were many logistical difficulties. On 12/14/1076 the prefect of Taiyuanfu, Han Jiang, memorialized that the people's greatest tribulation was the lack of salt. The present policy forced them to venture to salterns to buy it, but poor people who lived far away found it next to impossible to travel in inclement weather. It was an ordeal to provide for their families, and since every family needed salt, smuggling could not be stemmed. In addition, the privately sold salt was both tasty and cheap. So who could resist trading? The number of armed Hedong salt smugglers was mounting, and Han Jiang feared the problem would become as serious as in the southeast. Those who proposed the monopoly sought revenue to cover expenditures, yet after paying for transport and rewards for apprehending smugglers, there was little left. Furthermore, in the past, vouchers had been used to pay for border supplies. Now, proceeds from the sale of vouchers were dispersed at the center, while border expenses grew. This led to daily suffering for the people and provided no benefit to the state (*SHY* 24.12b–13a).

[4] *Pei* was a punishment, also termed *juepei*, *cipei*, or *liupei*, in which the offender was beaten with the heavy bamboo, tattooed on the face, then sent to perform hard labor. Originally it had represented a pardon of the death penalty, but then it became a regular punishment. Offenders sent into the army were called *peijun*. Grades of exile location ranged from inside the city, to a neighboring prefecture,

Further, if blue or white salt entered Hedong, the violator would be exiled to the frontier (*liu*) and any responsible officials who did not investigate would be punished as well. In 1081 (Yuanfeng 4) [Chen] Anshi himself reported a surplus in salt production that year and an increase in salt tax revenues from the Xinzhou[a] saliferous earth salters and Macheng Pond. The emperor decreed to promote [Chen] Anshi and reward his subordinates.[5]

Hedong prefectures consumed both their own earth salt and Xie pond salt, but salt from one of their own ponds was rejected in the mid 1080s.

In 1086 (Yuanyou 1) the right policy critic (*you sijian*), Su Che, stated:

In the past, besides consuming Xie salt, Hedong also depended on table salt produced in Yongli's eastern and western saltworks, which gave a constant supply. After 1080 (Yuanfeng 3) *[p. 4471]* the former chief councilor, Cai Que, and his brother [Cai] Li and others began adding salt of Macheng Pond in Xinzhou[a] (Hedong). It has saltpeter in it and tastes bitter, so common folk are unwilling to purchase it. I beg to have the Fiscal Intendancy notified that if there is no need [for this product], its collection should please be stopped.[6]

---

to Guangnan, and to a sea island. McKnight discusses exile in the Tang and Song and charts average sentences by reign to show these were much shorter than would have been the case without periodic amnesties (McKnight 1981, 79–82).

[5] Chen Anshi reported increased prefectural revenues by 7/14/1081, was promoted, and had the time until his next review reduced. What goes unsaid here is that one factor in Chen's apparent success was his forcing shop owners to purchase the salt for resale, though it was so foul tasting no one wanted to eat it (*SHY* 24.21b; *XCB* 309.7495, 314.7605).

Around 5/yiwei/1083 the Hedong Fiscal Intendancy memorialized that with the war and occupation of conquered lands, which required additional personnel and troops, though it was decreed to allow vouchers to be used for purchases, the office was out of funds. It requested an emergency fund of 350,000 strings and permission to allow awards of bonus salt so that merchants would come with grain and fodder (*XCB* 335.8071). On 10/dingmao/1084 the emperor decreed 300,000 strings worth of vouchers be given to Hedong's Fiscal Intendancy to buy fodder (*XCB* 349.8365).

[6] Su Che memorialized on 4/26/1086 (*SHY* 24.26b–27a; *XCB* 376.9125).

The emperor approved.

Chen Anshi was tried in the wake of a struggle over the use of salt wells in Hedong. The controversy involved whether the wells should come under government monitoring or be shut down, even at the risk of creating a shortage. Chen and the Hedong issue were part of a larger effort to control the new small-mouth wells, most in Sichuan, which were eventually allowed to operate privately. Chen was caught in the line of fire during a period when the circuits declared that digging such wells was prohibited. Wang Anshi would have gone after greater controls and crackdowns on anything that smacked of privatization, which the small-mouth wells certainly did.

In 1089 (Yuanyou 4) Chen Anshi was tried for implementing the current proposal to set up salt wells when he was serving as the Hedong fiscal intendant. That [program had] undermined [the revenue base of] the entire circuit. He was demoted to [the post of] prefect of Zhengzhou.[7] Prior to this, however, during the Xining period (1068–1077), there had been discussion of taking over the salt wells of Baoshun in Xihe Circuit's tribal region, which some thought inadvisable.[8] Wang Anshi said that if border generals managed affairs rationally, what was the harm? Those deliberating could not gainsay [Wang].

As elsewhere, Hedong policy at the turn of the eleventh century under Zhezong and Huizong alternated between merchant and government sales or a combination of the two. There were no entries made for Hedong once it was lost to the Jin.

In 1091 (Yuanyou 6) the emperor decreed that Daizhou's annual salt sales quota be determined on the basis of an average 850,000 catties, which was to be divided properly among its jurisdictions.[9] In 1094 (Shaosheng 1) Hedong restored a government sales policy. In 1104

---

[7] It was recorded for 12/18/1089 that Chen Anshi was demoted to Dengzhou, then to Zhengzhou in 1090 (*XCB* 436.10504–5).

[8] Xihe Circuit, near present-day Lanzhou (Gansu), underwent numerous changes. In 1072 it was called Xizhou and came under the jurisdiction of Qinfeng Circuit (*SS* 87.2162).

[9] On 2/6/1091 the emperor approved the Hedong military intendant's request, which had the support of the Hedong Fiscal Intendancy (*SHY* 24.29b–30a; *XCB* 455.10905). On 2/17/1093 a number of Hedong prefectures abolished the silkworm salt exactions (*SHY* 24.30b).

(Chongning 3), because vouchers in the three circuits [Hedong, Hebei, Shaanxi] had no set price, the price was especially low in Hedong and adversely affected [salt] procurement. Hence salt vouchers supplied to these three circuits were cancelled and only ready-cash certificates were available there, while other circuits followed Hebei's newly decreed voucher policy.[10] In 1105 (Chongning 4) the emperor decreed that the briny earth salt of Hedong's two Yongli directorates remain government-procured, to be sold for strings of cash. Merchants were to exchange cash for the [salt] vouchers, then head [with their salt stocks] to designated Hedong prefectures. Merchant sales of northeastern salt were no longer permitted in Hedong.

---

[10] Department of Ministries memorial of 1/27/1104 (*SHY* 24.38a–b).

Section 4
WELL SALT

The category of well salt comprises eleven pages, almost a fifth of the salt discussion. Well salt was produced primarily in four circuits in the region of today's Sichuan: Chengdufu, Zizhou, Kuizhou, and Lizhou^a. Together they were commonly referred to as Chuan ("the Rivers"), Chuanxia ("Rivers and Gorges"), or Liangchuan (the "Two Rivers," east and west). Well salt entailed sophisticated drilling technology and considerable labor. While it did not contribute a large percentage of central government revenues, it was important for regional finances. First, the Songshi lists production places and wells, which could be run by individuals who were then taxed.

Chapter 9: Sichuan

Northern Song

[p. 4471] The boiling of salt from well brine was carried out in four circuits: Yizhou^d, Zizhou [or Tongchuanfu], Kuizhou, and Lizhou^a (Map 15).[1] The 98 [salt] wells (*jing*) of Yizhou^d Circuit's single directorate annually produced 84,522 piculs. The 385 wells of Zizhou Circuit's two directorates produced 141,780 piculs. The 20 wells of Kuizhou Circuit's three directorates produced 84,880 piculs. And the 129 wells of Lizhou^a Circuit produced 12,200 piculs. Each provided [product and revenue] for its own circuit.[2] [As in other salt-producing regions] large units were

---

[1] For the Northern Song, Yizhou^d refers to Chengdufu Circuit. For Chengdufu's alternating status as prefecture (*zhou*) and higher level prefecture (*fu*) and its structure, see *SS* 89.2210–11.

[2] *CYZJ jia* 14.10a–b. Thus the four circuits of Sichuan had, at the beginning of the Song, six directorates with 632 wells, which annually produced 323,382 piculs. Chuanxia's "standing tube well" salt amounted to 12,251,683 catties (*SHY*

283

called directorates, while the small were called wells; the government managed the former, while at wells, native inhabitants took charge of boiling. The locals paid taxes according to output and were allowed to sell their excess in neighboring areas so long as they did not exit Chuanxia. In the beginning Chuanxia observed the old policy and the government sold salt. In 974 (Kaibao 7) the emperor [Taizu] decreed that [the price of] a catty be reduced by ten cash and ordered sellers to hand over 90 percent of their surplus revenues, should there be any.[3]

Powerful individuals bought salt low from the state and sold it high to the people. Officials also levied high taxes on producers.

[p. 4472] In 977 (Taipingxingguo 2) the right completioner, Guo Bi, submitted:

Jiannan's prefectural governments sell salt at seventy cash per catty. Salt wells must be dug deep and the boiling is difficult.[4] Tinder is expensive and cart transport arduous. Added to this are the worries of water transport, which at times results in [boats] drifting and [people] drowning. Then wealthy people and sly clerks collaborate to no good; they buy cheap from the government and sell dear to the common people. For one catty of salt they may reap several hundred cash. The government loses annual tax revenues, and the

---

23.10a). The *Yuhai* counts 608 wells (*YH* 181.34b–35a). In 1132 over 4,900 wells are recorded (*CYZJ jia* 14.9a–b). Production figures for the wells are listed by circuit and prefecture in *SHY* (23.11b–12b).

[3] Decreed 7/974 (*SHY* 23.19a). The state set up directorates near "fire wells," but elsewhere allowed people to boil and sell upon paying a tax. On 1/965 it was decreed that the old price, 160 cash per catty, was to be reduced by 60 cash; prefectures were to cut the price by one-third (*SHY* 23.18a). This year also marked the first recorded salt shortage in the Song and the collapse of the major well at Lingzhou (*XCB* 8.194, 4/wuzi/967). Accounts of trade in the region are littered with reports on shortages (Guo Zhengzhong 1981, 79–94).

[4] Valley people examined locations and drilled wells sixty to seventy *zhang* deep; if lucky, they would find a briny spring. They lined wells with stone and made bags out of cow hide. Groups of men pulled a rope that brought up bags of brine all day until the vein was exhausted. Then men were let down into the well to scoop up the brine by hand; when they filled a bagful, it was pulled up. The briny solution was sent to the stoves, and salt was produced (*Xu Zizhi tongjian* [*XZTJ*] 146.5a–b; *HSZLS* 55.22b–23a).

populace eats costly salt. I wish that the government selling price might be raised slightly, to 150 cash, so that powerful and slippery elements will have no source of profit, and the people will be provided for.

The emperor [Taizong] approved.[5] A responsible official stated:

Changzhou[a] annually collects an "empty" (or approximate) quota (*xu'e*) of over 18,500 catties of salt. During the Kaibao period (968–975) its prefect, Li Pei, squeezed [the people] harshly in hopes of attaining the record for the highest tax revenues. He abolished the wells' fuel money allowance and, in addition to the annual quota, taxed those in his jurisdiction extra amounts. The people were not accustomed to this and suffered hardship to the point of bankruptcy. Many have fled to other places yet cannot avoid their accumulated tax debts of many years.

When well salt was insufficient, the court allowed merchants to sell a variety of other kinds of regionally produced salt.

The emperor decreed to excuse all of these debts and restored the quota to 27,060 catties as before.[6] In the seventh month of 988 (Duangong 1) western Chuan's salt was insufficient. Merchants could sell, duty-free, blue and white salts from Jiezhou and Wenzhou[b], Xia Circuit well salt, and Yongkangjun "cliff salt" (*yayan*).[7]

---

[5] *XCB* 18.402 (4/xinmao/977). A decade before, on 1/dingyou/965, the emperor had issued pardons, including a reduction of the price of Chengdu salt from 160 to 100 cash per catty. The price in other prefectures was reduced by one-third (*XCB* 6.146).

[6] Reported on 2/guihai/978 (*SHY* 23.21a–b; *XCB* 19.423).

[7] Decreed 7/988 (*SHY* 23.22b). Cliff salt, also known as *yanyan*, came from salt blocks in cliffs, particularly in Qinfeng (present-day Gansu) Circuit's Jiezhou and Chengzhou (Wang Leiming 1985, 387n5). On 12/3/988 Luzhou[b] in Zizhou Circuit reported that a well had become depleted, but when people entered it to take a look, a huge roar like thunder arose from below, a blazing fire erupted, and eight persons were incinerated (*SHY* 23.22b). Such "fire wells" were natural gas veins. Linqiong County (Sichuan) had two wells, one a fire well, the other a salt well. When water drawn from the salt well was boiled using the fire well, each bushel produced four to five pecks of salt; otherwise only one to two pecks were produced (*Weilüe* [*WL*] 11.29a–b). The natural gas fire could produce more salt due to its greater heat. The Linqiong well is described elsewhere: when one needed a fire, one tossed a light into the fire well and immediately there would

At the turn of the eleventh century well salt was drawn into the border provisioning system. The state gave salters a measure of rest and reduced their taxes.

After the rebellion of Li Shun, border troops in Chuanxia's prefectures were increased, and people were called upon to bring in grain in exchange for salt.[8] In 1005 (Jingde 2) the provisional finance commissioner, Ding Wei, stated:

> Chuanxia's stores of grain are plenty. I petition to have salt hereafter exchanged for silk.

The emperor decreed that prefectures with stockpiles of food for two years and those near rivers and caves with three years' worth [of food] be allowed to do so.[9] In 1008 (Dazhongxiangfu 1) Zhenzong decreed that the stove salters of Luzhou[b]'s Nanjing[b] be given three days of rest at New Year's, the winter and summer solstices, and the "Cold Eats Festival" (*Hanshijie*), and be excused from their daily quotas.[10] In 1010 (Dazhong-xiangfu 3) the salt tax of Luzhou[b]'s Yujing directorate was cut by one-third.

---

come a boom and a flame that leaped skyward, lighting the area for ten *li* around (see Liu Yuanlin's commentary on "Shudu fu" [Song of the Shu capital], by Zuo Si, *WX* 4.10a). Such wells could also be found in Fushun, Jianwei, Yilong, and Pengxi counties.

[8] Li Shun (?–995), a Sichuan native with a tea farming background, led an uprising in 994 in western Sichuan. His rallying cry was to "equalize rich and poor" by redistributing property. After occupying Chengdu, he was proclaimed king of Great Shu. His power extended from eastern to western Sichuan, and his forces numbered 250,000. Taizong suppressed the rebellion in 995. Although Li Shun was taken captive and died, a portion of his rebel force continued to fight; see "Li Shun zhi bian" (The rebellion of Li Shun) in *Huang Song tongjian changbian jishi benmo* [*HSJS*] 13.1a–10b.

[9] "Rivers and caves" refer to the minority areas around the Sichuan-Hunan-Guizhou[b] border; minorities living nearby were called the Five Rivers Tribe. Ding Wei's memorial and the succeeding decree appear under 5/wuchen/1005 (*XCB* 60.1341).

[10] Well salters rested on these four festivals (*XCB* 81.1842, 7/dingwei/1013). The Cold Eats Festival, during which only cold provisions were eaten, occurred in the spring just before the Clear and Bright Festival (*Qingmingjie*) and 105 days after the winter solstice (Wang Leiming 1985, 387n8).

Wells were added, quotas reduced.

During the reign of Renzong (1022–1063) the three circuits of Chengdu[fu], Zi[zhou], and Kui[zhou] had the same six directorates as at the beginning of the Song, except that Chengdu Circuit added thirty-nine more wells and had its annual tax quota decreased by 56,597 piculs; Zizhou Circuit added twenty-eight more wells and had its annual tax quota decreased by 110,019 piculs; Lizhou[a] Circuit added fourteen more wells and had its annual tax quota decreased by 492 piculs and three-odd pecks; Kuizhou Circuit added fifteen more wells and had its annual tax quota decreased by 3,184 piculs. Each provided its own circuit [with salt], but Kuizhou also provided [salt to] the *[p. 4473]* southern minority peoples.[11] Based on its salt revenue, each circuit made 50 percent of its annual tribute payments in strings of cash, 50 percent in silver and fine silk. In addition, merchants were summoned to transport cash to the prefectures and to high-production areas to obtain salt, while in the Shizhou[a] and Qianzhou[c] border prefectures, they were called on to bring in grain.

Salt payments and taxes were settled in silver, which the region did not produce; in 1040 a request was made that they be paid in kind or cash. Border provisioning in

---

[11] On 6/dingchou/1024 the Kuizhou fiscal intendant, Diao Zhan, memorialized that tax revenues of the Yunanjun well were great, but previous prefects were military men who had neglected the records. He requested that the court appoint a high official to serve as Yunanjun prefect (*XCB* 102.2359). On 8/9/1025 a vice-director memorialized that three salterns of Zhongzhou in Kuizhou Circuit had a quota of over 454,500 catties, which included over 93,000 catties the Fiscal Intendancy had ordered. This bankrupted households and detained men were unable to deliver what they owed. Zhongzhou was excused the increase (*SHY* 23.33a–b; *XCB* 103.2386). In 2/renzi/1033 well households of the Fushun directorate were pardoned their salt taxes (*XCB* 112.2606). Sichuan wells had been depleted for many years, and the region's iron foundries and water mills abandoned. Yet households still had to pay taxes. Further, the state raised the salt price so people could not afford it. On 11/bingyin/1041 Suizhou[b] and Zizhou's taxes added for the intercalary month of the leap year were forgiven (*XCB* 134.3199). On 3/23/1074 a Zizhou Circuit official, Xiong Ben, requested to be permitted to keep two stoves for officials to boil salt at Yu Well and to sell the remaining brine (to local people to boil), as suggested by Xianyu Zhishao, a scholar from Luzhou[b] (*SHY* 24.6b).

exchange for well salt turned lucrative for merchants and lingered even after the need for it passed.

In 1040 (Kangding 1) the Huainan judicial intendant, Guo Wei, stated:

> Chuanxia heretofore has never produced silver but calls on people to exchange silver for its salt. Salt and liquor producers also have to pay annual taxes in silver. Thus merchants hasten to the capital and Shaanxi and return with silver. The government, after receiving the silver, has it transported to the capital again, which is laborious and costly for both the government and the people. I petition to allow merchants to make silver payments to the capital's Monopoly Goods Bureau or to Shaanxi prefectures, then that they be given vouchers with which they can obtain salt at Chuanxia, or that they pay annual taxes in salt and liquor. Those who wish to pay in cash may do so at a ratio of 2,000 cash to one ounce of silver.

The emperor decreed that this should be carried out. When subsequently only a few merchants brought silver to Shaanxi, adding twenty catties of salt to every hundred catties was discussed, as was recruiting traders to provision Fengxiang and Yongxing. At that time, with fighting in the west and military provisions running short, the emperor again decreed for provision of fodder and grain to the border until it was sufficiently supplied. Fodder and grain prices soared while the salt price sagged, so merchants profited; even after the crisis in the west had passed, they continued provisioning as before. The Kuizhou fiscal intendant, Jiang Ben, pointed out that over the more than ten years border provisioning had been practiced, inflated prices for provisions amounted to a waste of over 200,000 strings worth of Kui salt. Now that Shaanxi had profited from using pond salt and its military stores were full, he petitioned to return to the initial policy [of no provisioning]. The emperor approved.[12]

Well salt regions also consumed pond salt; in the 1040s charges on well salt imports from other circuits hiked up the well salt price.

---

[12] In 1/wuzi/1046 the Chengdufu, Zizhou, and Kuizhou fiscal intendants requested an increase in the well tax so that they could collect 100,000 (strings) annually (*XCB* 158.3817).

Prior to this, because Yizhou[d] and Lizhou[a] [circuits'] salt production was the lowest [of the Sichuan circuits], they also consumed salt from the Daning directorate [Kuizhou Circuit] and the Xie ponds, which merchants resold to them. During the Qingli period (1041–1048) merchants who paid cash to Yizhou[d] for the Daning directorate's salt were directed to pay an added charge of 1,000 strings of "small cash" (*xiaoqian*) for every 10,000 catties. Ten "small cash" were equal to one "big cash" (*daqian*). Sellers were few and far between, [however,] and Shu salt became extremely expensive. A catty cost 2,200 small cash. When the prefect of Yizhou[d], Wen Yanbo, related this, the emperor decreed to restore the previous policy.

Salt taxes could be paid in silver, silks, or gold. The Sichuan circuits' tribute was bought with salt tax revenues, and this commutation put a great burden on the people.

Local governments relied on the four circuits' salt revenues. Of well sites, however, some yielded, while some were depleted, yet taxes kept rising, just as before. Most of those in responsible positions tried to [collect] increased taxes to show their merit, often leaving behind a calamity for their successors [to deal with]. By then there was an urgent need to alleviate the people's misery, especially in remote areas. So whenever someone reported their difficulties to the emperor, he granted immediate pardons or reductions. Initially 50 percent of the salt tax revenues could be paid in silver or silks. One catty of salt was calculated at twenty to thirty cash, while one ounce of silver and one bolt of silk were calculated at an exchange rate of from 600 to 1,200 cash. Later the emperor decreed the commutation of salt taxes *[p. 4474]* to gold and silk at the current trading price.[13] Jinghu's Guizhou[a] and Xiazhou (Map 14)

---

[13] This 5/wuzi/1046 passage in the main *SS* text was taken verbatim from *XCB* (158.3827). Salt wells in ancient Weizhou[b], in Qinfeng Circuit, near the Xixia border and previously occupied by the Linzhan tribe, gradually fell into the hands of the Qingtang tribe. As the Song debated building a fort there, the Qingtang tribe rebelled and the Xixia also claimed possession of the land. The Song official Fu Qiu discussed the issue with Qingtang tribal leaders and declared that the Song would build a fort but leave the salt wells to the Qingtang (*XCB* 175.4226, intercalary 7/jichou/1053).

each had two wells, generating annual tax revenues of 2,820 piculs worth; each supplied the income for the needs of its respective prefecture.

Shu salt smuggling was rampant because the government could not monitor the many private wells. But the government decided against closing down all wells and importing Xie salt, which might have permitted it better control over supply and revenues.

During the Xining reign period (1068–1077) prohibitions could not deter the hordes of Shu salt smugglers.[14] Some wished to fill in private wells entirely and have Xie salt imported to fill needs, but no decision was reached. Shenzong inquired about this with the compiler of the imperial records (*xiu qijuzhu*),[15] Shen Kuo, who answered:

> Since it is permitted to purchase the right to operate private salt wells, private trade is inevitable. If we fill in all the wells, bring in Xie salt, and have all salt sold via government sales, this will help eliminate sentencing and punishments, as well as be a method to take over profits. Among the Zhongzhou, Wanzhou, Rongzhou^c, and Luzhou^b minority-populated areas, however, small wells are especially numerous and would be difficult to eradicate.[16] Should we marshal forces to monitor them, I am afraid that what we would gain would not be worth the cost.

So the suggestion died.

---

[14] Another glut of Shu salt occurred before this, between 1065 and 1066, in Qiongzhou^b (*SS* 266.9188–89).

[15] The position of compiler of the imperial records in 1071 was to be concurrently filled by the remonstrance official. The Imperial Recording Bureau (*qijuyuan*) and the chancellery imperial recorder (*qijulang*) recorded the emperor's words and actions (Wang Leiming 1985, 389n3).

[16] These four prefectures were located in eastern and southern Sichuan, close to minority areas of Hubei, Hunan, Guizhou^b, and Yunnan. There were frequent conflicts between Han and minority peoples in the basin; salt was produced in Han areas, but the scattered minority peoples had to rely on outside sources. Competition for wells ensued, creating more hardship and instability of receipts. Finally in the Southern Song a new policy opened up the trade and allowed minorities to participate (by selling firewood), thereby co-opting them (Jia Daquan 1983, 45–47).

In the 1070s the court discontinued the import of Xie salt; wells remained open and eastern Chuan salt continued to supply western Chuan.

In 1076 (Xining 9) Liu Zuo went to Shu to manage tea affairs and had 100,000 mats of Xie salt transported in one year.[17] The general censor, Zhou Yin, memorialized:

Chengdufu Circuit has always relied on salt produced in eastern Chuan. Recently the Fiscal Intendancy suggested selling [the salt of] Lingjing saltern, so eastern salt has been halted, the "standing tube" wells sealed [to restrict manufacture], and great numbers are unemployed.[18] Concerned with profit, ministers have brought in Xie salt, but the hazardous routes make for an extremely arduous journey. Chengdu's salt price has leaped while eastern Chuan salt is cheap, which encourages people to flout the law. I entreat that eastern salt continue to enter Chengdu, that standing tube wells remain open, and that government transport of Xie salt be discontinued.[19]

---

[17] Liu Zuo memorialized on 4/22/1076 that Shaanxi merchants profited from selling Xie salt and Shaanxi tea in Sichuan. He requested that the government use 2.01 million strings to buy salt and tea and prohibit merchant trade in Sichuan (*SHY* 24.9a–b). On 7/25/1076 the prefect of Yangzhou[b] in Lizhou[a] Circuit memorialized that while the tea trade in his prefecture had been going on for a long time, there were many irregularities. Although the surpluses generated were great, there were also problems with the monopoly: smuggling, which caused gluts, transport difficulties, and lack of cash, which halted trade. He cautioned the court to consider each policy thoroughly before implementing it (*SHY* 24.10a–11a).

[18] The standing tube technique revolutionized Sichuan wells. Before, extraction from large wells (*dajing*) was a labor-intensive process that produced only tens to hundreds of catties per day (*Yuanfeng jiuyuzhi* [*YFJYZ*] 7.1a–35b). Small-mouth well drilling with bamboo pipes to obtain brine was begun in the 1040s. Workers lowered interlocking sections of giant bamboo tubing into a well to channel the flow of water, then used a fanned mud (*shanni*) technique to clear mud from the bottom (*Shuzhong guangji* [*SZGJ*] 66.21b–25b). The mechanism involved a derrick, gears, and a conveyor belt. The wells were several tens of *zhang* deep with an opening the diameter of a bowl (*DPZ*, 76–77, (4); and *Su Shi wenji* [*SSW*], vol. 6, 2367. The new wells led to increased production and a drop in prices, but when they threatened government salt, some memorialized to close them (*Jingde ji* [*JDJ*] 4.4b–5a).

[19] Zhou Yin memorialized on 11/27/1076 that merchant trade in eastern Chuan salt would benefit both public coffers and private well being. It was 2,000 *li* from Shaanxi to Chengdufu where salt cost 250 to 260 cash per catty, equal to two bushels of rice; in eastern Chuan salt cost only 70 cash. Sichuan's four circuits

The emperor decreed for merchants to act as before. The sale of Xie salt was to be in accord with regulations on merchant trade, and exactions upon the people were prohibited. Before long, government transport of Xie salt indeed ended.[20]

Government-sold Xie salt in Chengdufu and Lizhou[a] was contaminated; merchant salt in Zizhou and Kuizhou was cheaper but taxed at a higher rate, or had other fees imposed.

In 1086 (Yanyou 1) the emperor [Zhezong] decreed that the Chengdu judicial intendant, Guo Gai, look into salt matters. The right policy critic, Su Che, accused [Guo] Gai of hedging, sycophancy, and unreliable memorials. Su also said:

Several Sichuan prefectures sell the government salt of Qiongzhou[b]'s Pujiang well at 120 cash per catty.[21] In recent years its salt springs have become

---

were actually one unit. For eastern Chuan to use Xie salt from several thousand *li* away was unreasonable and would mean a loss in taxes. Zhou Yin proposed merchant trade of Xie salt and also that from eastern Chuan (*SHY* 24.11a–12a; *XCB* 279.6826–27).

[20] A proposal supporting merchant trade was made by co-intendant of Chengdufu tea, Lu Shimin, on 3/wushen/1083 (*XCB* 334.8044–45). The Kuizhou fiscal intendant, Wang Zongwang, requested on 7/xinchou/1084 that Chengdufu set up a Monopoly Goods Bureau and salterns. Well salt was to be monopolized by the government. There were about 600 wells in operation: large ones produced 1,000 catties daily; small ones, 200 catties. Daily production reached 180,000 catties; annual production 63,720,000 catties. One hundred catties were priced at 4,000 cash, which meant 2,548,800 strings annually. Every string saw a profit of 1 *fen* 5 *li*; annual surpluses were 382,320 strings. Lu requested that 500 Buddhist ordination certificates and 100,000 ounces of silver be loaned to the Fiscal Intendancy as capital, which would be paid back in three years' time (*XCB* 347.8321).

On 6/jiayin/1086 the executive censor, Liu Zhi, impeached Lu Shimin for abuse of power. While serving as tea and horse intendant of Chengdufu and Yongxingjun, Lu had terrorized the populace. Since the intendancy was above the locales, he was not easily checked. Liu Zhi requested Lu's immediate dismissal so that witnesses could testify without fear; this was decreed (*XCB* 381.9272). Huang Lian, sent to investigate the Qiongzhou[b] well, replaced Lu; his memorial on Lu's measures continues in interstitial comment, 6/jiayin/1086 (*XCB* 381.9273–74).

[21] Sichuan should probably read Xichuan (western Chuan) (*XCB* 369.8906, intercalary 2/18/1086).

depleted, with much sand and dirt mixed in with the salt. Yet the price of merchant salt in Zizhou and Kuizhou circuits, as well as of small-well white salt sold among the people, costs only 70 to 80 [cash], so offices resort to extra fees and charges. [Guo] Gai does not care that the people must eat dear salt daily.[22]

The emperor thus decreed to dismiss [Guo] Gai and ordered Huang Lian to investigate and report on the matter. A petitioner stated:

Apart from tax revenues, the responsible office has charged well operators fifty strings of "government stream fees" (*guanxiqian*) annually.[23]

The emperor decreed for [Huang] Lian to abolish this [fee]. The emperor decreed that from now on, there should be no extra charges beyond the salt well tax payments.

In 1103 (Chongning 2) Chuanxia's Lizhou[a], Yangzhou[b], Xingzhou[a], Jianzhou[b], Pengzhou, Langzhou, Bazhou[a], Mianzhou, Hanzhou, Xingyuan-fu, and other prefectures all circulated northeast salt.[24] In 1105 (Chongning 4) *[p. 4475]* the salt of Zizhou, Suizhou[b], Kuizhou, Mianzhou, Hanzhou, Daningjian and so on was still sold in Sichuan but prohibited from encroaching upon Xie salt territory [i.e., Yizhou[d] and Lizhou[a] circuits].

---

[22] Su Che memorialized on 2/bingwu/1086 (*XCB* 369.8906). The palace censor, Lü Tao, memorialized on 10/guichou/1086 ten points concerning popular suffering and lack of governance in Chengdufu, including the government allowing operation of the private standing tube wells [probably by default] (*XCB* 390.9496). On 3/22/1191 the Ministry of Finance memorialized that Chengdufu's Longzhou well sold little, even though the price had fallen (*SHY* 28.34a–b).

[23] The petitioner was Huang Qian, a *jinshi* from Lingjingjian, a salt directorate in Chengdufu, who asked that this fee be eliminated (*XCB* 376.9125–26, 4/guichou/1086; *XCB* 392.9542, 11/gengchen/1086). Lingjingjian was the only place that charged the "government stream fees." On 1/24/1089 it was decreed that Chengdufu's 160 wells were the limit. Large and standing tube wells were both allowed. If a large well became depleted, a standing tube well could be drilled nearby to fill the original quota and taxes. The number of wells and their tax quotas were to be in accord with official decision. A defunct well had to be sealed. This was in response to the memorial of the censor, Lü Tao (*SHY* 24.29a; *XCB* 421.10195).

[24] This was owing to the 11/13/1103 petition of Li Cheng, salt intendant of Shaanxi and Hedong (*SHY* 24.37a).

Southern Song

The number of wells multiplied seven times over the Northern Song, and the monopoly was broken. In fact, private wells became the major source of Sichuan salt, with the government unable to curb the digging of new wells. The Southern Song administration charged Sichuan merchants numerous fees at contract markets, where they dealt directly with salters, but under government supervision.

It was in 1132 (Shaoxing 2) that the Sichuan quartermaster, Zhao Kai, initially changed the salt policy. In imitation of the Daguan period (1107–1110) policy, he established contract markets where tax fees on vouchers (*yinshui qian*) were collected.[25] This resembled the tea policy but was much more detailed. For each catty, [merchants] paid 25 [cash] in voucher tax fees, about 9.4 cash in native product taxes, 0.7 cash in transit taxes (*guoshui*) when crossing borders [that is, for itinerant merchants], 1.5 cash in stationary taxes (*zhushui*) on salt shops [for shop merchants], 60 cash in other transaction fees [on paper money payments], and later, exchange fees.[26] Sichuan's over 4,900 wells altogether produced approximately 60 million-odd catties of salt per year. When the voucher policy was first implemented, 100 catties counted as one load (*dan*), to which 10 additional catties could be added without being counted in, as an incentive. Later the amount increased to over 4 million strings worth. In 1159 (Shaoxing 29) Xihezhou's salt price to merchants was cut in half.[27]

---

[25] On 11/3/1129 a decree stated that people had petitioned to close exhausted wells but that prefectures and counties, aiming to increase taxes, would not agree. When people developed new wells, they dared not report the fact. If local officials would look into the matter and allow new wells, the government and the people would benefit (*SHY* 25.34a). It was proposed on 4/4/1133 that merchant trade in Kuizhou be allowed until Zhe and Huai salt arrived (*SHY* 26.11b–12a).

[26] *CYZJ jia* 14.9a; *XNYL* 58.16a. Zhao Kai's biography also tells that he managed Sichuan salt as he did tea, by contract markets designed to consolidate producers and merchants, control the flow of salt, and guarantee revenues. The court's aim was to monopolize wells in the Chengdu, Zizhou, and Lizhou[a] circuits. The markets confirmed the salt's weight to prevent merchants from taking more than their quota (*SS* 374.11596–600; Wang Leiming 1985, 390n1).

[27] Where wells were distant and waterways ran shallow, boiling and transport were problematic. While officials ignored petitions to shut down storehouses, Xiaozong granted numerous pardons, in 1165, 1167, 1170, and 1173 (*SHY* 27.18a). On 5/20/1176 the former prefect of Rongzhou[d], Cheng Jie, memorialized to close

The government rated wells to determine quotas, but administrators extracted more than they should have.

In 1179 (Chunxi 6) under Xiaozong the Sichuan regulator, Hu Yuanzhi, and the quartermaster, Cheng Jie, stated:

In assessing the four [Sichuan] circuits' 2,375 salt wells in 450 saltworks, aside from the 1,174 wells in 150 saltworks which follow the old quota in boiling and submission, 125 wells and 24 saltworks have either requested themselves or had the government decide to increase their quota.[28] There are 479 restored old wells that now wish to be registered for production. Wells that produce no salt will be eliminated, while those that are insufficient producers will have their [quota] quantity reduced. The reduction amounts to 409,888 vouchers and the increase amounts to 137,349 vouchers. So well households will be spared the hardship of heavy quotas.[29]

In 1180 (Chunxi 7) [Hu] Yuanzhi further stated:

The rating of salt wells is geared to increase the quota of those that produce plenty and decrease those that are not producing sufficiently. Since offices in charge focus on profit, they extract more than they should from productive wells and cut but little from those that have dried up. This stems entirely from selfish motives. From now on, whenever an assessment is used to

---

depleted wells. But if an old well could again be made operational, it could fill tax losses; this was approved (*SHY* 28.6b).

[28] *Tuipai* was a method by which taxes were based on registered property assets and reassessed every three years. Here, wells were checked to determine the level of tax quotas, usually with an eye toward raising revenues, as when the Sichuan salt and liquor monopoly's income was insufficient (Wang Leiming 1985, 390n6).

[29] Before "137,349 vouchers" it should read "increased salt sales in the prefectures amount to" as memorialized 5/13/1179 (*SHY* 28.8b–9a). On 9/16/1179 a pardon was issued from the Imperial Ancestral Hall concerning production funds, well closings, and quotas (*SHY* 28.9a–b). On 11/24/1179 the Sichuan consul-general, Li Changtu, memorialized that salterns operated by the Military Intendancy abused inhabitants, such as [those in] in Jinzhou[a], where they consumed salt from Tongzhou[b] and Taizhou[b] (Huaidong). When merchants arrived with salt, officials sold it at an elevated price, then hoarded the money. Merchants had to beg, sometimes for three or four years, before being paid. Li recommended abolishing the Military Intendancy and assigning salt administrators to the quartermaster's office (*SHY* 28.9b–10a).

increase quotas to cover expenditures, the addition imposed on producing wells may not exceed the amount cut [from eliminated wells].[30]

In the 1180s the military forced purchases of merchant salt at high prices.

In 1184 (Chunxi 11) the Jingxi assistant fiscal intendant, Jiang Pu, stated that the military commanders of Jinzhou[a] established markets to compel the purchase of merchant salt, then sold it to people as a tax (*kemai*) at a high price.[31] This led to hardship for the merchants, and the people had to eat expensive salt. The emperor decreed for Jinzhou[a] to follow the law in allowing merchants to buy and sell at their convenience and never to establish markets to press [sellers or buyers].

In the 1180s the voucher policy collapsed as officials paid salters in depreciated bills, forced them to give extra salt, and charged merchants taxes they could not pay. The state then ameliorated the policy.

Initially Zhao Kai's monopoly policy was to have merchants bring money in for vouchers, while well salters boiled salt according to the quota and paid only a native products tax. The salt veins, however, often changed. They either grew *[p. 4476]* or shrank, and monthly production rose or fell. [Officials] gave worthless vouchers to merchants and collected payments from them.[32] This ruined the voucher policy. Pressed by merchants, well salters [were forced to] give extra quantities. For every load [100 catties] up to as many as 160 catties were added. Again, depleted wells were assigned an extra quota to work on. Because people wanted to own wells they accepted the high salt quota. When they had nothing to sell, they were unable to meet payments for the native product taxes.

---

[30] Hu proposed this on 1/18/1180 (*SHY* 28.11a).

[31] When Jiang Pu presented this memorial on 4/3/1184, Jinzhou[a] was already under the Quartermaster Bureau, not the circuit military authority (*SHY* 28.23a–b). In the Northern Song Jinzhou[a] was in Jingxi; in the Southern Song it was a part of Lizhou[a] (*SS* 89.2221, 2224).

[32] *Jian* ("at times") can also be taken to mean *guan* (government officials), who also paid salters with fraudulent voucher bills, as in *CYZJ jia* 14.9b.

Many resorted to slitting their throats or hanging themselves. Both the government and the people were in distress.[33]

In 1192 (Shaoxi 3) under Guangzong the minister of personnel (*libu shangshu*), Zhao Ruyu, stated:

> During the Shaoxing period (1131–1162), according to the salt policy deliberated by Zhao Kai, none of the wells had quotas; there were only prohibitions against private selling. Prefectures, counties, and towns all set up contract markets to muster merchants. The weight of salt was standardized so that all markets had one uniform price and there was no manipulation; the price, be it dear or cheap, depended on conditions of the time. Now, however, this policy has been totally abandoned. It is appropriate to direct the Sichuan Quartermaster Bureau (*zong[ling]suo*) to refer to the old policy.[34]

At the time Yang Fu was commissioner of general accounts (*zongji*). He eliminated above-quota taxes, closed exhausted wells, strictly enforced the contract market policy, prohibited the catty weight from exceeding what

---

[33] On 12/18/1187 the Sichuan military intendant and regulator reported on Kuizhou's quota salt distribution. He suggested that the fiscal intendant and quartermaster share the deficit to spare the people. This was approved (*SHY* 28.27b). On 3/22/1191, the Ministry of Finance addressed the Chengdufu fiscal intendant's memorial concerning 368,900 piculs of Longzhou well salt distributed to Pengzhou, Chongqingfu, Yongkangjun, Meizhou, and Chengdufu. It was not selling because salt prices generally had fallen in recent years, so that government salt would not sell [at high rates]. The Ministry requested a price reduction; this was approved (*SHY* 28.34a–b). On 4/7/1191 the Sichuan regulator requested that a procedure be completed before quota assessments [went forward] (*SHY* 28.34b–35a). On 7/9/1191 the Ministry of Finance supported Kuizhou's request to sell irregular salt; this was approved (*SHY* 28.35a). On 11/27/1191 a Nanjiao sacrificial pardon was issued for barren wells; there had been petitions [by those officials hoping to curb abuses] to close them and halt the charging of fraudulent taxes (*SHY* 28.35b).

[34] Zhao Ruyu memorialized on 6/9/1192: Zhao Kai, a Sichuan native and fiscal intendant in the 1130s, ran a tight administration under which there was no salt quota and private trade was prohibited. Each town had a trading center so merchants could trade easily. The salt price was the same everywhere so there was no competition. Unfortunately Zhao Kai's practices were forgotten. Now people drilled wells at will so the supply grew and the price fell. Zhao Ruyu requested a return to former ways; this was approved (*SHY* 28.37a).

was proper, and made punishments for private sales more severe.[35] The value of salt thus immediately shot up. [Yang] Fu further petitioned to abolish six salt shops set up by Lizhoudong Circuit's Military Intendancy and to give the salt money collected at fords and crossings to the salt shops of Xingzhou in [Lizhou]xi Circuit. Later the quartermaster, Chen Ye, eliminated the government wells' increased quotas.

In 1194 (Shaoxi 5) the Ministry of Finance stated:

> Tongchuanfu [Circuit]'s salt and liquor are major problems in Shu. Not only is salt subject to the native products tax when sold for government vouchers but also to other levies apart from the quota imposed by the prefectures and counties. The liquor purchase fee, arrival fee, and landing fee, for instance, are all new creations.

So prohibitions [on excess charges] were extended to offices in Chengdu, Tongchuan, and Lizhou[a] circuits.[36] In 1207 (Jiading 7) the emperor decreed for Sichuan salt wells to be controlled solely by the Quartermaster Bureau, but then the pacification commissioner, An Bing, on the pretext of bolstering the military for the autumn defense against barbarian raids, took over it again.[37]

---

[35] "Former" has been omitted before "contract market policy" (*CYZJ jia* 14.9a).

[36] This was memorialized on 1/1/1194 (*SHY* 28.39a). On 2/11/1195 the Lizhou[b] prefect memorialized that Lizhou[b], in southwestern Chengdufu, was a bleak place with paltry revenues. Its expenses were paid through well salt [sales] from the directorate in Pujiang (Qiongzhou[b]), in the amount assigned by the fiscal intendant. Since sales were low, a quota was imposed, which made the people flee. He suggested abolishing [the quota] and having the Quartermaster Bureau, the high commissioner, and the Fiscal Intendancy share costs as a long-term solution; this was approved (*SHY* 28.46b–47a).

[37] On 1/20/1211 the Sichuan regulator and quartermaster petitioned that annual tribute included 300,000 bolts of silk, or about 900,000 in cash used to reward the army. This had begun as a temporary measure but had been required every year since. They requested its abolition and put in its place an additional salt tribute for three years, after which it would be abolished except in Luzhou[b] and Xuzhou[c], where the taxes were light; this was approved (*SHY* 28.52a–b).

APPARATUS

Song Reign Periods: The Northern Song

Emperor	Reign Period	Years
Taizu 太祖	Jianlong 建隆	960-962
	Qiande 乾德	963-967
	Kaibao 開寶	968-975
Taizong 太宗	Taipingxingguo 太平興國	976-983
	Yongxi 雍熙	984-987
	Duangong 端拱	988-989
	Chunhua 淳化	990-994
	Zhidao 至道	995-997
Zhenzong 真宗	Xianping 咸平	998-1003
	Jingde 景德	1004-1007
	Dazhongxiangfu 大中祥符	1008-1016
	Tianxi 天禧	1017-1022
	Qianxing 乾興	1022
Renzong 仁宗	Tiansheng 天聖	1023-1031
	Mingdao 明道	1032-1033
	Jingyou 景祐	1034-1038
	Baoyuan 寶元	1038-1039
	Kangding 康定	1040
	Qingli 慶曆	1041-1048
	Huangyou 皇祐	1049-1053
	Zhihe 至和	1054-1055
	Jiayou 嘉祐	1056-1063
Yingzong 英宗	Zhiping 治平	1064-1067
Shenzong 神宗	Xining 熙寧	1068-1077
	Yuanfeng 元豐	1078-1085
Zhezong 哲宗	Yuanyou 元祐	1086-1093
	Shaosheng 紹聖	1094-1097
	Yuanfu 元符	1098-1100
Huizong 徽宗	Jianzhongjingguo 建中靖國	1101
	Chongning 崇寧	1102-1106
	Daguan 大觀	1107-1110
	Zhenghe 政和	1111-1117
	Chonghe 重和	1118
	Xuanhe 宣和	1119-1125
Qinzong 欽宗	Jingkang 靖康	1126

Song Reign Periods: The Southern Song

Emperor	Reign Period	Years
Gaozong 高宗	Jianyan 建炎	1127–1130
	Shaoxing 紹興	1131–1162
Xiaozong 孝宗	Longxing 隆興	1163–1164
	Qiandao 乾道	1165–1173
	Chunxi 淳熙	1174–1189
Guangzong 光	Shaoxi 紹熙	1190–1194
Ningzong 寧宗	Qingyuan 慶元	1195–1200
	Jiatai 嘉泰	1201–1204
	Kaixi 開禧	1205–1207
	Jiading 嘉定	1208–1224
Lizong 理宗	Baoqing 寶慶	1225–1227
	Shaoding 紹定	1228–1233
	Duanping 端平	1234–1236
	Jiaxi 嘉熙	1237–1240
	Chunyou 淳祐	1241–1252
	Baoyou 寶祐	1253–1258
	Kaiqing 開慶	1259
	Jingding 景定	1260–1264
Duzong 度宗	Xianchun 咸淳	1265–1274
Gongzong 恭宗	Deyou 德祐	1275
Duanzong 端宗	Jingyan 景炎	1276–1277
Zhao Bing 趙昺	Xiangxing 祥興	1278–1279

Weights and Measures

The following equivalents are approximate and largely follow Liangzhe and Huainan practices, which changed even over the course of the Song.

Unit of Measure	Chinese	English	Equivalent
liang	兩	tael	1 1/3 ounces
jin	斤	catty	16 taels; 1 1/3 pounds avoidupois
dou	斗	peck	5 catties
hudou	斛斗	bushel	10 pecks, later 5 pecks
dan	石	picul	50 catties
shuo	碩	picul	
nang	囊	"pocket"	approximately 500 catties
chou	籌	batch	100 catties
dan	檐	load	100 catties
xi	席	mat	116.5 catties or 220 catties
yin	引	load	200 catties
dai	袋	bag	300 catties; 6 piculs
luo	籮	basket	variable
guan	貫	string	1,000 cash (*wen*)
sheng	升	pint	1/10 peck
zhong	鐘		4 pecks; 6 bushels and 4 pecks
zhang	丈		10 Chinese feet
li	里	Chinese mile	0.25 mile
mu	畝	Chinese acre	1/6 acre
qing	頃	hectare	100 *mu*; about 15 acres

Place Names

Place names in the original text are often given in a shortened form. For readers' convenience the glossary provides geographical tags and administrative units, such as *lu* (circuit); *fu, zhou, jun* (prefectures); *xian* (county); *jian* (directorate); and *yanchang* (saltworks), which may have been omitted in the original, in both pinyin and characters.

Anhua (xian) 安化縣 (Yongxingjun)
Ansujun 安肅軍 (Hebeixi)
Anyi 安邑 (Yongxingjun)
Anzhou 安州 (Jinghubei)

Bazhou^a 巴州 (Lizhou)
Bazhou^b 霸州 (Hebeidong)
Baichi 白池 (Xixia)
Baima 白馬 (Jingxibei)
Baipo 白波 (Jingxibei)
Baishi (zhen) 白石鎮 (Qinfeng)
Baizhou 白州 (Guangnanxi)
Banpu 板浦 (Huainandong)
Baoanjun 保安軍 (Yongxingjun)
Baodejun 保德軍 (Hedong)
Baodingjun 保定軍 (Hebeidong)
Baoshun 包順 (Xihe)
Baoxingjun 寶興軍 (Hedong)
Baozhou 保州 (Hebeixi)
Beijing 北京 (Hebeidong)
Beiliu (xian) 北流縣 (Guangnanxi)
Beizhou 貝州 (Hebeidong)
Bian (he) 汴河
Bianliang 汴梁 (Jingji)
Binzhou^a 邠州 (Shaanxi/Yongxingjun)
Binzhou^b 濱州 (Hebeidong)
Binzhou^c 賓州 (Guangnanxi)

Bingzhou 并州 (Hedong)
Bozhou^a 博州 (Hebeidong)
Bozhou^b 亳州 (Huainandong)

Caizhou 蔡州 (Jingxibei)
Cangzhou 滄州 (Hebeidong)
Caozhou 曹州 (Jin)
Chanyuan 澶淵 (Hebeidong)
Chanzhou 澶州 (Hebeidong)
Changguo (xian) 昌國縣 (Liangzhe)
Changhuajun 昌化軍 (Guangnanxi)
Changqing 長清 (Liao)
Changting 長汀 (Fujian)
Changweichi 長尾池 (Xixia)
Changxi (xian) 長溪縣 (Fujian)
Changyuan 長垣 (Jingji)
Changzhou^a 昌州 (Zizhou)
Changzhou^b 常州 (Liangzhe)
Chaozhou 潮州 (Guangnandong)
Chengongtang 陳公塘 (Huainandong)
Chenliu 陳留 (Jingji)
Chenzhou^a 郴州 (Jinghunan)
Chenzhou^b 陳州 (Jingxibei)
Chengdufu (lu) 成都府路
Chengshi 乘氏 (Jingdongxi)
Chengzhou 成州 (Qinfeng)
Chizhou 池州 (Jiangnandong)

305

Chongmingzhen 崇明鎮 (Huainandong)

Chongqingfu 重慶府 (Kuizhou)

Chuzhou[a] 處州 (Liangzhe)

Chuzhou[b] 楚州 (Huainandong)

Chuzhou[c] 滁州 (Huainandong)

Chuan 川

Chuanxia 川峽

Chunzhou 春州 (Guangnandong)

Cixi (xian) 慈溪縣 (Liangzhe)

Cizhou[a] 慈州 (Hedong)

Cizhou[b] 磁州 (Hebeixi)

Daming (fu) 大名府 (Hebeidong)

Daning (jian) 大寧監 (Kuizhou)

Dashizhai 大石寨 (Hedong)

Datong (fu) 大同府 (Liao)

Daishan 岱山 (Liangzhe)

Daixian 代縣 (Qin-Han, Period of Division)

Daizhou 代州 (Hedong)

Danzhou[a] 丹州 (Shaanxi/Yongxingjun)

Danzhou[b] 儋州 (Guangnanxi)

Daozhou 道州 (Jinghunan)

Deqing (jun) 德清軍 (Liangzhe)

Deshunjun 德順軍 (Qinfeng)

Dezhou 德州 (Hebeidong)

Dengzhou[a] 登州 (Jingdongdong)

Dengzhou[b] 鄧州 (Jingxinan)

Dizhou 棣州 (Hebeidong)

Dingshuzhai 定戍寨 (Qinfeng)

Dingyuan (jun) 定遠軍 (Huainanxi)

Dingzhou[a] 鼎州 (Jinghubei)

Dingzhou[b] 定州 (Hebeixi)

Dongbeizhou 東北州 (Huainandong)

Dongguan 東莞 (Guangnandong)

Dongjing 東京 (Jingji)

Dongming 東明 (Jingji)

Douzhou 竇州 (Guangnanxi)

Duanzhou 端州 (Guangnandong)

Ezhou 鄂州 (Jinghubei)

Enzhou 恩州 (Hebeidong)

Fangzhou[a] 房州 (Jingxinan)

Fangzhou[b] 坊州 (Shaanxi/Yongxingjun)

Fenzhou 汾州 (Hedong)

Fengqiu 封丘 (Jingji)

Fengxiangfu 鳳翔府 (Qinfeng)

Fengzhou 鳳州 (Qinfeng)

Fugou 扶溝 (Jingji)

Fuguozhen 富國鎮 (Zizhou)

Fujian (lu) 福建路

Fushun (jian) 富順監 (Zizhou)

Fuzhou[a] 鄜州 (Shaanxi/Yongxingjun)

Fuzhou[b] 福州 (Fujian)

Fuzhou[c] 府州 (Hedong)

Fuzhou[d] 撫州 (Jiangnanxi)

Fuzhou[e] 復州 (Jinghubei)

Gan (shui) 贛水

Gaoling 高陵 (Yongxingjun)

Gaoyoujun 高郵軍 (Huainandong)

Gaozhou 高州 (Guangnanxi)

Gongjingzhen 公井鎮 (Zizhou)

Gongzhou[a] 龔州 (Guangnanxi)

Gongzhou[b] 鞏州 (Qinfeng)

Gongzhou[c] 拱州 (Jingji)

Gou (he) 溝河

Guduidu 骨堆渡 (Liao)

Guan 關

Guancheng 管城 (Jingxibei)

Guangdejun 廣德軍 (Jiangnandong)

Guanghuajun 光化軍 (Jingxinan)

Guangjijun 廣濟軍 (Jingdongxi)

Guangnandong (lu) 廣南東路

Guangnanxi (lu) 廣南西路

Guangxinjun 廣信軍 (Hebeixi)

Guangze 光澤 (Fujian)

Guangzhou^a 光州 (Huainanxi)

Guangzhou^b 廣州 (Guangnandong)

Guiyangjian 桂陽監 (Jinghunan)

Guizhou^a 歸州 (Jinghubei)

Guizhou^b 貴州 (Guangnanxi)

Guizhou^c 桂州 (Guangnanxi)

Guozhou 虢州 (Yongxingjun)

Haikou (zhen) 海口鎮 (Fujian)

Hailing 海陵 (Huainandong)

Haimen (dao) 海門島 (Huainandong)

Haiyan 海鹽 (Liangzhe)

Haiyan (yanchang) 海㝉鹽場 (Guangnandong)

Haizhou 海州 (Huainandong)

Hanyangjun 漢陽軍 (Jinghubei)

Hanzhou 漢州 (Chengdufu)

Hangzhou 杭州 (Liangzhe)

Haozhou 濠州 (Huainanxi)

He 河 (Yellow River)

Hebeidong (lu) 河北東路

Hebeixi (lu) 河北西路

Hedong (lu) 河東路

Hejian (fu) 河間府 (Hebeidong)

Henan (fu) 河南府 (Jingxibei)

heshuo 河朔 (N. of Yellow River)

Heyang 河陽 (Jingxibei)

Hezhong (fu) 河中府 (Yongxingjun)

Hezhou 和州 (Huainanxi)

Hengshanzhai 橫山寨 (Guangnanxi)

Hengzhou^a 衡州 (Jinghunan)

Hengzhou^b 橫州 (Guangnanxi)

Hongtaochi 紅桃池 (Xixia)

Hongzhou 洪州 (Jiangnanxi)

Huzhou 湖州 (Liangzhe)

Huating 華亭 (Liangzhe)

Huazhou^a 華州 (Shaanxi/Yongxingjun)

Huazhou^b 滑州 (Jingxibei)

Huazhou^c 化州 (Guangnanxi)

Huaidong 淮東 (Huainandong)

Huainan 淮南

Huainandong (lu) 淮南東路

Huainanxi (lu) 淮南西路

Huai (shui) 淮水

Huaixi 淮西 (Huainanxi)

Huaiyang (jun) 淮陽軍 (Jingdongdong)

Huaizhou 懷州 (Hebeixi)

Huanzhou 環州 (Yongxingjun)

Huangyan 黃巖 (Liangzhe)

Huangzhou 黃州 (Huainanxi)

Huize 惠澤 (Huainandong)

Huizhou^a 惠州 (Guangnandong)

Huizhou^b 會州 (Qinfeng)

Huoshanjun 火山軍 (Hedong)

Huozhou 貨州 (Guangnanxi)

Jiyin 濟陰 (Jingdongxi)

Jizhou^a 吉州 (Jiangnanxi)

Jizhou^b 濟州 (Jingdongxi)

Jizhou^c 冀州 (Hebeidong)

Jiawa 賈瓦 (Yongxingjun)

Jiaxing (fu) 嘉興府 (Liangzhe)

Jianchangjun 建昌軍 (Jiangnanxi)

Jiankang (fu) 建康府 (Jiangnandong)

Jiannan (xilu) 劍南西路 (central Sichuan)

Jianning (fu) 建寧府 (Fujian)

Jianwei　犍爲 (Chengdufu)

Jianweizhai　鹼隄寨 (Qinfeng)

Jianzhou[a]　建州 (Fujian)

Jianzhou[b]　劍州 (Lizhou)

Jiangdong　江東 (Jiangnandong)

Jianglingfu　江陵府 (Jinghubei)

Jiangnan　江南

Jiangnandong (lu)　江南東路

Jiangnanxi (lu)　江南西路

Jiangningfu　江寧府 (Jiangnandong)

Jiangxi　江西 (Jiangnanxi)

Jiangyin (jun)　江陰軍 (Liangzhe)

Jiangzhou[a]　江州 (Jiangnandong)

Jiangzhou[b]　絳州 (Hedong)

Jiaozhi　交趾 (N. and central Vietnam)

Jie (he)　界河

Jiezhou　階州 (Qinfeng)

Jincheng (xian)　晉城縣 (Hedong)

Jinzhou[a]　金州 (Jingxinan)

Jinzhou[b]　晉州 (Hedong)

Jingdongdong (lu)　京東東路

Jingdongxi (lu)　京東西路

Jinghu (lu)　荊湖路

Jinghubei (lu)　荊湖北路

Jinghunan (lu)　荊湖南路

Jingji (lu)　京畿路

Jingjiangfu　靜江府 (Guangnanxi)

Jingkang (yanchang)　靜康鹽場 (Guangnandong)

Jingxi (lu)　京西路

Jingxibei (lu)　京西北路

Jingxinan (lu)　京西南路

Jingyang　涇陽 (Yongxingjun)

Jingzhaofu　京兆府 (Yongxingjun)

Jingzhou　涇州 (Qinfeng)

Junzhou[a]　均州 (Jingxinan)

Junzhou[b]　筠州 (Jiangnanxi)

Kaifeng (fu)　開封府 (Jingji)

Kaocheng　考城 (Jingji)

Kelanjun　岢嵐軍 (Hedong)

Kuaiji　會稽 (Liangzhe)

Kuizhou　夔州 (Kuizhou)

Kuizhou (lu)　夔州路

Laizhou　萊州 (Jingdongdong)

Lanzhou　嵐州 (Hedong)

Leizhou　雷州 (Guangnanxi)

Lifeng (jian)　利豐監 (Huainandong)

Liyang　櫟陽 (Yongxingjun)

Lizhou[a] (lu)　利州路

Lizhou[b]　黎州 (Chengdufu)

Lizhoudong (lu)　利州東路 (Lizhou)

Lizhouxi (lu)　利州西路 (Lizhou)

Liancheng (xian)　蓮城縣 (Fujian)

Lianjiang (xian)　連江縣 (Fujian)

Lianshui (jun)　漣水軍 (Huainandong)

Lianzhou[a]　連州 (Guangnandong)

Lianzhou[b]　廉州 (Guangnanxi)

Liangchuan　兩川

Liangguang　兩廣

Liangzhe (lu)　兩浙路

Liangzhedong (lu)　兩浙東路 (Liangzhe)

Liangzhexi (lu)　兩浙西路 (Liangzhe)

Liaozhou　遼州 (Hedong)

Lin'an (fu)　臨安府 (Liangzhe)

Linjiangjun　臨江軍 (Jiangnanxi)

Linpingjian　臨平監 (Liangzhe)

Linqiong　臨邛 (Chengdufu)

Linyixian　臨猗縣 (Shanxi Province)

Linzhou　麟州 (Hedong)

Lingjing (jian)　陵井監 (Chengdufu)

Lingnan　嶺南 (S. China)

Lingzhou 靈州 (Xixia)

Liuzhou 柳州 (Guangnanxi)

Longdefu 隆德府 (Hedong)

Longxingfu 隆興府 (Jiangnanxi)

Longzhou 隴州 (Qinfeng)

Luzhou[a] 廬州 (Huainanxi)

Luzhou[b] 瀘州 (Zizhou)

Luzhou[c] 潞州 (Hedong)

Luo (shui) 洛水

Luoyang 洛陽 (Jingxibei)

Luoyao 洛要 (Huainandong)

Luoyuan (xian) 羅源縣 (Fujian)

Machengchi 馬城池 (Hedong)

Meizhou 梅州 (Guangnandong)

Mengzhou[a] 蒙州 (Guangnanxi)

Mengzhou[b] 孟州 (Jingxibei)

Miying 密鸚 (Liangzhe)

Mizhou 密州 (Jingdongdong)

Mianzhou 綿州 (Chengdufu)

Min 閩

Minqing 閩清 (Fujian)

Minyue 閩越 (Fujian)

Minzhou 岷州 (Qinfeng)

Minghe (yanchang) 鳴鶴鹽場 (Liangzhe)

Mingzhou[a] 洺州 (Hebeixi)

Mingzhou[b] 明州 (Liangzhe)

Mozhou 莫州 (Hebeidong)

Muzhou 睦州 (Liangzhelu)

Nan'anjun 南安軍 (Jiangnanxi)

Nanenzhou 南恩州 (Guangnandong)

Nanjianzhou 南劍州 (Fujian)

Nanjing[a] (fu) 南京府 (Jingdongxi)

Nanjing[b] (jian) 南井監 (Zizhou)

Nankangjun 南康軍 (Jiangnandong)

Nanling 南嶺 (mountains of S. China)

Nanxiong (zhou) 南雄州 (Guangnandong)

Nanyi (zhou) 南儀州 (Guangnanxi)

Ningde (xian) 寧德縣 (Fujian)

Ningguo 寧國 (Jiangnandong)

Ninghua (jun) 寧化軍 (Hedong)

Ningzhou 寧州 (Yongxingjun)

Pengxi 蓬溪 (Zizhou)

Pengzhou 蓬州 (Zizhou)

Pingdingjun 平定軍 (Hedong)

Pingjiangfu 平江府 (Liangzhe)

Pujiang (jian) 蒲江監 (Chengdufu)

Puzhou 濮州 (Jingdongxi)

Qizhou[a] 齊州 (Jingdongxi)

Qizhou[b] 祁州 (Hebeixi)

Qizhou[c] 蘄州 (Huainanxi)

Qianning (zhen) 乾寧鎮 (Hebeidong)

Qianqingzhen 錢清鎮 (Liangzhe)

Qiantang (jiang) 錢塘江

Qiantang (xian) 錢塘縣 (Liangzhe)

Qianzhou[a] 虔州 (Jiangnanxi)

Qianzhou[b] 乾州 (Shaanxi/Yongxingjun)

Qianzhou[c] 黔州 (Kuizhou)

Qinfeng (lu) 秦鳳路

Qinzhou[a] 欽州 (Guangnanxi)

Qinzhou[b] 秦州 (Shaanxi/Qinfeng)

Qingchengjun 慶成軍 (Yongxingjun)

Qingliu (xian) 清流縣 (Fujian)

Qingzhou 青州 (Jingdongdong)

Qiongzhou[a] 瓊州 (Guangnanxi)

Qiongzhou[b] 邛州 (Chengdufu)

Quxian 衢縣 (Zhejiang Province)

Quzhou 衢州 (Liangzhe)

Quanzhou[a] 全州 (Jinghunan)

Quanzhou[b] 泉州 (Fujian)

Raozhou 饒州 (Jiangnandong)

Renhe (xian) 仁和縣 (Liangzhe)

Ronghe 榮河 (Yongxingjun)

Rongzhou[a] 容州 (Guangnanxi)

Rongzhou[b] 融州 (Guangnanxi)

Rongzhou[c] 戎州 (Zizhou)

Rongzhou[d] 榮州 (Zizhou)

Rugao 如皋 (Huainandong)

Ruzhou 汝州 (Jingxibei)

Runzhou 潤州 (Liangzhe)

Sanmen 三門 (Yongxingjun)

Shanfu 陝府 (Yongxingjun)

Shanzhou[a] 單州 (Jingdongxi)

Shanzhou[b] 陝州 (Shaanxi/Yongxingjun)

Shanghang 上杭 (Fujian)

Shangqiu 商丘 (Henan Province)

Shangyu 上虞 (Liangzhe)

Shangzhou 商州 (Yongxingjun)

Shaowujun 邵武軍 (Fujian)

Shaoxingfu 紹興府 (Liangzhe)

Shaozhou[a] 韶州 (Guangnandong)

Shaozhou[b] 邵州 (Jinghunan)

Shezhou 歙州 (Jiangnandong)

Shenzhou 深州 (Hebeixi)

Shengzhou 昇州 (Jiangnandong)

Shikang (xian) 石康縣 (Guangnanxi)

Shiyan 石堰 (Liangzhe)

Shizhou[a] 施州 (Kuizhou)

Shizhou[b] 石州 (Hedong)

Shouzhou 壽州 (Huainanxi)

Shu 蜀

Shuzhou 舒州 (Huainanxi)

Shuangsui (yanchang) 雙遂鹽場 (Liangzhe)

Si (shui) 泗水

Sizhou 泗州 (Huainandong)

Songcheng 宋城 (Jingdongxi)

Suzhou[a] 蘇州 (Liangzhe)

Suzhou[b] 宿州 (Huainandong)

Suanzao 酸棗 (Jingji)

Suizhou[a] 隨州 (Jingxinanlu)

Suizhou[b] 遂州 (Zizhou)

Taikang 太康 (Jingji)

Taining (xian) 泰寧縣 (Fujian)

Taipingzhou 太平州 (Jiangnandong)

Taiyuan (fu) 太原府 (Hedong)

Taizhou[a] 台州 (Liangzhe)

Taizhou[b] 泰州 (Huainandong)

Tanzhou 潭州 (Jinghunan)

Tangcun 湯村 (Liangzhe)

Tangzhou 唐州 (Jingxinan)

Taoluo 濤洛 (Jingdongdong)

Taoshan 桃山 (Liao)

Tengzhou 藤州 (Guangnanxi)

Tianfu (yanchang) 天富鹽場 (Liangzhe)

Tingzhou 汀州 (Fujian)

Tongchuanfulu 潼川府路 (S. Song Zizhou)

Tonglijun 通利軍 (Hebeixi)

Tongyuanzhai 通遠寨 (Qinfeng)

Tongzhou[a] 同州 (Shaanxi/Yongxingjun)

Tongzhou[b] 通州 (Huainandong)

Wachi 瓦池 (Xixia)

Wan'anjun 萬安軍 (Guangnanxi)

Wanzhou 萬州 (Kuizhou)

Weicheng 韋城 (Jingxibei)

Weishengjun 威勝軍 (Hedong)

Weishi 尉氏 (Jingji)

Wei (shui) 渭水

Weizhou[a] 濰州 (Jingdongdong)

Weizhou[b] 渭州 (Shaanxi/Qinfeng)

Weizhou[c] 衛州 (Hebeixi)

Wenquanchi 溫泉池 (Xixia)

Wenxi (xian) 聞喜縣 (Yongxingjun)

Wenzhou[a] 溫州 (Liangzhe)

Wenzhou[b] 文州 (Lizhou)

Wuchi 烏池 (Xixia)

Wuping (xian) 武平縣 (Fujian)

Wushatouzhen 烏沙頭鎮 (Jinghubei)

Wuweijun 無爲軍 (Huainanxi)

Wuxing (jun) 吳興郡 (Liangzhe)

Wuzhou[a] 梧州 (Guangnanxi)

Wuzhou[b] 婺州 (Liangzhe)

Xihe (lu) 熙河路 (Qinfeng)

Xihezhou 西和州 (Lizhou)

Xijiang 西江

Xijing 西京 (Jingxibei)

Xixia 西夏

Xizhou 隰州 (Hedong)

Xiasha (yanchang) 下砂鹽場 (Liangzhe)

Xiazhou 峽州 (Jinghubei)

Xianping 咸平 (Jingji)

Xianzhou 憲州 (Hedong)

Xiangfu 祥符 (Jingji)

Xiangyi 襄邑 (Jingji)

Xiangzhou[a] 相州 (Hebeixi)

Xiangzhou[b] 襄州 (Jingxinan)

Xiangzhou[c] 象州 (Guangnanxi)

Xiaohai (zhai) 小海寨 (Huainandong)

Xieliang 解梁 (Yongxingjun)

Xie (xian) 解縣 (Yongxingjun)

Xiezhou 解州 (Yongxingjun)

Xin'anjun 信安軍 (Hebeidong)

Xinyangjun 信陽軍 (Jingxibei)

Xinzheng 新鄭 (Jingxibei)

Xinzhou[a] 忻州 (Hedong)

Xinzhou[b] 信州 (Jiangnandong)

Xing'an (xian) 興安縣 (Guangnanxi)

Xingguojun 興國軍 (Jiangnanxi)

Xinghuajun 興化軍 (Fujian)

Xingrenfu 興仁府 (Jingdongxi)

Xingyuanfu 興元府 (Lizhou)

Xingzai 行在 (Liangzhe)

Xingzhou[a] 興州 (Lizhou)

Xingzhou[b] 邢州 (Hebeixi)

Xiongzhou 雄州 (Hebeidong)

Xiuzhou 秀州 (Liangzhe)

Xuzhou[a] 徐州 (Jingdongxi)

Xuzhou[b] 許州 (Jingxi)

Xuzhou[c] 敘州 (Jinghubei)

Xuanzhou 宣州 (Jiangnandong)

Xunzhou[a] 循州 (Guangnandong)

Xunzhou[b] 潯州 (Guangnanxi)

Yazhou 崖州 (Guangnanxi)

Yancheng 鹽城 (Huainandong)

Yanchuanzhai 鹽川寨 (Qinfeng)

Yanguan (chang) 鹽官場 (Liangzhe)

Yanling 鄢陵 (Jingji)

Yanshan 鹽山 (Hebeidong)

Yanzhou[a] 兗州 (Jingdongxi)

Yanzhou[b] 延州 (Shaanxi/Yongxingjun)

Yangcun 楊村 (Liangzhe)

Yangjiang (xian) 陽江縣 (Guangnandong)

Yangwu (xian) 陽武縣 (Jingji)

Yangzhou[a] 揚州 (Huainandong)

Yangzhou[b] 洋州 (Lizhou)

Yaozhou 耀州 (Yongxingjun)

Yilong 儀隴 (Lizhou)

Yizhou[a] 沂州 (Jingdongdong)

Yizhou[b] 宜州 (Guangnanxi)

Yizhou[c] 儀州 (Shaanxi/Qinfeng)

Yizhou[d] (lu) 益州路 (S. Song Chengdufu)

Yinxian 鄞縣 (Liangzhe)

Yingchangfu 潁昌府 (Jingxibei)

Yingtianfu 應天府 (Jingdongxi)

Yingzhou[a] 瀛州 (Hebeidong)

Yingzhou[b] 潁州 (Jingxibei)

Yingzhou[c] 郢州 (Jingxinan)

Yongding (jun) 永定軍 (Guangnanxi)

Yongfeng (qu) 永豐渠 (Yongxingjun)

Yongjia (yanchang) 永嘉鹽場 (Liangzhe)

Yongjingjun 永靜軍 (Hebeidong)

Yongkangjun 永康軍 (Chengdufu)

Yongli (jian) 永利監 (Hedong)

Yongqiu 雍丘 (Jingji)

Yongxingjun (lu) 永興軍路

Yongzhou[a] 邕州 (Guangnanxi)

Yongzhou[b] 永州 (Jinghunan)

Youxi (xian) 尤溪縣 (Fujian)

Yujing (jian) 淯井監 (Zizhou)

Yulinzhou 鬱林州 (Guangnanxi)

Yuyao (xian) 餘姚縣 (Liangzhe)

Yuanzhou[a] 原州 (Shaanxi/Qinfeng)

Yuanzhou[b] 袁州 (Jiangnanxi)

Yuezhou[a] 越州 (Liangzhe)

Yunzhou[a] 鄆州 (Jingdongxi)

Yunzhou[b] 筠州 (Jiangnanxi)

Zezhou 澤州 (Hedong)

Zhangzhou 漳州 (Fujian)

Zhaozhou[a] 昭州 (Guangnanxi)

Zhaozhou[b] 趙州 (Hebeixi)

Zhedong 浙東 (Liangzhe)

Zhejiang 浙江

Zhexi 浙西 (Liangzhe)

Zhezhong 浙中 (Liangzhe)

Zhendingfu 真定府 (Hebeixi)

Zhenjiang (fu) 鎮江府 (Liangzhe)

Zhenrongjun 鎮戎軍 (Qinfeng)

Zhenzhou[a] 真州 (Huainandong)

Zhenzhou[b] 鎮州 (Hebeixi)

Zhengzhou 鄭州 (Jingxibei)

Zhongli (xian) 鍾離縣 (Huainanxi)

Zhongmou 中牟 (Jingji)

Zhongzhou 忠州 (Kuizhou)

Zhucheng 諸城 (Shandong Province)

Zhuyajun 朱崖軍 (Guangnanxi)

Zhuolunzhai 濁輪砦 (Hedong)

Zizhou 梓州 (Zizhou)

Zizhou (lu) 梓州路

Zuocheng 阼城 (Jingxibei)

People

An Bing　安丙
An Dun　安惇
An Lushan　安祿山

Bao Zheng　包拯

Cai Jing　蔡京
Cai Li　蔡礪
Cai Que　蔡確
Cai Ting　蔡挺
Chen Anshi　陳安石
Chen Chengzhi　陳誠之
Chen Cisheng　陳次升
Chen Shu　陳恕
Chen Si (also pron. Cai)　陳偲
Chen Sunzhi　陳損之
Chen Xian　陳峴
Chen Ye　陳曄
Cheng Jie　程价
Cheng Kan　程戡
Chi You　蚩尤

Dai Xiaoba　戴小八
Deng Runfu　鄧潤甫
Diwu Qi　第五琦
Diao Zhan　刁湛
Ding Du　丁度
Ding Wei　丁謂
Du Chengrui　杜丞睿
Du Jie　都潔

Fan Chengda　范成大
Fan Chunren　范純仁
Fan E　范鍔
Fan Xiang　范祥
Fan Xun　范峋
Fan Zhongyan　范仲淹
Fan Ziqi　范子奇
Fan Zongjie　范宗傑
Fan Zuyu　范祖禹
Fang La　方臘
Fu Qiu　傅求
Fu Zide　傅自得

Gao Bo　高鎛
Gong Wei　拱偉
Guan Zhong　管仲
Guo Bi　郭泌
Guo Gai　郭概
Guo Wei　郭維

Han Bi　韓壁
Han Dunli　韓敦立
Han Jiang　韓絳
Han Qi　韓琦
Han Tuozhou　韓侂冑
Han Zhen　韓縝
Hao Zongchen　郝宗臣
He Tan　何郯
He Zhongli　何中立
Hou Shuxian　侯叔獻
Hu Tingzhi　胡庭直

Hu Wufu　胡吳傅
Hu Yuanzhi　胡元質
Huang Bing　黃炳
Huang Jiang　黃降
Huang Lian　黃廉
Huang Lü　黃履
Huang Qian　黃遷
Huang Qianhou　黃潛厚
Huang Shou　黃受
Huang Zhen　黃震
Huang Zhuogui　黃捉鬼

Jia Dan　郟亶
Jia Qing　賈青
Jia Sidao　賈似道
Jian Xuchen　謇序辰
Jian Zhoufu　謇周輔
Jiang Ben　蔣賁
Jiang Fei　蔣芾
Jiang Pu　江溥
Jiang Zhiqi　蔣之奇

Kong Yanzhi　孔延之

Li Bailu　李百祿
Li Biru　李弼孺
Li Can　李參
Li Cha　李察
Li Changtu　李昌圖
Li Cheng　李憕
Li Chengmai　李承邁
Li Chengzhi　李承之
Li Cong　李琮
Li Deming　李德明
Li Fu　李敷
Li Fugui　李復圭

Li Ji　李稷
Li Jihe　李繼和
Li Jipeng　李繼捧
Li Jiqian　李繼遷
Li Nangong　李南公
Li Pei　李佩
Li Ping　李平
Li Shan　李善
Li Shun　李順
Li Suzhi　李肅之
Li Weiqing　李惟清
Li Yan　李彥
Li Yigeng　李夷庚
Li Yuanhao　李元昊
Li Yuqing　李餘慶
Li Yuquan　李與權
Li Zhixiao　李知孝
Li Zi　李諮
Liang Chengda　梁成大
Liang Ding　梁鼎
Liang Rujia　梁汝嘉
Liang Shicheng　梁師成
Liao En　廖恩
Lin Jie　林邑
Lin Te　林特
Lin Yu　林豫
Liu Anshi　劉安世
Liu Bi　劉壁
Liu Shu　劉淑
Liu Wei　劉威
Liu Yan　劉晏
Liu Yi　劉誼
Liu Zhi　劉摯
Liu Zuo　劉佐
Lou Yi　樓異
Lu Bing　盧秉

Lu Shimin　陸師閔
Lü Gongzhu　呂公著
Lü Tao　呂陶
Lü Yihao　呂頤浩

Ma Cheng　馬城
Mao Zhu　毛注
Meng Kui　孟揆
Meng Yu　孟庾
Ming Tuo　明槖

Ouyang Xiu　歐陽修

Pang Chong　龐崇
Pi Gongbi　皮公弼

Qian Duanli　錢端禮
Qin Gui　秦檜
Qu Tingfa　瞿霆發

Sang Hongyang　桑弘羊
Shangguan Jun　上官均
Shao Dashou　邵大受
Shen Diao　沈調
Shen Fu　沈扶
Shen Kuo　沈括
Shen Li　沈立
Shen Xiyan　沈希顏
Sheng Du　盛度
Shi Miyuan　史彌遠
Shi Yuanchang　施元長
Sima Guang　司馬光
Song Di　宋迪
Song Xiang　宋庠
Su Che　蘇轍
Susha Juzi　夙沙瞿子 or 宿沙瞿子

Su Shi　蘇軾
Su Song　蘇頌
Sun Fu　孫甫
Sun Jiong　孫迥
Sun Lu　孫路
Sun Mian　孫冕
Sun Sheng　孫升
Sun Zixiu　孫子秀

Tang Zhongyou　唐仲友
Tang Zhuo　唐琢
Tian Jing　田京
Tian Kuang　田況
Tong Guan　童貫

Wan Qi　萬奇
Wang Anshi　王安石
Wang Bowen　王博文
Wang Boyu　王伯瑜
Wang Buzhi　王補之
Wang Di　王覿
Wang Ding　王鼎
Wang Fu　王黼
Wang Gongchen　王拱辰
Wang Guangzu　王光祖
Wang Jing　王景
Wang Qi　王琪
Wang Sui　王隨
Wang Xianfu　王咸孚
Wang Xu　王序
Wang Yansou　王巖叟
Wang Yao　王繇
Wang Zhongqian　王仲千
Wang Zijing　王子京
Wang Zongwang　王宗望
Wei Bochu　魏伯芻

Wei Lun　魏綸

Wen Yanbo　文彥博

Weng Zhongtong　翁仲通

Wu Chuan　吳傳

Wu Juhou　吳居厚

Xia Zhiwen　夏之文

Xianyu Zhishao　鮮于之邵

Xiong Ben　熊本

Xu Erbaijiu　徐二百九

Xu Fu　徐俯

Xu Shou　徐壽

Xu Yuan　許元

Xue Sichang　薛嗣昌

Xue Xiang　薛向

Yan Mengbiao　晏夢彪

Yan Shilu　顏師魯

Yan Zhenqing　顏真卿

Yang Fu　楊輔

Yang Youyi　楊由義

Yang Yungong　楊允恭

Yao Xian　姚憲

Ye Fen　葉份

Ye Heng　葉衡

Ye Sanqiansi　葉三千四

Ye Shi　葉適

Yin Zhuang　尹椿

Ying Mengming　應孟明

Yu Jing　余靖

Yu Xianqing　俞獻卿

Yu Zhaohu　俞召虎

Yu Zhouxun　魚周詢

Yue Fei　岳飛

Zeng Bu　曾布

Zeng Dian　曾點

Zeng Lian　曾連

Zeng Mo　曾默

Zhan Yizhi　詹儀之

Zhang Cha　張察

Zhang Chu　張芻

Zhang Chun　張純

Zhang Dexiang　張得象

Zhang Dun　章惇

Zhang Fangping　張方平

Zhang Gen　張根

Zhang Guan　張觀

Zhang Jie　張頡

Zhang Jing[a]　張靖

Zhang Jing[b]　張覿

Zhang Jingwen　張景溫

Zhang Lun　張綸

Zhang Qiyun　張其昀

Zhang Ruji　張汝楫

Zhang Ruxian　張汝賢

Zhang Shangying　張商英

Zhang Shi　張栻

Zhang Shicheng　張士澄

Zhang Xiangzhong　張象中

Zhang Yong　張詠

Zhang Yuan　張愿

Zhang Yuanfang　張元方

Zhao Bian　趙抃

Zhao Buliu　趙不流

Zhao Buyi　趙不已

Zhao Ding　趙鼎

Zhao Gonghuan　趙公澣

Zhao Gou　趙構

Zhao Kai　趙開

Zhao Kuangyin　趙匡胤

Zhao Kui　趙奎

Zhao Lingrong 趙令鑠

Zhao Pu 趙普

Zhao Ruyu 趙汝愚

Zhao Shu 趙樞

Zhao Yancao 趙彥操

Zhao Yong 趙用

Zhao Zhidao 趙至道

Zhao Zi 趙滋

Zheng Wenbao 鄭文寶

Zhou Ge 周革

Zhou Yin 周尹

Zhou Zhan 周湛

Zhu Chuping 朱初平

Zhu Chuyue 朱處約

Zhu Mian 朱勔

Zhu Taifu 朱台符

Zhu Xiyan 朱晞顏

Zhu Yanbo 朱彥博

Zhu Yi[a] 朱異

Zhu Yi[b] 朱熠

Zou Hao 鄒浩

Salt Monopoly and General Terms

ancang 庵倉 (hut storehouse for pond salt)

anchasi 按察司 (intendant-inspector)

anfushi 安撫使 (military intendant)

anfusiganban gongshi 安撫司幹辦公事 (Military Intendancy staff and supervisors)

anfu zhizhishi 安撫制置使 (military intendant)

anzhi 安置 (detention)

aobo 熬波 ("simmering the waves"; to boil sea water for salt)

aodi yanqian 敖底鹽錢 (a fee, for clerks)

ba 霸 ("hegemon")

baiyan 白鹽 (white salt)

baojia 保甲 (peasant militia unit)

beiding 備丁 ("preparation-workers"; salt laborers)

ben 本 (lit. "root"; foundation)

benji 本紀 (emperors' biographies)

benqian 本錢 (production funds)

bijiao 比較 (official performance evaluation)

bishucheng 祕書丞 (executive assistant of Palace Library)

bianguan 編管 (exile under custody)

biannianti 編年體 (chronological annalistic history)

bianpei 編配 (exile under surveillance)

bianqian huizi 便錢會子 ("convenience currency"; paper money)

bianxiu sansi tiaoliguan 編修三司條例官 (compiler of regulations for Ministry of Finance)

bing'an 兵案 (Military Section of *yantiesi*)

bingbu 兵部 (Ministry of War)

bingzhi 兵制 (military system)

caifu 財賦 (wealth and taxes)

canyan 蠶鹽 ("silkworm salt")

canzhi zhengshi 參知政事 (vice-chief councilor)

caochen 漕臣 (supply official fiscal intendant; fiscal vice-intendant)

caoqian 漕錢 (cash for transport)

caosi 漕司 (Fiscal Intendancy; short term for *zhuanyunsi*)

cha'an 茶案 (Tea Section of the Salt and Iron Bureau)

chafangshi 察訪使 (investigation commissioner)

chanyanfa 產鹽法 (salt production tax policy)

chang 場 (production site, procurement site or sales site for sea salt)

changliqian 常例錢 (customary delivery fee charged transporters)

changpingqian 常平錢 (Ever-normal Granary reserves)

changyin 長引 ("long" salt voucher for outside the circuit, valid for one year)

chao 鈔 (vouchers of exchange; salt vouchers)

chaofa 鈔法 (voucher law; salt voucher policy)

chaoyin 鈔引 (vouchers in exchange for cash, bills, gold, silver)

chenghu 鐺戶 ("pan household"; earth salt producer household)

chengwulang 承務郎 (gentleman-for-rendering-service)

chengyilang 承議郎 (gentleman-for-discussion)

chi 敕 (category of law)

chidie 敕牒 (official certification; document of appointment)

chiyan 赤鹽 (red salt)

chiyan 池鹽 ("pond salt"; lake salt)

chongyishi 崇儀使 (commissioner for fostering propriety)

chou 籌 (an instance of firing a salt stove)

chouyan 臭鹽 (smelly salt)

cipei 刺配 (see *pei*)

cishi 刺史 (prefect)

cuijianchang 催煎場 (production-supervisory saltern)

cuijianguan 催煎官 (production-supervisory official)

cuijianzhi 催煎制 ("production-supervisory system"; saltern boiling)

dajing 大井 (large-mouthed salt wells)

dali sicheng 大理寺丞 (assistant minister of High Court of Justice)

danong 大農 (Office of Agricultural Supervision)

daqian 大錢 ("big cash"; equal to 10 "small cash")

Daqing Hall 大慶殿 (the Daqing Hall)

dasinong 大司農 (Office of Agricultural Supervision)

dasinong zhongcheng 大司農中丞 (privy councilor)

daxu 大胥 (chief clerk)

daimai 帶賣 ("carrying sales"; additional government salt sales to resolve gluts)

daizhi 待制 (edict attendant)

danzi 單子 (a sort of tax notification)

dangshichao 當十鈔 ("equal to 10 vouchers")

daoxiao 倒硝 ("pouring saltpeter"; to refine saltpeter)

dibian 糴便 (government payment in vouchers)

difangzhi 地方志 (local gazetteer)

dianli 典禮 (institutions)

dianzhong shi yushi 殿中侍御史 (palace censor)

ding yanjuan 丁鹽絹 ("adult male salt silk" tax)

ding yanqian 丁鹽錢 ("adult male salt money" tax)

duchachang 都茶場 (Tea Office)

duda xunzhuo siyanguan 都大巡捉私鹽官 (smuggled-salt intendant)

dudie 度牒 (Buddhist ordination license)

dusheng 都省 (Department of Ministries; variant of *shangshu sheng*)

dutongzhi 都統制 (supreme commandant)

duyan'an 都鹽案 (Capital Salt Supply Section of the Salt and Iron Bureau)

duyancang 都鹽倉 (city salt storehouse)

duyanyuan 都鹽院 (Salt Directorate)

duyanyuan jianguan 都鹽院監官 (director of salt)

duzhang 都長 (superintendant)

duzhi 度支 (commissioner of revenue)

duzhi langzhong 度支郎中 (director of Office of Funds)

duzhi panguan 度支判官 (supervisor of funds)

duzhishi 度支使 (commissioner of revenue)

duzhisi 度支司 (Tax Bureau)

duzhi yuanwailang 度支員外郎 (vice-director of the Office of Funds)

du zhuanyunshi 都轉運使 (fiscal intendant-general)

duanyin 短引 ("short" salt voucher for within the circuit, valid 3 months)

duidai 對帶 (exchange of vouchers at a stipulated proportion of old to new issues)

duihuanquan 兌換券 (bills of exchange; *huizi*)

duitie 對貼 ("direct subsidization"; merchant cash payment for goods)

Erya 爾雅 (earliest Chinese lexicographical work)

fayun fushi 發運副使 (assistant intendant of transport)

fayunshi 發運使 (transport intendant)

fayunsi 發運司 (Transport Intendancy)

fangchangqian 坊場錢 ("shops and yards" money)

feiqian 飛錢 ("flying money"; bill of exchange for various goods)

fengzhuang 封樁 (reserves)

fengzhuangku 封樁庫 (Emergency Reserves Storehouse)

fu 府 (prefecture)

fu 復 (exempt)

fubingzhi 府兵制 (self-supporting Tang garrison militia system)

fugan 撫幹 (Military Intendancy staff member; abbreviation of *anfusi ganban gongshi*)

fuguo qiangbing 富國強兵 ("enrich the country, strengthen the army")

fumu guan 父母官 (prefects and county magistrates)

fushi 副使 (assistant commissioner)

fuyan 浮鹽 ("floating salt"; above-quota salt)

ganban gongshi 幹辦公事 (managing supervisors; circuit intendant staff)

gang 綱 (government salt convoy; salt flotilla)

gangyunren 綱運人 (government convoy laborers)

gaochi 告敕 (imperial certificates of appointment for lesser officials; also, *guan'gao*)

gaoshen 告身 (appointment certificate; also, *guan'gao*)

Gaozong Xinianlu 高宗系年錄 (The annals of Gaozong)

ge 格 (type of legal regulation)

gongbu 工部 (Ministry of Works)

gongju 公據 ("public deed")

gongping 公憑 (proof of identity or ownership; *pingyou*)

gongshi 貢士 (nominee for office)

gongshiku 公使庫 (local office with funds earmarked for official expenses)

goudang gongshi 勾當公事 (managing supervisors; circuit intendant staff)

gouyuan 勾院 (supervisor)

gu 鹽 (salt; "to pickle")

guyan 鹽鹽 (pond salt)

guajian 刮鹼 (to scrape sea salt crystals off drying bed soil)

guatu 刮土 (to scrape sea salt crystals off drying bed soil)

guan 官 (government officials)

guan'gao 官告 (certificate conferring office, esp. for high officials)

guanmai 官賣 (government sales of salt)

guanxiqian 官溪錢 ("government stream fees")

guanyu 官鬻 (government sales of salt)

guanzi 關子 (exchange certificates; silver and gold currency)

Guochao huiyao 國朝會要 (Song dynasty institutions)

guohu 鍋戶 ("cauldron households"; sea salt producers)

guoshi 國史 (national histories)

guoshui 過稅 (transit tax)

haicang 海倉 (sea salt storehouse)

haiyan 海鹽 (sea salt)

Hanlin xueshi 翰林學士 (Hanlin academician)

Hanshijie 寒食節 ("Cold Eats Festival")

haobu guan 號簿官 (registering official)

haoyan 耗鹽 (tare allowance for wastage salt)

hedi 和糴 (government grain purchase)

hemai 和買 ("harmonious purchase"; pre-purchase salt)

hetongchang 合同場 (contract market)

heiyan 黑鹽 (black salt)

hongyan 紅鹽 (red salt)

hu 戶 (family, household unit)

hubaodou 護寶都 ("Protecting Treasure Guards"; patrolmen)

hubu 戶部 (Ministry of Revenue; Ministry of Finance)

hubu fushi 戶部副使 (vice-commissioner of the Office of the Census)

hubu panguan 戶部判官 (supervisor of the census)

hubu shilang 戶部侍郎 (executive of Office of the Census)

hubusi 戶部司 (Ministry of Finance)

hufang 戶房 (Finance Section of *zhongshu sheng*)

huzhang 戶長 (head of unit of households)

huashigang 華石綱 ("flower and rock flotilla")

huangyu longxieyan 黃魚籠挾鹽 ("yellow-fish baskets" of salt)

hui 灰 (reed ashes used in Zhexi salt production)

huiyao 會要 (collected documents)

huiyi ku 回易庫 (government "trade treasuries")

Huiyouge 徽猷閣 (Huiyou Palace Hall)

huizi 會子 (check notes, paper money)

huo 貨 (money; goods)

huojing 火井 ("fire well"; natural gas vein)

jishizhong 給事中 (reviewing policy advisor)

jixian 畿縣 (imperial capital)

jixiandian xiuzhuan 集賢殿修撰 (Jixian Library compiler)

jizhisi 計置司 (Budget Office)

jia 甲 (mutual surveillance and assistance group)

jia'na 加納 (additional payments; extra fee)

jiarao 加饒 (bonus of salt to attract merchants where there was a backlog)

jiatou 甲頭 (furnace foreman)

jian 間 ("at times"; government official)

jian 監 (salt directorate; industrial prefecture; director of a ministry)

jian 鹼 (earth salt; alkaline soil)

jianbing 兼并 ("engrosser"; private monopolist)

jiancha yushi 監察御使 (investigating censor)

jiancha zhuyan 監察煮鹽 (salt-boiling inspector)

jianguan 諫官 (inspector; remonstrance official)

jianlinguan 監臨官 (investigating commissioner)

jiansi 監司 (circuit intendancy)

jiantu 鹼土 (saliferous earth; alkaline soil)

jianyanhu 煎鹽戶 (earth salt households)

jianzhengguan 檢正官 (examiner)

Jiang He Huai Hai zhuozei xunjian 江河淮海捉賊巡檢 (bandit-catching military inspector of the Yangzi River, Yellow River, Huai River, and the Sea)

jiangyan 絳鹽 (deep red salt)

jiaoyin 交引 (vouchers for salt and other goods for border provisioning

jiaozi 交子 (exchange notes; paper money)

jiaozi 腳子 ("foot carrier"; porter)

jie 解 (to rend)

jieliu 節流 (to reduce expenditures)

jieluqian 借路錢 ("road usage" fee charged salt merchants)

Jin 金 (Jurchen empire)

Jin 晉 (state in Spring and Autumn period)

jinbing 禁兵 (palace army)

jinjun 禁軍 (palace army)

jinshi 進士 (presented scholar)

jing 井 (salt well)

jinghu 井戶 (well salt producer household)

jingjiang 井匠 ("well artisans"; supervising technicians)

jinglue 經略 (abbreviation of *jinglue anfushi*)

jinglue anfu panguan 經略安撫判官 (Military Intendancy Supervisory Office)

jinglue anfushi 經略安撫使 (military intendant especially in frontier areas)

jingyan 井鹽 (well salt)

juepei 決配 (see *pei*)

jun 軍 (military prefecture; army)

juncang 軍倉 (military salt storehouse)

junqi jian 軍器監 (Directorate for Armaments)

junshufa 均輸法 (policy of balanced distribution)

kaiyuan 開源 (to broaden sources of income)

kao 考 (critical examination; annual merit rating)

kefu 科敷 (imposed government distribution of salt by head count)

kehu 客戶 ("guest households"; dependent tenant families)

kemai 科賣 (sale of salt to households as a levy)

keyan[a] 顆鹽 ("kernel salt"; pond salt)

keyan[b] 課鹽 (tax salt; quota salt)

koushiyan 口食鹽 (forced purchase of salt for consumption, a form of poll tax)

kuanshengqian 寬剩錢 (tax for emergencies)

lanru 闌入 (illegal trade)

langguan 郎官 (unofficial reference to a director or vice-minister)

leyü 鱸魚 (type of fish)

libu langzhong 吏部郎中 (Ministry of Personnel director)

libu shangshu 吏部尚書 (minister of personnel)

libu shilang 吏部侍郎 (Ministry of Personnel executive; office chief)

lishengqian 力勝錢 (salt boat tax)

lisheng shui 力勝稅 (tax on merchant boat)

lizheng 里正 (head of a unit of households)

liangshui 兩稅 (Double Tax)

Liao 遼 (Khitan empire)

liezhuan 列傳 (biographies)

Linzhan 藺氈 (tribal people)

ling 令 (legal articles)

liu 流 (exile to the frontier)

liupei 流配 (see *pei*)

Longtuge zhi xueshi 龍圖閣直學士 (auxiliary academician of Longtu Pavilion)

lu 路 (circuit)

lushi canjun 錄事參軍 (executive inspector of prefectures)

Luoyuan shi 洛苑使 (commissioner of the Luoyang Gardens)

machiyan 馬齒鹽 ("horse-teeth" salt)

mainachang 買納場 (procurement sales center or saltern)

mainaguan 買納官 (procurement sales official)

maipu 買撲 (franchising of a monopoly good; contracting out of tax collection)

menxia sheng 門下省 (Chancellery Department)

mifei qian 糜費錢 ("expenditure fees")

miaohao 廟號 (temple name)

miaomi 苗米 (tribute rice and grain)

min 緡 (string of cash)

mingtang 明堂 ("Hall of Enlightened Rule"; Imperial Ancestral Hall)

mo 末 (lit. "branch"; incidental)

mokan 磨勘 (evaluation system; official review)

mo-shio 藻鹽 (salt refined in ancient Japan by burning seaweed)

moyan 末鹽 ("powder salt"; sea salt)

neidian chongban 內殿崇班 (imperial warder of the Inner Hall)

neifu 內府 (Palace Treasury)

neizang 內藏 (Inner Palace Treasury)

nianyunsi 輦運司 (Imperial Transport Intendancy)

Nüzhen 女真 (Jurchen)

panguan 判官 (circuit supervisory official; staff supervisor)

pan hubu gouyuan 判戶部勾院 (Ministry of Finance supervisory comptroller)

pei 配 (punishment of beating, tattooing, and banishment to hard labor)

peijun 配軍 (convict sent to serve in army)

pingyou 憑由 (certificate or proof of identity or ownership)

pingzhang junguoshi 平章軍國事 (executive of military and state matters)

pu 撲 (sell)

pu 鋪 (courier station; salt shipping station)

pubing 鋪兵 (courier soldier)

puhu 鋪戶 (shop owner; shop household)

puhu shangfan yan 鋪戶商販鹽 (merchant shop-sold salt; franchising)

pumai 撲買 / 撲賣 (franchising; tax farming)

pumai (yan) 撲買鹽 (franchised salt)

puyan 撲鹽 ("gambled salt"; franchising)

puyi 鋪驛 (courier serviceman; salt shipper)

qi 畦 (section; embankment; pond salt field)

Qi 齊 (state in Spring and Autumn period)

Qidan 契丹 (Khitan)

qifu 畦夫 ("section worker"; pond salt producer)

qihu 畦戶 ("section household"; pond salt household)

qijulang 起居郎 (Chancellery imperial recorder)

qijuyuan 起居院 (Imperial Recording Bureau)

qiyan 畦眼 ("section eyes"; sections of pond salt fields; irregularities on their surfaces)

qianpan 簽判 (abbreviated reference to *qianshu panguan ting gongshi*)

qianshu 簽書 (signatory official)

qianshu panguan ting gongshi 簽書判官庭公事 (notary of the administrative assistant in a prefecture)

qianggan ruozhi 強幹弱枝 ("strengthen the trunk, weaken the branches")

qingji 輕齎 (lightweight payment instruments for ease of travel)

qingmiaofa 青苗法 ("green sprouts" policy of farm loans)

Qingmingjie 清明節 ("Clear and bright" festival)

Qingtang zu 青唐族 (tribal people)

qingyan 青鹽 (blue salt)

quan 券 (proof of set price; sometimes refers to *jiaoyin*; also called *yaoquan*)

quanyou 勸誘 (government "persuasion" of inhabitants to register as salters)

quehuowu 榷貨務 (Monopoly Goods Bureau)

quejin 榷禁 (monopoly prohibitions; government distribution)

quemai 榷賣 (monopoly sales)

queyan 榷鹽 (monopoly salt)

rongbing 冗兵 (supernumerary soldiers)

rongfei 冗費 (excessive spending)

rongyuan 冗員 (supernumerary officials)

rouyan 柔鹽 (soft salt)

ruzhong 入中 (merchant provisioning of the border in exchange for the right to make salt shipments)

sanban shichen 三班使臣 (commissioners of the three ranks)

sanguan 散官 (prestige title)

sanpin fu 三品服 (robes of the third rank)

sanshuofa 三說法 (Three Items Policy)

sansi 三司 ("Three Fiscal Agencies"; Finance Commission)

sansi fushi 三司副使 (assistant commissioner of Finance Commision)

sansishi 三司使 (finance commissioner)

sanyan 散鹽 ("loose salt" produced from sea brine, well brine, or saliferous earth)

seyi 色役 (corvee labor)

shaihui 曬灰 ("sunning the ashes"; Zhexi method of salt production)

shanni 扇泥 (fanned mud technique to drill salt wells)

shangfanyan 商販鹽 (merchant-sold salt; franchising)

shanghu 上戶 (upper class of salt producers)

shangshusheng 尚書省 (Department of Ministries)

shangshu zuopuye 尚書左僕射 (left executive of Department of Ministries)

shangshuian 商稅案 (Commercial Tax Section of the Salt and Iron Bureau)

shang sizhou 上四州 (Fujian's "upper" interior salt-consuming prefectures)

shean 設案 (Special Preparations Section of the Salt and Iron Bureau)

shengzhuan 乘傳 (postal carriages)

shi 什 (a unit of ten households)

shi 食 (food)

shibo 市舶 (maritime trade supervisor)

shihuozhi 食貨志 (monograph on economy)

shilianshi 石蓮試 ("stone lotus" technique using dried lotus seeds to test brine salinity)

shilu 實錄 (veritable records)

shiyan 石鹽 (rock salt)

shiyi wu 市易務 (State Trade Bureau)

shi yü 鮪魚 (a type of fish)

shiyushi 侍御史 (attendant censor)

shiyushi zhizashi 侍御史知雜事 (censor of miscellaneous affairs)

shouchen 守臣 (custodian)

shumi fushi 樞密副使 (assistant commissioner of Military Affairs)

shumiyuan 樞密院 (Bureau of Military Affairs)

shumi zhixueshi 樞密直學士 (auxiliary academician of Bureau of Military Affairs)

shuxiang 樞相 (unofficial reference to *shumishi*)

shuaichen 帥臣 (military intendant field marshall)

shuaifu 帥府 (military intendant)

shui 水 (river)

shuibo 水柏 (bog bean plant, *Menianthus trifoliata*)

sifu 四輔 ("four territories"; region around the capital)

sikong 司空 (grand master of works)

sishuofa 四說法 (Four Items Policy)

sui 歲 (year)

taichang boshi 太常博士 (erudite of imperial sacrifices)

taichangcheng 太常丞 (executive assistant of Court of Imperial Sacrifices)

taifusi 太府寺 (Court of Imperial Treasury)

tanchang 灘場 (raised drying beds used in sea salt production)

Tanggu 唐古 (Tangut)

tidian xingyu 提點刑獄 (judicial intendant)

tidian zhuqianshi 提點鑄錢事 (mint intendant)

tihuodan 提貨單 (bill of lading)

tiju chayan changping gongshi 提舉茶鹽常平公事 (intendant of tea, salt, and Ever-normal Granaries)

tiju changping chayan gongshi 提舉常平茶鹽公事 (intendant of ever-normal granaries, tea, and salt)

tiju changping gongshi 提舉常平公事 (ever-normal granary intendant)

tiju changpingguan 提舉常平官 (ever-normal granary intendant)

tiju changpingsi 提舉常平司 (Ever-normal Granary Intendancy)

tijusi 提舉司 (intendancy)

tiju yanshiguan 提舉鹽事官 (salt intendant)

tiju yanshisi 提舉鹽事司 (Salt Intendancy)

tiliang anfushi 體諒安撫使 (sympathetic military intendant)

tiling 提領 (superintendant)

tixia 提轄 (controller)

tixing anchashi 提刑安察使 (variant of *tidian xingyu*)

tixingsi 提刑司 (Judicial Intendancy)

tianfu 田賦 (land tax)

tie'an 鐵案 (Iron Section of the Salt and Iron Bureau)

tiena 貼納 (surtax; cash surcharge when exchanging vouchers)

tienafa 貼納法 (surcharge policy)

tienaqian 貼納錢 (cash surcharge on salter households)

tieqian 鐵錢 (iron cash)

tieshuqian 貼輸錢 (surcharge; exchange fee)

tietou 帖頭 ("recorded heads" who performed government service duty)

tingchang 亭場 (sea salt saltern; salt yard; saline)

tinghu 亭戶 ("pavilion household"; sea salter household)

tong 通 (comprehensive)

tongcui 統催 (collector-general)

tonghuoqian 通貨錢 (commercial tax)

tongling 統領 (commander-general, less prestigious than *tongzhi*)

tongpan 通判 (prefectural vice-administrator)

tongqian 銅錢 (copper cash)

tongshang 通商 (merchant distribution of salt)

tongshang difen 通商地分 (free-trade zone)

tongxia 統轄 (supervisor-in-chief)

tongyi dafu 通議大夫 (grand master for thorough counsel)

tongzhi 統制 (commander-general)

tongzhiguan 統制官 (commander-general)

touziqian 頭子錢 (agricultural surtax)

touzi shiliqian 頭子市例錢 (supplementary trade tax)

tuan 團 ("regiment"; guarded government salter settlement with furnaces)

tuangang 團綱 (government convoy)

tuanlian fushi 團練副使 (assistant military training commissioner)

tuanzha 團柵 ("regiments and palisades"; salt enclosure system)

tuipai 推排 ("investigate and clear out"; regular assessment of salter ranks and production quotas)

tuntian 屯田 (agricultural colony; state farm)

wei 尉 (sheriff district defender)

wenchao 文鈔 (previous voucher issues)

wenpingqian 文憑錢 ("certificate fee" deducted from salter capital)

wenxue xianliang 文學賢良 ("the literate and virtuous")

woyun 斡運 (an effort to work out a solution)

wu 務 (small saltern)

wu 五 (a unit of five households)

wulue dafu 武略大夫 (grand master for military strategy)

Wuyue 吳越 (kingdom of Five Dynasties period)

xi 畦 (pond salt field)

xihu 畦戶 ("section household"; pond salt producer household)

Xiqiang 西羌 (tribal people)

Xixia 西夏 (Tangut empire)

Xia guozhu 夏國主 ("Master of the Xia state")

xiahu 下戶 (lower salter households)

xia sizhou 下四州 (Fujian's "lower" coastal salt-producing prefectures)

xian 縣 (county)

xianjiushi 閑廄使 (commissioner for the palace corrals and stables)

xianling 縣令 (county magistrate)

xiang 相 (chief councilor)

xiang 鯗 (dried salt fish)

xiangbing 廂兵 (prefectural troops)

xiangjun 廂軍 (prefectural troops)

xiaochao 小鈔 (small salt voucher)

xiaohuo 小火 ("small fires"; originally independent salt boiling households)

Xiaojing 孝經 (Classic of filial piety)

xiaoqian 小錢 ("small cash")

xingbu shilang 刑部侍郎 (executive of the Ministry of Justice)

xingfa 刑法 (penal law)

xiu qijuzhu 修起居注 (compiler of imperial records)

xu 胥 (government clerk)

xu'e 虛額 ("empty" quota; approximate quota)

xuanfushi 宣撫使 (pacification commissioner)

xuanju 選舉 (selection of officials)

xuanyu 宣諭 (pacification commissioner)

xunhuanfa 循環法 (policy of rotational exchange of vouchers with repeated cash surcharges)

xunjian 巡檢 (military inspector)

xunjian dujian 巡檢都監 (chief military inspector)

xunzhuo sichayan 巡捉私茶鹽 (arresting agent for tea and salt smugglers)

yagangren 押綱人 (convoy overseer)

yamen 衙門 (government office)

yaqian 衙前 (service runners hired by local units)

yayan 崖鹽 ("cliff salt"; rock salt)

Yance 鹽策 (The Salt Policy)

yanchang 鹽場 (saltern; saline)

yanchao 鹽鈔 (salt vouchers for cash)

yanding 鹽丁 (sea salter)

yanfeng 鹽風 (the "salt" wind; south wind)

yangan 鹽幹 (a subordinate official in charge of overseeing salt revenues and audits)

yangang 鹽綱 (salt boat convoy, salt flotilla)

yangou 鹽勾 (subordinate official in the Salt and Iron Bureau)

yanjiang 鹽匠 ("salt artisans"; well salt laborers)

yan jiaoyin 鹽交引

yantieshi 鹽鐵使 (salt and iron intendant)

yantiesi 鹽鐵司 (Salt and Iron Bureau)

yantie zhuanyunshi 鹽鐵轉運使 (salt and iron transport commissioner)

yanyan 岩鹽 (cliff salt)

yanyin 鹽引 (salt voucher)

Yan Yun shiliuzhou 燕雲十六州 (16 prefectures ceded to the Liao)

yanzhu 鹽主 (salt master)

yaoling 遙領 (remote controller)

yin 引 (salt voucher)

yin 廕 ("shadow privilege"; *yin* protection)

yinqian 引錢 (paper money)

yinshuiqian 引稅錢 (voucher tax fees)

yong 庸 (corvee)

Yongle dadian 永樂大典 (the Yongle encyclopedia)

you jianyi dafu 右諫議大夫 (right grand master of remonstrance)

you shiyi 右拾遺 (right completioner)

you sijian 右司諫 (right policy critic)

youzi 由子 (a sort of tax notification)

yumai 豫買 (prepurchase of silk)

yuqian dajun 御前大軍 (imperial army; regular Southern Song army)

yushi 御使 (censor)

yushi dafu 御史大夫 (censor-in-chief)

yushitai 御史臺 (Censorate)

yushi zhongcheng 御史中丞 (executive censor)

yuanwailang 員外郎 (vice-director of bureau)

yunfu 運副 (see *zhuanyun fushi*)

yunpan 運判 (transport assistant)

zaqian 雜錢 ("miscellaneous fees"; supplementary taxes)

zaixiang 宰相 (chief councilor)

zao 灶 (sea salt stove; sea salt furnace)

zaohu 灶戶 ("stove household"; sea salter household)

zaojia 灶甲 (salt stove head system)

zaosang 遭喪 (mourning for a parent)

zhang 杖 (flogging with heavy bamboo)

zhebo 折博 (see *zhezhong*)

zhebowu 折博務 (Exchange Bureau)

zhe'na 折納 (commutation of taxes)

zhezhong 折中 ("equitable exchange" of merchant delivery of provisions in exchange for salt and other vouchers)

zhengque 征榷 (monopolies)

zhengyan 正鹽 (regular quota salt)

zhifang 職方 (Bureau of Operations in Ministry of War)

zhi jixianyuan 直集賢院 (auxiliary in Academy of Scholarly Worthies)

zhishiguan 直史館 (auxiliary official of Historiographical Office)

zhixian 知縣 (county magistrate)

zhiyi 職役 (corvee labor)

zhizheng 執政 (assisting councilor of state)

zhizhi chayansi 制置茶鹽司 (Tea and Salt Intendancy)

zhizhigao 知制誥 (special drafting official of the Secretariat)

zhizhi sansi tiaolisi 制置三司條例司 (Finance Planning Commission)

zhizhishi 制置使 (military regulator)

zhizhi Xie yan 制置解鹽 (Xie salt commissioner)

zhizhi Xie yanshi 制置解鹽使 (high commissioner of Xie salt)

zhizhou 知州 (prefect)

zhongcheng 中丞 (executive censor; abbreviation of *yushi zhongcheng*)

zhongmai 中賣 (salt sales to central authority, also see *ruzhong*)

zhongshusheng 中書省 (Secretariat Department)

zhongyan 種鹽 ("planting" of pond salt)

zhou 州 (prefecture)

zhouan 冑案 (Armaments Section in the Salt and Iron Bureau)

Zhouguan 周官 (original title of *Zhouli*, the Rites of Zhou)

zhoujun 州軍 (prefectures, civil and military)

zhuguanguan 主管官 (subordinate official)

zhuguansi 主管司 (supervising office)

zhuguan wenzi 主管文字 (subordinate official charged with ensuring quotas were met)

zhuhu 主戶 (household chief; powerful household)

zhujunqian 助軍錢 ("aiding the military" fee)

zhushui 住稅 (stationary tax on salt shops)

zhuzuo zuolang 著作佐郎 (assistant staff writer)

zhuanbancang 轉般倉 (storage depot)

zhuangliu 樁留 (reserve)

zhuanlang 轉廊 ("transfer ways"; merchant use of vouchers in a location other than where they had been purchased)

zhuanyun fushi 轉運副使 (assistant fiscal intendant)

zhuanyun panguan 轉運判官 (circuit fiscal supervisory official)

zhuanyunshi 轉運使 (commissioner for transport; fiscal intendant)

zhunbeiyan 准備鹽 ("preparatory salt"; stockpiled salt)

zhuotongjing 卓筒井 ("standing tube" well)

zichang 子場 (small branch saltern)

zongji 總計 (commissioner of general accounts)

zonglingsuo 總領所 (Quartermaster Bureau of regional military command)

zongxia 總轄 (furnace foreman)

zu 族 (tribe)

zuyongdiao 租庸調 (Tang agrarian system of taxes paid in grain, corvee, cloth)

zuo cao 左曹 (Left Section of *hubu*)

zuo shiyi 左拾遺 (left completioner)

zuo zang 左藏 (Left Storehouse)

zuo zhengyan 左正言 (left policy monitor)

Works Cited

Primary Sources

ABT   *Aobo tu* 熬波圖 (Salt production illustrated). Chen Chun 陳椿 (fl. 14th cent.). 1334. *Jishi'an congshu* 吉石庵叢書 edition.

BG   *Bizhou gaolüe* 敝帚稿略 (Collected works of Bao Hui). Bao Hui 包恢 (Song). In *SKQS*, vol. 1178, 703–804. Shanghai: Shanghai guji chubanshe, 1986.

BS   *Beishi* 北史 (History of the Northern dynasties). Compiled by Li Yanshou 李延壽 (Tang). 100 *juan*. Punctuated edition. Beijing: Zhonghua shuju, 1974.

BX   *Bao Xiaosu zouyi ji* 包孝肅奏議集 (Memorials of Bao Zheng). Bao Zheng 包拯 (999–1062). In *SKQS*, vol. 427, 73–182. Shanghai: Shanghai guji chubanshe, 1987.

BZ   "Ben zhuan" 本傳 (Huang's biography). Reprinted from *Yinxian zhi* 鄞縣志 (Yin County gazetteer). Huang Zhen 黃震 (1213–1280). In *Gujin jiyao yibian* 古今紀要逸編 (Important lost events recollected), *Siming congshu* 四明叢書 (Collected works of the Siming area), vol. 26, first series. Taipei facsimile, 1964.

BZB   *Bozhai bian* 泊宅編 (Collected works of Fang Shao). Fang Shao 方勺 (1066–post-1141). 3 *juan*. In *SKQS*, vol. 1037, 507–32. Shanghai: Shanghai guji chubanshe, 1987.

CMZ   *Caomuzi* 草木子 (Collected works of Ye Ziqu). Ye Ziqi 葉子奇 (fl. late Yuan, early Ming). Punctuated edition. Beijing: Zhonghua shuju, 1959.

CYZJ   *Jianyan yilai chaoye zaji* 建炎以來朝野雜記 (Notes on events of the Jianyan period, 1127–1130). Li Xinchuan 李心傳 (1166–1234). 2 vols. In *Songshi ziliao cuibian* 宋史資料萃編 (A collection of Song history sources), compiled by Zhao Tiehan 趙鐵寒. Taipei: Wenhai chubanshe, 1968.

DCJS   *Ducheng jisheng* 都城紀勝 (Famous sites of Lin'an). Naideweng 耐得翁 [pseud.] (13th cent.). Beijing: Zhongguo shangye chubanshe, 1982.

DGJ   *Duguan ji* 都官集 (Collected works of Chen Shunyu). Chen Shunyu 陳舜俞 (?–1076). In *SKQS*, vol. 1096, 405–551. Shanghai: Shanghai guji chubanshe, 1987.

DML   *Dongjing menghua lu* 東京夢華錄 (Past splendors of the eastern capital). Meng Yuanlao 孟元老 (fl. 1126–1147). 10 *juan*. Shanghai: Shanghai gudian wenxue chubanshe, 1956.

DPZ *Dongpo zhilin* 東坡志林 (Recollections of Su Dongpo). Su Shi 蘇軾 (1036–1101). Revised by Wang Songling 王松齡. In *Tang Song shiliao biji congkan* 唐宋史料筆記叢刊 (Collected Tang–Song historical materials and notes). Beijing: Zhonghua shuju, 1981.

DYDZ *Da Yuan shengzheng guochao dianzhang* 大元聖政國朝典章 (State code of the Yuan Dynasty). 60 *juan*. 1307. Taipei: Guoli gugong bowuyuan, 1976.

FWZY *Fan Wenzhenggong zouyi* 范文正公奏議 (Fan Zhongyan's memorials to the emperor). Fan Zhongyan 范仲淹 (989–1052). In *Fan Wenzhenggong ji* 范文正公集 (The collected works of Master Fan Wenzheng), *SBSB* 四部叢刊初編縮本, vols. 176–77. Taipei: Taiwan shangwu yinshuguan, 1965.

FZXJ *Fan Zhongxuan ji* 范忠宣集 (Collected works of Fan Chunren). Fan Chunren 范純仁 (1027–1101). In *SKQS*, vol. 1104, 541–843. Shanghai: Shanghai guji chubanshe, 1987.

GCZY *Guochao zhuchen zouyi* 國朝諸臣奏議 (Memorials presented by Northern Song officials). Compiled by Zhao Ruyu 趙汝愚 (1140–1196). In *Songshi ziliao cuibian* 宋史資料萃編, compiled by Zhao Tiehan 趙鐵寒. Taipei: Wenhai chubanshe, 1968.

GSJ *Gongshi ji* 公是集 (Works of Liu Chang). Liu Chang 劉敞 (1019–1068). 54 *juan*. Shanghai: Shanghai guji chubanshe, 1987

GZ *Guanzi* 管子 (The *Guanzi*). Taipei: Taiwan Zhonghua, 1973.

HDYFZ *Hedong Yanfa zhi* 河東鹽法志 (Hedong salt administration). Edited by Jueluo Shilin 覺羅石麟 (fl. 18th cent.). Taipei: Taiwan xuesheng shuju, 1966.

HNZG *Hainingzhou zhi gao* 海寧州志稿 (A draft of Hainingzhou gazetteer). 1896. Revised by Li Gui 李圭, edited by Xu Chuanpei 許傳霈, amended by Liu Weiren 劉蔚仁, re-edited by Zhu Xien 朱錫恩. Shanghai: Shanghai shudian, 1993.

HS *Hanshu* 漢書 (Han dynastic history). Ban Gu 班固 (32–92). 100 *juan*. Punctuated edition. Beijing: Zhonghua shuju, 1962.

HSJS *Huang Song tongjian changbian jishi benmo* 皇宋通鑑長編紀事本末 (Topical history of the Song). Yang Zhongliang 楊仲良 (Song). In *XSKQS*, vols. 386–87. Shanghai: Shanghai guji chubanshe, 1995.

HSRC *Huangshi richao* 黃氏日抄 (Daily writings of Mr. Huang). Huang Zhen 黃震 (1213–1280). 97 *juan*. Taipei: Dahua shuju 大化書局, 1984.

HSZLS *Huang Song zhongxing liangchao shengzheng* 皇宋中興兩朝聖政 (Imperial ordinances, 1127–1189: A chronological account of the early Southern Song administration). Anonymous. Reprinted in *Songshi ziliao cuibian* 宋史資料萃編, compiled by Zhao Tiehan 趙鐵寒. Taipei: Wenhai chubanshe, 1968.

HXZ *Huating xianzhi: Jiangsu sheng* 華亭縣志: 江蘇省 (Huating County gazetteer: Jiangsu Province), revised edition. 1879. Edited by Yang Kaidi 楊開第. In *Zhongguo fangzhi congshu* 中國方志叢書 (Chinese local gazetteers series), no. 45.

HYGSZ *Haiyan Ganshui zhi* 海鹽澉水志 (Haiyan County, Ganshui [Zhejiang] gazetteer). Chang Tang 常棠. In *SKQS*, vol. 487. Shanghai: Shanghai guji chubanshe, 1987.

HYJ *Han Yu ji* 韓愈集 (Collected works of Han Yu). Han Yu 韓愈 (768–824). In *TSBQ*, vol 1, 3–364. Beijing: Guoji wenhua chubanshe, 1997.

JDJ *Jingde ji* 淨德集 (Collected works of Lü Tao). Lü Tao 呂陶 (1027–1103). In *SKQS*, vol. 1098. Shanghai: Shanghai guji chubanshe, 1987.

JHH *Jinhua Huang xiansheng wenji* 金華黃先生文集 (Literary collection of Huang Jin 黃溍 [1277–1357]). 43 *juan*. In *SBSB*, vols. 304–5. Taipei: Taiwan shangwu yinshuguan, 1965.

JKZ *Jiankang zhi (Jingding)* 建康志 (景定) (Gazetteer of Jiankang, Jingding period 1260–1264). Zhou Yinghe 周應合 (1213–1280). 50 *juan*. In *SKQS*, vols. 488–89. Shanghai: Shanghai guji chubanshe, 1987.

JLB *Jile bian* 雞肋編 (Collected works of Zhuang Chuo). Zhuang Chuo 莊綽 (fl. 12th cent.). 1133. Edited by Fang Yuegong 方岳貢 and Chen Jiru 陳繼儒. Beijing: Shumu wenxian chubanshe 書目文獻出版社, 1991.

JNTZ *Jiangnan tongzhi* 江南通志 (Jiangnan gazetteer). Revised by Zhao Hongsi 趙弘恩, edited by Huang Zhijun 黃之雋 et al. 200 *juan*. In *SKQS*, vols. 507–512. Shanghai: Shanghai guji chubanshe, 1987.

JS *Jinshi* 金史 (Jin dynastic history). Edited by Tuo Tuo 脫脫 (1314–1355) et al. 135 *juan*. Punctuated edition. Beijing: Zhonghua shuju, 1975.

JSJ *Jushi ji* 居士集 (Collected works of Ouyang Xiu). Ouyang Xiu 歐陽修 (1007–1072). In *TSBQ*, vol. 1, 743–1745. Beijing: Guoji wenhua chubanshe, 1997.

JTS *Jiu Tang shu* 舊唐書 (Old Tang dynastic history). Edited by Liu Xu 劉昫 (887–946) et al. 200 *juan*. Punctuated edition. Beijing: Zhonghua shuju, 1975.

JYSJ *Jingyusheng ji* 景於生集 (Collected works of Chao Yuezhi). Chao Yuezhi 晁說之 (1059–1129). 20 *juan*. In *SKQS*, vol. 1118, 1–412. Shanghai: Shanghai guji chubanshe, 1987.

KJZ *Kuaiji zhi (Jiatai)* 會稽志(嘉泰) (Gazetteer of Kuaiji in the Jiatai period, 1201–1204). Edited by Shi Su 施宿 (1164–1222), et al. 20 *juan*. In *SKQS*, vol. 486, 1–439. Shanghai: Shanghai guji chubanshe, 1987.

LAZ *Lin'an zhi (Xianchun)* 臨安志 (咸淳) (Gazeteer of Lin'an in the Xianchun period, 1265–1274). Qian Yueyou 潛說友. 100 *juan*. In *SKQS*, vol. 490, 1–1020. Shanghai: Shanghai guji chubanshe, 1987.

LC	*Luancheng ji* 欒城集 (Su Che's collected works). Su Che 蘇轍 (1039–1112). 50 *juan*. In *SKQS*, vol. 1112. Shanghai: Shanghai guji chubanshe, 1987.

LCHJ	*Luancheng hou ji* 欒城後集 (Second series of Su Che's collected works). Su Che 蘇轍 (1039–1112). In *TSBQ*, vol. 3, 4037–4685. Beijing: Guoji wenhua chubanshe, 1997.

LMZ	*Lidai mingchen zouyi* 歷代名臣奏議 (Memorials of well-known great ministers). Compiled by Yang Shiqi 楊士奇 (1365–1444) et al. 350 *juan*. 1416. Taipei: Taiwan xuesheng shuju, 1985.

LS	*Liaoshi* 遼史 (Liao dynastic history). Edited by Tuo Tuo 脫脫 (1314–1355) et al. 116 *juan*. 1334. Punctuated edition. Beijing: Zhonghua shuju, 1974.

LZYF	*Liangzhe yanfa zhi* 兩浙鹽法志 (Salt administration of Liangzhe). Edited by Li Wei 李衛 (fl. 17th cent.). Taipei: Taiwan xuesheng shuju, 1966.

MBT	*Mengxi bitan* 夢溪筆談 (Notes taken in Mengxi). Shen Kuo 沈括 (1031–1095). 1 *juan*. 1086–1093. Beijing: Wenwu chubanshe, 1975.

MLL	*Mengliang lu* 夢梁錄 (Remembered splendors of Hangzhou). Wu Zimu 吳自牧 (Southern Song). 20 *juan*. 1274. Beijing: Zhongguo shangye chubanshe, 1982.

MS	*Mingshi* 明史 (Ming dynastic history). Edited by Zhang Tingyu 張廷玉 (1672–1775) et al. 332 *juan*. Punctuated edition. Beijing: Zhonghua shuju, 1974.

MZJ	*Mianzhaiji* 勉齋集 (Collection of Huang Gan). Huang Gan 黃幹 (1152–1221). In *SKQS*, vol. 1168, 1–68. Shanghai: Shanghai guji chubanshe, 1987.

NSZJ	*Nianer shi zhaji* 廿二史劄記 (Commentaries on the twenty-two dynastic histories). Zhao Yi 趙翼 (1727–1814). In *SBBY*, vol. 339. Taipei: Zhonghua shuju, 1981

QSG	*Qingshi gao* 清史稿 (A draft of the Qing dynastic history). Edited by Zhao Erxun 趙爾巽 (1844–1927) et al. 529 *juan*. Punctuated edition. Beijing: Zhonghua shuju, 1977.

QYSL	*Qingyuan tiaofa shilei* 慶元條法事類 (Statutes of the Qingyuan period (1195–1200) arranged topically). Edited by Xie Shenfu 謝深甫 (fl. late 12th cent.). 80 *juan*. Taipei: Xinwen, 1976.

QZCG	*Qingzheng cungao* 清正存稿 (Collection of Xu Luqing). Xu Luqing 徐鹿卿 (1189–1250). In *SKQS*, vol. 1178, 805–958. Shanghai: Shanghai guji chubanshe, 1987.

RTQF	*Ru Tang qiufa xuanli xingji* 入唐求法巡禮行記 (Ennin's diary of Tang China). Yuanren (釋) 圓仁 (fl. 9th cent.). Reprint with editorial corrections. Shanghai: Shanghai guji chubanshe, 1986.

SBBY	*Sibu beiyao* 四部備要 (Collectanea of the four classifications). Compiled by Gao Yehou 高野侯 et al. Taipei: Taiwan zhonghua shuju, 1981.

SBCK   *Sibu congkan* 四部叢刊 (Collection of the four classifications). Compiled by Zhang Yuanji 張元濟 (1867–1959) et al. First series. Shanghai: Shangwu yinshuguan, 1919.

SBSB   *Sibu congkan chubian suoben* 四部叢刊初編縮本 (*Sibu congkan* first condensed edition). Taipei: Taiwan shangwu yinshuguan, 1965.

SDZJ   *Song dazhaoling ji* 宋大詔令集 (A collection of Song decrees). Anonymous. 196 *juan*. 1210. Revised and punctuated. Beijing: Zhonghua shuju, 1997.

SHY   *Song huiyao* 宋會要 (Documents pertaining to matters of state in the Song). Edited by Zhang Dexiang 章得象 (978–1048) and Xu Song 徐松 (1781–1848). 460 *juan*. Tōyō bunko 東洋文庫 edition.

SHYJ   *Song huiyao jigao* 宋會要輯稿 (A draft of the *Song huiyao*). Compiled by Xu Song 徐松 (1781–1848). 366 *juan*. Reprinted in *Zhongguo lidai shihuozhi xubian* 中國歷代食貨志續編 (Economic monographs in Chinese history), edited by Xuehai chubanshe bianjibu 學海出版社編輯部, vols. 121–163. Taipei: Xuehai chubanshe, 1971.

SJ   *Shiji* 史記 (Records of the Grand Historian). Sima Qian 司馬遷 (ca. 145 B.C.–?). 130 *juan*. Punctuated edition. Beijing: Zhonghua shuju, 1959.

SJFZc   *Songjiang fuzhi (Chongzhen)* 松江府志 (崇禎) (Songjiang prefectural gazetteer, Ming Chongzhen edition [1628–1644]). Edited by Chen Jiru 陳繼儒 (1558–1639). Beijing: Shumu wenxian chubanshe 書目文獻出版社, 1991.

SJFZj   *Songjiang fuzhi (Jiaqing)* 松江府志 (嘉慶) (Songjiang prefectural gazetteer, Qing Jiaqing edition [1796–1820]). Compiled by Song Rulin 宋如林 (18th–19th cents.) and Sun Xingyan 孫星衍 (1753–1818) et al. 84 *juan*. Reprinted in *Zhongguo difang zhi jicheng* 中國地方志集成 (A collection of Chinese local gazetteers). Shanghai: Shanghai shudian, 1991.

SJZS   *Shisan jing zhushu* 十三經注疏 (Commentaries on the Thirteen Classics). Kong Yingda 孔穎達 (574–648). Hebei: Guoji wenhua chubanshe, 1996.

SKQS   *Siku quanshu* 四庫全書 (Complete texts of the four repositories). Compiled by Ji Yun 紀昀 (1724–1805) and Lu Xixiong 陸錫熊. 1773–1782. Shanghai: Shanghai guji chubanshe, 1987.

SLZY   *Shilin zouyi* 石林奏議 (Memorials of Ye Mengde). Ye Mengde 葉夢得 (1077–1148). 15 *juan*. 1205–1207. Reprinted in *XSKQS*, vol. 474. Shanghai: Shanghai guji chubanshe, 1995.

SMZ   *Siming zhi (Baoqing)* 四明志 (寶慶) (Gazetteer of Siming in the Baoqing period 1225–1227). Edited by Hu Ju 胡榘 and Luo Jun 羅濬 (12th–13th cents.). 21 *juan*. 1227. In *SKQS*, vol. 487, 1–492. Shanghai: Shanghai guji chubanshe, 1987.

SP   *Shupu* 鼠璞 (Unworthy writings: Collected works of Dai Zhi). Dai Zhi 戴植 (*jinshi* 1238). Shanghai: Shangwu yinshuguan 商務印書館, 1939.

SS   *Songshi* 宋史 (Song dynastic history). Edited by Tuo Tuo 脫脫 (1314–1355) et al. 496 *juan*. Punctuated edition. Beijing: Zhonghua shuju, 1977.

SSJ   *Su Shi ji* 蘇軾集 (Collected works of Su Shi). Su Shi 蘇軾 (1036–1101). In *TSBQ*, vols. 2–3. Beijing: Guoji wenhua chubanshe, 1997.

SSJW   *Sushui jiwen* 涑水記聞 (Recollections of Sima Guang). Sima Guang 司馬光 (1019–1086). 16 *juan*. Taipei: Shijie shuju, 1969.

SSQJ   *Su Shunqin ji* 蘇舜欽集 (Collected works of Su Shunqin). Su Shunqin 蘇舜欽 (1008–1048). Shanghai: Zhonghua shuju, 1961.

SSW   *Su Shi wenji* 蘇軾文集 (Literary collection of Su Shi). Su Shi 蘇軾 (1037–1101). 6 vols. Reviewed by Kong Fanli 孔凡禮. Beijing: Zhonghua shuju, 1986.

STKS   *Shantang xiansheng qunshu kaosuo* 山堂先生群書考索 (also known as *Shantang kaosuo* 山堂考索; Bibliographical inquiries of Zhang Ruyu). Zhang Ruyu 章如愚 (fl. 12th cent.). 212 *juan*. 1184, 1210. Beijing: Zhonghua shuju, 1992.

SWJZ   *Shuowen jiezi* 說文解字 (A dictionary of Hanzi). Xu Shen 許慎 (ca. 58–147). Hong Kong: Zhonghua shuju, 2000.

SXFZ   *Shaoxing fuzhi* 紹興府志 (Shaoxingfu gazetteer). In *Zhongguo fangzhi congshu* 中國方志叢書 (Chinese local gazetteer series), edited by Li Hengte 李亨特, reviewed by Ping Shu 平恕 et al, no. 221. Facsimile reproduction of 1792 edition. Taipei: Chengwen chubanshe, 1975.

SYXA   *Song Yuan xuean* 宋元學案 (Schools of thought in the Song and Yuan periods). Huang Zongxi 黃宗羲 (1610–1695) et al. 100 *juan*. In *SBBY*, vols. 388–93. Taipei: Taiwan zhonghua shuju, 1981.

SZGJ   *Shuzhong guangji* 蜀中廣記 (Notes on Sichuan). Cao Xuequan 曹學佺 (1571–1646). In *SKQS*, vols. 591–92. Shanghai: Shanghai guji chubanshe, 1987.

TABT   "Ti *Aobo tu*" 題熬波圖 (A poem on *Salt Production Illustrated*). Chen Chun 陳椿 (fl. 14th cent.). In *Liangzhe yanfa zhi* 兩浙鹽法志 (Salt administration of Liangzhe), edited by Li Wei 李衛 (1686–1738). Taipei: Taiwan xuesheng shuju, 1966.

TD   *Tongdian* 通典 (A comprehensive history of institutions). Edited by Du You 杜佑 (735–812) et al. 200 *juan*. Taipei: Xinxing shuju 新興書局, 1965.

TPZT   *Taiping zhiji tonglei* 太平治蹟統類 (Record of various topics pertaining to the politics of the Northern Song). Peng Baichuan 彭百川 (fl. late 12th cent.). Yangzhou: Jiangsu guanglin guji keyinshe 江蘇廣陵古籍刻印社, 1990.

TSBQ   *Tang Song badajia quanji* 唐宋八大家全集 (Collected works of the eight great literary figures of the Tang and Song). Edited by Yu Guanying 余冠英 et al. 3 vols. Beijing: Guoji wenhua chubanshe, 1997.

WASJ   *Wang Anshi ji* 王安石集 (Collected works of Wang Anshi). Wang Anshi 王安石 (1021–1086). In *TSBQ,* vol. 2, 2089–2670. Beijing: Guoji wenhua chubanshe, 1997.

WDHY   *Wudai huiyao* 五代會要 (Institutions of the Five Dynasties). Edited by Wang Pu 王溥 (922–982). 30 *juan.* Shanghai: Shanghai guji chubanshe, 1978.

WL   *Weilüe* 緯略 (Abstracts of the appendices to the Classics). Gao Sisun 高似孫 (ca. 1160–1230). 12 *juan.* In *SKQS,* vol. 852. Shanghai: Shanghai guji chubanshe, 1987.

WLJS   *Wulin jiushi* 武林舊事 (Remembrances of Hangzhou). Zhou Mi 周密 (1232–1298). Ca. 1280. Beijing: Zhongguo shangye chubanshe, 1982.

WS   *Weishu* 魏書 (Northern Wei dynastic history). Compiled by Wei Shou 魏收 (ca. 506–572). 114 *juan.* Punctuated edition. Beijing: Zhonghua shuju, 1974.

WX   *Wenxuan* 文選 (Literary selections). Edited by Xiao Tong 蕭統 (501–531), annotated by Li Shan 李善 (d. 689). 60 *juan.* In *SBBY,* vols. 561–64. Taipei: Taiwan zhonghua shuju, 1981.

WXTK   *Wenxian tongkao* 文獻通考 (Comprehensive study of the records). Ma Duanlin 馬端臨 (1254–1325). 348 *juan.* Shanghai: Tushu jicheng ju 圖書集 成局, 1901.

XCB   *Xu Zizhi tongjian changbian* 續資治通鑑長編 (Collected data for a continuation of the *Comprehensive Mirror to Aid in Government*). Li Tao 李燾 (1115–1184). 520 *juan.* Revised and punctuated. Beijing: Zhonghua shuju, 1979–1995.

XCBt   *Xu Zizhi tongjian changbian* 續資治通鑑長編 (Collected data for a continuation of the *Comprehensive Mirror to Aid in Government*). Li Tao 李燾 (1115–1184). Edited by Yang Jialuo 楊家駱, 15 vols. Taipei: Shijie shuju, 1961.

XCJ   *Xuechuang ji* 雪窗集 (Collected works of Sun Mengguan). Sun Mengguan 孫夢 觀 (fl. Song dynasty). 3 *juan.* In *SKQS,* vol. 1181, 61–112. Shanghai: Shanghai guji chubanshe, 1987.

XNYL   *Jianyan yilai xinian yaolu* 建炎以來系年要錄 (A digest of important affairs since the Jianyan period 1127–1130). Li Xinchuan 李心傳 (1166–1234). 200 *juan.* In *Songshi ziliao cuibian* 宋史資料萃編 (A collection of Song historical sources), compiled by Zhao Tiehan 趙鐵寒. Taipei: Wenhai chubanshe, 1968.

XSKQS   *Xuxiu Siku quanshu* 續修四庫全書 (Sequel to the *Siku quanshu*). Edited by Gu Tinglong 顧廷龍 (1904–1998) et al. Shanghai: Shanghai guji chubanshe, 1995.

XTS *Xin Tangshu* 新唐書 (New Tang dynastic history). Ouyang Xiu 歐陽修 (1007–1072) and Song Qi 宋祁 (998–1061). 225 *juan*. Punctuated edition. Beijing: Zhonghua shuju, 1975.

XWS *Xin Wudai shi* 新五代史 (New Five Dynasties dynastic history). Edited by Ouyang Xiu 歐陽修 (1007–1072) et al. Beijing: Zhonghua shuju, 1974.

XXCY *Xixi congyu* 西溪叢語 (Melanges of West Stream). Yao Kuan 姚寬 (1105–1162). 2 *juan*. In *SKQS*, vol. 850, 913–72. Shanghai: Shanghai guji chubanshe, 1987.

XYZY *Xihu youlan zhi yu* 西湖游覽志余 (West Lake travels). Tian Rucheng 田汝成 (1503–?). Beijing: Zhonghua shuju, 1958.

XZTJ *Xu Zizhi tongjian* 續資治通鑑 (A sequel to the *Comprehensive Mirror to Aid in Government*). Bi Yuan 畢沅 (1730–1797). 1801. In *SBBY*, vols. 264–277. Taipei: Taiwan zhonghua shuju, 1981.

YFJYZ *Yuanfeng jiuyuzhi* 元豐九域志 (Yuanfeng gazetteer of the nine regions (1078–1085)). Edited by Wang Cun 王存 (1023–1101). 10 *juan*. 1080. In *SKQS*, vol. 471, 1–231. Shanghai: Shanghai guji chubanshe, 1987.

YH *Yuhai* 玉海 (Encyclopedia of institutions). Compiled by Wang Yinglin 王應麟 (1223–1296). Nanjing: Jiangsu guji chubanshe, 1987.

YJZ *Yunjian zhi* 雲間志 (Gazetteer of Yunjian, or Huatingxian). Yang Qian 楊潛 (fl. 12th cent.). 3 *juan*. In *XSKQS*, vol. 687, 1–77. Shanghai: Shanghai guji chubanshe, 1995.

YLMC *Yunlu manchao* 雲麓漫抄 (Random notes from Cloudy Foothills: Zhao Yanwei's journal). Zhao Yanwei 趙彥衛 (fl. 12th cent.). Punctuated edition. Shanghai: Gudian wenxue chubanshe, 1957.

YS *Yuanshi* 元史 (Yuan dynastic history). Edited by Song Lian 宋濂 (1310–1381). 200 *juan*. Revised and punctuated. Beijing: Zhonghua shuju, 1976.

YSJ *Ye Shi ji: Shuixin bieji* 葉適集: 水心別集 (Collected works of Ye Shi). Ye Shi 葉適 (1150–1223). Revised and punctuated by Liu Gongchun 劉公純, Wang Xiaoyu 王孝魚, Li Zhefu 李哲夫. Beijing: Zhonghua shuju, 1961.

YTL *Yantie lun* 鹽鐵論 (Discourses on salt and iron). Huan Kuan 桓寬 (fl. 1st cent.). 10 *juan*. In *SBBY*, vol. 358. Taipei: Taiwan zhonghua shuju, 1981.

YXTZ *Yinxian tongzhi* 鄞縣通志 (Yin County [Zhejiang] gazetteer). In *Zhongguo fangzhi congshu* 中國方志叢書 (Chinese local gazetteer series), no. 216. Taipei: Chengwen chuban gongsi, 1974.

ZHG "Zhu hai ge" 煮海歌 (Song of sea-brine boilers). Liu Yong 柳永 (fl. 11th cent.). In *Songshi jishi* 宋詩紀事 (Events recorded in Song poems), edited by Li E 厲鶚 (1692–1752), vol. 2, 316–17. Taipei: Taiwan zhonghua shuju, n.d.

ZL   *Zhouli* 周禮 (Rites of the Zhou). In *SJZS*, vol. 3. Hebei: Guoji wenhua chubanshe, 1996.

ZS   *Zhoushu* 周書 (Northern Zhou dynastic history). Compiled by Linghu Defen 令狐德棻 (583–666) et al. 50 *juan*. Beijing: Zhonghua shuju, 1971.

ZZTJ   *Zizhi tongjian* 資治通鑒 (Comprehensive mirror to aid in government). Sima Guang 司馬光 (1019–1086). 294 *juan*. Beijing: Zhonghua shuju, 1956.

Secondary Sources

Aoyama Sadao 青山定雄. 1963. *Tō Sō jidai no kōtsū to chishi chizu no kenkyū* 唐宋時代の交通と土地地誌地圖の研究 (Studies of transport and maps of the Tang and Song periods). Tokyo: Yoshikawa Kōbunkan 吉川弘文館.

Balazs, Etienne. 1964. *Chinese Civilization and Bureaucracy: Variations on a Theme*. Translated from the French by H. M. Wright. Edited by Arthur F. Wright. New Haven: Yale University Press.

Balazs, Etienne, and Yves Hervouet, eds. 1978. *A Sung Bibliography (Bibliographie des Sung)*. Hong Kong: Chinese University Press.

Bao Xiaona 鮑曉娜. 1982. "Cong Tangdai yanfa de gaige lun jinque zhidu de fazhan guilu" 從唐代鹽法的改革論禁榷制度的發展規律 (Developmental patterns of the monopoly system as seen in the evolution of Tang salt laws). *Zhongguo shehui jingjishi yanjiu* 中國社會經濟史研究 (Chinese socio-economic history research) 2: 16–23.

Cai Chongbang 蔡崇榜. 1991. *Songdai xiushi zhidu yanjiu* 宋代修史制度研究 (A study of the Song system of historiography). Taipei: Wenjin chubanshe.

Chen Ran 陳然, and Zeng Fanying 曾凡英. 1991. "Yan, yizhong wenhua xianxiang" 鹽，一種文化現象 (Salt as a cultural phenomenon). In *Zhongguo yanyeshi guoji xueshu taolunhui lunwenji* 中國鹽業史國際學術討論會論文集 (Theses from the International Symposium on the History of the Chinese Salt Industry), edited by Peng Zeyi 彭澤益 and Wang Renyuan 王仁遠, 505–23. Chengdu: Sichuan renmin chubanshe.

Chen Yande 陳衍德. 1991. "Han Tang yan zhuanmai bijiao yanjiu" 漢唐鹽專賣比較研究 (A comparative study of the Han and Tang salt monopolies). In *Zhongguo yanyeshi guoji xueshu taolunhui lunwenji* 中國鹽業史國際學術討論會論文集 (Theses from the International Symposium on the History of the Chinese Salt Industry), edited by Peng Zeyi 彭澤益 and Wang Renyuan 王仁遠, 93–106. Chengdu: Sichuan renmin chubanshe.

Chen Zhichao 陳智超. 1995. *Jiekai Song huiyao zhi mi* 揭開宋會要之迷 (Puzzles of the *Song huiyao* resolved). Beijing: Shehui kexue wenxian chubanshe.

Dai Yixuan 戴裔煊. 1957. *Songdai chaoyan zhidu yanjiu* 宋代鈔鹽制度研究 (A study of the salt voucher system in the Song). Shanghai: Shangwu yinshuguan 商務印書館.

Franke, Herbert. 1961. "Some Aspects of Chinese Private Historiography in the Thirteenth and Fourteenth Centuries." In *Historians of China and Japan*, edited by W. G. Beasley and E. G. Pulleyblank, 115–34. London: Oxford University Press.

Gao Zhenduo 高振鐸, ed. 1982. *Zhongguo lishi yaoji jieshao ji xuandu* 中國歷史要籍介紹及選讀 (Introduction to and selected readings from important sources of Chinese history). Harbin: Heilongjiang renmin chubanshe.

Gardella, Robert. 1992. "Squaring Accounts: Commercial Bookkeeping Methods and Capitalist Rationalism in Late Qing and Republican China." *Journal of Asian Studies* 51.2 (May): 317–39.

Gernet, Jacques. 1962. *Daily Life in China on the Eve of the Mongol Invasion: 1250–1276*. Translated by H.M. Wright. Stanford: Stanford University Press.

Guo Dongxu 郭東旭. 1997. *Songdai fazhi yanjiu* 宋代法制研究 (A study of Song law). Baoding: Hebei daxue chubanshe.

Guo Zhengzhong 郭正忠. 1996. "Bei Song zhongqi de yique shi" 北宋中期的議榷詩 (Poems critical of the monopoly in the mid-Northern Song). In *Dierjie Songshi xueshu yantaohui lunwenji* 第二屆宋史學術研討會論文集 (Papers of the second symposium on Song studies), 37–60. Taipei.

———. 1990a. *Songdai yanye jingjishi* 宋代鹽業經濟史 (An economic history of the salt industry in Song). Beijing: Renmin chubanshe.

———. 1990b. *Song yan guankui* 宋鹽管窺 (A peek at Song salt). Taiyuan: Shanxi jingji chubanshe 山西經濟出版社.

———. 1984. "Lun Liang Song de zhouqixing shiyan 'guosheng' weiji: shi zhi shisan shiji Zhongguo shiyanye fazhan guilu chutan" 論兩宋的周期性食鹽 "過剩" 危機: 十至十三世紀中國食鹽業發展規律初探 (On the periodic salt 'glut' crises during the Northern and Southern Song: a preliminary investigation of the developmental patterns of the Chinese consumption salt industry from the tenth to the thirteenth centuries). *Zhongguo shehui jingjishi yanjiu* 中國社會經濟史研究 (Chinese social and economic history research) 1: 43–58.

———. 1983. "Songdai dongnan zhulu yanchan kaoxi" 宋代東南諸路鹽產考析 (An investigation of salt production in southeastern circuits in the Song). *Zhonghua wenshi luncong* 中華文史論叢 (Chinese culture and history) 26 (June): 77–115.

———. 1981. "Bei Song Sichuan shiyan weiji kaoxi" 北宋四川食鹽危機考析 (Analysis of the crises of Northern Song Sichuan consumption salt). *Zhongguoshi yanjiu* 中國史研究 (Chinese historical research) 1 (March): 79–94.

————, ed. 1997. *Zhongguo yanye shi: Gudai bian* 中國鹽業史: 古代編 (History of the Chinese salt industry: The ancient period). Beijing: Renmin chubanshe.

Hartwell, Robert M. 1988. "The Imperial Treasuries: Finance and Power in Song China," *Bulletin of Sung–Yuan Studies* 20: 18–89.

He Weining 何維凝. 1966. *Zhongguo yanzheng shi* 中國鹽政史 (The history of the salt administration in China). Taipei: He Long Lifen 何龍澧芬.

Hino Kaisaburo. 1963. "Government Monopoly on Salt in T'ang in the Period before the Enforcement of the Liang-shui fa." *Memoirs of the Research Department of the Toyo Bunko* 22: 1–56.

Jia Daquan 賈大泉. 1983. "Jingyan yu Songdai Sichuan de zhengzhi he jingji." 井鹽與宋代四川的政治和經濟 (Well salt in Song period Sichuan politics and economy). *Xinan shifan xueyuan xuebao* 西南師范學院學報 (Journal of the Xinan Teacher's College) 28 (July): 44–50.

Jin Yufu 金毓黻. 1944. *Zhongguo shixue shi* 中國史學史 (History of Chinese historiography). Taipei: Shangwu yinshuguan 商務印書館.

Ju Qingyuan 鞠清遠. 1935. "Nan Song guanli yu gongshang ye" 南宋管理與工商業 (Industrial and commercial management in the Southern Song). *Shihuo* 食貨 (Economy) 2.8 (September): (37–39).

Kawahara Yoshirō 河原由郎. 1979. "Sōsho ni okeru en kōin (enin) no keizaiteki yigi—shu toshite 'Han Shō no shōhō' settei izen no mondai" 宋初にぉける塩交引(塩引)の經濟的意義—主として范祥の鈔法設定以前の問題 (The economic impact of salt *jiaoyin* (salt *yin*) at the beginning of Song—particularly problems before Fan Xiang's voucher policy). *Fukuoka daigaku keizaigaku ronsō* 福岡大學經濟學論叢 (Fukuoka University economic studies) 19–2.3 (November): 331–52.

————. 1977. "Hoku Sō chō yū ka shōken toshite no enkōin enshō no kenkyū" 北宋期有價証券としての塩交引塩鈔の研究 (Study of salt *jiaoyin* and *chao* as securities under the Northern Song). *Fukuoka daigaku kenkyū shohō* 福岡大學研究所報 (Fukuoka University research journal) 28 (March): 1–14.

Kawakami Kōichi 河上光一. 1992. *Sōdai engyōshi no kiso kenkyū* 宋代塩業史の基礎研究 (Basic research on the history of salt in the Song). Tokyo: Yoshikawa ko bunkan 吉川弘文館.

————. 1974. "Sōdai Kai en no seisan to seisan keitai" 宋代解塩の生産と生産形態 (The system of salt production in the Xie lake district during the Song). In *Aoyama hakushi koki kinen Sōdaishi ronsō* 青山博士古稀記念宋代論叢 (Collection of essays on Song history in memory of Dr. Aoyama), 35–70. Tokyo: Seishin shobō 省心書房.

Kiyokoba Azuma 清木場東. 1984. "Godai Sōsho no ensen ni tsuite" 五代宋初の塩錢について (On the salt money system in the Five Dynasties and early Song). *Tōhō gaku* 東方學 (Eastern studies) 68 (July): 61–75.

Kracke, E.A., Jr. 1978. *Translations of Sung Civil Service Titles, Classification Terms, and Governmental Organ Names*, 2nd rev. ed. San Francisco: Chinese Materials Center, Inc.

Kusano Yasushi 草野靖. 1961. "Nan Sō jidai no Wai Setsu enshōhō" 南宋時代の淮浙鹽鈔法 (The salt voucher system of Huai-Zhe in Southern Song). *Shien* 史淵 (On history) 86 (December): 123–54.

Legge, James, trans. 1960. *The Chinese Classics*. Vol. 3: *Shangshu*; vol. 5: *The Ch'un Ts'ew with the Tso Chuen*. Hong Kong: Hong Kong University Press.

Levy, Margaret. 1988. *Of Rule and Revenue*. Berkeley: University of California Press.

Li Zongtong 李宗侗. 1953. *Zhongguo shixue shi* 中國史學史 (History of Chinese historiography). Taipei: Zhonghua wenhua chuban shiye weiyuanhui 中華文化出版事業委員會.

Liang Gengyao 梁庚堯. 1997. "Nan Song de Huai Zhe yanchang" 南宋的淮浙鹽場 (The Huai-Zhe salt centers in the Southern Song). In *Songshi yanjiuji* 宋史研究集 (Series on Song history), vol. 27. Taipei: Songshi zuotanhui 宋史座談會.

———. 1988. "Nan Song Huai Zhe yan de yunxiao" 南宋淮浙鹽的運銷 (Transport and sales of Huai-Zhe salt in the Southern Song). *Dalu zazhi* 大陸雜誌 (Mainland magazine), Part 1: 77.1 (July 15): 1–13; Part 2: 77.2 (August 15): 14–30; Part 3: 77.3 (September 15): 31–45.

Liang Taiji 梁太濟, and Bao Weimin 包偉民. 1994. *Songshi shihuozhi buzheng* 宋史食貨志補正 (Corrections of and addenda to the *Songshi*'s economic monograph). Hangzhou: Hangzhou daxue chubanshe.

Lin Zhenhan 林振翰. 1988. *Yanzheng cidian* 鹽政辭典 (Dictionary of salt administration terms). Zhengzhou: Zhongzhou guji chubanshe 中州古籍出版社.

Liu Jun 劉雋. 1973. "Song Yuan guan zhuanmai yinfa de chuangli yu wancheng" 宋元官專賣引法的創立與完成 (The establishment of the Yin system in the Song and Yuan). Originally published in *Zhongguo jingji shi jikan* 中國經濟史集刊, 6:2 (December 1939). Reprinted in *Song Liao Jin shehui jingji shi lunji* 宋遼金社會經濟史論集, ed. Zhou Kangxie 周康燮, 259–308. Hong Kong: Cuncui xueshe 存萃學社.

Ma Chujian 馬楚堅. 1997. *Zhongguo gudai de youyi* 中國古代的郵驛 (The ancient Chinese postal system). Beijing: Shangwu yinshuguan.

Ma Shuqin 馬淑琴. 1989. "Xixia yu Bei Song de qingbaiyan maoyi" 西夏與北宋的青白鹽貿易 (The trade of blue and white salts between the Western Xia and Northern Song). *Ningxia shehui kexue* 寧夏社會科學 (Ningxia social science) 2: 71–76.

Ma Zun 馬儔, Xiang Bin 項斌, Liang Baozhu 梁寶柱, Chen Shuming 陳書明, eds. 1993. *Zhongguo gudai caizheng sixiang shi gao* 中國古代財政思想史稿 (A draft history of financial thought in ancient China). Beijing: Zhongguo caizheng jingji chubanshe 中國財政經濟出版社.

McKnight, Brian E. 1981. *The Quality of Mercy: Amnesties and Traditional Chinese Justice.* Honolulu: University Press of Hawaii.

Nan Song jingcheng Hangzhou 南宋京城杭州 (Hangzhou, the Southern Song capital). Compiled by Zhejiangsheng Hangzhoushi weiyuanhui bangongshi 浙江省杭州市委員會辦公室 (Office of the Commission on Hangzhou, Zhejiang Province). Hangzhou: Zhejiang renmin chubanshe, 1988.

Ou Delu 歐德祿. 1989. "Cong Nan Song moya tan dangshi dui shiyan de guanli." 從南宋摩崖談當時對食鹽的管理 (Southern Song salt controls as seen in cliffside inscriptions). *Wenbo* 文博 (Literary relics) 2: 62–64.

People's Republic of China Atlas. United States Central Intelligence Agency. Washington, D.C: US Government Printing Office, 1971.

Qian Gongbo 錢公博. 1974. "Bei Song Xieyan de shengchan, yunxiao, he caizheng shouru" 北宋解鹽的生產運銷和財政收入 (Xie salt production, distribution, and revenues in the Northern Song). In *Songshi yanjiuji* 宋史研究集 (Song history research series), edited by Songshi zuotanhui 宋史座談會. Vol. 7. Taipei: Zhonghua congshu bianshenhui 中華叢書編審會.

———. 1964. "Songdai Xieyan de shengchan he yunxiao zhidu" 宋代解鹽的生產和運銷制度 (The production and transport system of Xie salt in Song). *Dalu zazhi* 大陸雜誌 (Mainland magazine) 28.5: 160–64.

Quan Hansheng 全漢昇. 1948. "Songmo de tonghuo pengzhang ji qi duiyu wujia zhi yingxiang" 宋末的通貨膨脹及其對於物價之影響 (Inflation at the end of the Song and its effect on commodity prices). *Bulletin of the Institute of History and Philology, Academia Sinica* 歷史語言研究所集刊 10: 193–222.

Saeki Tomi 佐伯富. 1987. *Chūgoku enseishi no kenkyū* 中國鹽政史の研究 (A study of the history of China's salt administration). Kyoto: Hōritsu bunkasha 法律文化社.

Schumpeter, Joseph. 1954. "The Crisis of the Tax State." In *International Economic Papers: Translations Prepared for the International Economic Association,* edited by Alan T. Peacock, Ralph Turvey, Wolfgang F. Stoper, and Elizabeth Henderson. Vol. 4.

Schurmann, Herbert Franz. 1967. *Economic Structure of the Yuan Dynasty: Translation of Chapters 93 and 94 of the Yuanshi.* Cambridge, Mass.: Harvard University Press.

Seo Tatsuhiko 妹尾達彦. 1982a. "Tōdai Katō chien no seisan to ryūtsū" 東大河東池鹽の生産と流通 (The production and circulation of Hedong pond salt in the Tang). *Shirin* 史林 (Forest of history) 5.6 (November): 829–66.

―――. 1982b. "Tōdai go hanki ni okeru Kō Wai enzei kikan no ritchi to kinō" 唐代後半期における江淮鹽税機關の立地と機能 (The location and function of government salt taxation agencies in Jianghuai in the late Tang). *Shigaku zasshi* 史學雜誌 (Journal of historical studies) 91.2 (February): 1–37.

Shangshi tongjian 商史通鑒 (Encyclopedia of commercial history). Edited by Zhang Jingyue 張景月 and Liu Xinfeng 劉新風. Beijing: Jiuzhou tushu chubanshe 九洲圖書出版社, 1996.

Smith, Paul. 1991. *Taxing Heaven's Storehouse: Horses, Bureaucrats, and the Destruction of the Sichuan Tea Industry, 1074–1224.* Cambridge: Harvard University Press.

Tan Qixiang 譚其驤, ed. 1982. *Zhongguo lishi ditu ji* 中國歷史地圖集 (Historical atlas of China). Vol. 6: Song–Liao–Jin shiqi 宋遼金時期 (Song, Liao, and Jin period). Shanghai: Ditu chubanshe.

Tang Song shiliao biji congkan 唐宋史料筆記叢刊 (Collected historical materials and notes of the Tang and Song). Revised and punctuated by Kong Fanli 孔凡禮. Beijing: Zhonghua shuju, 1981.

Teraji Jun 寺地遵. 1995. *Nan Song chuqi zhengzhishi yanjiu* 南宋初期政治史研究 (A study of early Southern Song political history). Translated from the Japanese by Liu Jingzhen 劉靜貞 and Li Jinyun 李今蕓. Taiwan: Daohe chubanshe 稻禾出版社.

Twitchett, Denis C. 1992. *The Writing of Official History under the Tang.* Cambridge: Cambridge University Press.

―――. 1970. *Financial Administration under the Tang Dynasty*, 2nd ed. Cambridge: Cambridge University Press.

―――. 1954. "The Salt Commissioners after An Lu-shan's Rebellion," *Asia Major*, n.s. 4.1: 60–89.

Vogel, Hans Ulrich. 1993. "The Great Well of China." *Scientific American* (June): 116–21.

―――. 1992. *Bibliography of Works on Salt History Published in China* (special issue of the Commission Internationale d'Histoire du Sel). Austria: Berenkamp Verlag Schwaz.

―――. 1991. "Sichuan shen zuan jing jishu chuanbo dao xifang de zhenxiang he zhengyi" 四川深鑽井技術傳播到西方的真相和爭議 (Transmission of Sichuan deep drilling technique to the West: Facts and problems). In *Zhongguo yanyeshi guoji xueshu taolunhui* 中國鹽業史國際學術討論會 (Theses from the International Symposium on the History of the Chinese Salt

Industry), edited by Peng Zeyi 彭澤益 and Wang Renyuan 王仁遠, 39–58. Chengdu: Sichuan renmin chubanshe.

Wang Leiming 王雷鳴, comp. 1985. *Lidai shihuozhi zhushi* 歷代食貨志注釋 (Monographs on the economy through the ages with annotation), vol. 2: Five Dynasties and Song. Beijing: Nongye chubanshe.

Wang Shengduo 王聖鐸. 1995. *Liang Song caizhengshi* 兩宋財政史 (Financial history of the Song). Beijing: Zhonghua shuju.

Worthy, Edmund H. 1975. "Regional Control in the Southern Sung Salt Administration." In *Crisis and Prosperity in Sung China*, ed. John W. Haeger, 101–41. Tucson: The University of Arizona Press.

Xu Weiqin 許維勤. 1988. "Liang Song Fujian yanzheng lunlue" 兩宋福建鹽政論略 (A brief account of the salt administration of Fujian in the Northern and Southern Song). *Fujian luntan* 福建論壇 (Fujian tribune) (April): 17–23.

Yan Changyao 顏昌嶢. 1996. *Guanzi jiaoshi* 管子校釋. Changsha: Yuelu shushi 岳麓書社.

Yang Lien-sheng. 1961. "The Organization of Chinese Official Historiography: Principles and Methods of the Standard Histories from the Tang through the Ming Dynasty." In *Historians of China and Japan*, edited by W. G. Beasley and E. G. Pulleyblank, 44–59. London: Oxford University Press.

———. 1952. *Money and Credit in China: A Short History*. Cambridge: Harvard University Press.

Yoshida Tora 吉田寅. 1993. *Salt Production Techniques in Ancient China: The Aobo Tu*. Translated and revised by Hans Ulrich Vogel. Leiden: E. J. Brill.

———. 1963. "'Gōha zu' to Sō Gen jidai no seien gijutsu" 熬波圖と宋元時代の製鹽技術 (The *Aobo tu* and salt production techniques in the Song and Yuan). *Rekishi kyohiku* 歷史教育 (Historical education) 11.9 (September): 38–43.

Yuki Tōru 幸徹. 1984. "Sōdai no tōnan kanbai enhō (3)—Kinei Genhō nenkan chokuzen no kanbai enhō no taihai ni tsuite" 宋代の東南官賣塩法—熙寧元豐年間直前の官賣塩法の退廢について (Government sales salt policy in the Southeast in the Song: breakdown of the government sales salt policy on the eve of the Xining and Yuanfeng reign periods). *Rekishigaku chirigaku nenpō* 歷史學地理學年報 (History and geography annual) (March): 27–54.

———. 1982. "Sōdai no tōnan kanbai enhō (2)—kanbai matsuensen nenshūgaku no suii" 宋代の東南官賣塩法—官賣末塩錢年收額の推移 (Government sales salt policy in the southeast in the Song: the change in annual revenues of government sales powder salt money). *Rekishigaku chirigaku nenpō* 歷史學地理學年報 (History and geography annual) 6 (March): 1–31.

————. 1977. "Hoku Sō Keireki nenkan no kanbaihō ka matsuenshō ranhatsu no eigyō ni tsuite" 北宋慶曆年間の官賣法下末塩鈔亂發の影響について (The influence of overissuing of powder salt vouchers from 1041 to 1048 in Northern Song). *Rekishigaku chirigaku nenpō* 歷史學地理學年報 (History and geography annual) 1 (March): 25–66.

Zhang Jiaju 張家駒. 1935. "Nan Song Liangzhe zhi yanzheng" 南宋兩浙之鹽政 (The salt administration of Liangzhe in Southern Song). *Shihuo* 食貨 (Economy) 1.6 (February): 19–25.

Zhang Jingyue 張景月, and Liu Xinfeng 劉新風, eds. 1996. *Shangshi tongjian* 商史通鑒 (A comprehensive mirror of merchant history). Beijing: Jiuzhou tushu chubanshe 九洲圖書出版社.

Zhang Xiaoye 張小也. 2001. *Qingdai siyan wenti yanjiu* 清代私鹽問題研究 (A study of Qing dynasty salt smuggling). Beijing: Shehui kexue wenxian chubanshe 社會科學文獻出版社.

Zhang Xiuping 張秀平. 1983. "Songdai queyan zhidu shulun" 宋代榷鹽制度述論 (On the salt monopoly in the Song). *Xibei daxue xuebao* 西北大學學報 (Journal of Northwestern University) 37 (February): 56–64.

Zhang Xuejun 張學君. 1984. "Songdai Sichuan yanye zhong de suoyouzhi zhuanhua" 宋代四川鹽業中的所有制轉化 (The transformation of ownership in the Sichuan salt industry in the Song). *Zhongguo shehui jingjishi yanjiu* 中國社會經濟史研究 (Chinese social economic history research) 11: 58–66.

Zhao Tiehan 趙鐵寒, comp. 1968. *Songshi ziliao cuibian* 宋史資料萃編 (Collected essays on Song history). Taipei: Wenhai chubanshe.

Zhao Xiaogeng 趙曉耕. 1994. *Songdai fazhi yanjiu* 宋代法制研究 (A study on the Song legal system). Beijing: Zhongguo zhengfa daxue chubanshe 中國政法大學出版社.

Zheng Xuemeng 鄭學檬. 1982. "Wudai yanfa gouchen" 五代鹽法鉤沉 (Salt policy in the Five Dynasties). *Zhongguo shehui jingjishi yanjiu* 中國社會經濟史研究 (Studies of the history of Chinese society and economy) 1: 68–74.

Zhongguo yanyeshi guoji xueshu taolunhui lunwenji 中國鹽業史國際學術討論會論文集 (Theses from the International Symposium on the History of the Chinese Salt Industry). Edited by Peng Zeyi 彭澤益 and Wang Renyuan 王仁遠. Chengdu: Sichuan renmin chubanshe, 1991.

above-quota sales, 56, 237–238
above-quota salt, 40, 180, 237, 239,
  239n122; government procurement of,
  40, 176; illegal production, 234; tax
  payment with, 175; unfairly included as
  regular production, 227
administrative offices: competition
  between agencies, 79–80; offices and
  responsibilities, 14, 18–23; regional
  differences, 7n11, 231. See also central
  government; local government; officials
adult male salt money (ding yanqian), 57.
  See also silkworm salt (canyan)
agricultural surtax (touziqian), 217n52
aliases: for corvee exemption, 229; salters
  using, 175; used by officials, 78, 226,
  269n31
alum, 231
An Bing, 298
An Dun, 244n8
anfushi (military intendant). See military
  intendant (shuaifu, shuaichen, anfushi)
Anhua (xian) (Yongxingjun), 183
An Lushan Rebellion, 7n11, 8, 10
Ansujun (Hebeixi), 146
Anyi Pond (Yongxingjun), 41, 95–96n1;
  annual production, 96–97. See also
  Xiezhou pond salt policies (960-1047)
Aobo tu (Chen Chun), 88, 89, 141,
  233n111
aodi yanqian (clerical fees), 160n8

bagged salt, 171, 178, 182; bag size, 222,
  228; surtax on, 179

bag policy, 68–69, 75, 215; bonus salt, 228;
  Huai, 215, 221; seals, 69, 215,
  222–223n60
Baipo (Jingxibei), 125n82
Baishi saltern, 258
Baizhou (Guangnanxi), 258
bandits, 58, 113–114n52; drummers, 196;
  pirate fleets, 262n12; Qianzhou, 193,
  194n18; "Six Bandits," 221n57; Yao
  tribesmen, 193n17. See also smuggling
Banpu (Huainandong), 185
Baoanjun (Yongxingjun), 113–114n52
baojia law, 28, 29; applied to salters, 47–48,
  164
Baoqing period (Lizong): sea salt, 237, 254,
  272
Baoshun (Xihe), 280
Baoyou period (Lizong): sea salt, 238, 239,
  255
Baoyuan period (Renzong): pond salt, 109
Bao Zheng, 115, 116, 132, 132n100
Baozhou (Hebeixi), 146
Bazhou[a] (Lizhou), 293
Bazhou[b] (Hebeidong), 146
beiding (salt laborers), 141–142n2, 173. See
  also laborers
Beijing (Hebeidong), 11
Beizhou (Hebeidong), 146
Bian Canal, 125–126n82
Bian River, 202–203n34
Binzhou[a] (Shaanxi/Yongingian), 98
Binzhou[b] (Hebeidong), 146, 150, 275
Binzhou[c] (Guangnanxi), 258
Black and White Ponds, 113, 118
black salt (heiyan), 43, 93–94n1, 118–119

---

* NS=Northern Song; SS=Southern Song

blue and white salt trade, 100n12,
113–114, 118–119, 119n66, 127n87
blue salt (*qingyan*), 15, 43, 100–101,
100n12, 110n42, 278, 279, 285; impact
of import, 112–113n48
boat tax (*lishengqian*), 67, 80, 205n38
boiler households (*jianyanhu*), 44
boiling foremen (*cuijianguan*), 47
boiling salters: after fees, left with no
money, 234, 237; banishment, 230;
forced to sell licenses, 202–203n34;
incentives, 223–224n61; soldiers, 142
bonus salt (*jiarao*), 178, 182, 214, 215, 228,
278
border provisioning: about, 59, 62–63;
under Fan Xiang's policy, 113–114;
goods in exchange for salt vouchers
(*jiaoyin*), 59, 62–63, 110–111 (*see also*
vouchers); with Huai salt, 186–187,
190–192; inflation resulting from, 59,
109–110, 116–117, 120, 191, 208;
return from without commodities,
217–218
boundaries, restricted, 49, 97–98; 1980
discovery in Shaanxi, 98n7; factor in salt
shortages, 53; workers in, 105–106,
105n30
Bozhai bian (Fang Shao), 89–90
Bozhou[a] (Hebeidong), 146, 184n
Bozhou[b] (Huainandong), 97
bribes, 226, 229, 262–263n12
Bureau of Military Affairs, 19, 30

Cai Jing, 13–14, 135n119, 218, 219, 247;
one of "Six Bandits," 221n57; reforms,
30–32, 67–70, 204–205
Cai Li, 279
Cai Que, 279
Cai Ting, 195–196
Cangzhou (Hebeidong), 146, 150, 152
Caozhou (Jin), 97n6, 143
carrying sales, 155, 217, 221, 233
cash-for-vouchers system, 63–65, 66,
111–118, 134–135, 212

cash surcharges, 61, 73, 80; voucher
exchange, 69, 75, 134–135, 206, 211,
224n63
cauldron households, 239
central government: agencies, 20–23;
court expenses, 24–26, 82, 220; court
policy, 200–201n30, 209
centralization, 16–20; administrative,
18–19; fiscal, 19–20; military, 11, 17–18
chang. See salterns (*chang*)
Changguo directorate, 156
Changqing saltern, 241
changyin (long salt voucher), 68
chanyanfa (salt production tax policy), 247,
248n17
Chanyuan Treaty, 24, 25
chaoyin vouchers, 63–65, 66. *See also*
vouchers
Chaozhou, 257, 258–259n5, 266, 272n37
check notes (*huizi*), 38
Chen Anshi, 278, 279, 279n5
Chen Chengzhi, 249
Chen Chun, 89
Chen Cisheng, 244
Chengdufu Circuit, 124n80, 287, 291,
292
Cheng Jie, 295
Cheng Kan, 113
Chen Shu, 187, 187n7
Chen Si, 247n16
Chen Xian, 252
Chen Ye, 298
Chizhou (Jiangnandong), 184, 214
Chonghe period (Huizong): pond salt, 138
Chongning period (Huizong): earth salt,
281; pond salt, 133, 134, 135; sea salt,
206, 207, 208; well salt, 293
Chunhua period (Taizong): pond salt, 104
Chunxi period (Xiaozong): sea salt, 233,
234, 250, 252, 268, 269, 271; well salt,
295, 296
Chunyou period (Lizong), 238, 302
Chuzhou[a] (Liangzhe), 219
Chuzhou[b] (Huainan), 183, 185, 234
Cizhou[a] (Hedong), 146

cliff salt (*yayan*), 43, 285
commercial tax (*tonghuoqian*), 65, 75, 222,
    257, 259n6
commodities and services: high cost of,
    200–201n30; traded at border, 110, 114
consumption: mandatory purchase greater
    than, 56–57, 126. *See also*
    forced-purchase salt
consumption tax, 250n26, 252n31
container fees, 228
contamination of salt, 51, 107n34, 108,
    188–189, 195
contract markets (*hetongchang*), 76–77, 294,
    297
convoys: equipment, 50–51; laborers (*gang-
    yunren*), 50, 71; overseer (*yagangren*), 51
convoy transport, 50–51, 249, 251n27,
    255; back ups, 199–200n29; 500 boats
    sink, 202n34; cargo load, 159n7;
    construction target, 125–126n82;
    contamination, 108, 188–189 (*see also*
    contamination of salt); costs, 234, 268;
    crews can sell back extra salt, 196;
    criticized by Su Shi, 202–203n34;
    funding involving tax households,
    251n28; hazards of, 108, 284; officials
    illegally trade from, 161n10; state flotillas
    compete with prefecture's flotillas, 251,
    254–255; transport to capital, 119n68,
    125–126n82. *See also under specific region*
copper cash, 37, 180, 231
corruption, official, 183–184; abuses at
    salterns, 229, 295n29; abuses of salters,
    73, 77–78, 82–83, 89, 132n100,
    244–247, 244n8, 246, 247n16, 249, 255,
    259–260; aliases, 78, 226, 269n31;
    collusion with merchants, 148;
    embezzlement plan of Wei Bochu,
    219–221; forgery, 269n31; four cited
    abuses, 227; in Guang, 262–263n12; in
    Huai, 183–184n1; illegal trade, 67,
    77–78, 172, 222–223n60, 225, 238;
    interference with boat transport, 161n10,
    172; in Liangzhe, 161n10, 172, 181;
    production fund corruption, 73, 179,

227, 230; smuggling, 55, 78, 83 (*see also*
    illegal trade [*lanru*])
corvee exemptions, 9, 20, 48, 174–175,
    229
corvee-free tax, 200–201n30
corvee labor, 8, 20; blood and sweat of
    people, 153n16; criticized by Liu Yi,
    200; wages, 200–201n30; wealthy
    families elude, 229. *See also* laborers
Court of the Imperial Treasury (*taifusi*), 23
currency, 37–39, 108, 180, 288; *jiaoyin*
    distinguished from *jiaozi*, 110n43;
    non-standardized values, 73, 228,
    270–271n33; paper money, 35, 37–38
customs inspections, 202–203n34 (203)
customs taxes, 147n3, 194

Daguan period (Huizong): pond salt, 135;
    sea salt, 206, 207
daimai (carrying sales), 155, 217, 221, 233
Dai Xiaoba, 194n18
Daizhou, 104, 104n25
Daming (fu) (Hebeidong), 97n6, 146
Dazhongxiangfu period (Zhenzong): pond
    salt, 97n6; well salt, 286
death penalty, 103, 131n99, 183–184n1,
    278–279n4
deficits, 192, 208; causes, 26–27, 31, 35,
    39, 82; reforms, 27–32
Deng Runfu, 242
Dengzhou, 143
Deqing (jun) (Liangzhe), 146
Dezhou (Hebeidong), 146
Ding Du, 189
Dingzhou[h] (Hebeixi), 146
Directorate for Armaments (*junqi jian*), 22
directorates (*jian*), 45–47
distribution, government, 49–50, 58;
    imposed (*kefu*), 56. *See also* convoy
    transport
distribution, merchant, 49–50. *See also*
    merchant sales (*tongshang*); merchant
    transport
distribution sites, 180, 227; contention
    over, 46, 64n153

distribution storehouses (*zhiyancang*), 46, 227, 229
Diwu Qi, 8, 236
Dizhou (Hebeidong), 146
Dongguan saltern, 257
Dongjing (Jingji), 97n6, 194n19
Double Tax, 20, 174–175, 222, 250n26; Guangxi, 268n29; Sichuan, 217–218n52
drying pans, 6, 162, 163–164
Duangong period (Taizong): well salt, 285
Duanping period (Lizong): sea salt, 239
duchachang (Tea Office), 238n120
Du Chengrui, 101
dudie (Buddhist ordination license). *See* ordination certificates
duidai voucher policy (transfer ways), 205–210, 205n41
Du Jie, 178
dusheng (Department of Ministries), 237
duzhi (commissioner of revenue), 266
duzhi langzhong (director of Office of Funds), 267n26
duzhi panguan (supervisor of funds), 197
duzhishi (commissioner of revenue), 99
duzhi yuanwailang (vice-director of the Office of Funds), 202–203n34
du zhuanyunshi (fiscal intendant-general), 119n68
Duzong (SS emperor), 80

earth salt (*jian*), 42; producers, 44. *See also* Hedong earth salt policies
Eastern Capital, 97n6, 222n58
eastern salt, 105, 106, 113, 123n78, 124, 128–130
Emergency Reserves Storehouse (*fengzhuangku*), 202–203n34, 204
equitable exchange (*zhezhong*), 63, 186–187. *See also jiaoyin* voucher program
ever-normal granary intendant, 21–22, 79, 199n29
Exchange Bureau (*zhebowu*), 111
exchange notes (*guanzi*), 231
exchange notes (*jiaozi*), 38, 120, 231

exile, 175, 204n37, 206, 243; locations of, 278–279n4
Ezhou (Jinghubei), 185, 264, 267n27

Fan Chengda, 271–272n36
Fan Chunren, 119–120
Fan E, 152
fangchangqian (shops and yards money), 204
Fang La Uprising, 31, 89
Fang Shao, 89
Fan Xiang, 131–132n100; implementation of policy, 111–115, 117; policy overview, 64–65, 70; superiority of policy, 99
Fan Xun, 199–200
Fan Zhongyan, 27, 159, 189
Fan Zongjie, 111n46, 131–132n100
Fan Zuyu, 132n100
Fengxiangfu (Qinfeng), 288
Fenzhou (Hedong), 275
Finance Commission, 21, 22, 121, 127n86
fire wells, 42, 285–286n7
fiscal intendants (*zhuanyunshi*), 19, 21, 56, 119
fiscalism in Song, 12
Five Dynasties, 10, 11, 20, 103–104
floating salt, 239, 240. *See also* above-quota salt
floating salt tax, 250n26
flying money (*feiqian*), 38, 123n76, 134, 208
forced-purchase salt, 177, 179, 207, 244n8, 252, 269n30; according to summer tax, 195; by fisherman, 227; in Guangnan, 272n37; household salt, 260–261n9; Huai tax canceled, 196; per head, 260n7; in Sichuan, 296
Four Items Policy (voucher redemption), 63, 190–192
franchises, 40, 60–61, 161, 162n11, 175
fubing system, 8, 17, 27
fuel, 239, 290n16
Fujian sea salt policies (NS), 241–247; distribution areas, production and revenue, 241–242; gluts, 53, 241–242n1; lower prefectures, 241, 247; moves to

Fujian sea salt policies (NS), continued
curtail smuggling, 243; moves to
uniform pricing, 245n11; official
rewards, 243–244, 246; officials
punished for exacting exorbitant taxes,
244–247; prefectural policies change,
243–244; price increases under Cai Jing,
247; salt quota, 245–246n12; sold in
Huai, 193–194; upper prefectures, 241,
242, 247; voucher system implemented,
247–248
Fujian sea salt policies (SS), 247–256;
distribution areas, production and
revenue, 171, 224n63, 241–242; lower
prefectures, 248, 254; monks hired to
distribute salt, 249; official abuses of salt
policy, 249, 255; pardons of salter debts,
250n26, 255; reductions, 253–254;
revenue income, 248; smuggling, 182,
250, 252n29, 253; transport issues, 249,
251, 252, 255–256; upper prefectures,
248; vouchers, 249, 252
Fu Qiu, 289n13
furnace, salt (zao), 170
Fuzhou^b (Fujian), 241, 245, 254
Fuzhou^c (Hedong), 276
Fu Zide, 252, 252n29

gang (salt convoy), 195
Gan River, 197, 197n23
Gao Bo, 260n8
Gaozong (SS emperor), 32–33, 71; salt
policy, 74
gluts of salt: about, 64, 116; carrying sales,
155, 217, 221, 233; dumping on
merchants, 61–62, 217; Fujian,
241–242n1; Guang, 264; Hedong, 276;
Huai, 183–184n1, 189, 191n14,
202–203n34, 217, 221n56, 227,
228–229, 232–233n110; Liangzhe, 182,
265; Wenzhou, 52, 178; Xie, 64,
102–103, 107–108, 109n40, 116–117
gold currency, 37
Gongdi (SS emperor), 81
Gongzhou^a (Guangnanxi), 258

Gongzhou^b (Qinfeng), 132–133n103
government distribution (guanmai): about,
49–50, 58; convoy system (see convoy
transport); gluts (see gluts of salt);
pilfering and contamination (see contamination); smuggling (see smuggling)
government transport (boat). See convoy
transport
government transport (land), 109, 111,
113
grain and fodder, 110, 190, 191n15, 208,
209
granular salt (moyan), 41
"green sprouts" system, 198n24, 254
guan'gao (office certificates), 204n40, 205
Guangdejun (Jiangnandong), 213
Guangjijun (Jingdongxi), 143
Guangnan sea salt policies (NS):
distribution, salterns, production and
revenue, 257–259; eastern circuit, 257;
official abuses of salters, 259–260; sale
price, 259n6; smuggling, 193–194,
195n21, 197–199, 197n22, 199n27, 201;
stockpiles, 257–258n5; tax quota, 257;
transport issues, 259–260n6 (260);
western circuit, 257, 259
Guangnan sea salt policies (SS), 261–273;
distribution, salterns, production and
revenue, 257–259; eastern circuit, 257,
261; exports to Huai-Zhe, 171, 224n63;
gluts, 53, 270–271n33, 272n37;
Guangdong and Guangxi combined
administration, 265–268, 271–272;
official corruption, 262–263n12; price,
265–266; pros and cons of government vs.
merchant sales, 269–270; quotas, 271,
271n34, 272n37; revenue, 262n12,
263–264, 267, 269n31; revenue loss,
270–271n33; smuggling, 262n12,
270–271n33; transport issues, 261,
262–263n12, 267, 268; vouchers, 224,
263, 266, 267, 269–273; western circuit,
257, 261
Guangxi Circuit, 257–259, 261, 265

Guangxi Tea and Salt Intendancy, 262–263
Guangzhou (Guangnandong), 259, 265, 266
Guan Zhong, 81–82, 129n94; *Guanzi*, 4–5
guarantors, 64n152, 68, 222–223n60
Guizhou[a] (Jinghubei), 289
Guizhou[b] (Guangnanxi), 264
Guizhou[c] (Guangnanxi), 258
Guo Gai, 292, 293
Guo Zhengzhong, 4n1

Haikou saltern, 185
Hailing directorate, 183, 236
Haiyan (Liangzhe), 157n1
Haizhou (Huainandong), 185
Han Bi, 270–271n33
Han Dunli, 134
Hangzhou (Liangzhe), 11, 156, 165, 169
Han Jiang, 278
Han monopoly, 5–7
Han Qi, 112, 132
Han Tuozhou, 34
Han Wudi, 5
Han Yu, 9
Han Zhen, 197
haoyan (tare allowance for wastage salt), 228
Haozhou (Huainanxi), 156, 161–162, 232–233n110
Hao Zongchen, 130n95
Hebei sea salt policies, 15, 16, 41, 146–156, 153n16, 199; bagged salt sales, 150–153; distribution areas, production and revenue, 146; Double Tax, 149; duties not collected, 148; the emperor's benevolence, 149–150, 151–153, 154n20; higher cost of government sales, 147–148n5, 149; periods of government distribution, 152–155; surcharge system, 147; vouchers, 153, 155, 191–192
Hedong earth salt policies, 42, 275–281; blue and white salts policy, 191, 279; bonus salt, 279n5; consumption of pond

salt, 105, 276; directorates, distribution, production and revenue, 275–276; gluts, 276; Macheng Pond, 279; procurement price, 276; quotas, 280–281; salters' debts pardoned, 276n2; small-mouthed wells and competition, 280; transport issues, 277–278; vouchers, 276–278, 280–281
hemai (harmonious purchase), 57n140, 211n47
Henan (fu) (Luoyang), 97n6
Hengzhou[b] (Guangnanxi), 258, 262n12
Hengzhou (Jinghunan), 193n17
He Tan, 113–114n54, 148n5
hetongchang (contract market), 76–77, 294, 297
Heyang, 155
He Zhongli, 118n65
Hezhou (Huainanxi), 184
Hongzhou (Jiangnanxi), 184
horse-teeth salt, 43
horse trade, 24, 65, 119n67, 263–264, 265, 267n27
household chief (*zhuhu*), 56–57, 173
household ranking, 56, 71–72, 82–83, 260–261n9, 269n30
household registers, 141–142n2, 200–201n30
household taxes, 40, 56–57, 200–201n30, 207, 249
Hou Shuxian, 199–200n29
Huai sea salt policies (NS), 41, 183–221; advantages of merchant trade, 186–189; border provisioning, 186–187, 190–192; Cai Jing policy, 204–205, 214–216; directorates, production and distribution areas, 169, 183–185, 190; forced-purchase salt, 195, 196; glut salt, 52, 189, 221n56; Guang salt trade, 197–199, 201; illegal boiling, 186–187; price, 54, 185, 186n5, 196–197, 212, 213–214, 217; revenue allocation, 184–185, 190; revenue income, 183–184n1, 192, 196, 218–219; revenue loss, 186, 188, 202–203n34, 208; salter's

Huai sea salt policies (NS), *continued*
  hardships, 188–189, 203–204; selling
  price *vs.* procurement cost, 186;
  smuggling, 54–55, 195–196; stockpiles,
  212–213; storehouses and transfer
  facilities, 185–186; supply issues to
  Jiangnan and Jinghu, 193–195; tax
  pardons (salters), 188n9; Three Items
  and Four Items Policies, 190–192;
  transport issues, 187, 188–190, 192,
  195–199, 202–203n34, 214; voucher
  exchange, 206–207, 213–214, 221;
  vouchers, 188, 192–193, 205–218
Huai sea salt policies (SS), 70–71, 221–240;
  gluts, 52–53, 227–229; Guang and
  Fujian salt imports, 224n63, 245–246;
  merchant incentives, 224, 228;
  production funds, 222, 223–224n61,
  227, 230, 234; production issues, 227,
  232–233n110, 233n111, 234; quotas,
  239–240; respite declared for salters,
  237–238; revenue, 183–184n1, 236–237;
  revenue loss, 232; stockpiles, 228–229;
  summary, 224–231; transition period,
  221–224; transport issues, 232–233n110;
  vouchers, 228
Huai-Zhe salt, 72, 74, 76, 109, 156, 171.
  See also Huai sea salt policies; Liangzhe
  sea salt policies; powder salt
Huang Bing, 194–196
Huang Jiang, 131
Huang Lang, 245
Huang Lian, 292n20, 293
Huang Lü, 244, 244n8
Huang Qian, 293n23
Huang Qianhou, 222n58
Huang Shou, 273
Huangyan directorate, 156
Huangyou period (Renzong): earth salt,
  276; pond salt, 115; sea salt, 150, 160,
  192, 222
Huang Zhen, 181, 182, 228, 229–230;
  excess bureaucrats, 80, 180; salter
  advocate, 72–73, 80, 81; written works
  of, 88–89

Huangzhou (Huainanxi), 184
Huang Zhuogui, 193n17
Huanzhou (Yongxingjun), 119n67
Huating (Liangzhe), 89n226, 157n1, 174
Huazhou^a (Shaanxi/Yongxingjun), 132
Huazhou^b (Jingxibei), 155
Huazhou^c (Guangnanxi), 258
Huiyou Palace Hall, 219, 219n54
Huize saltern (Huainandong), 185
Huizong (NS emperor), 13, 30, 36, 89,
  132; fiscal policy and military strategy,
  30–32, 67; reign periods, 301
huojing (fire well; natural gas vein), 42,
  285–286n7
Hu Tingzhi, 269, 270–271n33
Hu Wufu, 233n111
Hu Yuanzhi, 295
Huzhou (Liangzhe), 162, 165, 257,
  258–259n5

illegal production, 74, 172–173, 222, 231,
  234n113; control mechanisms under Lu
  Bing, 47–48 (*see also* Lu Bing);
  conversion to cultivated fields, 155;
  implications of stone lotus test, 74 (*see
  also* stone lotus test); small-mouth wells,
  76–77 (*see also* small-mouth wells
  [*zhuotongjing*])
illegal trade (*lanru*), 15–16, 62, 172,
  239n122; aboard boats, 222–223n60; by
  officials, 62, 77–78, 172, 225 (*see also*
  corruption, official); punishments,
  103–104, 118–119, 172–173, 225; of salt
  for food, 143n4. *See also* blue and white
  salt trade; smuggling
imperial army, 33, 34, 35, 172
Imperial Recording Bureau, 290, 290n15
imposed distribution (*kefu*), 56
Inner Palace Treasury, 121
Intendancy of Tea and Salt, 76
intendants, 19, 55–56, 145n14; combined
  appointments, 79; establishment of Salt
  Intendancies, 22. *See also under specific
  type of intendant*

investigating and clearing out (*tuipai*), 71, 181, 294n28
investigation commissioner (*chafang*), 198n24
iodized salt, 84n209
iron cash, 37, 38, 136, 231
iron industry, 6, 37

Jia Dan, 198, 201, 245
Jiading period (Ningzong), 237, 302; sea salt, 235; well salt, 298
jianbing (private monopolist), 121, 213
Jiang Fei, 267
Jiangkang saltern, 257
Jiangnan, 159, 184–187, 192–193, 247n16, 258
Jiangningfu (Jiangnandong), 184, 213
Jiang Pu, 268, 296
Jiangxi sea salt policies, 153n15, 195–196, 201, 210, 238, 245–247
jiangyan (deep red salt), 137n111
Jiang Zhiqi, 55, 125–126n82, 201, 202–203n34, 202n34, 247n16
Jiangzhou^a (Jiangnandong), 158, 184, 214
Jiangzhou^b (Hedong), 276
Jianlong period (Taizu): pond salt, 104
Jianning (fu) (Fujian), 244
Jianyan period (Gaozong): sea salt, 222, 247, 261
Jianzhou^a (Fujian), 241, 244, 249, 250
Jianzhou^b (Lizhou), 242, 243, 244, 250
Jian Zhoufu, 145, 198, 199, 201, 242, 244, 245, 260n7
jiaoyin voucher program, 62–63, 109–111, 110n43. *See also* cash-for-vouchers system
jiaozi (exchange notes; paper money), 110n43, 120n70. *See also* paper money
Jia Qing, 243, 244, 245
Jia Sidao, 78
Jiatai period (Ningzong): sea salt, 235n117
jia units, 141–142n2, 164, 230, 250n26
Jiayou period (Renzong): pond salt, 119; sea salt, 159, 192, 194, 209
Jiezhou (Qinfeng), 132

Jincheng (xian) (Hedong), 275
Jingde period (Zhenzong): well salt, 286
Jingding period (Lizong): sea salt, 255
Jingdong sea salt policies, 105, 142–145, 154n20, 246
Jinghu, 158, 186–187, 192–193, 196–197
Jinghunan, 186n5
Jingkang period (Qinzong): pond salt, 139; sea salt, 221
Jingxi, 105–106, 131–132, 138, 154n20
Jingyou period (Renzong): sea salt, 190
Jingyuan Circuit, 137n111
Jingzhou, 258–259n5; Guangnan salt, 257
Jinzhou^a (Jingxinan), 296
Jinzhou^b (Hedong), 111, 276
Jizhou^a (Jiangnanxi), 184
Jizhou^b (Jingdongxi), 143
Jizhou^c (Hebeidong), 146
Judicial Intendancy (*tixingsi*), 21, 210
Jurchen Jin, 11, 15–16, 31–32, 34; regions acquired from Song, 70–71, 95, 142

Kaibao period (Taizu): sea salt, 147; well salt, 284
Kaifeng (fu) (Jingji), 23, 97n6
Kaixi period (Ningzong): sea salt, 235
Kangding period (Renzong): earth salt, 276; well salt, 288
kernel salt (*keyan*), 41, 98, 99n11
Khitan Liao, 11; Chanyuan Treaty, 24–25; close proximity to capital, 23; import-export products, 12; reference literature, 90; salt monopoly, 15; smuggling, 147, 149, 150n10; subdued by Jin, 31–32; trade relations, 12, 15–16, 147, 154
koushiyan (poll tax), 252n31
kuanshengqian tax (emergency fund), 200–201n30, 202–203n34, 261n10
Kuizhou, 283, 289, 292, 294n25, 297

laborers: eliminated under Fan Xiang policy, 113; exhaustion, 50–51, 108, 111; forced to pay clerk's wages, 200–201n30; numbers reduced by Xue Xiang,

laborers, *continued*
117–118; salter *vs.* government hiring
of, 105–106; sources, 33, 44, 141–142n2,
183–184n1, 183–184n1; systematized
hiring, 43–44, 105; temporary
differentiated from pond salters,
105–106n30, 107; wages, 51, 105
Laizhou (Jingdongdong), 143
land tax systems, 5, 7–8, 20, 250n26; large
source of revenue, 16, 20; nonarable
lands, 147, 150–151n10, 225; tax based
on registered assets, 295n28. *See also*
Double Tax
Later Jin, 103n20
Later Zhou, 10, 103n20, 149
Liang Chengda, 254–256
Liang Ding, 99, 100–102, 101
Liangguang, 257. *See also* Guangnan sea
salt policies
Liang Rujia, 172, 173
Liang Shicheng, 221n57
liangshui (Double Tax). *See* Double Tax
Liangzhe sea salt policies, 41–42, 156–182;
competition between eastern and
western circuits, 170; cost of storage and
transport, 158–162; franchising and
smuggling cut revenue, 161;
government support to salters, 160–162;
illegalities by officials, 173, 178, 179,
181; imported Huai sea salt, 185;
increased taxes, 179; model for other
circuits, 42, 262n11; official evaluations,
169; over staffing, 180–181; pardon for
uncollected taxes not implemented,
165–167, 182; point of distribution, 180;
procurement, 175; production and
processing supervised by officials, 171;
quota salt, 237–238; revenue, 157n2,
160n8, 166n28, 175, 177–178; Salt
Code (of 130 items), 167–168; saltern
ratings, 163; salterns, directorates and
production, 156–157, 170–171; salters,
71–72, 164, 174–175; salt policies of Lu
Bing, 162–167, 166n30; smuggling,
157n3, 159, 161, 176–177; storage, 180;

transport issues, 158, 161n10, 167, 172,
178–179; vouchers, 168, 180, 228;
zhuanlang policy, 67–68
Lianzhou (Guangnanxi), 258, 263, 265
Liao En, 242
Li Bailu, 137
Li Biru, 170
Li Can, 116
Li Cha, 144, 145
Li Changtu, 295n28
Li Cheng, 293n24
Li Chengmai, 262n11
Li Chengzhi, 121n74
Li Cong, 201, 201n32
Li Deming, 119n67
Lifeng directorate, 52, 183
Li Fu, 193
Li Ji, 129, 129n94
Li Jihe, 100n12
Li Jipeng, 110n42
Li Jiqian, 110n42, 112n48, 118, 119n67
Lin'anfu, 169–170, 176, 224, 238; Xingzai,
97n6
Li Nangong, 145
Lingjing (jian) (Chengdufu), 291
Lingnan (S. China), 197
Lingzhou (Xixia), 100n12
Linpingjian (Liangzhe), 157n1
Linqiong (Chengdufu), 285–286n7
Lin Te, 102
Lin Yu, 154
Linzhan (tribal people), 289n13
Li Pei, 285
Li Ping, 130n95
lishengqian (salt boat tax), 67, 205n38
Li Suzhi, 159
Li Tao, 87
Liu Anshi, 166–167n30
Liu Shu, 247n16
Liu Wei, 260–261n9
Liu Yan, 8, 9, 111, 112n47, 129n94
Liu Yi, 199, 200–201n30, 247
Liu Yong, 160–161n8
Liu Zhe, 245–246n12
Liu Zhi, 145n14, 292n20

Liu Zuo, 291
Li Weiqing, 186n5
Li Xhixiao, 237
Li Xinchuan, 87–88
Li Yuanhao, 110n42, 113–114n52, 118
Li Yuqing, 157n1
Lizhou^a, 283, 287, 289, 292, 293, 298
Lizhou^b (Chengdufu), 298
Lizong (SS emperor), 35, 36, 76, 80, 302
loans, 73, 179, 204, 206, 226–227, 251n27;
    certificates at 70% interest free, 203–204;
    "green sprouts" system, 198n24, 254;
    payment, 211, 211n47; salt vouchers at
    interest, 226; trade treasuries, 226
local government, 14, 56, 79–80, 207;
    magistrates, 19, 225, 248. *See also*
    officials
local histories, 90n229
local products tax, 76–77, 296–297, 298
long vouchers (*changyin*), 68
Lou Yi, 168
Lu Bing, 47–48, 162–166
Luoyao saltern, 185
Lu Shimin, 292n20
Lü Tao, 246, 293n22
Lü Yihao, 74, 75, 222, 223
Luzhou^a (Huainanxi), 184
Luzhou^b (Zizhou), 286
Luzhou^c (Hedong), 275

Ma Cheng, 133
Macheng Pond, 279
mainachang (procurement sales center or
    saltern), 45, 46, 47
mainaguan (procurement-sales official). *See*
    procurement-sales official (*mainaguan*)
maipu (franchising). *See* franchises
Mao Zhu, 70, 207–210, 210n44
Map referrals: Map **1**, 10; Map **2**, 11; Map
    3, 95–96; Map **4**, 97, 142, 185; Map **5**,
    97; Map **6**, 97, 146; Map **7**, 97, 146, 275;
    Map **8**, 97, 146; Map **9**, 124; Map **10**,
    141, 146, 156, 157, 185; Map **11**, 141,
    241; Map **12**, 141, 258; Map **13**, 185,
    258; Map **14**, 185, 289; Map **15**, 283

marsh reeds, 239n121
mats, drying and measurement, 96–97n5
Meng Kui, 262–263n12
Mengxi bitan (Shen Kuo), 89
Meng Yu, 262
merchants: driven to suicide, 218;
    disinterest in salt trade, 59, 61, 228;
    punishment for disinterest, 214;
    registration, 215, 217; results of no
    profits, 237; salt dumped on, 61–62, 216
merchant sales (*tongshang*): about, 49–50,
    64, 77, 94n2; advantages, 58–59, 187n6;
    contract markets, 76–77, 294, 297;
    franchises, 40, 60–61, 161, 162n11, 175;
    household requirements, 56–57; revenue
    allocation, 40; under Tang state, 8–10;
    transport, 49 (*see also* merchant transport);
    zhuanlang policy, 67–68. *See also* border
    provisioning; vouchers; specific
    distribution/production region
merchant shop-sold salt, 161, 217. *See also*
    franchises
merchant taxes, 40–41, 61, 75–76, 179; to
    cover production fund shortages, 227.
    See also taxes
merchant transport (boat): *lishengshui* tax,
    67, 205n38; officials interfere with
    transport, 172; passing protocol, 205n39;
    policy under Cai Jing, 204–205;
    regulations, 215
merchant transport (land), 50–51; privately
    owned vehicles, 263n13; road usage fee,
    222n58
military: archer squads, 29; *baojia* law, 28,
    29; centralization, 11, 17–18; *fubing*
    system, 8, 17, 27; imperial army, 33, 34,
    35; navy, 34, 176; palace army, 11, 17,
    33; prefectural armies, 11, 17, 35, 172;
    standing army, 11, 17
military events (table of major), 25
military inspectors, 222; chief (*xunjian*
    dujian), 150–151n10
Military Intendancy, 250n26, 269n31,
    295n29

military intendant (_shuaifu, shuaichen, anfushi_), 19, 21, 268
military maintenance: cost and size, 20, 267n27; effects of growth, 82; excessive, 24, 26–27, 31; size by reign, 17, 23, 24, 26, 30, 33–34, 34; at time of Song restoration, 32; unmet costs, 270–271n33
military personnel: command positions, 8, 10, 11; illegal actions, 78, 172–173, 176, 238, 296; salary cost burden, 8, 18, 24, 35; unfit for duty, 31, 35
military prefectures, 95, 146, 275
Mingdao period (Renzong): earth salt, 277; sea salt, 188
Minghe (yanchang) (Liangzhe), 168
Ming Tao, 262n12
Ming Tuo, 262–263n12
Mingzhou[a] (Hebeixi), 146
Mingzhou[b] (Liangzhe), 81, 156, 160n8, 168, 169, 171, 175
Ministry of Finance, 21, 38
Ministry of Justice, 224, 245
Ministry of Revenue, 22–23
Ministry of Works, 22
Minzhou (Qinfeng), 125n81, 132
Miying (Liangzhe), 156
Mizhou prefecture, 142–143
mokan (evaluation system;; official review). _See_ officials, evaluations
money. _See_ currency
money-lending. _See_ loans
Mongols, 35, 81, 110n42
monks hired to distribute salt, 249
monopolies: Han period, 5–7; Liao, 15; other than salt, 36–37, 231 (_see also_ tea monopoly; wine monopoly); post-Song, 84; pre-Qin unification, 4–5; Tang, 7–10. _See also_ salt monopolies
Monopoly Goods Bureau (_quehuowu_), 23, 115; about, 21; vouchers issued by, 63
mo-shio (Japanese) salt, 220n55
moyan (powder salt; sea salt), 41
Mozhou (Hebeidong), 146

Nan'anjun (Jiangnanxi), 258
Nanenzhou, 261–262, 266
Nanenzhou (Guangnandong), 261–262
Nanjianzhou (Fujian), 241, 242n3, 255
Nankangjun (Jiangnandong), 214
native products tax, 76–77, 296–297, 298
natural gas vein (_huojing_), 42
New Policies, 13, 66, 151n11, 165; criticized as failing, 29; institution of, 22, 27–28; Liu Yi cites 10 oppressive abuses of, 200–201n30; prefectures not implementing, 165; restored, 29–30
Ningguo (Jiangnandong), 126n84
Ningzong (SS emperor), 34, 35, 235; reign periods, 302; revenue, 36
nonstandard weights and measures, 73, 204, 227, 229–230
Northern Capital, 97n6; stone inscription to Renzong, 150, 154n20
Northern Song: fall, 31–32; historical reference sources, 87, 88; salt policy, 49–70. _See also under specific region_

Office of Agricultural Supervision, 6
officials: agency reorganization, 46; attitudes and opinions, 14, 83; awards given for above-quota sales revenue, 56; certificate conferring office, 205n40; clerical fees, 160n8; cross filing of annual reports, 22, 79; dual appointments, 79, 176; evaluations, 55–56, 62, 83, 202–203n34, 220–221; excessive staffing and cost, 18, 24, 26–27, 180–181; interagency obstructionism, 78–79, 79–80, 254–256; privilege of position, 18; prohibited from salt trade, 77, 204, 225; replace military commanders, 11; rewards and punishments, 84, 85, 169, 202n34, 220–221, 225, 236n119; selection, 85, 177; shadow privilege, 18, 27, 204n36, 225; wages, 46, 200–201n30; _xu_ and _daxu_ terms, 218n53. _See also_ corruption, official
ordination certificates, 204, 205, 209, 292n20

Ouyang Xiu, 109n40, 113–114n52, 113–114n52, 150–151n10, 158n4, 160–161n8
palace army, 11, 17, 33
Pang Chong, 183–184n1
pan households (*chenghu*), 44, 275
paper money, 37–38; buy back, 38; over issue, 35, 38; printing, 180
patrolmen (*hubaodu*), 96, 177, 229
patrols: courier soldiers, 194n19; saltern, 225, 227, 229
pavilion household members (*yanding*), 141
pavilion households (*tinghu*), 44, 141, 239
pavilion salterns (*tingchang*), 44
peasant hardships, 81; under *baojia* system, 29, 164; Confucians sympathetic toward, 6–7; during famine, 143n4; forced to buy salt according to property value, 244n8; resulting bandits, 58, 159–162; salt shortages, 53–54, 81, 100n12, 158n4, 189; tax burden, 27, 57 (*see also* taxes)
peasant militia units. *See baojia* law; *fubing* system
pei (punishment), 278–279n4
People's Republic of China, 55n133, 84n209, 95–96n1
Pi Gongbi, 126, 128–130
Pingjiangfu (Liangzhe), 171
pingyou (proof of identity or ownership), 202–203n34, 203–204
planting the salt (*zhongyan*), 96
poll consumption tax, 252n31
pond salt (*chiyan*): distribution in three geographical areas, 105; producers, 43, 96; production regions, 41. *See also* Xiezhou pond salt
postal system, 102n17, 194n19
powder salt, 134, 142, 205, 213
prefects (*zhizhou*), 19
prefectural army, 11, 17, 35, 172
prefectures: compete with central government for income, 9–10, 79, 202–203n34, 255–256; funds diverted

into official pockets, 179; local expenses, 251; revenue, 20, 279
preparation workers, 141–142n2
preparatory salt (*zhunbeiyan*), 212
prepurchased salt, 57n140, 211n47
private trade, 59, 94, 144, 238
procurement cost, 40, 46
procurement funds, 203–204
procurement-sales official (*mainaguan*), 72
procurement salterns (*mainachang*), 45–47
procurement storehouses (*shouyancang*), 46, 64n153
producers: abuses of, 72–73, 80–81 (*see also* production funds); *jia* units, 141–142n2, 164, 230, 250n26; soldiers as, 142; stratification, 71–72, 82–83 (*see also* household ranking); wages and compensation, 43–45. *See also specific type of producer;* salters
production: about, 43–48, 232–233; effects of weather, 163n14, 181
production funds, 40, 48; abused by officials, 73, 179, 227, 230; according to household rank, 173–174; inequality in, 229; payment of funds owed, 80, 222, 223–224n61, 234; promised in two installments, 73, 227; purposes used for, 177; routine operating fees, 73, 228; shortages of, 177, 227–228; Zhe concerns, 181–182
production methods: boiling, 42, 141; evaporation, 41; historical literature describing, 89; large wells, 284n4, 291n18; mat evaporation, 41; pond salt, 41n95, 95–96n1; scraping the salty earth, 147n4, 170; sea salt, 147n4, 163–164; standing tube technique, 291n18; sunning the ashes, 170; time needed to produce sea salt quota, 232–233n110
production regions, 41–43; lost to Jin, 70–71, 95, 142
production-supervisory official, 47
production volume: effects of technological advances, 74; of Jin, 16; yield by type (c. 997), 43

production works (*cuijianchang*), 46
products tax, local, 76–77, 248
proportional voucher exchange (*duidai*), 69–70, 75, 224n63, 231
Pujiang (jian) (Chengdufu), 292
pumai (yan) (franchised salt), 162n11. *See also* franchises
Puzhou (Jingdongxi), 143

Qiandao period (Xiaozong): sea salt, 250n27, 266, 268
Qiande period (Taizu): pond salt, 104
Qian Duanli, 228
Qianhua County, 194n18
Qiantang (Liangzhe), 158n4
Qiantang River, 156, 172
Qianxing period (Renzong): pond salt, 106, 118; sea salt, 188
Qianzhou (Jiangxi), 193–199, 195n20, 260n7, 261n10
Qinfeng Circuit, 289n13
Qingchengjun (Yongxingjun), 97n6
qingji (light weight currency), 231
Qingli period (Renzong), 301; earth salt, 278; pond salt, 111, 115, 118; sea salt, 143, 148, 152, 158, 191, 193, 196; well salt, 289
qingmiaofa. *See* "green sprouts" system
Qing salt monopoly, 84
Qingtang tribe, 289n13
Qin Gui, 32–33
Qingyuan period (Ningzong): sea salt, 235, 237
Qin Kuai, 171
Qinzhou[a] (Guangnanxi), 263n13, 264, 265
Qinzong (NS emperor), 32, 221n57; reign periods, 301
Qiongzhou[a] (Guangnanxi), 260n7
Qiongzhou[b] (Chengdufu), 290n14, 292, 292n20, 298
qiyan (section eyes), 133n104
Qizhou (Hebeixi), 146
Qizhou (Huainanxi), 184

quanyou (government "persuasion" of inhabitants to register as salters), 141–142n2
Quanzhou (Fujian), 241, 242, 255, 255n35
Quartermaster Bureau, 76, 298
quota salt: empty quota (*xu'e*), 285
quota salt (*zhengyan*), 40, 43, 44, 155, 237–240; ancestral salt quota, 72; grades, 272n37; monthly delivery, 181; stove head (*zaojia*) system, 47–48; time needed to produce (Huai), 232–233n110
Quzhou (Liangzhe), 162, 178

Raozhou (Jiangnandong), 162, 184, 214
rebellion and unrest, 81, 83, 183–184n1; result of unfair salt policies, 269n30; results in bandit uprising, 58; Yan Mengbiao Uprising, 255n35
records, flow and handling of: accounting, 252n30; bag policy, 69, 215; *bishucheng* (imperial collections), 186, 187n6; between circuits, 269–270n31; involved with salt bags, 215; maps, 195n20; production monitoring, 176; records forwarded to magistrate, 225; *shilu* (veritable records), 86; vouchers, 70, 231; *xiu qijuzhu* (compiler of imperial records), 290
red salt, 43, 137; at Xie pond, 137n111
regiments and palisades (*tuanzha*) system, 47–48
reign periods, 301–302
remonstrance official, 119, 120n69
Renzong (NS emperor), 26, 86, 118, 119n66, 124, 148, 151, 287
revenue: commercial taxes begin to surpass agrarian tax income, 9; expenditures equal, 34; expenditures twice over, 35; general flow, 40–41; local, 79–80; sources, 16, 20, 33, 36–37, 39; under government distribution, 58; surpluses in early Song, 23, 24. *See also* salt revenue
rewards and punishments, 78, 220, 225, 238. *See also* officials

right to trade, purchase of (*maipu*), 161, 162, 199
road usage fee (*jieluqian*), 222n58
rock salt (*shiyan*), 43, 93–94n1 (94), 132
rotation law, voucher (*xunhuanfa*), 69

sales to the central authority (*zhongmai*), 63, 275–276
salt: from alternate sources, 220; characteristics and types, 43, 93–94n1; preciousness of, 152; spoilage, 54, 227
Salt and Incense Intendancy, 210
Salt and Iron Bureau, 21–22, 37, 102
Salt and Iron Debate, 6–7
salt artisans (*yanjiang*), 44
Salt Code of 130 items, 167
salterns (*chang*), 45, 141; abuses occurring at, 229, 295n29; distribution, 46, 64n153, 180; fuel, 226; functions, 185; number of furnaces comprising, 170–171; order of merchant service, 222–223n60; patrols, 225, 227, 229; privately owned resources, 42; production per firing, 234; rating system, 163; regiments and palisades, 47–48, 171, 229; routine operating fees, 73, 228; small (*wu*), 146
salters: abandon positions, 81, 257, 269–270n31, 271–272n36; abuses by officials, 73, 77–78, 82–83, 89, 132n100, 244n8, 245–246n12, 245–247, 246, 259–260; bankruptcy, 61, 272n37; coerced into service, 246 (*see also* laborers); driven to extreme behavior, 165, 188n9, 296–297; highest number of households, 43; impoverished, 80–81, 188n9; incentives, 223–224n61; inspectors, 222; land transfer, 174; official position towards, 14; over taxed, 250n26 (*see also* taxes); poems about, 160–161n8; punishments, 175–176, 230; stratification, 173–174 (*see also* household ranking)
Salt Intendancy, 22

salt monopolies: fiscal stability gained by manipulation of, 39; historical sources on, 85–90; implications from historical perspective, 81–83; in modern day PRC, 84n209; post-Song, 84; pre-Song, 4–10
saltpeter, 108, 131, 279
Salt Policy (*Yance*) (Shen Li), 160
salt revenue, 39, 43, 65; allocation, 40–41; compared historically, 9, 36, 236; Guan Zhong quoted on, 5; Salt and Iron Debate, 6–7; southeastern salt, 186, 191. *See also under specific regions*
Sang Hongyang, 7, 129n94
Sanmen (Yongxingjun), 125n82
sea salt (*haiyan*): about, 41–42, 141–142; measurements (bags and pockets), 153n17; producers, 43 (*see also* pavilion households [*tinghu*]); scraping the salty earth, 147n4, 170; sea water ratings, 163. *See also under specific circuit*; southeastern salt; stone lotus test
seasonal tax, 200–201n30
sea water rating system, 163n17
seaweed, 220n55
section eyes (*qiyan*), 133n104
section households (*qihu* or *xihu*): about, 43–44, 96, 96n3; production statistics, 104–105
section workers (*qifu*), 96. *See also* laborers
Shaanxi, 208, 210; glut, 121n74; provisioning, 191; sales salterns, 121–122n76; salt and horse policies, 119–120; tea, 291n17; vouchers, 65–66; western salt, 106
shadow privilege (*yin*), 18, 27, 204n36, 225
Shangguan Jun, 154
Shangyu (Liangzhe), 237
Shanxi, 41, 95
Shao Dashou, 177, 227
Shaoding period (Lizong): sea salt, 237
Shaosheng period (Zhezong): earth salt, 280; pond salt, 131; sea salt, 153, 203, 212

Shaowujun (Fujian), 241, 242, 243, 244, 244n8, 255
Shaoxingfu (Liangzhe), 165, 171, 176, 178
Shaoxing period (Gaozong), 236, 302; sea salt, 224, 234, 249, 251, 261, 262–263, 264; well salt, 294, 297
Shaoxi period (Guangzong): well salt, 297, 298
Shaozhou[a] (Guangnandong), 247
Shaozhou[b] (Jinghunan), 247, 254
Shen Diao, 250n26
Shen Fu, 195
Sheng Du, 105–106n32, 107, 108n37
Shen Kuo, 89, 112n47, 126, 127, 290
Shen Li, 159, 160
Shen Xiyan, 131
Shenzhou (Hebeixi), 146
Shenzong (NS emperor), 13, 22, 27, 28, 127n89, 131, 151, 162, 165, 205n38, 210n44, 244; reign periods, 301; salt revenue, 36
Shezhou (Jiangnandong), 214
Shikang saltern, 258
Shi Miyuan, 35, 173
Shi Yuanchang, 194
Shizong (Later Zhou emperor), 34, 149
shop merchants, 294, 298
shops and yards money (*fangchangqian*), 204
shortages of salt, 53–54, 284n3. *See also* gluts of salt
short vouchers (*duanyin*), 68
Shuzhou (Huainanxi), 184
Sichuan money vouchers (*chuanyin*), 216
Sichuan region, 42, 53, 71–72, 111, 113, 120n69; horse breeding, 265; major tea producer, 37
Sichuan Tea and Horse Agency, 82n207
Sichuan well salt policies (NS), 283–298; additional charges for paying cash, 289; border provisioning, 286, 287, 288; currency issues, 288–290; depleted wells, 292–293, 294–295n27, 294n25; directorates, distribution and production, 283–284; government sales price, 284–285; illegal taxes, 293; minority

participation, 290n16; salt import, 285, 290, 291, 292–293; small mouthed wells, 290; smuggling, 290; wells increased, 287
Sichuan well salt policies (SS), 294–298; contract markets, 76–77, 294, 297; depleted wells, 294n25, 297n33; excess charges prohibited, 298; native products tax, 76–77, 296–297, 298; quotas, 295, 297; storehouses, 294n27; transport issues, 294n27; vouchers, 216, 296; well ratings, 295–296
silkworm salt (*canyan*), 57, 103–104n21, 144n8, 168
silver cash, 37, 288
Sima Guang, 13, 29, 87, 127n87, 194n18
sishuofa (Four Items Policy), 63, 190–192
Sixteen Prefectures of Yan Yun, 11, 23, 32
small-mouth wells (*zhuotongjing*), 42–45, 45n101, 280, 283n2, 291, 291n18, 293n22–23; break monopoly, 294, 297n34; franchised, 60–61; government closure, 76–77; monitoring, 44–45, 60
small vouchers. *See xiaochao* (small salt voucher)
smelly salt (*chouyan*), 43, 93–94n1
smuggling: about, 54–55; curtailment, 175–176, 232–233n110; 'holding' undeclared salt longer than ten days, 75, 222; Huai salt, 187n7, 196; Liao En, 242; official promotions to apprehenders, 150n10; officials in league with, 78, 83; punishments, 164, 223–224n61, 243n4, 278–279n4; in response to rising quotas, 47; reward for capture, 226. *See also under individual regions*; bandits
Song Di, 120
Song Xiang, 109
southeastern salt, 141, 168, 190–191; greatest revenue of empire, 186, 191. *See also* sea salt (*haiyan*)
Southern Capital, 97n6, 143
southern salt, 105, 106, 113, 124
Southern Song, 11, 31–34, 88, 261n10; monopoly abuse, 73, 77–80; regions lost

to Jin, 70–71, 95, 142. *See also under specific region*
speculators (*jianbing*), 121, 213
Spring and Autmn period, 4
standing tube wells. *See* small-mouth wells (*zhuotongjing*)
State Trade Bureau, 121–128, 130, 189
statism in Song, 12
stone lotus test, 72, 74, 233n111; implications, 74; procedure, 233n111
storehouses, 46, 54, 64n153, 110n43, 158, 180, 185–186, 202n34, 227, 230
stove head (*zaojia*) system, 47–48
stove households (*zaohu*), 44, 141–142n2
stratification of salter households, 82, 173–174. *See also* household ranking
stream fees, government, 293n23
Su Che, 153n16, 279, 292, 293n22
Sun Fu, 113–114n52 (114)
Sun Jiong, 131n100
Sun Mian, 186–187, 187n6
Sun Sheng, 246–247
Sun Zixiu, 182
surcharge policy (*tienafa*), 75, 179, 228
surpluses, 23–26, 144, 239. *See also* gluts of salt
Susha Juzi, 4
Su Shi, 149n7, 158n4, 160–161n8, 202–203n34
Suzong (Tang emperor), 236

taifusi (Court of Imperial Treasury), 23
Taipingxingguo period (Taizong): pond salt, 104; well salt, 284
Taipingzhou (Jiangnandong), 184, 213
Taizhou^a (Liangzhe), 161–162, 168, 169, 171, 182, 183, 188
Taizhou^b (Huainandong), 52, 183, 219, 228, 230, 234n112, 236
Taizong (NS emperor), 16, 23, 24, 285; reign periods, 301
Taizu (NS emperor), 10, 23, 147, 149n7; reign periods, 301
Tang, 7–10, 20, 112, 236

Tangut Xixia, 12, 15–16, 31–32, 110n42; as military threat, 11, 28, 30, 31, 65, 191n15; Qingtang tribal land, 289n13. *See also* blue and white salt trade
Tang Zhongyou, 226
Tang Zhou, 266
Tang Zhuo, 267n26
Taoluo (Jingdongdong), 142
Taoshan (Liao), 104n25
Tax Bureau (*duzhisi*), 21
taxes, 56–57; based on property value, 211n47, 242, 250, 254; collection, 21, 60; evasion, 260; exemptions, 231; increasing, 20, 61, 82, 179, 244–247, 250n26, 257, 272n37; on merchants, 40–41, 75, 227; under the New Policies, 200–201n30; payment in salt (*chanyanfa*), 248n17. *See also under specific tax*
tax households, 251n28
Tea and Horse Agency, 82n207, 98n7
Tea and Salt Intendancy, 76
tea monopoly, 37, 38, 291, 291n17, 294; forced purchases, 244n8; vouchers, 110n43, 238n120
three capitals and twenty-eight prefectures, 97, 105, 105n30, 108
Three Items Policy (voucher redemption), 63, 190–192
Tianfu directorate, 156
Tian Kuang, 112, 115
Tiansheng period (Renzong): pond salt, 105, 105–106n30, 108, 301; sea salt, 156, 185, 192, 241, 259
Tianxi period (Zhenzong): pond salt, 106; sea salt, 188, 189, 196–197
tienafa (surcharge policy), 75
tihuodan (bill of lading), 110n43
Tingzhou (Fujian), 196, 241–244, 244n8, 249, 252; counties of, 253n33; Guangnan salt, 197n22; uprising, 255n35
Tongchuanfulu (S. Song Zizhou), 298
Tong Guan, 31–32, 137, 138, 221n57
Tonglijun (Hebeixi), 146
Tongyuanjun (Qinfeng), 132–133n103

Tongzhou[a] (Shaanxi/Yongxingjun), 111, 132
Tongzhou[b] (Huainandong), 183, 185, 188, 222–223n60, 230, 234n112
touziqian (agricultural surtax), 217n52
transfer depots, 186
transfer ways voucher policy, 67–68, 205–217
transit taxes (guoshui), 294
transport: officials, 9; routes, 97n6, 105–106n32; systems, 9, 50, 67
Transport Intendancy (Zhe), 202n34, 203
tribute goods, 119n68, 195, 262–263n12 (263), 267
tuanzha (regiments and palisades), 47–48
tuipai (investigate and clear out), 71, 181, 295n28
tuntian (agricultural colony), 194

voucher exchange, 206–207, 213–214, 218; exchange ratio, 222–223n60, 228, 231; grades of (Huai), 210; proportional, 69–70, 75, 224n63; regional differences, 270–271n33
vouchers, 59–60, 65–70, 66n159; cash-for-vouchers system, 63–65, 66, 111–118, 134–135, 212; chuanyin, 216n51; devalued, 116; embezzlement of funds, 226; exchange ratio, 222–223n60, 228, 231; fraudulent, 216, 296n32; inflated cost of goods, 59, 63, 64, 101, 109–110 (see also border provisioning); issued by fleeing Northern Song court, 32; issuing agencies, 23, 63, 116, 127n86, 230; jiaoyin vouchers, 62–63, 69, 109–111; old pond salt vouchers, 209, 235–236; order of service at saltern, 222–223n60; over issued, 65, 70, 121–123, 121n72, 216n51; proportional exchange, 69–70, 224n63, 231; redemption during transition to SS, 222–223n60; rotation, 69, 218, 235; speculators, 121, 213; Three Items and Four Items Policies, 63, 190–192; transfer ways method and

modifications, 67–68, 205–217; universal voucher policy, 67–70; voucher quota, 121n76, 123; xiaochao vouchers, 65–66, 117–118, 141–142. See also under specific region
voucher tax fees, 294

Wang Anshi, 120n71, 126, 160n8, 162n13, 198, 210n44; disapproval of franchising, 61; on Liangzhe salt policy, 162; poem by, 160n8; reforms, 13, 22–23, 27–28; salt crime policy, 47; support of Xue Xiang, 65, 119–120
Wang Bowen, 143n4
Wang Boyu, 150–151
Wang Di, 202–203n34, 245–246n12
Wang Fu, 219, 221, 221n57
Wang Gongchen, 113n52
Wang Jing, 107n34
Wang Qi, 196
Wang Sui, 51, 105–106n32, 107, 188, 189n11
Wang Xianfu, 194n18
Wang Xu, 155
Wang Yansou, 152
Wang Yao, 193
Wang Zhongqian, 133, 136
Wang Zijing, 244n8, 245, 251
Wang Zongwang, 292n20
Wan Qi, 161–162, 162n11
weapons manufacture, 18, 31
Wei Bochu, 170, 218–221
Wei Lun, 247n16
Weizhou[a] (Jingdongdong), 143
Weizhou[b] (Shaanxi/Qinfeng), 289n13
Weizhou[c] (Hebeixi), 97n6, 146
well artisans (jingjiang), 44
well households (jinghu), 42
wells: types of, 42–43, 291n18; large, 293n23; small-mouth, 42–45, 45n101. See also small-mouth wells
well salt, 42–43; fire wells, 42, 285–286n7; large well extraction, 284n4, 291n18; rating, 295–296. See also Sichuan well salt policies

Weng Zhongtong, 166
Wen Yanbo, 119n66, 151
Wenzhou[a] (Liangzhe), 52, 81, 156,
    161–162, 171, 178, 180–182
Wenzhou[b] (Lizhou), 285
Western Capital, 97n6
western salt, 105, 106, 123n78, 124,
    128–130
white salt (*baiyan*), 15, 43, 100n12,
    118–119, 278, 279, 285
wide-mouth wells. *See* wells, large
wine merchants, 60, 162, 164, 188, 188n9
wine monopoly, 36–37, 257
Wu Chuan, 234
Wu Juhou, 144, 145, 154n20, 245n12
Wuweijun (Huainanxi), 184
Wuzhou[b] (Liangzhe), 178

xiangbing (prefectural troops). *See*
    prefectural army
xiang (dried salt fish), 220
Xiangzhou[a] (Hebeidong), 146
Xianping period (Zhenzong): earth salt,
    276
xiaochao (small salt voucher), 65–66,
    117–118, 141–142n2, 153, 171, 249
Xiaohai saltern, 183
Xiaozong (SS emperor), 34, 72, 164n19,
    231; reign periods, 302; revenue, 34, 36
Xiasha (yanchang) (Liangzhe), 89, 174
Xiazhou (Jinghubei), 289
Xieliang (Yongxingjun), 133
Xie Pond, 41n95, 95–96n1; brine depth,
    133
Xiezhou pond salt policies (960-1047):
    about, 95–100; advantages of
    government trade (Liang Ding),
    101–102; advantages of merchant sales,
    five (Sheng Du, Wang Sui), 107–108;
    advantages of merchant trade, restoration
    (pre-Liang Ding), 102–103; cash
    payment for salt, 106, 108, 111;
    distribution areas, 95, 97–98, 105–106,
    108n37; gluts, 102–103, 107–108,
    109n40; *jiaoyin* vouchers, 63, 109–110

(*see also jiaoyin* voucher program); price
    of salt, 99, 112n47, 113; revenues, 109;
    smuggling, 100n12, 101, 112–113n48;
    southern, western and eastern salt, 106;
    vacillation between government and
    merchant sales, 107, 111
Xiezhou pond salt policies (1048–1067),
    50, 99, 111–119; market stabilization
    under Fan Xiang, 111, 116–117;
    merchants pay in cash for salt vouchers
    (Fan Xiang), 63–65, 112–119
Xiezhou pond salt policies (1068-1127):
    call for resumption of Fan Xiang's policy,
    130–131; distribution areas, 120–123,
    125, 131–132, 138–139; eastern/western
    salt price differential, 127n86, 128–129;
    eight point policy changes (collaboration),
    121–123; forced-purchase salt, 126–127;
    over issued vouchers and buy back,
    120–123, 120–139; price stabilization
    between east and west (Pi Gongbi),
    128–130; production after flooding
    resumes, 137–139; production halts after
    flooding, 132–133; sea salt sales in pond
    distribution areas, 133–135, 138n113,
    171; surcharge system (Cai Jing),
    132–137, 218; *xiaochao* vouchers (Xue
    Xiang), 65–66, 117–118, 117n62
Xiezhou (Yongxingjun), 95, 105–106n30.
    See also Xiezhou pond salt policies
Xihe (lu) (Qinfeng), 280n8
Xinghuajun, 241, 242, 254
Xingxhou[b] (Hebeixi), 146
Xining period (Shenzong), 165, 301; earth
    salt, 277, 280; pond salt, 119, 125, 129;
    sea salt, 150–151, 161, 166n28, 197, 199,
    201, 208, 209, 210, 247; well salt, 290,
    291
Xinzhou[a] (Hedong), 275
Xinzhou[b] (Jiangnandong), 162, 184, 214
Xiohai saltern, 183
Xiong Ben, 120
Xiongzhou (Hebeidong), 146
Xiuzhou (Liangzhe), 156, 170
Xiuzhou saltworks, 81, 156, 161–162

Xixia salt: blue and white salt trade, 100n12, 101 (*see also* blue and white salt trade); quality of, 15

Xixia (Tangut empire). *See* Tangut Xixia

Xizhou (Hedong), 280n8

xuanfushi (pacification commissioner), 137–138n112

Xuanhe period (Huizong): sea salt, 155, 216, 217

Xuanzhou (Jiangnandong), 184

Xue Sichang, 133

Xue Xiang, 119n67, 162n11, 209; about, 65–66, 208–209; as Shaanxi fiscal intendant, 162; as Xie salt military regulator, 117, 119, 120

Xu Gongyu, 177

Xunxhou[b], 264

Xu Shou, 246

Xu Song, 86

Xuzhou[b] (Jingxi), 97n6

Yancheng directorate, 183

Yang Fu, 76–77, 297, 298

Yangjiang (xian) (Guangnandong), 261

Yanguan (*chang*) (Liangzhe), 157n1

Yang Youyi, 252

Yang Yungong, 186n5

Yangzi River, 34, 172, 228

Yan Mengbiao, 255n35

Yanshan (Hebeidong), 150

Yan Shilu, 182

yantieshi (salt and iron intendant), 8

Yanzhou[a] (Jingdongxi), 143

Yao Xian, 178

Ye Heng, 74, 176

Yellow Emperor, 4, 41n95

yellow flag privilege, 67, 80

Yellow River, 97–98n6, 98n8, 153n16, 200–201n30, 276n2

Ye Longli, 90

Yingchangfu (Jingxibei), 97n6

Ying Mengming, 253, 271–272

Yingtianfu (Jingdongxi), 143

Yingtianfu (Songzhou), 97n6

Yingzhou[a] (Hebeidong), 146

yinshuiqian (voucher tax fees), 294

Yinxian (Liangzhe), 160n8

Yin Zhuang, 273

Yizhou[a] (Jingdongdong), 143

Yizhou[d], 283, 289, 293

Yongdingjun (Guangnanxi), 146

Yongfengqu (Ever-bountiful Canal), 105–106n30

Yongjia saltern, 156

Yongjingjun (Hebeidong), 146

Yongli directorate, 53, 275, 276n2, 279

Yongxingjun Circuit, 66, 95, 288. *See also* Xiezhou pond salt

Yongxi period (Taizong): pond salt, 104

Yuanfeng period (Shenzong): earth salt, 278, 279; pond salt, 129; sea salt, 144, 152, 167–168, 167n32, 202n34, 207, 208, 209, 210, 211, 212, 243, 251, 259

Yuanfeng Salt Code, 166n28, 167–168, 207

Yuanfu period (Zhezong): pond salt, 132; sea salt, 154

Yuan salt monopoly, 84

Yuanyou period (Zhezong): earth salt, 279, 280; pond salt, 130; sea salt, 152, 166, 166–167n30, 166n28, 202–203n34 (203), 236; well salt, 292

Yuanzhou[b] (Jiangnanxi), 184

Yue Fei, 32, 33

Yuezhou[a] (Liangzhe), 165, 168, 169

Yulinzhou (Guangnanxi), 259–260n6

yumai (prepurchase of silk), 211n47

Yunzhou[a] (Jingdongxi), 143

Yunzhou[b] (Jiangnanxi), 184

Yu Xianqing, 188n9

Yuyao (xian) (Liangzhe), 237

Yu Yuan, 194

Yu Zhaohu, 228, 230

Zeng Bu, 13

Zeng Dian, 163n14

Zeng Lian, 266

Zeng Mo, 163

Zhang Cha, 210, 210n45, 212

Zhang Chun, 74, 75, 171, 222

Zhang Dexiang, 143n6
Zhang Dun, 13, 151, 151n11, 198, 246
Zhang Fangping, 58, 116, 149
Zhang Gen, 210
Zhang Guan, 143n6
Zhang Jie, 199–200n29 (200)
Zhang Jing[a], 119, 119n68
Zhang Jing[b], 165
Zhang Jingwen, 126, 129, 260–261n9
Zhang Ruji, 249
Zhang Ruxian, 245, 246
Zhang Ruyu, 89
Zhang Shangying, 67, 135, 210
Zhang Shi, 268
Zhang Shicheng, 201, 246
Zhang Xiang, 132n100
Zhang Xiangzhong, 102–103
Zhang Yong, 102, 158n4
Zhang Yuan, 175, 176
Zhangzhou, 241, 242, 250n26, 255,
    255n35
Zhan Yizhi, 268n29, 270, 271, 271n34
Zhao Bian, 161, 162
Zhao Buliu, 234n114
Zhao Buyi, 251
Zhao Ding, 75
Zhao Gonghuan, 268
Zhao Kai, 76, 294n26, 296, 297
Zhao Kuangyin, 10
Zhao Kui, 259–260n6, 259–260n6
Zhao Lingrong, 183–184n1
Zhao Ruyu, 252
Zhao Shu, 194n18
Zhao Yancao, 253
Zhao Yong, 150–151n10, 151n10
Zhao Zhan, 121, 152
Zhao Zhidao, 237
Zhaozhou[a] (Guangnanxi), 258
Zhaozhou[b] (Hebeixi), 146
Zhao Zi, 150n10
Zhedong sea salt policies, 166n28,
    170–172, 179. *See also* Liangzhe sea salt
    policies
Zhendingfu (Hebeixi), 146

Zhenghe period (Huizong): pond salt, 136;
    sea salt, 212, 214, 216, 218, 219, 247
Zhenzong (NS emperor), 24; decrees on
    Xie salt, 103, 106, 107n34, 108; reign
    periods, 301; revenue, 24, 36
Zhexi (Liangzhe), 156, 170. *See also*
    Liangzhe sea salt policies
Zhexi Salt and Tea Intendancy, 72, 73
Zhexi sea salt policies. *See* Liangzhe sea salt
    policies
zhezhong (equitable exchange). *See*
    equitable exchange (*zhezhong*)
Zhezong (NS emperor), 13, 29, 131, 219,
    244; policy, 29–30
Zhidao period (Taizong): sea salt, 142
Zhihe period (Renzong): earth salt, 277;
    pond salt, 115; sea salt, 144
Zhiping period (Yingzong): sea salt, 157n1,
    192, 196, 197
Zhou Ge, 151
Zhou Yin, 126n85, 291, 291n18
Zhou Zhan, 194
Zhu Chuping, 198, 259
Zhu Chuyue, 194n18
Zhu Mian, 221n57
zhunbeiyan (stockpiled salt), 212
Zhu Taifu, 102n16
Zhu Yanbo, 247n16
Zhu Yi[a], 175
Zhu Yi[b], 238, 239
Zizhou, 283, 287, 292, 298
Zou Hao, 167
zuyongdiao (Tang agrarian system of tax), 8

Printed and bound by CPI Group (UK) Ltd, Croydon, CR0 4YY

13/04/2025

14656536-0003